BUILDING AN EU SECURITIES MARKET

This highly topical book considers some of the fundamental issues concerning the legal framework that has been established to support a single EU securities market. It focuses particularly on how the emerging legal framework will affect issuers' access to the primary and secondary market. The Financial Services Action Plan (FSAP, 1999) was an attempt to equip the Community better to meet the challenges of monetary union and to capitalise on the potential benefits of a single market in financial services. It led to extensive change in securities market regulation: new laws; new law-making processes; and more attention to the mechanisms for the supervision of securities market activity and legal enforcement. With the FSAP nearing completion, it is a good time to take stock of what has been achieved, and to identify challenges that lie ahead.

EILÍS FERRAN is a Reader in the Law Faculty, University of Cambridge, specialising in corporate and securities law. She is a former Director of the Faculty's Centre for Corporate and Commercial Law. She is the author of *Company Law and Corporate Finance* (1999), and of various articles on corporate law, securities law and financial regulation and is an editor of the *Journal of Corporate Law Studies*. In 2000 she was a special adviser to the UK Parliamentary Joint Committee on the Financial Services and Market Bill, and more recently has advised the UK Department of Trade and Industry on the Company Law Reform Project. Dr Ferran is a graduate (MA and PhD) of Cambridge University and is a qualified solicitor.

BUILDING AN EU SECURITIES MARKET

EILÍS FERRAN

CAMBRIDGE
UNIVERSITY PRESS

PUBLISHED BY THE PRESS SYNDICATE OF THE UNIVERSITY OF CAMBRIDGE
The Pitt Building, Trumpington Street, Cambridge CB2 1RP, United Kingdom

CAMBRIDGE UNIVERSITY PRESS
The Edinburgh Building, Cambridge, CB2 2RU, UK
40 West 20th Street, New York, NY 10011–4211, USA
477 Williamstown Road, Port Melbourne, VIC 3207, Australia
Ruiz de Alarcón 13, 28014 Madrid, Spain
Dock House, The Waterfront, Cape Town 8001, South Africa
http://www.cambridge.org

First published 2004

Printed in the United Kingdom at the University Press, Cambridge

Typeset in 10.17/12.75 pt Minion

A catalogue record for this book is available from the British Library

ISBN 0521 847222 hardback

To Rod, Aoife and Oliver

CONTENTS

Preface   xiii

Table of legislation and cases   xv

1 **Overview and introduction to terminology**   1

  A The FSAP   1
  B General background to the development of the FSAP   2
  C From FSAP to Lamfalussy and CESR   5
  D EU securities law – explanation for
      terminological approach   7

2 **Law's role in the building of an integrated EU**
  securities market   8

  A Scope of chapter   8
  B Financial development and the promotion of
      economic growth   11
      The benefits of financial market development:
      expectations and evidence   11
      Growth in securities market activity in the EU   15
        Market changes   15
        Forces that propelled the growth in securities market
        activity within the EU   22
        An omission?   24
  C Did EU law matter to the development of
      securities market activity in the EU during the 1980s
      and 1990s?   25
      Law as market-creator: what the debate is about   25
      How does this debate relate to EU securities regulation?   28
        Controlling market abuse: banning insider dealing   30
        Issuer disclosure: prospectuses and ongoing disclosure   34
        EU law was a catalyst for changes in Member States' law
        but it does not necessarily follow that it was a catalyst for
        securities market development   38

D Strategic policy choices in EU law-making to promote
   a single securities market   41
      Implications of uncertainty surrounding law's
      contribution to the development of securities markets   41
      The FSAP favoured regulatory intervention as the
      primary policy tool (despite the dangers)   43
      Is there an EU policy alternative? Placing the emphasis
      more on supervision and enforcement than on
      additional regulation   46
      Making future policy choices on EU regulatory
      intervention: should there be some room for
      regulatory competition?   50

3 The regulatory process for securities law-making in
   the EU   58

   A Scope of chapter   58
   B Recent refinement of the regulatory process – the
      Lamfalussy model   61
      The path towards reform of the regulatory process   61
      Co-operation between the Commission, Council and
      European Parliament in the Lamfalussy process   67
      Formal allocation of regulatory responsibilities as
      between the Commission, Council and European
      Parliament under the Lamfalussy process   67
      The establishment of new committees to assist the
      regulatory process   75
         Existing committees and bodies that contribute to
         securities law-making   75
         New committees under the Lamfalussy process (1):
         European Securities Committee   77
         New committees under the Lamfalussy process (2):
         Committee of European Securities Regulators   78
         The mechanics of Level 2 legislation   81
      Role of the private sector and a new emphasis
      on transparency and consultation   82
   C Assessing the Lamfalussy process   84
      Expansion of the Commission's role: empire-building
      or advancing towards a new model of collaborative
      governance?   86

Consultation and transparency by the Commission and
CESR: the development and management of dialogic webs   92
Consultation and transparency as quality-enhancing devices   92
*Consultation and transparency processes: the functioning
of the machinery*   95
*Consultation and transparency as mechanisms for
improving accountability and legitimacy*   96
*Consultation and transparency: can there be too much
of a good thing?*   98
Boundaries between levels of regulation within the
Lamfalussy process   99
Level 1 and Level 2   99
*Level 2 and Level 3 – a new 'boundaries' issue that could
become increasingly significant*   100
CESR's relations with the Commission and with interest
groups: legitimacy and accountability concerns   102
The role of the European Securities Committee (ESC)   107
The role of the European Parliament   109
D   The limitations of processes   111
E   An alternative model: a pan-European securities
regulatory (and supervisory) agency   119
F   Conclusions   122

4   **The centrality of disclosure as a regulatory strategy**   127

A   Scope of chapter   127
Disclosure as the first-choice regulatory strategy
generally, and for issuers in particular   127
Functions that issuer disclosure regimes can perform   127
The policy choice, and how the EU has chosen to
exercise it   129
How well does the EU manage the high risk of making
regulatory mistakes? Analysing issuer disclosure
provides an opportunity to test the Lamfalussy process
for securities law-making   131
The importance of credible disclosure; and what the EU
is doing about it by way of organisation of supervisory
oversight of issuer disclosure   132
The role of stock exchanges in the regulation and
supervision of issuers within the EU   133

5 **Issuer disclosure**   **134**

   A Scope of chapter   134
   B Prospectus and periodic disclosure: the legislative
      background and the emerging new regime   135
   C Building a comprehensive, standardised disclosure
      regime at the expense of loss of opportunities for
      competition between Member States – a move in the
      right direction?   138
         Prospectus disclosure requirements – a new world of
         'maximum harmonisation'   138
         But compare the Transparency Directive   145
         Allocation of regulatory and supervisory responsibilities
         for issuers amongst the competent authorities of EU
         Member States   147
            Prospectus Directive – identification of home State is
            important for supervisory rather than regulatory
            purposes (because the rules are the same)   147
            Identifying an issuer's EU home State for the Prospectus
            Directive   149
            Where the Prospectus Directive led, the Transparency
            Directive (broadly) followed   149
            Concerns about the rigidity of the rules on the
            determination of home States   150
            Potential implications for EU issuers   153
            Potential implications for non-EU issuers   155
         Are Member States likely to exceed the Transparency
         Directive – or is de facto convergence on periodic
         disclosure requirements a more likely prospect?   156
         Assessment – moving in the right direction?   159
   D Demolishing the tower of Babel – standardising
      the language of financial and other information   160
         Financial information in prospectuses and periodic
         disclosures – treatment of foreign issuers   160
         The language(s) of non-financial information   164
            Translations of prospectus summaries   166
   E Adapting the prospectus and periodic disclosure
      regime for specialist debt securities markets   167
         Exemptions from the requirement to produce
         a prospectus   169

Modified disclosure requirements for prospectuses
relating to wholesale securities that are to be admitted
to trading on regulated markets 170
Periodic disclosure requirements and specialist
securities 173
But a different threshold for a special regime on the
allocation of supervisory responsibilities 173
F Tailoring prospectus and periodic disclosure
requirements to cater for retail investors 175
G The impact of the new regime for prospectuses
and periodic disclosures on smaller/younger
issuers and on second-tier market infrastructure
providers 179
SMEs and start-ups as a deserving case for a lighter
touch – only limited success for this argument in the
Prospectus Directive 180
But more success in the Transparency Directive 182
Implications for second-tier stock markets 185
H Ensuring candid and careful compliance with
prospectus and periodic disclosure requirements 188
I Dissemination of information 193
J The Market Abuse Directive and issuer disclosure 197
K Concluding remarks – moving closer to a genuine single
securities market? 200
The new rules should facilitate exempt offers of
unlisted securities to the wholesale markets 200
Cross-border offers/multiple listings making use
of the passport are likely to remain rare 201
The new regime does not seek to address the
home State bias in primary equity listings and may
have only limited impact on home bias in investment
portfolios 202
The interests of non-EU issuers have received
insufficient attention and this could have adverse
long-term consequences 205
Non-ISD/ISD2 regulated markets and alternative
trade execution mechanisms could benefit at the
expense of ISD/ISD2 regulated markets 206

6   Institutional supervision of issuer disclosure within
    the EU   208

    A   Scope of chapter   208
    B   Issuer disclosure obligations outside core securities law   212
        Financial disclosures   212
            No post-Enron reassessment of EU policy choices on the
            content of financial disclosure obligations   215
        Corporate governance disclosures   218
    C   Supervision of issuer disclosure   219
    D   US regulatory requirements as a catalyst for institutional
        remodelling in Member States: recent experience on
        auditor oversight   228
    E   Does lack of uniformity in EU-wide supervision
        of securities market activity matter?   233

7   Regulatory competencies: the end of exchange-based
    regulation and supervision of issuers in the EU?   236

    A   Scope of chapter   236
    B   Exchanges as regulators of issuers and the
        impact of demutualisation: issues and responses   239
        Demutualisation: changes to organisational structures
        as a response to growing competitive pressures   239
        Exchanges as regulators and supervisors of issuers:
        possible functions, and how the assessment of their
        role is affected by demutualisation   243
        Post-demutualisation cutting of the regulatory and
        supervisory pies: different approaches around the world   247
    C   Competitive exchanges and EU market integration   254
        Existing diversity in the regulatory and supervisory
        roles played by exchanges in Member States   254
        Exchange-based regulation and supervision as a
        mechanism for promoting EU market integration   255
        Counter considerations   257
        A way forward   259

Bibliography   267

Index   293

PREFACE

The European Union is the world's leading example of regional economic integration. Whilst integration of European securities markets has been on the policy agenda since the 1970s, this aspect of the market integration project acquired a new intensity after the European Commission's announcement in 1999 of an ambitious five-year Action Plan of policy objectives and specific measures to improve the single market for financial services. The Commission's Financial Services Action Plan has largely been adopted within its original timeframe, which is a remarkable achievement. However, many fascinating questions still remain and in this book I explore some of them.

Regulation, in its narrow rule-making sense, was the favoured policy tool employed in the Financial Services Action Plan. The new laws move significantly beyond early interventions, which concentrated on removing national barriers to cross-border activity by issuers, investors and intermediaries, and put in place increasingly detailed, standardised EU-wide re-regulation in the interests of market efficiency and investor protection. There is room for disagreement on whether the details are right in every respect. Certainly the close examination of the new regime for issuer disclosure contained in this book identifies a number of areas where the rules could be counterproductive in their practical operation. More fundamentally, it is open to question whether the emphasis on regulation in the Financial Services Action Plan was the right strategic approach. Even if we assume that the rule-makers have done a good job and that whatever regulatory mistakes they may have made are not too significant, the point remains that high-quality rules are just one of the factors that can help to build a strong, deep securities market and, in fact, the value of their contribution may be quite small. EU policy-makers might thus have done better to have been more open to policy alternatives to regulation. In particular, the recent recognition of the importance of ensuring that there is in place a system of supervisory oversight that can support the effective implementation of an increasingly heavy body of rules might have received closer attention at an earlier stage.

This book looks critically at EU policy and law-making processes for securities law to see how successfully the risks of regulatory mistake are managed and controlled. It also examines substantive new EU securities laws on issuer disclosure with a view to establishing whether they are likely to enhance the attractiveness of the EU marketplace for issuers and investors, or whether they are likely to detract because they are too rigid, too standardised, and involve excessive compliance costs.

I would like to record my gratitude to various people who provided valuable assistance in the process of writing this book. Without Niamh Moloney's magisterial work, *EC Securities Regulation* (Oxford, Oxford University Press, 2002), finding relevant background material and assessing its significance would have been much harder tasks. It has been rightly said of her book that it helps to define and develop the law in this field. I have also benefitted from Niamh's personal support and encouragement throughout this project and her comments on early drafts of the main chapters.

Howell Jackson read and commented on a number of the chapters and provided welcome general encouragement. He also gave me an opportunity to discuss some of the draft chapters with his International Securities LL.M. Class 2003/4 at Harvard Law School. Those sessions helped to clarify my thinking in certain key respects.

Others who assisted by providing helpful comments on drafts of individual chapters, answering specific questions, supplying useful material, suggesting new lines of inquiry or discussing issues with me include Albertina Albors-Llorens, Kern Alexander, Jesús Alfaro, Philip Augar, Chris Brayford, Didier Cahen, Brian Cheffins, Wolfgang Ernst, Christophe Hillion, Angus Johnston, Steffen Kern, Ian Mackintosh, Clive Maxwell, Colin Mayer, Michael McKee, Nigel Phipps, Pippa Rogerson, Anibal Sanchez, Jochen Seitz, Alberto Vaquerizo, Philip Wynn-Owen, Eddy Wymeersch, the Partners at Herbert Smith (particularly Charles Howarth, Malcolm Lombers, James Palmer, Jonathan Scott and Carol Shutkever), and two anonymous referees.

The staff of the Squire Law Library answered my queries and located material with their customary efficiency and cheerfulness. The Law Faculty's Computer Officers dealt well with occasional technological challenges along the way. Daud Khan provided timely assistance in the closing stages of writing the book by finding outstanding references and checking notes.

My thanks go the staff at Cambridge University Press, especially Kim Hughes and Jane O'Regan, for guiding the book through to production with calm professionalism and efficiency.

My biggest debt is owed to my children, Aoife and Oliver, who had to put up with a mother who was often preoccupied with arcane aspects of securities regulation and my husband, Rod, who not only provided thoughtful comments on individual chapters, but also supported and encouraged me in countless other ways throughout this project. The book is dedicated to him and to our children.

TABLE OF LEGISLATION AND CASES

Treaties

Consolidated Version of the Treaty
Establishing the European
Community (2002), OJ 2002
C325/1 (EC Treaty), 7, 100
Art. 3, 29
Art. 5, 29
Art. 14, 29
Art. 47(2), 29
Art. 94, 29
Art. 95, 29
Art. 105.4, 76
Art. 202, 66, 74
Protocol 30, para. 6, 70–71
Draft Treaty Establishing a Constitution
for Europe (18 July 2003) OJ 2003
C169/01, 7
Maastricht Treaty, 8

Commission Decisions

Commission Decision (2001/527/EC)
Establishing the Committee of
European Securities Regulators,
OJ 2001 L191/43 (CESR
Decision), 65, 78
Art. 4, 84
Art. 5, 84
Commission Decision (2001/528/EC)
Establishing the European
Securities Committee, OJ 2001
L191/45 (ESC Decision), 65, 77, 78
Commission Decision (2004/5/EC)
Establishing the Committee of
European Banking Supervisors,
OJ 2004 L3/28, 48

Commission Decision (2004/6/EC)
Establishing the Committee
of European Insurance and
Occupational Pensions
Supervisors, OJ 2004 L3/30, 48

Commission Recommendations

Commission Recommendation 2001/
256/EC of 15 November 2000 on
quality assurance for the statutory
audit in the European Union:
minimum requirements, OJ 2001
L191/91, 230
Commission Recommendation
2002/590/EC of 16 May 2002 on
statutory auditors' independence
in the EU: a set of fundamental
principles, OJ 2002 L191/22, 230

Council Decisions

Council Decision 99/468/EC Laying
Down the Procedure for the
Exercise of Implementing Powers
Conferred by the Commission
(Comitology Decision), OJ 1999
L184/23, 66

Council Resolutions

Council of Ministers Resolution on
More Effective Securities Market
Regulation in the European
Union (Stockholm, 23 March
2001), 61, 65, 83

para. 2, 67
para. 3, 68
para. 5, 74

European Parliament Resolutions

European Parliament Resolution on
the Implementation of Financial
Services Legislation (2001/
2247(INI) P5_TA(2002)0035),
66, 83
para. 5, 67

Regulations

Council Regulation (EC) 1103/97 of 17
June 1997 on certain provisions
relating to the introduction of
the euro, OJ 1997 L162/1, 171
Regulation (EC) 1606/2002 of the
European Parliament and of
the Council of 19 July 2002 on
the application of international
accounting standards, OJ 2002
L243/1, 35, 44, 69, 209, 213
Recital 16, 222, 225
Art. 6, 214

Directives

Fourth Council Directive 78/660/EC on
the annual accounts of certain types
of companies, OJ 1978 L222/11, 35
Council Directive 79/279/EEC of 5
March 1979 coordinating the
conditions for the admission of
securities to official stock exchange
listing, OJ 1979 L66/21 (Admission
Directive), 3, 34, 35, 135, 145, 260
Council Directive 80/390/EEC of 17
March 1980 coordinating the
requirements for the drawing up,

scrutiny and distribution of the
listing particulars to be published
for the admission of securities to
official stock exchange listing, OJ
1980 L100/1 (Listing Particulars
Directive), 34, 35, 136, 138, 186
Art. 15, 149
Council Directive 82/121/EEC of 15
February 1982 on information to
be published on a regular basis by
companies the shares of which
have been admitted to official
stock exchange listing, OJ 1982
L48/26 (Interim Reports
Directive), 35, 136, 186
Seventh Council Directive
83/349/EEC of 13 June 1983
on consolidated accounts,
OJ 1983 L193/1, 35
Eighth Council Directive 84/253/EEC
of 10 April 1984 on the approval
of persons responsible for
carrying out the statutory
audits of accounting documents,
OJ 1984 L126/20, 35
Council Directive 85/611 relating
to undertakings for collective
investment in transferable
securities (UCITS), OJ 1985
L375/3, 4
Council Directive 89/298/EEC of 17
April 1989 coordinating the
requirements for the drawing-up,
scrutiny and distribution of the
prospectus to be published when
transferable securities are offered
to the public, OJ 1989 L124/8
(Public Offers Directive), 3, 35,
36, 136
Art. 2.1(a), 170
Art. 2.1(b), 169
Art. 20, 149

Council Directive 89/592 of 13 November 1989 coordinating regulations on insider dealing, OJ 1989 L334/30, 30

Council Directive 93/22/EEC of 10 May 1993 on investment services in the securities field, OJ 1993 L141/27 (Investment Services Directive), 3, 38, 93, 186, 217, 239

Directive 2001/34EC of the European Parliament and of the Council of 28 May 2001 on the admission of securities to official stock exchange listing and on information to be published on those securities, OJ 2001 L184/1 (CARD), 34, 35, 145, 146, 186

Recital 40, 72
Recital 41, 73
Recital 42, 73
Art. 24, 72, 73
Art. 37, 149
Art. 68, 198
Art. 81, 198

Directive 2002/87/EC of the European Parliament and of the Council of 16 December 2002 on the supplementary supervision of credit institutions, insurance undertakings and investment firms in a financial conglomerate and amending Council Directives 73/239/EEC, 79/267/EEC, 92/49/EEC, 93/6/EEC and 93/22/EEC, and Directives 98/78/EC and 2000/12/EC of the European Parliament and of the Council, OJ 2003 L35/1 (Financial Conglomerates Directive), 73

Directive 2003/6/EC of the European Parliament and of the Council of 28 January 2003 on insider dealing and market manipulation (market abuse), OJ 2003 L96/16 (Market Abuse Directive), 44, 54, 68, 73, 81–2, 92, 97, 131, 134, 135, 208

Recital 1, 200
Recital 2, 200
Recital 7, 71
Recital 9, 71
Recital 36, 220
Recital 39, 220
Recital 40, 220
Recital 42, 71
Recital 43, 71
Art. 1.1, 197
Art. 6, 44
Art. 6.1, 197, 198, 199
Art. 6.2, 198
Art. 6.3, 199
Art. 9, 198
Art. 10, 71, 199
Art. 11, 220
Art. 12, 220
Art. 14, 220
Art. 16, 220
Art. 17.2, 71
Art. 17.4, 72

Directive 2003/71/EC of the European Parliament and of the Council of 4 November 2003 on the prospectus to be published when securities are offered to the public or admitted to trading and amending Directive 2001/34/EC, OJ 2003 L345/64 (Prospectus Directive), 44, 72, 92, 93, 95–6, 97, 109, 131, 134, 138, 147–9, 155–6, 159, 208

Recital 4, 137, 180, 200
Recital 10, 130, 137
Recital 12, 187
Recital 14, 150
Recital 15, 141
Recital 20, 141
Recital 21, 166, 179

Recital 22, 140
Recital 24, 263
Recital 37, 220
Recital 38, 220
Recital 39, 220
Recital 43, 220
Art. 1(m)(iii), 137
Art. 1.2(h), 180
Art. 2(m)(i), 149
Art. 2(m)(iii), 149, 156
Art. 2.1(b), 171
Art. 2.1(c), 171
Art. 2.1(e), 169
Art. 2.1(m)(ii), 174
Art. 2.2, 169
Art. 3.2, 169, 201
Art. 3.2(a), 169
Art. 3.2(b), 169
Art. 3.2(c), 169
Art. 3.2(d), 169
Art. 3.2(e), 180
Art. 5.1, 139, 179
Art. 5.2, 166, 171, 179
Art. 6, 189
Art. 6.1, 189
Art. 6.2, 189
Art. 7.2(b), 168, 171
Art. 7.2(e), 180, 181
Art. 10, 137, 206
Art. 13.5, 151
Art. 14, 195
Art. 14.2, 195
Art. 15, 169
Art. 17, 142
Art. 18, 142
Art. 19, 164
Art. 19.2, 151, 166
Art. 19.3, 166
Art. 19.4, 167
Art. 20.3, 162
Art. 21, 220, 238, 263
Art. 21.3(a), 141
Art. 22, 220

Art. 23, 192
Art. 25, 220
Art. 29, 137
Directive 2004/25/EC of the European
        Parliament and of the Council of
        21 April 2004 on takeover bids, OJ
        2004 L142/12 (Takeover
        Directive), 54, 110, 116–18
Art. 9, 117
Art. 11, 117
Directive 2004/39/EC of the European
        Parliament and of the Council of
        21 April 2004 on markets in
        financial instruments amending
        Council Directive 85/611/EEC and
        93/6/EEC and Directive 2000/12/
        EC of the European Parliament
        and of the Council and repealing
        Council Directive 93/22/EEC, OJ
        2004 L145/1 (Financial
        Instruments Markets Directive or
        ISD2), 44, 73, 83, 93, 98, 106, 186
Art. 27, 94
Arts. 36–46, 262
Art. 40, 261
Art. 53, 50
Transparency Directive, 44, 69–70, 83, 131,
        134, 145–7, 155–6, 159, 217, 260
Recital 1, 138, 200
Recital 10, 189, 190
Recital 15, 196
Recital 18, 220, 224
Recital 22, 73
Recital 24, 73
Recital 25, 73
Recital 26, 73
Recital 26a, 73
Recital 27, 220
Art. 2.1(1), 149
Art. 2.1(1)(ii), 174
Art. 3, 145
Art. 4, 138, 161
Art. 4.2, 189

Art. 5, 138, 161
Art. 5.2, 189
Art. 6, 138, 189
Art. 7, 189
Art. 16, 165
Art. 17, 196
Art. 17.3, 196
Art. 19, 161
Art. 19.3, 162
Art. 20, 220, 238, 264
Art. 21, 220
Art. 22, 149, 192
Art. 23, 73
Art. 24, 220
Art. 26, 161

Commission Regulations and Directives (Level 2)

Commission Directive 2003/124/EC of
    22 December 2003 implementing
    Directive 2003/6/EC as regards the
    definition and public disclosure
    of inside information and the
    definition of market manipulation,
    OJ 2003 L339/70, 82
  Art. 1, 197
  Art. 2, 199
  Art. 3, 198
Commission Directive 2003/125 of 22
    December 2003 implementing
    Directive 2003/6/EC as regards the
    fair presentation of investment
    recommendations and the
    disclosure of conflicts of interest, OJ
    2003 L339/73, 82
Commission Regulation (EC) 2273/2003
    of 22 December 2003
    implementing Directive 2003/6/
    EC as regards exemptions for
    buy-back programmes and
    stabilisation of financial instruments,
    OJ 2003 L336/33, 82

Commission Regulation (EC) 809/2004
    of 29 April 2004 implementing
    Directive 2003/71/EC of the
    European Parliament and of the
    Council as regards information
    contained in prospectuses as
    well as the format, incorporation
    by reference and publication
    of such prospectuses and
    dissemination of advertisements,
    OJ 2004 L149/1
  Recital 9, 140
  Recital 22, 140, 181
  Recital 23, 141
  Art. 3, 139
  Art. 4, 139
  Art. 5, 140
  Art. 5.1, 139
  Art. 7, 139
  Art. 9, 140
  Art. 10, 139
  Art. 11, 139
  Art. 12, 139
  Art. 14, 139
  Art. 15, 139
  Art. 16, 139
  Art. 19, 139
  Art. 20, 139
  Art. 21, 139
  Art. 23, 140, 181
  Art. 23.1, 181
  Art. 23.3, 141
  Art. 25, 179
  Art. 26, 179
  Art. 27, 137
  Art. 32, 195
  Art. 35, 161, 162
  Annex I, 139, 179
  Annex I, para 20.1, 161
  Annex II, 140
  Annex IV, 139
  Annex VI, 140
  Annex VII, 139

Annex VIII, 139
Annex IX, 139
Annex IX, para. 11.1, 171
Annex XI, 139
Annex XII, 139
Annex XIII, 139
Annex XVI, 139
Annex XVII, 139
Annex XIX, 140, 181

Committee of European Securities Regulation (CESR) constitutional documents and standards

CESR Charter
    Art. 4, 80
    Art. 4.5, 80
    Art. 5, 80, 81, 84
    Art. 6, 79
Standards for Alternative Trading Systems
    (CESR/02–086b, 2002),
    80, 240
Enforcement of Standards on
    Financial Information in Europe
    (CESR Standards on Financial
    Information, No.1, CESR/03–073),
    221, 222, 223
    Principle 3, 222
    Principle 6, 222
    Principle 7, 222
    Principle 20, 222
Coordination of Enforcement Activities
    (CESR Standards on Financial
    Information, No.2, CESR/03–317c,
    2004), 222
    Principle 4, 223

National legislation and regulatory standards

France
    Financial Security Act 2003, 229

Germany
    Securities Trading Act 1994, 39
    Exchange Act 2002, 249
Ireland
    Companies (Audit and Accounting)
        Act 2003, 229
United Kingdom
    Public Offers of Securities
        Regulations 1995
        (SI 1995/537)
        reg. 13, 37
        reg. 14, 37
        reg. 15, 37
    Financial Services and Markets Act 2000,
        54, 251
        s. 90, 37
    Financial Services and Markets
        Act 2000 (Recognition
        Requirements for Investment
        Exchanges and Clearing
        Houses) Regulations 2001
        (SI 2001/995), 237
    Financial Services and Markets Act
        2000 (Official Listing of Securities)
        Regulations 2001 (SI 2001/
        2956), 37
    Companies (Audit, Investigations
        and Community Enterprise)
        Bill 2003, 226
    UKLA, Listing Rules, 146, 250–1, 252
        Sch. 12, 193

United States

Public Company Accounting
    Reform and Investor
    Protection Act of 2002
    (Sarbanes-Oxley), 113
Final Rules Relating to the Oversight
    of Non US. Public Accounting
    Firms (PCAOB Release No.
    2004–005, June 2004), 114

CASES

European Court of Justice

Case 120/78, Rewe-Zentrale AG v. Bundesmonopolverwaltung für Branntwein (Cassis de Dijon) [1979] ECR 6, 4

Case C-212/97, Centros Ltd v Erhvervs-og Selskabsstyrelsen [1999] ECR I-1459, [1999] 2 CMLR 551, [2000] 2 BCLC 68, 56

Case C-376/98, Germany v. Parliament and Council (the Tobacco Advertising Case) [2000] ECR I-8419, 29

Case C-208/00, Überseering BV v. Nordic Construction Company Baumanagement GmbH (NCC) [2002] ECR I-9919, 56

Case C-167/01, Kamer van Koophandel en Fabriekn voor Amsterdam v. Inspire Art Ltd, 56

United Kingdom

Caparo Industries plc v. Dickman [1990] 2 AC 605, 190

Hedley Byrne & Co Ltd v. Heller & Partners Ltd [1964] AC 465, 190

Henderson v. Merrett Syndicates Ltd [1995] 2 AC 145, 190

Overview and introduction to terminology

A   The FSAP

Promoting the smooth and efficient flow of capital from savings to investment is a policy priority for Governments around the world. An important aspect of this policy agenda is the development of securities markets to facilitate access to capital by issuers.

Within the EU enthusiasm for improving issuers' access to capital is entwined with interest in building a properly integrated pan-European financial market. Such a market, it is believed, will offer a range of benefits including lower capital costs for issuers and better returns for investors that should, if projections are right, impact positively on the real economy.

The Financial Services Action Plan (FSAP) was an attempt by the European Commission to equip the Community better to meet the challenges of monetary union and to capitalise on the potential benefits of a single market in financial services.[1] The FSAP set out a detailed action plan for the adoption by 2005 of legislative measures to support a single, integrated financial market in which a strong securities market was envisaged as a major component.

The FSAP led to extensive change in securities market regulation: new laws; new law-making processes; and more attention to the mechanisms for the supervision of securities market activity and enforcement. With the FSAP nearing completion, it is now a good time to take stock of what has been achieved, and to identify challenges that lie ahead. Paradoxically, the programme of activity that was heralded by the FSAP is vulnerable to charges of both excess – that there has been intervention that is liable to inhibit legitimate business activity – and underachievement – that the reality of a common regulatory system, embracing common supervisory standards and practices as well as common legal rules, is still much further off than some political rhetoric might suggest.

---

[1] European Commission, *Financial Services: Implementing the Framework for Financial Markets: Action Plan* (COM (1999) 232).

Concern about what has been created by the FSAP is evident in a number of recent reports.[2] This book shares some of the concerns and identifies problems in three key areas: the balance between regulatory harmonisation and diversity, where some recent changes may have shifted the balance too far in favour of a standardised approach; excessive reliance on regulation as the first-choice policy tool at the expense of due attention to supervision; and insufficient regard to the consequences of EU regulation on the global competitiveness of its securities markets.

Although this book acknowledges some serious deficiencies in the recent developments, it does not see a pan-European securities market regulator and supervisor as offering a superior way forward. The preferred option is to build upon and refine the existing regulatory and supervisory framework. The book suggests that a dedicated pan-European securities regulatory and supervisory agency would not solve existing problems and that it could generate a host of new concerns about transparency, accountability, efficiency and effectiveness.

The FSAP was wide-ranging in scope but this book concentrates particularly on how the new legal framework will affect issuers' access to the primary and secondary securities market. Since any market would struggle to grow without a good supply of its basic commodities, the attractiveness, or otherwise, of a securities market to issuers, that is to the providers of fundamental securities, is a crucial determinant of its likely success. In line with international norms, disclosure is the primary regulatory strategy within the EU for regulating issuers' access to securities markets. The essays in this book therefore pay special attention to the new issuer disclosure regime. Examining such an intrinsically important area provides an opportunity to assess the achievements and failings of the FSAP more generally.

B   General background to the development of the FSAP

A properly integrated financial market is one where capital can move freely within the economic area and in which investment services are gen-

---

[2] HM Treasury, *Flexibility in the UK Economy* (March 2004), p. 25, available via www.hm-treasury.gov.uk (accessed April 2004); Securities Expert Group, *Financial Services Action Plan: Progress and Prospects* (Final Report, Brussels, May 2004), available via http://www.europa.eu.int/comm/internal_market/en/finances/actionplan/docs/stocktaking/fasap-stocktaking-report-securities_en.pdf (accessed May 2004).

erally available. Free movement of capital implies the removal of barriers hindering issuers from raising capital from wherever they like within the economic area and investors from investing anywhere they like within the economic area. Freedom to provide services, and the associated freedom for people to establish businesses, imply the removal of barriers hindering financial intermediaries and market infrastructure providers (trading systems, settlement services and so forth) from operating throughout the economic area. Free movement of capital, services and persons are freedoms enshrined in the Treaty Establishing the European Community.[3] This Treaty provides the base for Community legislative competence in the economic field.

The creation of a strong, deep securities market to facilitate the free movement of capital and pan-European provision of investment services and products was on the policy agenda of the central institutions by the 1960s[4] but it was not until 1979 that the first legislative measure directly relating to issuers was adopted – a Directive on admission to official listing.[5] The fairly narrowly confined area of admission of securities to official listing remained the focus for centralised legislative activity during the first part of the 1980s.

A significant expansion in securities laws emanating from the central institutions resulted from the drive towards the establishment of the single market that was launched by the European Commission in the mid-1980s. The Directives adopted during this second phase of securities law-making within the EU included the Investment Services Directive,[6] often described as the cornerstone of EU securities regulation,[7] and the Public Offers of Securities Directive.[8] These Directives made use of the passport

---

[3] Title III.

[4] Report by a Group of Experts, *The Development of a European Capital Market* (Brussels, European Commission, 1966) (Segré Report), discussed in N. Moloney, *EC Securities Regulation* (Oxford, Oxford University Press, 2002), pp. 22–5. This paragraph draws heavily on Moloney's work.

[5] Council Directive 79/279/EEC of 5 March 1979 coordinating the conditions for the admission of securities to official stock exchange listing, OJ 1979 No. L66/21.

[6] Council Directive 93/22/EEC of 10 May 1993 on investment services in the securities field, OJ 1993 No. L141/27.

[7] European Commission, *Upgrading the Investment Services Directive* (COM (2000), 729); Moloney, *EC Securities Regulation*, p. 24.

[8] Council Directive 89/298/EEC of 17 April 1989 coordinating the requirements for the drawing-up, scrutiny and distribution of the prospectus to be published when transferable securities are offered to the public, OJ 1989 No. L124/8.

concept.[9] The essence of the passport concept is that issuers, investment firms and market structure providers authorised in one Member State can gain access to other Member States without the need for further, local regulatory approvals. The passport concept was conceived as being crucial to the development of a properly integrated pan-European financial market in which issuers, investment firms and investors could operate freely and seamlessly, unimpeded by national boundaries.

Despite these developments a new mood of pessimism took hold during the latter part of the 1990s. There was a widespread view that insufficient had been done to equip the European Community to make the most of monetary union and to capitalise on its benefits.[10] The European Commission felt that Europe was still a long way from realising the potential benefits of the single market in financial services.[11] Although some progress had been made in the previous decade, the passage of time had exposed deficiencies in laws that often had been political compromises representing the lowest common denominator on which the Member States could agree. Member States retained much discretion to add to the centralised requirements and to interpret them in different ways, and this practice was felt to hinder the realisation of an effective integrated market. One of the more obvious failings of the existing regime was the passport provision for securities offerings.[12] Host Member States could require

---

[9] P. Clarotti, 'The Completion of the Internal Financial Market: Current Position and Outlook' in M. Andenas and S. Kenyon-Slade (eds.), *EC Financial Market Regulation and Company Law* (London, Sweet & Maxwell, 1993), pp. 1–17, provides an overview of the use of the passport concept across banking, securities and insurance law. He notes (at p. 8) that Council Directive 85/611/EEC relating to undertakings for collective investment in transferable securities (UCITS), OJ 1985 No. L375/3 was the first securities law Directive to make use of the passport concept. See also, E. Lomnicka, 'The Internal Financial Market and Investment Services' in ibid., pp. 85–6.

The landmark decision of the European Court of Justice in Case 120/78, *Rewe-Zentrale AG v. Bundesmonopolverwaltung für Branntwein (Cassis de Dijon)* [1979] ECR 6 marked a general shift in the internal market harmonisation programme, away from the imposition of the same standards in all Member States to mutual recognition regimes whereby Member States were obliged to accept compliance with the regulatory requirements of other Member States: G. Hertig, 'Imperfect Mutual Recognition for EC Financial Services' (1994) 14 *International Review of Law and Economics* 177, 178.

[10] Moloney, *EC Securities Regulation*, pp. 26–32 discusses the background to the FSAP and the Lamfalussy Report; R. S. Karmel, 'Reconciling Federal and State Interests in Securities Regulation in the United States and Europe' (2003) 28 *Brooklyn Journal of International Law* 495, 529.

[11] European Commission, *Financial Services: Building a Framework for Action* (COM (1998) 625), p. 1.

[12] Ibid., p. 9.

issuers seeking to rely on the passport to translate the prospectus into the local language and to add additional information for local investors. These additional requirements added significantly to the transaction costs of a cross-border issue making the passport route unattractive to issuers with the result that for most practical purposes it became irrelevant.[13] The passport regime for investment services providers was plagued by similar problems in that passported firms were generally subject to host Member State conduct of business rules, which were not harmonised and which could therefore differ from State to State.[14]

It was thus largely out of a desire to redress the deficiencies of the existing regulatory regime as a pan-European integration mechanism that the FSAP was born. This marks it out as unusual. Revisions of securities laws are more typically driven by market collapses or major scandals that unmask deficiencies in existing law and generate strong political imperatives for Governments to be seen to be moving quickly to correct the mistakes of the past and to repair investor confidence.[15] Although various crisis-response measures were grafted onto the detail of the FSAP during its life, its priorities and principles were originally shaped in a different environment. This is a relevant consideration in assessing the achievements of the FSAP.

C   From FSAP to Lamfalussy and CESR

One of the complicating aspects of studying the development of securities law and supervision within the EU is the bewildering array of acronyms

---

[13] A. B. St John, 'The Regulation of Cross-border Public Offerings of Securities in the European Union: Present and Future' (2001) *Denver Journal of International Law and Policy* 239.

[14] European Commission, *Financial Services: Building a Framework*, pp. 11–12; European Commission, *Upgrading*, p. 3 ('the usefulness of the single passport has been impaired by extensive exemptions from its scope and widespread application of host country requirements'). Generally, M. G. Warren, The Harmonization of European Securities Law' (2003) 37 *International Lawyer* 211, 213–15.

[15] S. Banner, 'What Causes New Securities Regulation? 300 Years of Evidence' (1997) 75 *Washington University Law Quarterly* 849; F. Partnoy, 'Why Markets Crash and What Law Can Do About It' (2000) 61 *University of Pittsburgh Law Review* 741; B. A. K. Rider, 'The Control of Insider Trading – Smoke and Mirrors!' (2000) 19 *Dickinson Journal of International Law* 1, 31–5; E. Ferran, 'Examining the United Kingdom's Experience in Adopting the Single Financial Regulator Model' (2003) 28 *Brooklyn Journal of International Law* 257.

and other terms whose meaning is not immediately obvious.[16] Alongside 'FSAP', there are two other terms whose significance is such that they merit an early introduction.

The first is the 'Lamfalussy' law-making process. In 2001 the process for making securities laws within the EU was overhauled with a view to providing a more nimble legislative machinery that would be better adapted to the pace of global financial market change.[17] The need for change in the legislative process, and a model for its achievement, had been laid out in a powerful report from an influential committee headed by Baron Alexandre Lamfalussy, a Belgian central banker and distinguished economist.[18] It has been said of Baron Lamfalussy's achievement in this field that he is one of very few people outside the world of politics to have an eponymous legislative process.[19]

The Lamfalussy process was applied to many of the new EU laws that are considered in this book. However, those laws were first formally proposed in the FSAP, an initiative which preceded the adoption of the new legislative process. This sequence of events deserves emphasis. Whilst it is legitimate to ask whether the adoption of the Lamfalussy process has helped produce better-quality laws governing securities market activity within the EU, it is important also to bear in mind that the Lamfalussy process came late, after certain important strategic policy decisions had been made and, crucially, after the timetable for the adoption of the FSAP had been set. These considerations must qualify whatever blame for the substantive quality of the recent laws is laid at the feet of the legislative process.

The second significant term is 'CESR', which stands for the Committee of European Securities Regulators. This Committee, which comprises the heads of the securities regulators from the EU Member States and certain

---

[16] 'The Tower of Babble', *Economist*, 2 August 2003, p. 45 notes that this is a general problem within the EU, it being a key EU strategy, honed over many years, 'to avoid calling anything by a name that might let an outsider guess what is being talked about'.

[17] The adoption of the new legislative process is considered in detail in ch. 3.

[18] *The Regulation of European Securities Markets: Final Report* (Brussels, 15 February 2001), in which *The Regulation of European Securities Markets: Initial Report* (Brussels, 9 November 2000) appears as Annex 5. The reports are available via http://www.europa.eu.int/comm/internal_market/en/finances/general/lamfalussyen.pdf (accessed April 2004). Baron Lamfalussy was the one-time general manager of the Bank for International Settlements, and president of the European Monetary Institute, the forerunner of the European Central Bank.

[19] P. Norman, 'Brussels Wise Man 'Satisfied' With Reform', *Financial Times*, 2 June 2003, FT Fund Management, p. 4.

other European countries, was established as part of the adoption of the Lamfalussy process.[20] CESR performs a range of functions, including participating in the process whereby laws are made and helping to develop pan-European consistency in supervisory practices and policies.

D   EU securities law – explanation for terminological approach

It is now widespread practice for legal instruments relating to the securities market that emanate from the central institutions to be described as "EU" measures. Thus, for example, the index to regulation on the European Commission's website proclaims that 'EU Directives ensure the development of a single securities market for both new issues and trading of securities.'[21] Likewise CESR's website describes it as an advisor to the Commission 'in particular in its preparation of draft implementing measures of EU framework Directives in the field of securities'.[22] The strict technical position is that securities laws are made within the legal framework of the European Community (EC, formerly European Economic Community or EEC), which is a Community within the common structure of the European Union.[23] The EU, as such, has a limited role, although this will change if the Constitutional Treaty for the EU is finally adopted because this is intended to confer legal personality and powers on the EU and to provide for it to succeed to all of the rights and obligations of the EC.[24] This book generally follows the looser practice that has developed in the securities field but references are made to EC law or to the EC Treaty where technical accuracy is demanded by the context.

---

[20] See further ch. 3.

[21] http://europa.eu.int/comm/internal_market/securities/index_en.htm (accessed April 2004).

[22] *CESR In Short*, statement on CESR website, http://www.cesr-eu.org/ (accessed April 2004).

[23] J. Shaw, *Law of the European Union* (3rd edn, Basingstoke, Palgrave Macmillan, 2000) pp. 4–11.

[24] Draft Treaty Establishing a Constitution for Europe (18 July 2003), OJ 2003 No. C169/1. A heavily amended version of the Constitution was agreed by the EU Heads of State/ Government in June 2004. The Constitution will now need to be approved unanimously by Member States. Various Member States have indicated their intention to hold a referendum on the issue. Since the process of securing all of the necessary approvals is likely to be time-consuming and politically contentious, with no guarantee of eventual success, the essays in this book refrain from speculating on how the new constitutional framework may affect securities law.

2

Law's role in the building of an integrated EU securities market

A Scope of chapter

Two fundamental, and interlinked, issues relating to the development of an integrated EU securities market are considered in this chapter.

The first concerns the policy objectives that underpin the interest of the central EU institutions and Member States in the development of an integrated securities market, the extent to which these policy objectives have already been achieved, and the forces that have contributed to that achievement. A pan-European, fully integrated financial market, of which a securities market is an important component element, represents a key part of the political and economic vision for the EU. Establishing a common market for certain sorts of economic activity was where the massive structure that is now the European Union all began in the 1950s.[1] If originally this was conceived as a post-World War II plan to avoid further armed conflict, by the 1960s the economic advantages that could be secured by the creation of a large trading bloc were becoming highly valued in their own right.[2] Promotion of economic integration has continued to occupy a central position in EU policy-making down to the present day. With regard to financial markets, the integration programme received a massive boost at the end of the 1980s with the formal commencement of the process for the realisation of economic and monetary union.[3] This process produced the Maastricht Treaty, which paved the way for the establishment of the European Central Bank and resulted in the introduction of the Euro

---

[1] With the establishment of the European Coal and Steel Community by the Treaty of Paris in 1951: S. Weatherill and P. Beaumont, *EU Law* (3rd edn, London, Penguin, 1999), p. 2. Generally on the origins of the EU: J. Gillingham, *European Integration 1950–2003: Superstate or New Market Economy* (Cambridge, Cambridge University Press, 2003), pt 1.

[2] Weatherill and Beaumont, *EU Law*, p. 5.

[3] Ibid., pp. 767–83.

as a unit of account in 1999 and its adoption in 2002 as the physical national currency in the countries of the Eurozone.[4]

From an economic perspective, the policy of promoting the development of an integrated securities market that combines fragmented pools of capital in a stronger and deeper single source has much to commend it. Evidence reviewed in this chapter strongly suggests significant linkages between financial market development and economic growth. The existence of a strong securities market matters to financial development and hence to economic growth because banks and securities markets are complementary sources of finance and each has potential advantages over the other depending on the type of economic activity for which funding is being sought.

In recent years, the European corporate sector has shifted away from its traditional reliance on bank-based financing towards greater use of the securities markets. European investor interest in securities markets has also grown. However, particularly on the retail side, investor interest is still largely fragmented along national lines and thus, despite some movement in that direction, it cannot yet be claimed that the EU has a fully integrated single securities market. That the single securities market is not yet a reality is significant because it implies that there remain important policy questions about tools that might be put to use to complete the building project.

Regulation, in its narrow rule-making sense, is a favoured EU policy tool. It is therefore appropriate to pay particular attention to the historical contribution made by EU regulation towards the development of securities market activity within the EU, and also to consider its potential further contribution towards completion of the task. The role of regulation is the second key issue considered in this chapter but the discussion of it is preceded by a strong caveat to the effect that the development of securities market activity is contingent upon a range of variables and is not simply a creature of central planning.

In contemporary law and economics scholarship there is much discussion of the relationship between law and financial development, a central question being whether law drives financial development or follows after it to regularise and formalise the norms that market participants have already come to expect as a matter of established practice. Superficially,

---

[4] The origins of European Monetary Union (EMU) are reviewed by J. Dermine, 'European Capital Markets: Does the Euro Matter?' in J. Dermine and P. Hillion (eds.), *European Capital Markets with a Single Currency* (Oxford, Oxford University Press, 1999), pp. 1–30 and D. Gros and K. Lannoo, 'EMU Monetary Policy and Capital Markets', ibid., pp. 33–75.

this debate appears relevant in the context of EU securities market regulation for two reasons. First, in the rhetoric often seen in EU policy discussions relating to the development of a single securities market, legal
changes are frequently described as having a creative effect. Taken at face
value, such commentary appears to suggest that historical study of the
ways in which the EU has used regulation to advance its single market
goals could usefully inform the wider debate on the relationship between
law and financial development. However, this chapter suggests that an
examination of the EU's record in regulating securities markets from this
perspective is likely to disappoint. Stripped of its rhetoric, historically the
EU's agenda for securities market regulation was mainly concerned with
the task of dismantling barriers to doing business or investing on a cross-
border basis. As such, it had a different focus from, and therefore tells us
little that is useful to, the general debate on law as a creative force since
that debate is essentially concerned with the contribution that credibly
enforced investor protection laws can make to financial development.
Even narrowing down the inquiry to aspects of established EU law that
can properly be regarded as attempts to improve pan-European investor
protection, the chapter suggests that there is little concrete evidence to
link the growth in securities market activity that has taken place within the
EU in the past two decades to the existence of these laws.

The second reason why the general 'law matters' debate could be relevant
to the analysis of EU securities market regulation is its normative dimension. As the need for barrier-dismantling laws has diminished, the attention
of EU policy-makers has turned increasingly to investor protection
issues,[5] a potentially worrying change of emphasis if looked at through the
lens of the 'law matters' debate. That debate has failed thus far to establish
convincingly that better-quality investor protection laws actually do promote
securities market development or, even if a linkage is assumed, to pinpoint
precisely which laws matter most in this respect. This uncertainty suggests
that EU policy-makers should proceed cautiously in pursuing an investor
protection regulatory agenda because they are, broadly speaking, shooting
in the dark. Arguably they would do better to leave some room for
continuing diversity between Member States with regard to investor protection laws. This alternative would not necessarily preclude a gradual
shift towards common standards because it could allow for a process of de

---

[5] N. Moloney, 'Confidence and Competence: The Conundrum of EC Capital Markets Law'
[2004] *Journal of Corporate Law Studies* 1.

facto convergence by Member States around the regulatory requirements that have proved to be the most successful in attracting issuers and investors. This quasi-Darwinian mechanism implies a form of competition between Member States to supply the rules that are liked most by the market.

This chapter argues for a mixed approach in which there is a continuing role for both harmonisation and regulatory competition in the development of the EU regulatory framework. However, the opposite trend is evident in some measures adopted under the Financial Services Action Plan (FSAP[6]), the five-year programme of action announced by the European Commission in 1999, since these evidence a move towards greater uniformity imposed from the centre and a corresponding reduction of the scope for regulatory competition between Member States. This trend could be difficult to reverse despite the potential merits of doing so. A more encouraging sign is that, as the FSAP nears completion, there are indications that policy priorities are shifting away from regulation and onto supervision and enforcement, aspects of the overall regulatory system that could in fact matter more to securities market growth than continual refinement of the substantive rules.

The chapter is organised as follows. Section B outlines the benefits of financial development, examines the growth in securities market activity in the EU and considers some of the forces that propelled it. Section C looks specifically at the question whether EU laws banning insider dealing and promoting issuer disclosure encouraged the development of European securities market activity during the 1980s and 1990s but finds no strong evidence of linkages. Section D examines the strategic approach adopted in the FSAP and suggests some lessons for the future.

B   Financial development and the promotion of economic growth

The benefits of financial market development: expectations and evidence

Promoting securities market integration as part of a wider financial market integration objective can be regarded as a step towards achievement of the long-term political vision of a fully integrated European super-State.[7] The EU is at a point in its evolution where it is acquiring some significant

---

[6] European Commission, *Financial Services: Implementing the Framework for Financial Markets: Action Plan* (COM (1999) 232) ('*FSAP Action Plan*').

[7] 'There are forces at work here that are grander than a desire to shape up economically: A Survey of Europe's Internal Market', *Economist*, 8 July 1989, p. 55.

State-like attributes – such as the Euro, a growing military capacity and a Constitution. Closer European political union remains, however, highly controversial, being seen by some as threatening an unacceptable erosion of the national sovereignty of Member States.[8]

Looking more narrowly at the economic objectives underlying the drive towards an integrated European financial market takes the debate into somewhat less contentious territory. Since it is a key function of financial markets, defined here as including equity markets, bond markets and the banking sector,[9] to facilitate the allocation of resources to their most productive use, it is intuitively persuasive to expect connections between the depth and sophistication of a region's financial markets and its economic prosperity. A well-functioning integrated financial market that brings together previously fragmented pools of capital into a single source should offer a range of potential benefits to enhance the allocative efficiency of the market for the benefit of the real economy.[10] For investors it should offer the potential for higher returns through enhanced opportunities for portfolio diversification in more liquid and competitive capital markets. For companies it should provide easier access to financing capital and to a wider choice of financial products at attractive prices.[11]

Studies support these intuitive expectations. The European Commission commissioned its own research measuring the projected economic benefits of a fully integrated pan-European financial market.[12] That research found that the cost of equity capital would fall by about 40 basis points on average as a result of full European financial market integration, and that there would be a similar reduction in the cost of bond financing. Among the key results indicated by the report's macroeconomic simulations incorporating these reductions in the cost of capital for companies were that the

---

[8] E.g., 'The Perils of Political Europe', *Economist*, 28 June 2003, p. 52. See further Weatherill and Beaumont, *EU Law*, pp. 32–3 and references there to the debate on the desirability of aspiring to convert the EU into a State.

[9] London Economics, *Quantification of the Macro-Economic Impact of Integration of EU Financial Markets* (Final Report to the European Commission Directorate-General for the Internal Market, November 2002) sec. 2.4 provides the definition which is adopted here. This report is available via http://europa.eu.int/comm/internal_market/en/finances/mobil/overview.htm (accessed April 2004).

[10] Ibid.

[11] Ibid.

[12] Ibid. The results are summarised in the executive summary and developed further in the report.

level of EU-wide real GDP would rise by 1.1 per cent in the long-run, total business investment would be almost 6 per cent higher and total employment would be 0.5 per cent higher.

Although self-commissioned research which is supportive of an institution's agenda merits a degree of scepticism, other empirical work involving firm-level studies, industry studies, individual country studies and cross-country studies, also identifies positive linkages between financial market development and economic growth.[13] Levine and Zervos show that active (though not necessarily large) stock markets and a strong banking sector are good predictors of growth.[14] Demirgüç-Kunt and Maksimovic support the significance of an active stock market to growth.[15] There are some doubts about causality – does financial development generate economic growth or follow after it?[16] Supporters of causality from development to growth concede the difficulties of proving this but point to the large body of evidence that is consistent with this view.[17] Another plausible view is that the causal relationship is two-way: financial development can spawn economic growth but, equally, economic growth can increase participation in financial markets thereby facilitating the creation and expansion of financial institutions.[18] Overall, economic theory and empirical work offer much support for the existence of a strong, statistically significant relationship between financial development and growth.[19] As Levine, a leading authority, puts it: 'Although conclusions must be started hesitantly and with ample qualifications, the preponderance of theoretical reasoning and empirical evidence suggests a positive, first-order relationship between financial development and growth.'[20]

[13] Ibid., sec. 2.3 provides a literature survey.

[14] R. Levine and S. Zervos, 'Stock Markets, Banks, and Economic Growth' (1998) 88 *American Economic Review* 537.

[15] A. Demirgüç-Kunt and V. Maksimovic, 'Law, Finance, and Firm Growth' (1998) 53 *Journal of Finance* 2107.

[16] J. Jayaratne and P. Strahan, 'The Finance-Growth Nexus: Evidence from Bank Branch Deregulation' (1996) 111(4) *Quarterly Journal of Economics* 639 summarises the long-standing causality debate. So too does R. Levine, 'Financial Development and Economic Growth: Views and Agenda' (1997) 35 *Journal of Economic Literature* 688.

[17] Jayaratne and Strahan, 'The Finance-Growth Nexus'.

[18] London Economics, *Quantification*, sec. 2.3.

[19] M. S. Khan and A. S. Senhadji, 'Financial Development and Economic Growth: An Overview' *IMF* Working Paper WP/00/209 (2000), available via http://www.imf.org/external/pubs/ft/wp/2000/wp00209.pdf (accessed April 2004).

[20] Levine, 'Financial Development'.

European politicians and civil servants can thus draw upon impressive support for the view that financial market development will lead to the economic growth that they envisage for Europe. As part of this, the growth of a liquid securities market does seem to be crucial if Europe is to come anywhere close to achieving its publicly-expressed grand ambition of becoming the most innovative, dynamic, knowledge-based economy in the world.[21] Studies suggest that arms-length securities market-based financing is better than bank-based relationship-orientated financing at financing innovation.[22] Newer companies lose out in a bank-based system because the system is less competitive, its inherently conservative players lack the mindset and incentive to innovate, and its opacity tends to discriminate against newcomers.[23]

The relative merits of securities market and bank-based financing systems are much discussed.[24] A compelling view is that this debate is somewhat misplaced and that, rather than it being a choice of one rather than the other, a well-functioning sophisticated financial market should comprise both banks and securities markets providing complementary financial products and services.[25] As well as being better equipped to meet the varying needs of different types of issuer, this model is particularly appropriate for the EU because of the differences in Member States' economies, especially after the May 2004 enlargement of the EU. Studies suggest that bank-based financing is almost always the best route for the development of less mature economies.[26]

---

[21] At its Lisbon Summit Meeting in 2000 the European Council adopted this as its new strategic goal for the upcoming decade: *Presidency Conclusions*, Lisbon European Council, 23–24 March 2000, available via http://ue.eu.int/en/info/eurocouncil/index.htm (accessed April 2004).

[22] R. G. Rajan and L. Zingales, 'Banks and Markets: The Changing Character of European Finance', *National Bureau of Economic Research* Working Paper No 9595 (2003); W. Carlin and C. Mayer, 'Finance, Investment and Growth' (2003) 69 *Journal of Financial Economics* 191.

[23] Rajan and Zingales, 'Banks and Markets'.

[24] Khan and Senhadji, 'Financial Development' 6–7 provide a helpful summary. See, too, B. S. Black, 'The Legal and Institutional Preconditions for Strong Securities Markets' (2001) 48 *UCLA Law Review* 781, 832–3 which sets out a number of potential advantages that securities markets may have over bank financing and internal financing as a means to finance firm growth.

[25] Levine, 'Financial Development'.

[26] D. C. North, *Institutions, Institutional Change and Economic Performance* (Cambridge, Cambridge University Press, 1990).

Growth in securities market activity in the EU

Within Continental Europe the corporate sector has historically relied heavily on bank-based financing and made little use of securities market-based financing. This is changing, and the extent of change merits attention to establish how far existing market conditions fall short of the desired policy goal of a pan-European financial market in which bank and securities market financing both play a significant role. Forces that propelled the shift towards greater securities market activity within the EU are also worth examining to set within an appropriately broader context questions about the extent to which regulatory intervention, which is the main policy tool that EU institutions have at their disposal, historically contributed to the growth of securities market activity, and its possible future contribution.

Market changes

Since the 1980s the corporate sector in Continental Europe has been gradually moving away from traditional bank-based financing and towards an increasingly securities market-based approach to raising capital.[27] During the last 20 years or so, the number of listed companies in France, Germany and Spain rose substantially.[28] European IPOs became increasingly common: in 1999, for example, public offerings in Spain, Germany and Italy raised more equity than those in the UK.[29] Secondary public offerings also grew in significance, particularly in the Netherlands.[30] According to one study, in the two decades since 1980 in Continental Europe the stock market capitalisation to GDP ratio went up thirteen times while the proportion of investments financed through equity issues went up sixteen times.[31]

---

[27] London Economics, *Quantification*, sec. 1.1; European Commission, *Proposal for a Directive of the European Parliament and of the Council on investment services and regulated markets* (COM (2002) 625), explanatory memorandum, pp. 3–5.

[28] C. van der Elst, 'The Equity Markets, Ownership Structures and Control: Towards an International Harmonization' in K. J. Hopt and E. Wymeersch (eds.), *Capital Markets and Company Law* (Oxford, Oxford University Press, 2003), pp. 3–46. Also E. Nowak, 'Investor Protection and Capital Market Regulation in Germany' in I. P. Krahnen and R. H. Schmidt (eds.), *The German Financial System* (Oxford, Oxford University Press, 2004), pp. 426–7 noting German developments suggesting a gradual evolution towards a market-orientated equity culture.

[29] Nowak, 'Investor Protection'.

[30] Ibid.

[31] Rajan and Zingales 'Banks and Markets'.

During the global boom in mergers and acquisitions activity during the 1990s, European companies relied extensively on the bond markets to finance their acquisitions.[32] European companies also became more outward looking in their search for investors, with the number of them with cross-listings, in the US or in European countries other than their home State, increasing significantly.[33]

Just as the European corporate sector became increasingly interested in raising finance from the securities markets, so too did European investors wake up to attractive opportunities offered by stock market investing. The European institutional investment industry (principally, insurance companies, pension funds and mutual funds)[34] grew significantly, with funds under management recently estimated to be valued at around $2.2 trillion (life funds), $2 trillion (pension funds) and $2.5 trillion (mutual funds).[35] European pension funds, which had traditionally concentrated their investments in bonds, began to invest much more heavily in the equity securities markets.[36] European mutual funds, again traditionally bond-based, also began to shift towards equity.[37]

New securities markets and trading platforms sprang up to compete for new issuance and secondary trading business from issuers and investors.[38] The European banking sector also changed significantly under the influence of the securities markets.[39] One change was that an explosion of new derivative and securitised products provided banks with opportunities to manage their traditional commercial lending business in new ways by enabling them to remove assets from their balance sheets and convert them into sophisticated capital markets financial instruments. Another

---

[32] G. Galati and K. Tsatsaronis, 'The Impact of the Euro on Europe's Financial Markets' *Bank for International Settlements* Working Paper No 100 (July 2001), para. 3.2.

[33] M. Pagano, A. A. Röell and J. Zechner, 'The Geography of Equity Listing: Why Do Companies List Abroad?' (2002) 57 *Journal of Finance* 2651.

[34] E. P. Davis and B. Steil, *Institutional Investors* (Cambridge, Mass., MIT Press, 2001), pp. 14–18.

[35] Ibid., p. 165.

[36] Ibid., pp. 167–8; Hopt and Wymeersch (eds.), *Capital Markets and Company Law*, pt V.

[37] Davis and Steil, *Institutional Investors*, pp. 172–3.

[38] European Commission, *Proposal for a Directive on investment services*, explanatory memorandum, pp. 8–12.

[39] 'Deregulation of European financial systems, competition from home and abroad, the need to tap the capital markets of the US – these trends have created the global investment bank. Universal banks in Switzerland and Germany have decided that their future lies in competing in this wider league, not in continuing to fight yesterday's battles at home.' P. Martin, 'Ghost of Business Future', *Financial Times*, 11 December 1997, p. 20.

was that growth in interest in securities market financing presented some of them with potentially lucrative business opportunities to expand out of traditional lending.[40] Major European banks, particularly German and (outside the EU) Swiss ones, long ago recognised opportunities to generate superior returns on investment banking and asset management to those achievable through traditional relationship banking.[41] Building up an investment banking and asset management franchise (a process that frequently involved the acquisition of established British investment banks)[42] enabled European banks to respond to growing interest in securities market-based financing by the European corporate sector, and to compete with foreign, particularly US, investment banks for that business.[43] It also equipped them with the capability to sell new products and services to existing customers, and to reach out to new customers and markets. How things have changed is illustrated by the position of Deutsche Bank, once known for its role as provider of traditional banking finance for German industry, but now in competition with Wall Street investment houses for global investment banking business.[44]

Admittedly European developments pale by international comparison. Collectively European securities markets are estimated to be only about

---

[40] European Commission, *Financial Integration Monitor* (SEC (2004) 559), p. 19. This is the Commission's first annual report on indicators of economic benefits from financial integration. An accompanying report from a group of securities market specialists which was established by the Commission to take stock of the FSAP takes the view that it is too early to judge the impact of the FSAP on the trend towards integration within EU securities markets: Securities Expert Group, *Financial Services Action Plan: Progress and Prospects* (Final Report, May 2004), p. 5. This report is available via http://www.europa.eu.int/comm/internal_market/en/finances/actionplan/docs/stocktaking/fasap-stocktaking-report-securities_en.pdf (accessed May 2004).

[41] Davis and Steil, *Institutional Investors*, pp. 198–9.

[42] Including the acquisition of Morgan Grenfell by Deutsche Bank (Germany), Barings by ING Bank (Netherlands), Kleinwort Benson by Dresdner (Germany), Hoare Govett by ABN Amro (Netherlands) and BZW by Crédit Suisse (Switzerland): Dermine 'European Capital Markets', p. 26.

[43] W. Gerke, M. Bank and M. Steiger, 'The Changing Role of Institutional Investors – A German Perspective' in Hopt and Wymeersch (eds.), *Capital Markets and Company Law*, p. 383. According to a survey by the *Financial Times* in February 2001 (*Europe Reinvented*, http://specials.ft.com/europereinvented1/FT3VDDT1WHC.html (accessed April 2004)) giant investment banks such as Goldman Sachs and Morgan Stanley Dean Witter were changing Europe's corporate landscape beyond recognition by putting together multi-billion dollar cross-border deals. See also, Gillingham, *European Integration 1950–2003*, pp. 453–4 (on US-employed bankers sending shock waves through the European financial system).

[44] T. Major, 'Deutsche Bank Faces Up to Its Identity Crisis', *Financial Times*, 28 September 2001, p. 23.

half the size of those in the US.[45] Although IPOs have become more common in Continental Europe, the size of the 'free float' – the portion of securities offered to the market – tends to remain much smaller than in the US and the UK, with the result that concentrated ownership of firms persists.[46] Institutional investment in European equity markets is still nothing like the dominant force that it is in the US.[47] The growth of an equity culture in Europe took a severe knock with the deep downturn in securities markets in the early 2000s. As the price of securities fell and dividends were cut, retail investor sentiment turned away from the markets.[48] This affected some market infrastructure providers badly. For example, the German Neuer Markt, once a poster child for the growth in European securities markets, went from being lauded in the mid to late 1990s as a highly successful market for young, fast-growing technology companies, through a period of challenge as share prices fell and IPOs were postponed,[49] to a serious loss of capitalisation that led to its closure in 2002.[50] The market downturn at the turn of the millennium also exposed the mixed success of efforts by European banks to turn themselves into 'bulge bracket' investment houses to rival the likes of Morgan Stanley and Goldman Sachs.[51] During the early 2000s several European banks had to scale back significantly their loss-making investment banking activities.[52]

---

[45] Lamfalussy Committee, *The Regulation of European Securities Markets: Final Report* (Brussels, 15 February 2001) (*Lamfalussy Report*), pp. 78–83. The *Lamfalussy Report* is available via http://www.europa.eu.int/comm/internal_market/en/finances/general/lamfalussyen. pdf (accessed April 2004).

[46] For example, about 90 per cent of companies listed on the London Stock Exchange do not have a major shareholder owning 25 per cent or more of the voting rights, whereas 85 per cent of listed German companies have such a shareholder: M. Goergen and L. Renneboog, 'Why Are The Levels of Control (So) Different in German and UK Companies? Evidence From Initial Public Offerings' (2003) 19 *Journal of Law, Economics and Organization* 141.

[47] *Lamfalussy Report*, p. 80.

[48] A. Skorecki, 'Equity Ship is Becalmed', *Financial Times*, 11 January 2003, Money Section, p. 3.

[49] T. Barber, 'The Neuer Markt: Celebrations Turn to Sober Reflections', *Financial Times*, 2 December 1999, European Private Equity Survey, p. 3.

[50] Skorecki, 'Equity Ship'.

[51] 'Is Deutschland AG Kaputt?', *Economist*, 7 December 2002, A Survey of Germany, p. 8.

[52] 'The Perils of Not Sticking to Your Knitting', *Economist Global Agenda*, 12 November 2002, via www.economist.com (accessed June 2004) (noting problems at Commerzbank and commenting 'It is hard not to feel sorry for Germany's private-sector commercial banks. It is no wonder that they were tempted into pastures new, such as insurance and investment banking. After all, the commercial-banking market in Germany is barely profitable thanks to a surfeit of state-subsidised Landesbanks and mutually owned savings institutions. Unfortunately, Germany's banks have found, like other banks that were seduced by the idea of being a one-stop-shop for a range of financial services, that the practice is a lot more difficult than the theory.'

Yet, despite a period of depressed conditions in European securities markets, there remains strong support for the view that the strengths of market-based financing are now sufficiently embedded to withstand occasional market corrections.[53] Certainly on the bonds side, the market is growing and appears likely to continue to do so in the absence of major political or economic upheavals.[54]

Greater securities market activity within the EU does not necessarily indicate the emergence of a truly integrated pan-European securities market. In fact, there is strong evidence to counter any suggestion to this effect since it points broadly towards the conclusion that although wholesale financial markets are integrating, retail financial services in the EU are still fragmented along largely national lines.[55]

Fragmentation can be seen in the structure of issuance activity. Although gross issuance of international equity by Eurozone companies during 1999–2000 almost doubled compared with the previous two-year period to reach the equivalent of $199 billion,[56] it cannot be said that truly pan-European offerings of equity securities to institutional and retail investors are a reality. Where pan-European equity securities offerings take place,

See also 'Big, Bigger, Biggest', *Economist*, 6 April 2002, p. 77 (discussing the problems faced by ABN Amro (Netherlands), Commerzbank (Germany) and Société Générale (France) in breaking into global investment banking business). Deutsche Bank Research, 'Consolidation in European Banking: Great Progress – Except in Germany' (2004) 11 *EU Monitor* 4, 10 notes that investment banking in Europe is increasingly being left to the most successful players from the USA and Europe.

[53] European Commission, *Upgrading the Investment Services Directive* (COM (2000) 729) 5; European Commission, *Proposal for a Directive on investment services*, explanatory memorandum, pp. 3–5.

[54] P. Coggan, 'Considering Equity Supply', *Financial Times*, 28 July 2003, p. 28 reporting that long-term bond issuance was $2,193bn (£1,367bn) in the first half of that year, up 15.5 per cent on the same period in 2002 but that the annual growth in European equity issuance had slowed by 10–15 per cent (as a proportion of market value) in the late 1990s to 2–3 per cent in 2002. European Commission, *Financial Integration Monitor*, p. 8 also reports significant increase in cross-border volume of trade settlements in bond markets.

[55] European Commission, *Financial Integration Monitor*, pp. 4–5; HM Treasury, Financial Services Authority and Bank of England, *The EU Financial Services Action Plan: A Guide* (July 2003), available via http://www.hm-treasury.gov.uk/documents/financial_services/eu_financial_services/fin_euf_actionplan.cfm (accessed April 2004). The OECD *Economic Survey – Euro Area 2003* also found uneven integration of financial markets across market segments. This report is available via http://www.oecd.org (accessed April 2004).

A specific example is provided by the example of therapeutics and diagnostics company Innogenetics (Ghent, Belgium). Philippe Archinard, CEO, has been quoted as saying that despite listing on Euronext, the company's shares still attracted little interest from investors outside Belgium: S. Louët, 'Biotechs Await Single European Financial Market' (2003) 21(12) *Nature Biotechnology* 1417.

[56] Galati and Tsatsaronis, 'The Impact of the Euro', para. 4.

they are usually structured as a public offering to investors in the issuer's home market, with complementary private placements to institutional investors in other Member States. In this respect the EU has certainly not yet achieved the goal of a fully-integrated capital market.[57] Even in the bond markets, the pan-European market is immature in the sense that it is dominated by a few types of issuer, principally banks and media and telecommunications companies.[58] The pan-European market for high yield bonds remains underdeveloped.[59]

Fragmentation is also evident in common patterns of investment activity. Even on the institutional side, European investors still retain some bias towards their home – i.e. national – securities market in their investment decisions. This bias is to some extent linked to national protectionist legislation, which requires pension and investment funds to invest a considerable portion of their funds in Government securities.[60] Higher taxes on non-domestic investments are also a powerful disincentive against vigorous pursuit of a genuinely pan-European investment strategy.[61] However, and particularly in the fixed income bond market, European institutional investors are increasingly pursuing pan-European investment strategies.[62]

Amongst financial intermediaries, in the retail segment foreign fund managers have begun to challenge local providers of collective investment products.[63] However, it is US fund managers that have achieved the most notable early success in operating fund management businesses on a pan-European basis; European managers tend to remain divided on local, national lines.[64]

Investment analysts appear to be the vanguard in the establishment of an integrated pan-European market as a practical reality. Research on European bonds and equities is increasingly done by sector rather than by

---

[57] A. B. St John, 'The Regulation of Cross-border Public Offerings of Securities in the European Union: Present and Future' (2001) 29 *Denver Journal of International Law and Policy* 239.

[58] Galati and Tsatsaronis, 'The Impact of the Euro', para. 3.2.

[59] Ibid.

[60] 'A Ragbag of Reform', *Economist*, 3 March 2001, p. 93.

[61] T. Balk, 'Brussels Has to Bear Down on Unfair Taxes' *Financial Times*, 17 February 2003, FT Fund Management, p. 6.

[62] European Commission, *Financial Integration Monitor*, p. 9; Galati and Tsatsaronis, 'The Impact of the Euro', para. 5.

[63] F. Gimbel, 'US Managers Dominate Europe', *Financial Times*, 21 July 2003, FT Fund Management, p. 1.

[64] Ibid.

country.[65] The adoption of the Euro has accelerated the trend towards sectorally-orientated research.[66]

The provision of corporate finance advisory services is also becoming more integrated. This trend is particularly evident in the bond markets, where there is clear evidence of convergence in fee levels for intermediaries as a result of enhanced competition.[67] US investment banks have attracted a significant share of the European market in bond underwriting.[68]

With regard to market infrastructure provision, although more integrated market infrastructures are emerging,[69] Europe still has around 30 stock exchanges. Clearing and settlement remain fragmented. Ambitious plans to establish uniform trading platforms to facilitate seamless pan-European equities trading have encountered serious difficulties and have had to be scaled back.[70] Perhaps the clearest example of the problems was the collapse of the proposed merger between the London Stock Exchange and Deutsche Börse in 2000.[71] This foundered in the face of opposition by established market participants and difficulties in reconciling divergent local regulatory requirements.[72] The Amsterdam, Brussels, Lisbon and Paris stock exchanges have achieved a merger of sorts but its failure to attract large blue chip stocks has undermined its prestige to some extent.[73]

The persistence of fragmentation in some aspects of EU securities market activity indicates that the task of building an integrated EU-wide securities market is still incomplete. This is a finding that has obvious significant implications for the policy agenda, though it does not necessarily point towards the conclusion that the driving force for further progress towards completion of the project can, or should, come from EU regulatory intervention.

---

[65] 'A Ragbag'; Galati and Tsatsaronis, 'The Impact of the Euro', para. 4.3.

[66] S. Shojai, 'But I Thought I Was Part of a Pan-European Index', *Sunday Business*, 16 September 2001, p. 29.

[67] Securities Expert Group, *FSAP: Progress*, p. 5.

[68] European Commission, *Financial Integration Monitor*, p. 14.

[69] Ibid., p. 9.

[70] Galati and Tsatsaronis, 'The Impact of the Euro', para. 4.2.

[71] 'Signed But Not Sealed', *Economist*, 27 May 2000, p. 113.

[72] Generally on the regulatory challenges presented by exchange mergers: E. Wymeersch, 'Regulating European Markets: The Harmonisation of Securities Regulation in Europe in the New Trading Environment' in E. Ferran and C. E. Goodhart (eds.), *Regulating Financial Services and Markets in the 21st Century* (Oxford, Hart Publishing, 2001), pp. 189–210.

[73] Galati and Tsatsaronis, 'The Impact of the Euro', para. 4.2.

Forces that propelled the growth in securities market activity within the EU

The recent shift in Continental Europe towards securities market-based financing can be attributed to a range of factors, some of which affected securities markets around the world, some of which were exclusively, or particularly, EU-orientated. An outline of certain factors that appear to have been especially forceful agents of change is as follows.

At the broad international level, the collapse of the Bretton Woods system of fixed exchange rates in 1971 led to the disappearance of restrictions hindering the smooth international flow of capital.[74] International financial deregulation put new competitive pressures on national financing systems because it increased the possibilities for companies to tap into pools of capital outside their home markets.[75] Expansion in international trade also generated new competitive pressures that filtered through to national financing systems.[76] Technological innovation assisted the massive international development of securities market-based financing: this made possible electronic trading and settlement of securities transactions,[77] and facilitated speedy access to information thereby improving the transparency on which well-functioning market-based financing systems depend.[78] Technological advances also enhanced the capacity of the financial sector, making it possible for institutional investors to achieve more efficient management of complex, internationally diversified portfolios.[79]

Another important factor with international significance was that changing demographics – ageing populations, rises in life expectancy and declining birthrates – undermined existing social security systems and intensified Governmental and individual interest in private mechanisms for the provision of old-age financial security through pension funds and

---

[74] J. Eatwell, 'New Issues in International Financial Regulation' in Ferran and Goodhart, *Regulating Financial Services*, pp. 235–54, and more generally J. Eatwell and L. Taylor, *Global Finance at Risk: The Case for International Regulation* (Cambridge, Polity Press, 2000).

[75] Rajan and Zingales, 'Banks and Markets'.

[76] Ibid.

[77] M. Giovanoli, 'Legal Aspects of Standard-Setting' in M. Giovanoli (ed.), *International Monetary Law* (Oxford, Oxford University Press, 2000), pp. 3–59.

[78] Rajan and Zingales 'Banks and Markets'.

[79] H. J. Blommstein, 'The New Financial Landscape and Its Impact on Corporate Governance' in M. Balling, E. Hennessy and R. O'Brien (eds.), *Corporate Governance, Financial Markets and Global Convergence* (Dordrecht, Kluwer Academic, 1998), pp. 41–70.

other forms of institutional investment.[80] The high levels of return available on securities markets investments at the end of the 1990s gave the markets an obvious appeal as a means of satisfying this growing demand for forms of institutional saving.[81] Developments in modern portfolio theory, which emphasised the benefits of international diversification of portfolios, fuelled investor interest in markets outside their home base,[82] and contributed to the rise in foreign ownership of the equity of European companies.[83]

The evolving EU processes of political and economic integration also played a significant part in fostering the development of securities market-based financing.[84] The introduction of the Euro, which is at least a contender for the title of 'most important event in post-War monetary history',[85] intensified the trend for European-based companies to raise finance from European capital markets, as demonstrated by major growth in the Eurozone corporate bond market after its introduction.[86] Commentators also noted possible links between the surge in European equity markets in 1999 and the introduction of the Euro.[87] Monetary union eliminated currency risk within the Eurozone, thereby removing one of the considerations that had previously inhibited institutional investors in participating countries from investing outside their home market.[88]

At Member State level, political decisions by public authorities in Continental Europe to privatise State-owned enterprises through public offerings of equity securities attracted new investors into the securities

---

[80] Davis and Steil, *Institutional Investors*, pp. 42–9; W. R. White, 'The Coming Transformation of Continental European Banking?', *Bank for International Settlements* Working Paper No 54 (June 1998), pp. 3–9.

[81] J. W. Winter, 'Cross-border Voting in Europe' in Hopt and Wymeersch (eds.), *Capital Markets and Company Law*, pp. 388–9.

[82] Davis and Steil, *Institutional Investors*, pp. 75–8.

[83] Van der Elst, 'Equity Markets', pp. 28–9 provides some data. Between 1990 and 1998 foreign ownership rose in most European countries surveyed. By 1998 foreigners held more than 40 per cent of the shares in the Netherlands (in fact a small fall from the percentage holding in 1990) and foreign holdings in French and Spanish companies topped 35 per cent.

[84] Ibid.

[85] Ibid., p. 41.

[86] Rajan and Zingales 'Banks and Markets'. Other studies have established similar results: J. P. Danthine, 'European Financial Markets After EMU: A First Assessment' *National Bureau of Economic Research* Working Paper No 8044 (2000); Galati and Tsatsaronis, 'The Impact of the Euro'.

[87] Danthine, 'European Financial Markets'.

[88] Davis and Steil, *Institutional Investors*, pp. 196–8.

markets.[89] However, how much weight to attach to privatisation as a force propelling the development of securities market investment activity within the EU is doubtful in view of evidence demonstrating that surges in direct retail investment in securities prompted by privatisation programmes tend not be sustained over the longer term.[90]

An omission?

Missing from the list of agents for change just mentioned is EU regulatory intervention that might have made it easier or more attractive for issuers, investors and financial intermediaries to make use of securities markets. The omission is deliberate. The contribution made by past EU regulatory intervention that was designed directly to promote the development of securities markets is considered separately in the next section because the heavy EU reliance on regulation as a policy pool and the general scholarly interest in linkages between law, financial development and economic growth together mean that this issue deserves special attention. However, before embarking on that discussion it is worth pausing to make the point that many of the factors contributing to the growth of securities market activity within the EU arose from political and economic decisions that were not directly concerned with the building of a single securities market, and from social factors, such as demographics, that lay outside the direct control of policy-makers. That the development of a market is contingent on a wide range of different, and sometimes unpredictable, variables in itself is an entirely unsurprising conclusion. Yet, despite its obviousness, this conclusion deserves emphasis so as to counter any misleading impression that might otherwise arise to the effect that the development of a market is, or could be, simply the creature of some form of central planning. Although law's contribution may attract a great deal of attention from bureaucrats whose career aspirations are tied up with how well they do the job of devising rules and from theorists interested in the bureaucrats' outputs, in reality its contribution may not be that significant.

---

[89] E.g. through privatisation in 1996 Deutsche Telekom acquired some 3m small shareholders: Lex Column, 'Deutsche Bahn', *Financial Times*, 24 May 2003, p. 16.

[90] Van der Elst, 'Equity Markets', p. 25 notes the failure of efforts made in the 1980s French privatisation programme to promote individual share ownership. Between 1990 and 1998 the proportion of French equity held by individuals fell from over 37 per cent to just 11 per cent.

C   Did EU law matter to the development of securities market activity in the EU during the 1980s and 1990s?

Law as market-creator: what the debate is about

It is sometimes suggested that EU regulatory intervention will create a truly integrated European financial market. For example, a senior official from the European Commission has said that: 'Over the last five years, the European Union has been engaged in a process of integrating its financial markets...It has been doing so on the basis of a Financial Services Action Plan with a framework for action of 42 measures.'[91] This sort of statement merits attention because it can be interpreted as appearing to attribute a startlingly ambitious catalytic role to law reform. It seems to imply that the EU can accelerate the development of a liquid, deep securities market by refining legal rules and the regulatory infrastructure by which they are supported, or that by changing its legal framework the EU can make itself better able to compete internationally with US and other capital markets. It would be truly remarkable for reform of the legal system to be the key to securing the Holy Grail of economic growth fostered by financial development. That a flourishing, integrated pan-European securities market could emerge simply from an upgraded legal system looks rather too good and too easy to be true. Law reform[92] (albeit reform of limited value because it did not extend sufficiently into the supporting judicial and administrative infrastructure to reassure investors on the credibility of the enforcement threat) did not suddenly give formerly Communist transition countries securities markets to rival the capitalist West.[93] Suggestions

---

[91] A. Schaub, 'Testimony of Director-General, DG Internal Market of the European Commission before the Committee on Financial Services, U.S. House of Representatives', 13 May 2004, available via http://europa.eu.int/comm/internal_market/en/finances/general/2004-05-13-testimony_en.pdf (accessed May 2004).

[92] The formerly communist countries of Eastern Europe made extensive changes to their laws in the 1990s to improve shareholder and creditor protections: K. Pistor, 'Patterns of Legal Change: Shareholder and Creditor Rights in Transition Economies' (2000) 1 *European Business Organization Law Review* 59.

[93] This is supported by studies of the impact of legal changes in transition economies: K. Pistor, M. Raiser and S. Gelfer, 'Law and Finance in Transition Economies' (2000) 8 *Economics of Transition* 325. The authors conclude that a lesson to be drawn from the experience of transition economies is that economic change cannot be engendered only by improvements, however radical, in the legal framework for the protection of shareholder and creditor rights. An important additional constraint on financial market development is the absence of effective legal institutions. See also B. S. Black, R. Kraakman and A. Tarassova, 'Russian Privatization and Corporate Governance: What Went Wrong?' (2000) 52 *Stanford Law Review* 1731.

that regulatory intervention can kick-start a market deserve serious, but sceptical, attention.

There is certainly no dispute that well-judged legal intervention can reinforce the development of a market by lowering the transaction costs involved in doing business. However, transaction-cost reducing law reform is not in essence an example of the law acting as a creative, path-breaking force. Rather, in these situations, the law's role is secondary, following down the path already established by market participants smoothing out the potholes along the way. Admittedly, new business activities may sometimes develop indirectly from law reform that was originally conceived with a view to reducing transaction costs. For example, informed British commentators have claimed that the transaction costs savings offered by the FSAP initiative to improve the prospectus passport regime for cross-border issues of securities[94] will be meaningless for small and medium-sized UK companies because at present they tend to concentrate solely on sources of finance in their home market, and have predicted that it will be large companies with financing needs that are too big to be absorbed by the pool of investment capital available from investors in any one country that will more likely feel immediate transaction cost benefits.[95] However, it is plausible to suggest that the existence of an effective, efficient passport regime may act as an encouragement to smaller companies and their advisers to look outside their home markets and to build up a network of contacts with a much deeper multinational pool of business angels willing to invest in risky, early-stage businesses.[96] That new business opportunities may open up as a by-product of law reform that was originally designed to remove obstacles hindering the efficient operation of existing activities is not something that should be lightly dismissed. Yet, in asking whether law can drive financial development, it would be something of an exaggeration to claim a development of this sort as one of law's major creations.

In looking at law as a creative force, what is essentially an issue in contemporary general debate is the contribution that credibly-enforced

---

[94] This passport is considered in detail in ch. 5.

[95] P. Freeman, Director of Markets and Compliance, OFEX speaking at an OFEX Financial Services Action Plan Conference, 24 July 2003.

[96] C. Huhne MEP (Rapporteur to Economic and Monetary Affairs Committee, European Parliament) speaking at an OFEX Financial Services Action Plan Conference 24 July 2003.

investor protection laws can make to financial development.[97] In the words of La Porta, Lopez-de-Silanes, Shleifer and Vishny, the distinguished economists who have spearheaded research in this field:[98]

> Such diverse elements of countries' financial systems as the breadth and depth of their capital markets, the pace of new security issues, corporate ownership structures, dividend policies, and the efficiency of investment allocation appear to be explained both conceptually and empirically by how well the laws in these countries protect outside investors. According to this research, the protection of shareholders and creditors by the legal system is central to understanding the patterns of corporate finance in different countries.

It is not hard to see why a weak securities market and a weak legal system for the protection of investors might well go together.[99] Without a basic legal framework to guarantee contractual and property rights, a securities market will undoubtedly struggle to develop. To this extent, La Porta *et al.*'s work is consistent with intuitive expectations and with long-established understandings of the relationship between law and the marketplace.[100] Beyond this, however, things become very controversial. Of the extensive debate that the pioneering work of La Porta *et al.* has generated,[101] a point

---

[97] R. La Porta, F. Lopez-de-Silanes, A. Shleifer and R. W. Vishny, 'Legal Determinants of External Finance' (1997) 52 *Journal of Finance* 1131. Ideas in this paper are developed further in several papers including: R. La Porta, F. Lopez-de-Silanes, A. Shleifer and R. W. Vishny, 'Law and Finance' (1998) 106 *Journal of Political Economy* 1113; R. La Porta, F. Lopez-de-Silanes and A. Shleifer, 'Corporate Ownership Around the World' (1999) 54 *Journal of Finance* 471; R. La Porta, F. Lopez-de-Silanes, A. Shleifer and R. W. Vishny, 'Agency Problems and Dividend Policies Around the World' (2000) 55 *Journal of Finance* 1; R. La Porta, F. Lopez-de-Silanes, A. Shleifer and R. W. Vishny, 'Investor Protection and Corporate Governance' (2000) 58 *Journal of Financial Economics* 3; R. La Porta, F. Lopez-de-Silanes and A. Shleifer, 'Investor Protection and Corporate Valuation' (2002) 57 *Journal of Finance* 1147; R. La Porta, F. Lopez-de-Silanes and A. Shleifer, 'What Works in Securities Laws?' *National Bureau of Economic Research* Working Paper 9882 (July 2003).

[98] La Porta, Lopez-de-Silanes, Shleifer and Vishny, 'Investor Protection and Corporate Governance', 3.

[99] M. J. Roe, *Political Determinants of Corporate Governance* (Oxford, Oxford University Press, 2003), p. 184.

[100] R. H. Coase, 'The Institutional Structure of Production' in *Essays on Economics and Economists* (Chicago, University of Chicago Press, 1994), pp. 11–12.

[101] Among the commentary lies the following strong criticism: 'they are based on extremely tenuous statistical data . . . Not only the methodology, but also the mathematical assumptions of these studies, are questionable': F. Partnoy, 'Why Markets Crash and What Law Can Do About It' (2000) 61 *University of Pittsburgh Law Review* 741, 766–7. See also Roe, *Political Determinants*, pp. 183–93.

that stands out is that whilst the empirical work shows connections between good investor protection laws and strong securities markets, it does not resolve questions of causation: did good investor protection laws produce strong securities markets or did strong securities markets give rise to the presence of interest groups that were in a position to press Governments to enact laws to protect their interests?[102] Some commentators who have studied the development of large securities markets in the US and the UK have argued that the historical data supports the latter interpretation of the order of events.[103]

How does this debate relate to EU securities regulation?

In trying to consider in an EU context the La Porta *et al.* inspired debate on the significance of the law to financial market development the immediate difficulty that has to be confronted is that, once the surrounding rhetoric is peeled away, it becomes apparent that much of the EU's regulatory agenda has historically been focused in a different direction from that which is in issue in the general debate. Although the boundaries are somewhat fuzzy and there is some degree of overlap, overall it is the removal of regulatory hurdles hindering cross-border activity rather than the provision of better investor protection that has been at the heart of EU securities law-making historically.[104]

---

[102] J. C. Coffee, 'The Rise of Dispersed Ownership: The Roles of Law and the State in the Separation of Ownership and Control' (2001) 111 *Yale Law Journal* 1 (arguing that, in terms of cause and effect, much historical evidence suggests that legal developments tended to follow, rather than precede, economic change).

[103] Coffee, 'The Rise of Dispersed Ownership'; B. R. Cheffins, 'Does Law Matter? The Separation of Ownership and Control in the United Kingdom' (2001) 30 *Journal of Legal Studies* 459.
   J. Franks, C. Mayer and S. Rossi, 'Ownership: Evolution and Regulation', *European Corporate Governance Institute* Working Paper No 9 (2003), ssrn abstract=354381 presents the conclusions of a study of the evolution of fifty British companies over the twentieth century. The authors note the development of strong stock market activity despite weak investor protection laws. In their view, different laws, namely the legal framework for limited liability, were a more likely foundation for the rapid dispersion of ownership observed during the twentieth century. They accept that stronger investor protection could have been a factor contributing to the greater liquidity and turnover in shareholdings during the second half of the century.

[104] Even as late as the development stage of the FSAP the European Commission described the agenda as being to set out: 'A coherent programme of action to smooth out remaining legislative, administrative and fiscal barriers to crossborder floatations and investment-related activities': European Commission, *Financial Services: Building a Framework for Action* (1998), p. 2.

This focus is related to the orientation of the EC Treaty, from which law-making competencies in the securities field ultimately flow. This Treaty does not provide a specific basis for investor protection law-making[105] and is concerned instead with the creation of an internal market in which obstacles to the free movement of goods, persons, services and capital have been abolished.[106] This means that investor protection laws can only be adopted with a view to achieving the Treaty goal of market integration. The central institutions do not have legislative competence to regulate for investor protection simply because they judge this to be important in its own right. 'Protective harmonisation', as Moloney describes it, is only permissible where the 'diversity or obstructive nature' of Member States' national investor protection laws impedes freedom of movement within the internal market.[107] In such circumstances the EU can remove the blockages represented by diverse national rules and replace them with harmonised re-regulation on investor protection. The subsidiarity and proportionality doctrines, which are enshrined in the EC Treaty, are also relevant in this context because these impose further limitations on what can legitimately be legislated for at the central level.[108]

---

[105] Moloney, *EC Securities Regulation*, pp. 577–606 examines in detail the implications of the fact that the promotion of investor protection is not a specific Treaty competence. This section draws heavily on Moloney's powerful analysis. See also N. Moloney, 'Investor Protection and the Treaty: an Uneasy Relationship' in G. Ferrarini, K. J. Hopt and E. Wymeersch (eds.), *Capital Markets in The Age of the Euro: Cross-border Transactions, Listed Companies and Regulation* (London, Kluwer Law International, 2002), pp. 17–61.

[106] Arts. 3 and 14.

[107] Specifically arts. 47(2), 94 and 95 allow for investor protection harmonisation (in Treaty language 'for the approximation of such laws, regulations or administrative provisions of the Member States' (arts. 94 and 95)) but only where this is for the purpose of achieving market integration.

The ECJ judgment in Case C-376/98, *Germany* v. *Parliament and Council* (*the Tobacco Advertising Case*) [2000] ECR I-8419 makes it clear that arts. 47(2) and 95 do not give the Community legislature general power to regulate the internal market. Harmonisation measures must genuinely have as their object the improvement of the conditions for the establishment and functioning of the internal market. Mere findings of disparities between national rules and of the abstract risk of obstacles to the exercise of fundamental freedoms or of distortions of competition liable to result therefrom are insufficient to justify intervention.

[108] As provided by EC Treaty, art. 5 ('In areas which do not fall within its exclusive competence, the Community shall take action, in accordance with the principle of subsidiarity, only if and in so far as the objectives of the proposed action cannot be sufficiently achieved by the Member States and can therefore, by reason of the scale or effects of the proposed action, be better achieved by the Community. Any action by the Community shall not go beyond what is necessary to achieve the objectives of this Treaty.'). See further P. Craig and G. de Búrca, *EU Law Text, Cases, and Materials* (3rd edn, Oxford, Oxford University Press, 2003), pp. 132–7.

Yet, even though the primary focus was elsewhere, some of the EU securities laws that have been in place for some time have an investor protection dimension, particularly those relating to market transparency (disclosure requirements) and integrity (anti market-abuse measures). It is thus possible to inquire whether there is anything to link the growth of securities market activity in the EU in the 1980s and 1990s to improvements in pan-European investor protection laws during that period. Leaving aside constitutional concerns,[109] a positive response to this question could assuage some of the worries about the expansion of EU regulatory intervention that has recently taken place under the FSAP because it would indicate that EU policy-makers are in fact building upon a successful track record in following this course.

Controlling market abuse: banning insider dealing

Although it was by no means the EU's first foray into the regulation of securities markets, the adoption of an EU-wide ban on insider dealing in 1989[110] is a good place to start in looking for signs of linkages between law reform and financial development because there does now seem to be broad international political consensus that a ban on insider dealing is a good thing for countries that are seeking to support the existence of a strong securities market.[111] Not all European countries had laws banning

---

[109] Moloney, 'Confidence and Competence', 44–9.

[110] Council Directive 89/592/EEC of 13 November 1989 coordinating regulations on insider dealing, OJ 1989 No. L334/30. Regulation of insider dealing, one form of market abuse, is now generally regarded in the EU as an aspect of securities regulation though, historically, the British tended to view it as a specialist aspect of the regulation of the fiduciary position of company directors. On the evolution from company to securities law, see P. L. Davies, 'The European Community's Directive on Insider Dealing: From Company Law to Securities Market Regulation' (1991) 11 *Oxford Journal of Legal Studies* 92.

J. Black, 'Audacious but Not Successful? A Comparative Analysis of the Implementation of Insider Dealing Regulation in EU Member States' [1998] *Company Financial and Insolvency Law Review* 1 provides an overview of the Directive and its implementation in Member States. More generally, see K. J. Hopt and E. Wymeersch (eds.), *European Insider Dealing* (London, Butterworths, 1999), pt II.

[111] Of the 103 countries with stock markets, 87 of them have insider dealing laws: U. Bhattacharya and H. Daouk, 'The World Price of Insider Trading' (2002) 57 *Journal of Finance* 75.

Note Black, 'Legal and Institutional Preconditions', 803 who regards a ban on insider dealing as important but not absolutely critical: 'A stock market can be strong without controls on insider trading; it will be stronger with these controls.'

insider dealing before EU intervention obliged them to adopt them:[112] in particular Germany stood out as a country where the controls were only self-regulatory in nature.[113]

Did the new EU law reassure investors as to the integrity of the price formation process in European markets thereby making them more willing to invest? Did it level off the playing field for information-access so as to encourage the growth of an investment analyst community whose competitive efforts improved investors' understanding of the financial markets and enhanced their willingness to invest? Various, mainly anecdotal, commentary had sought to link low participation by Europeans in the equity markets to the absence of effective bans on insider dealing.[114] It would thus be nicely symmetrical to claim that the ban on insider dealing did make a difference and did promote the European shift into equities in

---

The wide consensus around the desirability of a ban on insider dealing stands at odds to the historical evidence regarding the strong development of securities markets in the UK and the US prior to its adoption and effective enforcement. Furthermore, there is evidence exposing limits on strong laws on insider dealing in legal systems that do not also clamp down on alternative mechanisms whereby controlling shareholders can exploit the private benefits of control such as diverting their firms' assets to themselves at an undervalue: A. A. Durnev and A. S. Nain, 'The Unanticipated Effects of Insider Trading Regulation', working paper (2004), ssrn abstract = 517766.

[112] France led the way in 1967. The UK's approach of using the criminal law to legislate against insider dealing (in 1980) was followed by Norway (1985), Sweden (1985), and Denmark (1986): J. lau Hansen, 'The New Proposal for a European Union Directive on Market Abuse' (2002) 23 *University of Pennsylvania Journal of International Economic Law* 241, 250–2.

Data on the date of adoption of insider dealing laws by all 103 countries with stock exchanges is provided by Bhattacharya and Daouk, 'World Price'.

[113] B. A. K. Rider and M. Ashe, 'The Insider Dealing Directive' in M. Andenas and S. Kenyon-Slade (eds.), *EC Financial Market Regulation* (London, Sweet & Maxwell, 1993), pp. 209–40; H. J. Schwarze, 'The European Insider Dealing Directive and its Impact on the Member States, Particularly Germany' in Hopt and Wymeersch (eds.), *European Insider Dealing*, pp. 151–7; Nowak, 'Investor Protection', p. 431.

[114] 'It is no coincidence that in many countries where insider dealing has been rife – for example, in southern Europe – stock exchanges have remained backwaters in their domestic economies': 'Outing the Insiders', *Financial Times*, 1 August 1994, p. 15; M. G. Warren, 'The Regulation of Insider Trading in the European Community' (1991) 48 *Washington & Lee Law Review* 1037, 1040–1 (suggesting that the explanation for a poor equity culture in Europe might have been that insider trading was regarded as a major tenet of trading strategy in the EU's securities markets). According to a 1989 survey of Europe's internal market published in *The Economist*: 'West Germany and France assumed until recently that insider trading was what financial life was all about.'

the 1990s.[115] No such claim can be made, however, because empirical data on the impact of insider dealing laws on market practices is too inconclusive to support such a strong assertion about their causal effect.[116]

In fact the German evidence with regard to the ban on insider dealing is consistent with the view that law tends to follow after financial development rather than lead it. Some key players in the German market had already been pressing for a ban on insider dealing before it became obligatory for Germany to enact one in order to comply with its EU obligations.[117] Why? Because that legal upgrade was thought to be necessary to enable Germany to compete for international financial business and to enable Frankfurt to challenge London more effectively for the position of focal point for European financial markets activity.[118] A statutory ban on insider dealing was thought to be needed to enhance Germany's commercial reputation as a trustworthy international, financial centre.[119] Why then did Germany not simply adopt a ban itself rather than wait for a lead from the EU? There could have been many reasons but it is worth noting at this point that States sometimes prefer to work through the EU in order to bypass pockets of entrenched opposition within their local environment.[120] Going through the EU can be a politically astute move to avoid direct confrontation between established powerful groups that benefit from the law as it is and newer communities that are growing in influence and who want the law to be changed.

Another basis for disputing the creative effect of the adoption of an EU-wide ban on insider dealing is by reference to the poor record of enforcement action in respect of it. Investors are unlikely to be fooled by shiny, new laws

---

[115] Though not specifically related to Europe, it has, for example, been claimed that the existence of a vibrant analysts community flows directly from the prohibition on insider trading and would not exist otherwise: Z. Goshen and G. Parchomovsky, 'On Insider Trading, Markets, and "Negative" Property Rights in Information' (2001) 88 *Virginia Law Review* 1229.

[116] Measuring the impact of insider dealing laws on market practices is notoriously difficult. Some of the extensive literature is surveyed in Moloney, *EC Securities Regulation*, pp. 739–42.

[117] E.g., prior to the adoption of the ban, Hilmar Kopper, the head of Deutsche Bank was quoted in the press as saying that legislation outlawing insider trading 'is clearly overdue and I cannot understand why it is taking so long': J. Eisenhammer, 'Red Faces at Failure to Enact EC law', *Independent*, 30 May 1993, Business on Sunday, p. 6. Press coverage suggested that he was speaking for many in the international financial community: ibid.

[118] O. August, 'Don't Mention the Euro as Germany Prepares for E-Day to Dawn in City', *Times*, 15 July 1997, Business Section.

[119] W. Munchau, 'Germany to Tighten Financial Regulation', *Times*, 18 January 1992, Business Section.

[120] A range of factors that may lead Member States to support the adoption of new EU laws is considered further in ch. 3.

appearing on the statute books. If they distrust the integrity and efficiency of a market they will still keep away from it despite the enactment of new laws if those laws lack credibility by not being supported by effective enforcement. This view about the (non)-effect of the mere existence of insider dealing laws is supported by an international empirical study by Bhattacharya and Daouk, which shows on a country-by-country basis that insider dealing laws which have never been enforced do not affect the cost of equity.[121]

The European ban on insider dealing is not a beacon of success so far as enforcement is concerned. Although there have been a few notable scalps, of which the most prominent in recent times was undoubtedly the successful French prosecution of George Soros (he was fined €2.2m),[122] overall across Europe the conviction rate for insider dealing is very low. Reportedly, only nineteen convictions for insider dealing were achieved in Britain, Germany, France, Switzerland and Italy in the five years before 2002, contrasting sharply with the forty-six successful prosecutions achieved in the same period by a single district court in Manhattan.[123] Low levels of enforcement are generally attributed to the fact that most Member States opted to implement the ban on insider dealing through their criminal law,[124] thereby presenting enforcement agencies with the problems of having to meet high standards of proof and grapple with various other safeguards enshrined in the criminal justice process.

Thus one plausible interpretation of the fact that European securities markets grew during the 1990s notwithstanding the absence of a vigorously enforced ban on insider trading is that this shows that the law and its enforcement 'didn't matter' in any practically meaningful way, that they were not a catalyst for financial development.[125] However, this view is challenged by Bhattacharya and Daouk's work, which shows a statistically significant drop in the cost of equity after the first insider trading prosecution.[126] Since one prosecution appears to be enough to give credibility to insider dealing

---

[121] Bhattacharya and Daouk, 'World Price'.

[122] M. Milner, 'Soros Fined £1.4m for Insider Trading over Privatisation of French Bank', *Guardian*, 21 December 2002, p. 2.

[123] R. Godson, 'But Europe is Worse', *Sunday Times*, 10 March 2002, Business Section.

[124] Black, 'Audacious but Not Successful?'. Also Nowak, 'Investor Protection', p. 431 on enforcement problems under German criminal law.

[125] Cheffins, 'Does Law Matter?', 478 looking at the British position, argues that it is doubtful whether the enactment of a ban on insider dealing had a major impact because of minimal enforcement activity (only twenty-four convictions in twenty years).

[126] Their numerical estimates range from a low of 0.3 per cent (on the basis of looking at credit ratings) to a high of 7 per cent (using the international asset pricing model).

laws it is thus not possible to rely on low levels of enforcement to rule out the possibility of European insider dealing law having had a significant practical impact. However, Bhattacharya and Daouk carefully avoid making strong claims about the causal implications of insider dealing enforcement.

Issuer disclosure: prospectuses and ongoing disclosure

It is well-established economic theory that investors will respond positively to increased levels of credible issuer disclosure and that issuers will reap the benefits of improvements in investor sentiment in their cost of capital.[127] This theory implies that issuers have an interest in committing themselves voluntarily to good disclosure. From this starting point has flowed considerable debate on whether States should intervene to impose disclosure obligations on issuers or should simply leave the market to its own devices in this respect. However, whilst the academic community continues to be divided about the merits of mandatory disclosure,[128] international securities regulatory practice has come down fairly unambiguously in its favour. Rather than challenging the underlying fundamental principle, intensive debate amongst those involved in designing issuer disclosure regimes tends often to focus more on fine-tuning their operation.

Mandatory issuer disclosure is a longstanding feature of EU securities law.[129] It was first introduced in 1979–80[130] and has grown incrementally since then. Under EU law all public offerings of securities now require a

---

[127] J. C. Coffee, 'Racing Towards the Top? The Impact of Cross-listings and Stock Market Competition on International Corporate Governance' (2002) 102 *Columbia Law Review* 1757, 1780–3.

[128] M. B. Fox, 'Retaining Mandatory Securities Disclosure: Why Issuer Choice is Not Investor Empowerment' (1999) 85 *Virginia Law Review* 1335, pt II provides a review of the empirical evidence concerning the welfare effects of mandatory disclosure.

[129] V. Edwards, *EC Company Law* (Oxford, Clarendon Press), pp. 228–31 helpfully and succinctly outlines the background to the adoption of these laws. In the mid 1970s the European Commission experimented with a voluntary code of conduct relating to securities transactions which included issuer disclosure requirements. The code did not have a strong practical impact.

[130] By Council Directive 79/279/EEC of 5 March 1979 coordinating the conditions for the admission of securities to official stock exchange listing, OJ 1979 No. L66/21 ('Admission Directive'); and Council Directive 80/390/EEC of 17 March 1980 coordinating the requirements for the drawing up, scrutiny and distribution of the listing particulars to be published for the admission of securities to official stock exchange listing, OJ 1980 No. L100/1 ('Listing Particulars Directive'); both now consolidated into Directive 2001/34/EC of the European Parliament and of the Council of 28 May 2001 on the admission of securities to official stock exchange listing and on information to be published on those securities, OJ 2001 No. L184/1 ('CARD').

prospectus;[131] there is an equivalent disclosure requirement where securities are admitted to official listing;[132] issuers of officially-listed shares must comply with periodic disclosure obligations,[133] and issuers with securities admitted to trading on regulated markets must make timely disclosure of material new information.[134] Alongside these securities laws, but historically categorised as part of the EU's company law regulatory programme, are mandatory harmonised requirements on accounting disclosures and auditing.[135] As a result of the FSAP, this regime is on the brink of a major upgrade which is designed to provide a comprehensive initial and on-going disclosure regime applying to all issuers whose securities are admitted to trading on regulated markets and which will implement International Accounting Standards(IAS)/ International Financial Reporting Standards (IFRS) on a mandatory basis across the EU.[136]

The initial impact of the first wave of EU issuer disclosure laws on the pre-existing national legal systems of Member States varied considerably. At one end of the spectrum, the UK already had a fairly detailed issuer disclosure regime and adapting this so as to conform to EU requirements was a relatively straightforward task.[137] Belgium, Luxembourg and France also

---

[131] Council Directive 89/298/EEC of 17 April 1989 coordinating the requirements for the drawing-up, scrutiny and distribution of the prospectus to be published when transferable securities are offered to the public, OJ 1989 No. L124/8 ('Public Offers Directive').

[132] Originally Listing Particulars Directive, now CARD.

[133] Council Directive 82/121/EEC of 15 February 1982 on information to be published on a regular basis by companies the shares of which have been admitted to official stock-exchange listing, OJ 1982 No. L48/26 ('Interim Reports Directive') now consolidated into CARD.

[134] Imposed initially on the officially-listed sector by the Admission Directive (later amended and consolidated into CARD), arts. 68 (shares) and 81 (debt securities). By virtue of the Insider Dealing Directive this obligation was extended to issuers with securities admitted to trading on ISD regulated markets.

[135] Fourth Council Directive 78/660/EEC on the annual accounts of certain types of companies, OJ 1978 No. L222/11; Seventh Council Directive 83/349/EEC of 13 June 1983 on consolidated accounts, OJ 1983 No. L193/1; Eighth Council Directive 84/253/EEC of 10 April 1984 on the approval of persons responsible for carrying out the statutory audits of accounting documents, OJ 1984 No. L126/20.

[136] Regulation (EC) No 1606/2002 of the European Parliament and of the Council of 19 July 2002 on the application of international accounting standards, OJ 2002 No. L243/1.
IAS are financial standards adopted by the International Accounting Standards Committee from 1973 to 2000. After an institutional reorganisation the International Accounting Standards Committee was replaced by the International Accounting Standards Board in 2001. IFRS are the new pronouncements being issued by the IASB.

[137] Edwards, EC Company Law, pp. 241–2. On the changes of detail triggered by the Public Offers of Securities Directive, which included an extension of the scope of the regime, A. Alcock, 'Public Offers in the UK: The New Regime' (1996) 17 Company Lawyer 262.

had well-developed systems.[138] However, there were significant gaps in the securities laws of other countries.[139] For example, public offers of securities not listed on a German exchange were not directly subject to disclosure requirements until the Sales Prospectus Act of 13 December 1990. This Act imported the Public Offers Directive into German law;[140] as with insider trading, German issuer disclosure law largely followed the EU lead.

Did, then, the upgrading and greater uniformity brought about by the adoption of EU issuer disclosure laws act as a magnet that attracted investors into the European market place? There is some commentary that attributes the growth of European securities markets in the 1990s to legislative reforms of issuer disclosure led by the EU.[141] However, against this, there is also clear evidence that some sectors of the market developed without the aid of regulatory intervention from the EU to force disclosure. Issues of international equity securities are usually structured so as to take advantage of exemptions from EU prospectus disclosure requirements, yet in practice the disclosure standards that are adhered to in respect of such issues are in fact higher than those required by EU prospectus laws.[142] At this specialised, sophisticated wholesale end of the market, European market participants voluntarily upgraded disclosure practices to international, largely US-driven, standards in order to compete more effectively for a slice of the huge amount of investment capital pouring into securities markets around the world in the 1990s. Although ultimately ill-fated, Germany's Neuer Markt provides another example of a situation where market participants, in this case the exchange operator, intentionally adopted disclosure standards that were designed to be more stringent than those mandated by the general law.[143]

Assessing the contribution (if any) made by better EU disclosure laws to the development of securities market activity in the EU during the 1980s and 1990s is further complicated by the growth in US cross-listings

---

[138] S. Suckow, 'The European Prospectus' (1975) 23 *American Journal of Comparative Law* 50.

[139] Ibid.

[140] D. B. Guenther, 'The Limited Public Offer in German and US Securities Law: A Comparative Analysis of Prospectus Act Section 2(2) and Rule 505 of Regulation D' (1999) 20 *Michigan Journal of International Law* 871; J. Adolff, B. Meister, C. Randell and K. D. Stephan, *Public Company Takeovers in Germany* (Munich, Verlag CH Beck, 2002), pp. 72–3; Nowak, 'Investor Protection', pp. 428–9.

[141] Guenther, 'Limited Public Offer', 873.

[142] H. E. Jackson and E. J. Pan, 'Regulatory Competition in International Securities Markets: Evidence from Europe in 1999 – Part I' (2001) 56 *Business Lawyer* 653.

[143] Coffee, 'Racing', 1804–6.

by European companies during the period.[144] News in one market can drive securities market activity in other locations.[145] Thus, even presupposing that mandatory disclosures do matter in some way, disclosures that European issuers were required to make in order to comply with US securities regulatory requirements could have done more to influence investor behaviour within the EU than homegrown EU disclosure requirements.

La Porta, Lopez-de-Silanes and Shleifer have provided recent statistical analysis suggesting that certain good disclosure laws, and their enforcement, are important to the growth of strong securities markets.[146] According to La Porta *et al.* certain disclosure requirements are positively correlated with larger stock markets. Their data suggests that improving certain disclosure requirements by two standard deviations is associated with an increase in the market-capitalisation-to-GDP ratio of 0.27. Their data also suggests that lowering the burden of proof by two standard deviations is associated with an increase in the market-capitalisation-to-GDP ratio of 0.20. La Porta *et al.* contend therefore that the development of stock markets is strongly associated with measures of private enforcement such as extensive disclosure requirements coupled with a relatively low burden of proof on investors seeking to recover damages resulting from inaccurate disclosures.

At a broad level La Porta *et al.*'s work could be taken to provide some support for the contention that EU intervention might well have stimulated the development of securities market activity within the EU by requiring Member States to upgrade their disclosure laws. Yet it is difficult to apply the La Porta *et al.* analysis credibly in this context because detailed aspects of disclosure enforcement, such as liability standards and burden of proof, fell outside the harmonisation programme and were left to the discretion of Member States.[147] To the

---

[144] Pagano, Röell and Zechner, 'The Geography of Equity Listing'.

[145] Securities Expert Group, *FSAP: Progress*, p. 5.

[146] La Porta, Lopez-de-Silanes and Shleifer, 'What Works'.

[147] Contrast, e.g., the UK position where liability is currently based on a negligence standard, does not require the investor to prove reliance on the false statement, and attaches to a range of persons, including professional advisers, as well as the issuer and its directors (Financial Services and Markets Act 2000, s. 90; Financial Services and Markets Act 2000 (Official Listing of Securities) Regulations 2001 (SI 2001 No. 2956), Pt 2; and Public Offers of Securities Regulations 1995 (SI 1995 No. 1537) regs. 13–15) and the German position where the liability standard is based on intention or gross negligence and attaches to a narrower range of persons (Nowak, 'Investor Protection', p. 429).

  On the sensitivities surrounding EU intervention in the area of sanctions, K. J. Hopt, 'Modern Company and Capital Market Problems: Improving European Corporate Governance after Enron' [2003] *Journal of Corporate Law Studies* 221, 246–7.

extent that the research emphasises claimant-friendly liability rules as being conducive to the growth of securities markets, it is therefore impossible for EU bodies to claim much direct credit for supplying legal improvements that may promote securities market growth.

Overall it is hard to come to any sort of definite conclusion about the impact of the first wave of mandatory EU disclosure requirements on the growth of European securities markets.[148] In sectors dominated by institutional investors[149] the market largely evolved without the need for legal underpinning of disclosure; and market participants tended actively to resist direct legislative controls.[150] At the retail end of the market, however, better disclosure, as required by EU law, could have played a part in boosting investor confidence. Yet there is little concrete support for any claim about the quality of EU disclosure law being a major factor fuelling investor interest in the securities markets in the 1990s.

EU law was a catalyst for changes in Member States' law but it does not necessarily follow that it was a catalyst for securities market development

A study of recent German legal changes powerfully makes the claim that the old picture of German law as a system that provided weak protections to shareholders may be out of date and due for reassessment.[151] The EU is cited as the impetus for much of the change, though not all of the laws surveyed were introduced into German law as a direct consequence of

---

[148] For a similarly qualified assessment of the impact of the passport for intermediaries provided by Council Directive 93/22/EEC of 10 May 1993 on investment services in the securities field, OJ 1993 No. L141/27 ('Investment Services Directive'), see G. Hertig, 'Regulatory Competition for EU Financial Services' in D. C. Esty and D. Geradin (eds.), *Regulatory Competition and Economic Integration* (Oxford, Oxford University Press, 2001), p. 225.

[149] E.g. the pan-European equity offerings sector: Jackson and Pan, 'Regulatory Competition'.

[150] The exemptions in EU securities law that permit pan-European offerings to be structured on a basis that does not trigger a prospectus requirement were the result of detailed negotiations between the European Commission and representatives of the international capital markets coordinated by the International Primary Market Association: P. Krijgsman, *Brief History: IPMA's Role in Harmonising International Capital Markets 1984–1994* (London, International Primary Market Association, 2000), available via http://www.ipma.org.uk/ne_index.asp (accessed April 2004).

[151] Nowak, 'Investor Protection'.

obligations on Germany, as a Member State, to implement EU law.[152] Thus the German experience suggests that EU law can not only be a trigger for certain specific measures that Member States must implement but can also open the door for additional home-grown measures too. This raises the question why powerful Member States would wait for a lead from the EU rather than simply pursuing their own domestic agenda directly, to which one response is that, as noted earlier in this chapter, in some instances national Governments may favour change at the EU level first as a strategy to break through opposition from national interest groups that could block progress on purely domestic legislative initiatives.[153]

The influence of EU law is most starkly seen in countries seeking accession to the EU because adjustment of national rules to EU standards is a precondition to entry.[154] EU officials also need to be satisfied as to the adequacy of supervisory structures.[155] The ten countries that joined the EU in May 2004 were deemed by the European Commission to have done enough to satisfy the entry criteria so far as giving effect to financial services legislation was concerned, though certain relatively

---

[152] Some 80 per cent of recent German capital markets law is attributed to EU initiatives: ibid., p. 426. The author does not give a qualitative analysis examining the relative importance of laws that were EU-led as against those that were home-grown. However, the Securities Trading Act 1994 is cited as 'the watershed event' (pp. 429–30). This Act established a new regulatory apparatus in the form of the Bundesaufsichtsamt für den Wertpapierhandel (BAWe, which was later collapsed into Bundesanstalt für Finanzdienstleistungsaufsicht (BaFin) Germany's integrated financial regulator), an initiative not directly linked to EU law requirements. It also prohibited insider dealing, imposed new issuer reporting requirements, and obligations for notification of changes in major holdings of voting rights, changes that were broadly necessary to conform to EU requirements.

[153] Underlying factors that may lead Member States to support proposals for new EU laws are considered further in ch. 3.

[154] The 'Copenhagen criteria', which are the preconditions of entry to the EU are that a country must: be a stable democracy, respecting human rights, the rule of law, and the protection of minorities; have a functioning market economy; and adopt the common rules, standards and policies that make up the body of EU law. On the accession process generally: P. Nicolaides, 'Preparing for Accession to the European Union: How to Establish Capacity for Effective and Credible Application of EU Rules' in M. Cremona, *The Enlargement of the European Union* (Oxford, Oxford University Press, 2003), pp. 43–78.

[155] D. Brennerman, 'The Role of Regional Integration in the Development of Securities Markets: A Case Study of the EU Accession Process in Hungary and the Czech Republic' (April 2004, unpublished LLM thesis, Harvard Law School, on file with author) looks at the EU's role in driving forward reform of the institutional arrangements for the oversight of securities market activity.

modest gaps were identified and addressed by means of transitional arrangements.[156]

In many ways, therefore, a country such as the UK can be regarded as the unusual case so far as EU-driven development of national law is concerned. The UK already had a mature legal framework to support its equity market culture prior to significant EU regulatory activity in the field, and so changes required during the 1980s and 1990s in order to conform national law to EU requirements were usually more by way of adjustment to the detail than fundamental reform.

Experience outside the UK makes it impossible to dispute the conclusion that the EU's securities law programme during the 1980s and 1990s helped some Member States to adopt laws that conform to broad international expectations on the sort of features that legal systems ought to have in order to support securities market development. Yet it is not clear that the gradual evolution towards an equity culture in the EU during the 1980s and 1990s owed much (if anything) to legal change. Furthermore, there is evidence from accession countries (where the influence of the EU in driving legal change was especially powerful) against legal upgrades acting as a catalyst for securities markets growth – for example only seven equity stocks trade in the system that handles the most liquid stocks on the Prague Stock Exchange and the bond market there is dominated by Government and bank bonds.[157] Overall stock market capitalisation in the new Member States at the time of accession (May 2004) was 16 per cent, measured against GDP, as compared to an EU-15 average of 67 per cent.[158] Though there is much growth potential, the non-banking financial sector in the accession countries is small and equity and debt securities markets are still at a developmental stage.[159]

---

[156] A. Doughty and E. Papp, 'Harmonising Legislation in Central Europe' (2004) 14 *European Financial Services Regulation* 11 (reviewing the position in the Czech Republic, Slovakia and Slovenia); H. Haabu, 'Country Report on Estonia' (2004) (2004) 14 *European Financial Services Regulation* 14; I. Gárdos, 'Country Report on Hungary' (2004) 14 *European Financial Services Regulation* 15; G. Cers and I. Sakarne, 'Country Report on Latvia' (2004) 14 *European Financial Services Regulation* 17; G. Reciunas and G. Stasevicius, 'Country Report on Lithuania' (2004) 14 *European Financial Services Regulation* 19; A. Lipska and J. Miller, 'Country Report on Poland' (2004) 14 *European Financial Services Regulation* 21; A. Zerafa, 'Country Report on Malta' (2004) 14 *European Financial Services Regulation* 23.

[157] Brennerman, 'The Role of Regional Integration'.

[158] European Commission, *Financial Integration Monitor*, p. 20.

[159] B. Inel, 'Impact of Enlargement on the Wholesale Banking Markets' (2004) 14 *European Financial Services Regulation* 3.

That the historical story of the linkages between law and securities market development is so bounded by uncertainty is a conclusion that has implications for the shaping of EU policy choices in relation to the securities markets.

D   Strategic policy choices in EU law-making to promote a single securities market

Implications of uncertainty surrounding law's contribution to the development of securities markets

Similar questions crop up in different branches of economic scholarship: is financial development a catalyst for economic growth or does financial development follow from economic growth;[160] are securities markets a precondition for the development of institutional investors or do institutions emerge first and then stimulate capital market development;[161] must good, effectively enforced investor protection laws be in place before a securities market can develop or do such laws get put in place after a market has established itself and its major players have acquired sufficient political influence to enable them to lobby effectively for laws to protect their interests? Causal uncertainty is evident in the debate on all of these questions. Unsurprisingly, lawyers have taken a particular interest in the last question though, interestingly, much legal scholarship has tended to be rather sceptical of the view that investor protection laws alone provide the key to understanding why some countries have bigger securities markets than others, particularly where the countries under comparison are developed economies with good, long-established legal systems. Whilst individual components of the protection afforded to investors by the legal system of any one developed country may look stronger than their equivalents in another such country, looked at overall, major differences of quality would be surprising.[162]

The previous section found little evidence to link the growth of securities market activity in the EU in the 1980s and 1990s to the adoption of EU investor protection laws. Thus EU policy-makers cannot easily look to their own history of securities law-making since the 1980s to resolve uncertainties that surround debate about linkages between financial development, law, institutions and economic growth or, in particular, to establish a direct causal link between the adoption of new securities laws

---

[160] As considered in sec. B above.
[161] Davis and Steil, *Institutional Investors*, pp. 226–7.
[162] Roe, *Political Determinants*, pp. 183–93.

and the growth of securities markets. Nor will they find much comfort in the general literature on the significance of investor protection laws to securities market growth. Although one specific finding that emerges from the literature is that claimant-friendly civil liability standards and procedural rules are associated with large securities markets,[163] this is not especially helpful to EU policy-makers because the widely differing legal systems and traditions in Member States give rise to major political and constitutional sensitivities that inhibit aggressive EU intervention in these areas.

These considerations suggest a state of uncertainty about the relationship between regulation and securities market growth that should give EU policy-makers pause for thought about the limitations of their foresight and wisdom, and curb their enthusiasm for regulatory intervention. EU Member States, including its ten new members as from 1 May 2004, already have the basic laws and the requisite accompanying administrative and judicial infrastructure to protect property and contractual rights.[164] At least in part thanks to the EU, they also have the sort of securities laws that are usually associated internationally with strong securities markets, such as in relation to issuer disclosure of financial and other information.[165] It is not certain which further refinements to those laws (if any) will work best to promote further securities market development. Furthermore, even if some package of laws can help securities markets to grow, other factors are also relevant so there is no room for over-optimism about what can be achieved through law reform.[166] Particularly where existing laws are already fairly good, policy-makers should not assume that the benefits of an upgrade will necessarily outweigh the costs of the upheaval associated with it. The law of diminishing returns is likely to kick in at some point – arguably it already does in the UK, where regulatory upheavals triggered by a need to conform existing requirements to EU securities law tend to be greeted with a degree of hostility[167] that may be rooted in lack of conviction that the benefits will

---

[163] La Porta, Lopez-de-Silanes and Shleifer, 'What Works'.

[164] As required in order to satisfy the Copenhagen criteria, on which see generally Nicolaides, 'Preparing for Accession'.

[165] In response to the question 'where to start to build a strong securities market?', Black, 'Legal and Institutional Preconditions', pp. 847–9 includes good disclosure-orientated capital market laws, of which accounting rules should be a central part.

[166] Pistor, Raiser and Gelfer, 'Law and Finance'.

[167] E.g. P. Norman, 'A Crucial Year for the Single Market', FT.com, 11 January 2004, noting the challenge facing the Commission and CESR 'to convince an increasingly sceptical industry that all this effort [on regulations to create an integrated market in financial services] is worth the trouble'.

outweigh the costs in a legal system that is already fairly well-attuned to the needs of the securities markets. This sort of reaction could spread to other Member States where past EU intervention may have attracted a broad coalition of support from interest groups seeking to exploit opportunities presented by a shift from bank-based to market-based financing and an emerging equity culture but where additions or adjustments to that body of law are likely to have less obvious potential appeal. Policy-makers should also bear in mind that choices on law reform, particularly those made against a background of fundamental uncertainty about how laws can help markets to grow after certain basic features are in place, could impact negatively rather than positively, and should therefore take careful note of the risk that regulatory intervention may prove counter-productive.[168]

EU securities market activity certainly needs a coherent regulatory structure if it is to flourish but if a pan-European securities market, the underlying policy goal, is to emerge this will ultimately depend on market participants rather than regulatory intervention. This implies that a sensible strategy for EU policy-makers would be to concentrate their attention on dismantling any remaining barriers that hinder efficient pan-European securities market activity and to hesitate to 're-regulate' the market on investor protection grounds. To be sure, a market will struggle to grow if investors do not feel protected against fraud and abuse or if they feel that, informationally, the odds are stacked too heavily against them, but judging precisely which regulatory 'package' delivers the best investor protection results is a delicate task and the consequences of mistakes, in terms of chilling market development, could be very severe indeed. Investors in the EU markets would still be protected by barrier-dismantling laws that incidentally serve an investor protection function (the categories are not watertight) and also by Member States' national law. Admittedly the quality of investor protection available under national laws would differ, but merely having common rules would not guarantee uniform investor protection in any event because the rules could be applied differently across Member States.

The FSAP favoured regulatory intervention as the primary policy tool (despite the dangers)

This is not, however, the direction that EU policy-makers took in the FSAP. The FSAP was an ambitious programme of regulatory intervention

---

[168] Coffee, 'The Rise of Dispersed Ownership'; Cheffins, 'Does Law Matter'.

embracing some forty-two measures in all, many of which have a strong investor protection dimension. Under the FSAP, the EU has imposed, amongst other things, a new issuer disclosure regime,[169] mandatory use of IAS/IFRS in consolidated accounts,[170] a wide-ranging regime on market abuse (including insider dealing)[171] and much more detailed common rules regulating the provision of investment services and the operation of exchanges and other trade execution mechanisms.[172] It is too early to single out any of the FSAP laws as definite mistakes because major measures will not start to take effect in Member States until October 2004 at the earliest.[173] Yet it is already possible to identify some laws that could prove counter-productive because they may impose excessive burdens on some categories of market participant supposedly in order to enhance investor protection. One example is the obligation on issuers admitted to trading on regulated markets to make prompt disclosure of inside information.[174] The scope of this disclosure obligation is very broad (and its boundaries are

---

[169] Directive 2003/71/EC of the European Parliament and of the Council of 4 November 2003 on the prospectus to be published when securities are offered to the public or admitted to trading and amending Directive 2001/34/EC, OJ 2003 No. L345/64 ('Prospectus Directive', which deals with prospectus disclosure); Transparency Directive 2004 ('Transparency Directive', which deals with annual and half-yearly financial disclosures, and with interim (quarterly) reporting requirements. In May 2004 the Council agreed the text of this Directive, as previously amended by the European Parliament (on first reading). The Directive is not expected to be formally adopted and published in the Official Journal until autumn 2004. Translating the text into the numerous official languages of the expanded EU is a cause for delay; an unofficial version of the final text is available via http://europa.eu.int/comm/internal_market/en/finances/mobil/transparency/directive-unofficial_en.pdf (accessed May 2004) and references to specific articles of the Directive are to this version; Directive 2003/6/EC of the European Parliament and of the Council of 28 January 2003 on insider dealing and market manipulation (market abuse) OJ 2003 No. L96/16 ('Market Abuse Directive', which deals with timely disclosure by issuers of inside information).

[170] IAS Regulation.

[171] Market Abuse Directive.

[172] Directive 2004/39/EC of the European Parliament and of the Council of 21 April 2004 on markets in financial instruments amending Council Directives 85/611/EEC and 93/6/EEC and Directive 2000/12/EC of the European Parliament and of the Council and repealing Council Directive 93/22/EEC, OJ 2004 No. L145/1 ('Financial Instruments Markets Directive', also known as the revised Investment Services Directive or 'ISD2').

[173] 12 October 2004 (eighteen months after publication in the Official Journal) is the implementation date for the Market Abuse Directive, i.e., the date by which Member States are bound to give effect to its provisions within their national law. Securities Expert Group, *FSAP: Progress*, p. 2 regards it as too early to judge the impact of the FSAP but see n. 178 below.

[174] Market Abuse Directive, art. 6.

uncertain).[175] There is a distinct risk that it could undermine the ability of EU regulated markets to compete for international business from issuers; if it does, the end result could be reduction, rather than expansion, of the pool of investments available to investors. Likewise the drive towards disclosure standardisation that is evident across the FSAP issuer disclosure regime could ultimately be detrimental to investors if there proves to be substance in the fears that this regime will repel issuers because it is insufficiently calibrated to the needs of certain categories (such as small and medium-sized enterprises) or is insufficiently sensitive to the way in which certain market segments actually operate (such as bond markets that are largely wholesale in orientation).[176]

Later chapters consider aspects of the issuer disclosure regime in greater detail.[177] Here it suffices to note that there are serious concerns about the damage that certain aspects of it could cause to EU securities market activity and that there are fears that it could reverse rather than, as intended, promote the growth of a properly integrated pan-European market. Whilst some of the more doom-laden predictions may have been coloured by the underlying agenda of lobbyists to secure favourable treatment during the legislative process for the particular concerns of certain interest groups, overall the worries about what has been created under the FSAP are too widespread to be dismissed simply as overstatements designed to attract attention.[178] Judged against the background of uncertainty on law's contribution to securities market development once the basics are in place that has been outlined in this chapter, it is not surprising that such worries have arisen.

---

[175] Herbert Smith, *Market Abuse: Key Implementation Issues* (Corporate Briefing, April 2004). The potentially adverse implications of the breadth of this disclosure obligation are discussed further in ch. 5. For a more positive assessment, however, J. lau Hansen, 'MAD in a Hurry: The Swift and Promising Adoption of the EU Market Abuse Directive' [2004] *European Business Law Review* 183.

[176] See further ch. 5.

[177] Ch. 5 (substantive content requirements), ch. 6 (institutional supervision of issuer disclosure) and ch. 7 (the role of exchanges).

[178] Despite reluctance to come to an over-hasty judgment on the FSAP, the group of securities markets experts that was established to take stock of the FSAP does record concern that the FSAP did not sufficiently recognise that European securities markets operate in a global and strongly competitive international environment: Securities Expert Group, *FSAP: Progress*, p. 13.

Is there an EU policy alternative? Placing the emphasis more on
supervision and enforcement than on additional regulation

Delivery of credible investor protection depends on legal and supervisory *systems*, not simply on the laws 'on the books'.[179] Within the EU, responsibility for supervision and enforcement of securities market activity remains concentrated at national level and Member States' national securities law supervisors and law enforcement bodies operate within widely-differing common and civil law legal traditions. Whatever appearance of standardisation is achieved through the imposition of common rules via EU regulatory intervention, its practical impact is thus liable to be compromised by differences in the way in which it is applied and enforced in Member States. Negative externalities could arise in that market segments that are within the supervisory jurisdiction of Member States that achieve high standards in supervision and enforcement could suffer by association with segments that are supervised by Member States with lower standards.

Whilst it is not politically feasible for EU policy-makers to dictate to Member States precisely how they should supervise and make arrangements for enforcement actions in relation to securities market activity that is within their jurisdiction,[180] it clearly would be unwise for them to ignore this dimension altogether. Yet the importance of effective implementation, supervision and enforcement has only gradually come to the foreground of the EU policy agenda. In the document establishing the FSAP, the European Commission emphasised steady EU-led convergence in regulatory standards as a mechanism for the development of sound supervisory structures for a truly single market in financial services.[181] The technique of using regulatory convergence to promote supervisory convergence was thereafter employed in various ways in laws adopted under the FSAP, which, to a significantly greater extent than earlier EU securities law, prescribe the minimum characteristics of the agencies to which Member

---

[179] Black, 'Legal and Institutional Preconditions', emphasises institutional arrangements (honest courts, regulators and prosecutors) as being in the forefront of the steps that countries need to take if they want to build a strong securities market. See also J. C. Coffee, 'Privatization and Corporate Governance: The Lessons from Securities Market Failures' (1999) 25 *Journal of Corporation Law* 1, 6.

[180] Hopt, 'Modern Company and Capital Market Problems'. The situation is different for countries seeking to join the EU. There the EU institutions (particularly the Commission) have considerable leverage because they can delay or refuse entry to countries whose institutional arrangements or detailed substantive legal framework are not up to scratch.

[181] European Commission, *FSAP Action Plan*, pp. 13–15.

States can entrust certain supervisory responsibilities and also standardise the powers and responsibilities of these agencies.[182]

The original FSAP document published by the Commission was noticeably reticent on other measures, aside from regulation, to promote supervisory convergence.[183] The Commission noted that regulatory organisations had themselves taken the initiative to develop a greater degree of uniformity in supervisory practices and philosophies by forming FESCO (Forum of European Securities Commissions), which was established on an informal basis in 1997. The Commission raised the possibility that a single EU authority to oversee securities markets might one day emerge as a meaningful proposition. Beyond this, its only specific proposal was for the establishment of a specialist committee to assist the EU institutions in the development and implementation of regulation (this recommendation largely reflecting the general FSAP emphasis on regulation as the first-choice policy tool).

The *Lamfalussy Report* on the regulation of European securities markets went further than the Commission had done in seeking to improve the consistency of the day-to-day transposition and implementation of legislation. This Report called for the establishment of a framework for enhanced and strengthened co-operation and networking between national regulators with a view to: ensuring consistent and equivalent transposition of legislation in Member States; and encouraging national regulators to agree joint protocols for improving implementation and a peer review process to ensure consistent enforcement practice.[184]

Later chapters note developments since the *Lamfalussy Report* and assess their significance in promoting supervisory convergence.[185] The key change is that CESR, the Committee of European Securities Regulators, has replaced FESCO[186] as the network organisation which is responsible for promoting supervisory convergence across the EU. CESR has assumed a wide-ranging role, which includes producing administrative guidelines, interpretative recommendations and common standards. CESR conducts peer reviews and comparisons of regulatory practice to improve consistent application and enforcement. Although it is early days, the CESR-network model has bedded down well. One indication of its early success is that it has inspired similar changes in the pan-European organisation of banking

---

[182] This strategy for promoting supervisory convergence is discussed further in ch. 6.
[183] European Commission, *FSAP Action Plan*, pp. 13–15.
[184] *Lamfalussy Report*, pp. 37–8.
[185] Ch. 3 and ch. 6.
[186] An outline of CESR's role is available via http://www.cesr-eu.org (accessed April 2004).

and insurance supervision.[187] Another is that it has removed some of the
heat from debate on the need for a single EU-wide securities regulator, at
least in the short term.[188]

From today's perspective, as the proposals that were set out in the
original FSAP document near completion, it is evident that policy priorities are shifting away from regulation and towards ensuring consistent
implementation and supervision, and effective enforcement. In a speech
in January 2004 reflecting on the lessons learnt from the FSAP, Frits
Bolkestein, the European Commissioner for the Internal Market for the
period of the FSAP, admitted that 'supervisory convergence' had become
the new buzz-word, adding: 'Regulators need to be humble. It is not
within their gift to force financial market integration by adopting EU
legislation.'[189] This shift may have various explanations, amongst them
regulatory fatigue, lack of resources to develop new regulatory proposals
and political manoeuvring between EU institutions so as to restrain the
Commission, which controls the power to initate new EU regulation. The
reassessment of priorities may have been influenced by the establishment
of CESR and an associated growing awareness of the limits of regulation as
a policy tool to promote the market integration objective.[190] Concern

---

[187] There have been established a Committee of European Banking Supervisors (CEBS) based
in London (Commission Decision (2004/5/EC) Establishing the Committee of European
Banking Supervisors [2004] OJ L3/28) and a Committee of European Insurance and
Occupational Pensions Supervisors (CEIOPS), based in Frankfurt (Commission Decision
(2004/6/EC) Establishing the Committee of European Insurance and Occupational
Pensions Supervisors [2004] OJ L3/30).

  With CESR based in Paris, this arrangement neatly shares out portions of the supervisory
pie between three major EU Member States. The new legal framework supporting this
committee structure, which also includes a Directive (European Commission, *Proposal for
a Directive of the European Parliament and of the Council amending Council Directives 73/
239/EEC, 85/611/EEC, 91/675/EEC, 93/6/EEC and 94/19/EC and Directives 2000/12/EC,
2002/83/EC and 2002/87/EC of the European Parliament and of the Council, in order to
establish a new financial services committee organisational structure* (COM (2003) 659))
received final approval in May 2004 and will come into force on formal adoption
(expected Autumn 2004). Progress on the development of the structure for the extension
of Lamfalussy is outlined by N. Reinhardt, *The Lamfalussy Process: A Guide and Evaluation*
(Brussels, Houston Consulting Europe, April 2004), pp. 31–3.

[188] See further ch. 3.

[189] F. Bolkestein, 'Learning the Lessons of the Financial Services Action Plan' Speech/04/50.
The text of this speech is available via http://europa.eu.int/rapid/start/cgi/guesten.ksh?
p_action.getfile=gf&doc=SPEECH/04/50‖RAPID&lg=EN&type=PDF (accessed April 2004).

[190] HM Treasury, FSA and Bank of England, *The EU Financial Services Action Plan*, p. 19, citing
D. Green, 'Philosophical Debate or Practical Wisdom: Competing Visions of the EU's
Financial Services Sector', Conference Speech (March 2003): 'There is room for debate about

about the quality of some of the laws resulting from the FSAP may have played a part.[191] There may also have been some cross-fertilisation from the processes leading up to the enlargement of the EU in May 2004 because the importance of ensuring effective implementation and enforcement of EU laws were prominent issues in that context.[192] A 'breathing space' to allow new laws to bed down without adding further to them has been identified as being of particular importance for the new Member States.[193]

Whatever the driving influences, the policy shift can be seen as a sign of maturity within EU securities regulation. Substantive rules may matter but their long term success or failure depends less on continual refinement and expansion of the rules themselves than on how they are applied in practice. There may sometimes be a case for more EU regulatory intervention[194] but a readjustment of the balance in favour of more emphasis on supervision and enforcement and less on regulation is appropriate given the already extensive body of harmonised law, the difficulty of establishing with certainty which refinements or additions to it will in fact achieve desired policy goals, and the opportunities that stronger linkages between supervisory bodies present to develop non-regulatory solutions to policy concerns. An example of an area where significant progress may be made otherwise than through formal regulatory intervention is with regard to out-of-court redress and dispute resolution mechanisms for retail investors.[195] Improving these private mechanisms on a cross-border basis could help to supply some of the credible enforcement that intuitive expectations and also empirical research suggest to be important to securities market growth. The strategy that the EU has adopted is the establishment of a redress network for financial services disputes, FIN-NET, which is

---

the degree of "singleness" required to complete the Single Market in financial services, but no clear or simple answer. New EU legislation may not be the best way of removing barriers that are peculiar to one Member State and are not common across the EU as whole.'

[191] In his 'Learning the Lessons' speech Frits Bolkestein acknowledged some defects in quality, particularly as regards the Takeover Directive and called for a raised awareness by Member States and the European Parliament of the opportunity costs associated with optionality, vague compromises and third-best solutions.

[192] Nicolaides, 'Preparing for Accession', pp. 45–7.

[193] Securities Expert Group, *FSAP: Progress*, p. 7.

[194] See, e.g., Securities Expert Group, *FSAP: Progress*, p. 7 identifying possible future initiatives, with cross-border settlement and clearing and custody services seen as a particular priority.

[195] On the importance of such mechanisms in a national context, see: E. Ferran, 'Dispute Resolution Mechanisms in the UK Financial Sector' [2002] *Civil Justice Quarterly* 135; A. Samuel, 'Consumer Financial Services in Britain: New Approaches to Dispute Resolution and Avoidance' (2002) 3 *European Business Organization Law Review* 649.

based on linking together national out-of-court settlement bodies.[196] This approach avoids the problems surrounding aggressive interference from the centre in sensitive areas of Member States' legal systems.[197] If it works (full stress-testing must await the growth of more cross-border retail investment activity), it could become an important element of a truly EU-wide system of investor protection.

Making future policy choices on EU regulatory intervention: should there be some room for regulatory competition?

Despite the welcome change of emphasis from regulation to supervision, it is unrealistic to rule out the possibility of new EU securities laws in the future.[198] It is therefore pertinent finally to consider some strategies that EU policy-makers might use to inform themselves on desirable regulatory choices. The option currently favoured within the EU is refinement of the policy formation process through earlier and closer involvement of market participants in the determination of regulatory needs.[199] However, this is not the only way forward.

Some critics of harmonisation advocate regulatory competition as a superior mechanism for discovering the best laws for international securities markets.[200] In broad terms, regulatory competition in this context means competition between States for business from issuers, investors and intermediaries through the provision of favourable national regulatory frameworks for securities transactions. Supporters of regulatory competition

---

[196] Moloney, 'Confidence and Competence' 18. Further on the arrangements between these bodies, see *Memorandum of Understanding on a Cross-border Out of-Court Complaints Network for Financial Services in the European Economic Area*, available via http://europa. eu.int/comm/internal_market/en/finances/consumer/mou-en.pdf (accessed April 2004).

[197] However, there is some central steering in this area in the Financial Instruments Markets Directive (ISD2), art. 53 which requires Member States to provide efficient and effective complaints and redress procedures for out of court settlement of disputes involving investment firms: Moloney, 'Confidence and Conundrum'.

[198] Despite acknowledging the need for regulatory humility, Frits Bolkestein added in the same speech: 'legislative harmonisation has played an important role in the past and may serve us well in the future: where a solid case can be made for targeted legislative action to overcome clearly identified legal or regulatory barriers, it should remain an option for the architects of the single financial market'.

[199] This strategy is considered further in ch. 3.

[200] One of the most commonly cited benefits of regulatory competition is that it provides a market-driven mechanism for discovering what people want: J. M. Sun and J. Pelkmans, 'Regulatory Competition in the Single Market' (1995) 33 *Journal of Common Market Studies* 67, 82–8 (cost-benefit analysis of regulatory competition v harmonisation).

argue that if issuers are free to choose their regulatory regime, they have incentives to select ones that offer good investor protection laws because such choices lower the cost of capital. Investors will, it is claimed, discount the price of securities that are regulated by a regime that offers poor investor protection.[201] In turn, Governmental responsiveness to regulatory competition should mean that countries around the world will adapt their standards so as to bring them into line with issuer and investor preferences.[202] From other quarters, however, come doubts about issuers' incentives to select regimes with good investor protection laws[203] and about investors' ability to collect and process all of the information that would be needed to make meaningful assessments of differences in quality between different investor protection regimes.[204] Whether there are sufficient regulatory jurisdictions to engage in meaningful competition is

---

[201] Fierce debate has raged amongst leading scholars on the merits of regulatory competition in securities market regulation. Key articles include: R. Romano, 'Empowering Investors: a Market Approach to Securities Regulation' (1998) 107 *Yale Law Journal* 2359; R. Romano, 'The Need for Competition in International Securities Regulation' (2001) 2 *Theoretical Inquiries in Law* 387 S. J. Choi and A. T. Guzman, 'Portable Reciprocity: Rethinking the International Reach of Securities Regulation' (1998) 71 *South California Law Review* 903; M. B. Fox, 'Securities Disclosure in a Globalizing Market: Who Should Regulate Whom' (1997) 95 *Michigan Law Review* 2498; M. B. Fox, 'Retaining Mandatory Securities Disclosure: Why Issuer Choice is Not Investor Empowerment' (1999) 85 *Virginia Law Review* 1335; M. B. Fox, 'The Issuer Choice Debate' (2001) 2 *Theoretical Inquiries in Law* 563. H. E. Jackson, 'Centralization, Competition, and Privatization in Financial Regulation' (2001) 2 *Theoretical Inquiries in Law* 649, 659–62 provides a valuable overview of the debate.

[202] Jackson and Pan, 'Regulatory Competition' note that an implicit assumption in the debate over regulatory competition is that at least some Governments will make meaningful changes in their legal regimes in order to preserve or expand the number of entities under their regulatory oversight.

[203] J. C. Coffee, 'Law and Regulatory Competition: Can They Co-exist?' (2002) 80 *Texas Law Review* 1729.

[204] J. D. Cox, 'Regulatory Duopoly in US Securities Markets' (1999) 99 *Columbia Law Review* 1200, 1234 ('Before we embrace multiple standards in the belief that a disclosure hierarchy will develop among the securities of a particular market, we need better evidence that securities markets are capable of making discrete judgments among issuers using different disclosure standards').

Being fully informed is one of the conditions which according to the classic theory of regulatory competition (the Tiebout model from C. Tiebout, 'A Pure Theory of Local Expenditures' (1956) 64 *Journal of Political Economy* 416) needs to be satisfied for it to operate effectively: J. P. Trachtman, 'Regulatory Competition and Regulatory Jurisdiction in International Securities Regulation' in Esty and Geradin (eds.), *Regulatory Competition and Economic Integration*, pp. 289–310. However, this exacting condition can never be fully met: ibid.; H. S. Scott, 'Internationalization of Primary Public Securities Markets' (2000) 63 *Law and Contemporary Problems* 71.

questioned.[205] Some commentators have identified enforcement as a likely weak spot in that issuer freedom of choice as regards investor protection could imply highly-contentious extraterritorial enforcement by the securities regulatory agency of the chosen national regime or unskilled and inexperienced enforcement of that regime by the agencies of other countries.[206] The assumption that States necessarily would respond to regulatory competition by shifting their national laws upwards is also disputed.[207]

The regulatory competition debate is relevant to inquiry about how far EU policy-makers should push the agenda for harmonised rules for the single market because it suggests that an alternative strategy could be to confine the legal changes to initiatives that would allow regulatory competition to flourish. That would put promotion of issuer mobility – freedom for issuers to move to their preferred regime – at the top of the policy agenda.[208] With the legal preconditions to issuer mobility and regulatory competition in place, EU policy-makers could then sit back and wait for the market to demonstrate which Member States have the best laws. According to theory, other Member States could then be expected to gravitate towards the 'winning' package of laws. Further, since the reality is that laws 'on the books' are meaningless if compliance is not properly monitored and enforced, Member States could also be expected to upgrade their supervisory and enforcement infrastructures so as to emulate those in place elsewhere.

However, the doubts about the practical operation of regulatory competition resonate strongly in the European context.[209] The continuing home bias amongst issuers and the low levels of institutional investor participation in markets outside the UK (a significant factor because the effective operation of regulatory competition depends on the presence of investors skilled in making accurate assessments of the differences in quality between regimes) mean that, even if the EU legal environment as regards issuer mobility were

---

[205] Cox, 'Regulatory Duopoly', 1232–3.

[206] Ibid., 1239–44; Coffee, 'Law and Regulatory Competition'.

[207] Cox, 'Regulatory Duopoly', 1201 (regulatory competition may produce a hierarchy among international capital markets but it is then for national policy-makers to decide where they want to place their country within that hierarchy).

[208] Recent developments in EU law corporate mobility are considered further below in this chapter.

[209] S. Woolcock, 'Competition Among Rules in the Single European Market' in W. Bratton, J. McCahery, S. Picciotto and C. Scott (eds.), *International Regulatory Competition and Coordination* (Oxford, Clarendon Press, 1996), pp. 315–16 (examining why the scope for competition among rules is fairly limited).

to be adjusted so as to be more conducive to the operation of regulatory competition, the practical preconditions for its effective operation might still be far from satisfied.[210] Moreover, even if regulatory competition did work so as to identify market preferences, Member States' political responsiveness to that data could not be assumed. An entirely plausible alternative course of events is that, instead of good laws spreading by imitation, forces of national protectionism could continue to operate within the EU and result in the persistence of substandard rules favouring local players and preserving national biases.[211]

This discussion appears then to be pointing towards an insoluble dilemma. If a harmonised approach is risky because our lack of a clear understanding of the ways in which the law can foster securities market growth means that the chances of counterproductive regulatory mistakes are high and a regulatory competition-orientated approach is flawed because the competition may operate imperfectly and cannot be relied upon to produce a common regime for the single market, what are EU policy-makers to do? The approach that is supported here is of a mixed strategy that combines some reliance on regulatory competition within the EU alongside judicious use of EU regulatory powers to impose harmonised regulation in certain situations. This approach is consistent with the EC Treaty presumptions about subsidiarity and proportionality that, broadly, mean that regulatory intervention should take place at local (i.e. national or lower) level wherever possible. Whether a centrally-dictated harmonised approach to a particular matter is appropriate and, if so, how far it should extend, are questions that need to be considered carefully on an individual basis, but the case for harmonisation should never be lightly assumed.

Notwithstanding the many limitations of regulatory competition, leaving some room for diversity does offer certain potential advantages. Given the different levels of securities market development across the EU (particularly the enlarged EU), it avoids the problem of trying to devise rules that are not either too rigorous or too weak for many of the countries in which they are meant to apply. Diversity may, on some occasions, eventually act as a helpful acclimatising precursor to harmonisation. If one Member State's

---

[210] G. Ferrarini, 'Pan-European Securities Markets: Policy Issues and Regulatory Responses' (2002) 3 *European Business Organization Law Review* 249.

[211] K. Heine and W. Kerber, 'European Corporate Laws, Regulatory Competition and Path Dependence' (2000) 13 *European Journal of Law and Economics* 47; Sun and Pelkmans, 'Regulatory Competition', 84–5.

innovative approach to regulation commends itself to market participants and to regulators in other Member States, this is valuable information that could be taken as evidence in favour of a harmonised rule to follow the lead set at national level. The European Commission's acknowledgement that UK law is often highly influential in determining the EU approach is consistent with this suggestion.[212] A specific illustration is provided by the Market Abuse Directive, adopted by the EU in 2003, the development of which owed a considerable debt to the market abuse regime enacted by the UK in its Financial Services and Markets Act 2000.[213] The influence of the British *City Code on Takeovers and Mergers* on the Takeover Directive[214] has also been noted.[215]

There is, admittedly, nothing novel about arguing for co-existence of regulatory competition and harmonisation within EU policy-making for the single market. Much of the existing body of EU securities law (consistently with the legislative framework for the single market more generally) was built on the basis of a principle of harmonisation of core standards with scope for Member States to add their own additional requirements on top (the 'minimum harmonisation' approach). Thus, from the European perspective, analysis that casts harmonisation and regulatory competition into diametrically opposing camps seems rather wide of the mark. In European debate, harmonisation and competition are often seen as complementary forces, in the sense that harmonisation of core standards can generate trust between Member States on the broad comparability of their requirements which, in turn, may foster a system of mutual recognition of national requirements that may well be over and above the harmonised 'core'.[216]

---

[212] The *Financial Times* has quoted an unnamed spokesperson for the European Commission as saying that: 'Given that the City is the EU's leading financial centre, UK financial legislation in practice tends to form the basis of measures in the financial services action plan' in T. Tassell, E. Rigby and D. Dombey, 'City Trade Bodies Issue Warning on Directives', *Financial Times*, 14 October 2003, p. 8.

[213] Lau Hansen, 'The New Proposal'.

[214] Directive 2004/25/EC of the European Parliament and of the Council of 21 April 2004 on takeover bids, OJ 2004 No. L142/12.

[215] M. Becht, 'Reciprocity in Takeovers' *European Corporate Governance Institute* Law Working Paper No. 14/2003, ssrn abstract = 463003.

[216] Sun, and Pelkmans, 'Regulatory Competition' argue for regulatory competition and harmonisation to be seen as complements, rather than substitutes, with the demarcation between the two being determined on a case-by-case basis according to the subsidiarity principle. See also, Woolcock, 'Competition Among Rules'.

However, there is good reason at this time to restate the case for preserving room for diversity to co-exist with, and to complement, harmonisation. With the FSAP the EU moved into a new and more aggressive phase of securities law-making. It has been remarkably successful, in the sense that much of the ambitious legislative programme has been, or is in the process of being, realised with no more than the usual amount of jockeying for position, lobbying, horsetrading and compromising necessary to achieve agreement at EU level. The European Commission has achieved this success in part by riding the crest of a wave of disillusionment about the failure of minimum harmonisation to deliver a barrier-free single market. That failure guaranteed a wide coalition of interests wanting to operate across the single market and therefore prepared to support a new approach. This new approach is characterised by increased use of 'maximum harmonisation', that is prescriptive rules dictated by the centre with no discretion for Member States to add their own additional requirements. This approach lies at the core of the new prospectus disclosure regime and there are some indications that it may eventually spread into the periodic disclosure regime too.[217] The Regulation providing the framework for the adoption of IAS/IFRS is also a maximum harmonisation measure.[218]

Maximum harmonisation reduces the scope for diversity at national level. There are, of course, benefits in more uniformity but they come at a cost, in terms of rigidity[219] and loss of a useful stream of feedback about regulatory innovations which have been tested out at national level. To be sure, feedback from the rest of the world will still be available – but ever-increasing reliance on the US for innovative ideas (a likely consequence of cutting off diversity within the EU) is not a self-evidently desirable outcome.[220]

As well as cutting down the scope for national regulation to exceed the standard mandated by the centre, the new approach heralded by the FSAP has also reduced the scope for regulatory competition within the EU in another direction by more firmly tying issuers to their State of incorporation for the purpose of obtaining supervisory approvals.[221] From the

---

[217] See further ch. 5

[218] D. Littleford, 'International Financial Reporting Standards: Harmonising Accounting Principles' (2004) 15(4) *Practical Law for Companies* 23.

[219] See further ch. 5.

[220] This would be a paradoxical and unsettling result from the viewpoint of those who see the drive towards a single market as being Europe's attempt to gear itself up to compete with the US on more equal economic terms.

[221] See further ch. 5.

perspective of this chapter, which advocates a mixed approach in which there is some scope for the operation of regulatory competition, this looks like a move in the wrong direction because it removes the threat hanging over national regulators of loss of business from their 'home' issuers if they fail to match up to the standards of competence, efficiency and effectiveness of other regulators in the EU. This wrong turn, which was largely politically driven by certain Member States that were anxious to preserve the position of their national regulators, is counterbalanced to an extent by the establishment of the CESR infrastructure for better communication and closer co-operation between national regulators.[222] However, whilst this structure should help develop a shared regulatory and supervisory philosophy between EU regulators that could well become reflected in national standards and practices, it is by no means certain that the version of uniformity that emerges from the regulators' 'club' will be as good as that which could have been generated by a degree of competition between them leading eventually to convergence.

The negative effects of the trend in EU securities law to link issuers ever more rigidly to their State of incorporation could also be counterbalanced by moves within EU company law to make it easier for issuers to change their State of incorporation. A powerful catalyst for change in this direction was a series of decisions by the European Court of Justice that held certain national restrictions on issuer mobility to be incompatible with EC Treaty freedoms.[223] The European Commission has since published a proposal for harmonising legislation to provide a clear framework so that companies can exercise freedom of movement by transferring their registered offices between Member States.[224] It is too early to ascertain what factors will in practice motivate issuers to make use of the greater mobility that is emerging within EU company law, but it is conceivable that a desire to opt into or escape from the securities regulatory regime of a particular Member State could be one of them.

A further aspect of the new infrastructure is also troubling when it is considered alongside the move towards greater reliance on maximum

---

[222] See further ch. 3.

[223] Case C-212/97, *Centros Ltd* v. *Erhvervs- og Selskabsstyrelsen* [1999] ECR I-1459 [1999] 2 CMLR 551, [2000] 2 BCLC 68; Case C-208/00, *Überseering BV* v. *Nordic Construction Company Baumanagement GmbH (NCC)* [2002] ECR I-9919; Case C-167/01, *Kamer van Koophandel en Fabrieken voor Amsterdam* v. *Inspire Art Ltd.*

[224] European Commission, 'Commission Consults on the Cross-border Transfer of Companies' Registered Offices', Commission Press Release 26 February 2004, IP/04/270, announcing Internet consultation.

harmonisation. This is the new institutional framework for securities law-making in which the detailed requirements are set by a form of delegated legislation.[225] In broad terms the establishment of a process that allows the detailed aspects of legislative proposals to be separated off from the fundamentals and dealt with under a less cumbersome legislative machinery represents a valuable and long overdue development in EU securities law-making; but there is a risk that a system that makes it easier to make laws could remove a de facto check on excessive legalism and increase the overall regulatory burden. A strategy of maximum harmonisation, coupled with access to a delegated law-making process, thus puts a particularly strong burden on law-makers to choose the 'right' rules and standards. In the absence of a developed and mature understanding of the interplay between law and securities market growth, it is hard to be confident about their chances of making successful choices.

Whether the reduction of regulatory competition that is evident in recent developments represents the best way forward for EU securities law-making is an issue to which policy attention could usefully return. To the extent that regulatory competition is deemed unsuitable for the EU because market conditions do not display the features on which its operation effectively depends (such as issuers with commercial incentives to exploit emerging relaxations on issuer mobility in EU corporate law, and a sophisticated investor and analyst community to decode the significance of issuers' actions and reflect it in securities prices), this justification should properly be kept under review in line with market developments. Post-FSAP, it seems likely that the EU will take a break from formulating new securities laws for a while. This breathing space could provide a useful opportunity for policy-makers to reflect on fundamental aspects of their regulatory strategy and, in particular, to reconsider the appropriate balance between harmonisation and regulatory competition.[226]

---

[225] See further ch. 3.
[226] Securities Expert Group, *FSAP: Progress*, p. 23 calls for 'correction of poor legislation'. It is not clear whether the group had in mind narrow, technical improvements or more fundamental change.

3

The regulatory process for securities law-making in the EU

A   Scope of chapter

This chapter is concerned with the making of EU regulation for the single securities market. Since our understanding of the ways in which laws may foster the development of strong securities markets is still in its infancy, it is not possible to claim that the bureaucrats and politicians involved in the regulatory process are on a sure path that has been legitimised by scientific proof as being exactly what needs to be done by way of refinements to the legal system in order to promote the development of a securities market.[1] The lack of definitive guidance on how law matters to the development of securities markets suggests that there could be dangerous uncertainty in the regulatory process, involving strong risks of counterproductive policy decisions about the necessary rules, potential for exploitation by agenda-controlling bureaucrats intent on empire-building or by powerful interest groups that have influence over them, and vulnerability to political distortions. The quality of the regulatory process influences how much weight we should attach to these concerns. If there are effective safeguards built into the process that minimise the chances of policy mistakes and curb opportunities for bureaucratic excess or political or private distortions, the fact that we do not have a clear starting point, in the form of a comprehensive blueprint of all the laws that are conducive to securities market growth, becomes a much less troubling concern than it might be otherwise.

Formulating policy in the EU is a complex and multi-faceted undertaking. These complexities, combined with wide variations in policy processes across the vast range of EU activity, make it hard to reduce policy-making down to a few key features.[2] What is sometimes said of EU policy-making is what it is not: the product of a rational model of

---

[1] See ch. 2.
[2] H. Wallace, 'The Institutional Setting' in H. Wallace and W. Wallace (eds.), *Policy-Making in the European Union* (4th edn, Oxford, Oxford University Press, 2000), p. 6.

decision-making.[3] Although the discussion here is selective, focusing on securities law, the regulatory process in this field is vulnerable to the difficulties that beset EU policy-making in general. These general concerns include:[4]

- difficulties in securing agreement because of the large number and diverse interests of the participating parties;
- persistent path-dependent differences between countries that can impede efforts at coordination;
- tactical manoeuvring between the parties that can slow up the processes and erode the clarity and coherence that may have existed in initiatives when they were first proposed;
- political compromises that can result in 'package deals' whereby seemingly unconnected matters become linked to each other as Member States trade off their competing interests;
- the division of policy-making responsibilities between the internal institutions (in particular as between the European Commission, European Parliament and Council of the European Union[5]) that can lead to disagreements and conflicts; and
- the openness of the processes to lobbyists that can result in regulation tainted by self-interest.

Yet somehow (some have suggested 'muddling through' as a good description[6]), EU policy-making has managed to transcend these difficulties and has evolved sophisticated policy capabilities that are beyond those of other transnational organisations.[7] The EU has provided a forum for consensus-building out of which has come remarkable regulatory achievements, particularly in the development of a single market. For example, the 1992 internal market programme contained some 300 legislative proposals to remove barriers and open up European markets.[8] Rather than being harmful, the involvement of many public and private actors, including significant support from big business, in the development of the single

---

[3] N. Nugent, *The Government and Politics of the European Union* (4th edn, Basingstoke, Palgrave Macmillan, 1999), p. 385.

[4] On EU policy-making generally Wallace and Wallace, *Policy-Making*; Nugent, *Government and Politics*; J. Richardson (ed.), *European Union: Power and Policy-Making* (2nd edn, London, Routledge, 2001).

[5] The Council of the Union (or Council of Ministers) comprises the Ministers of Member States.

[6] J. Richardson, 'Policy-making in the EU: Interests, Ideas and Garbage Cans of Primeval Soup' in Richardson (ed.), *European Union*, pp. 3–26.

[7] H. Wallace, 'The Policy Process' in Wallace and Wallace (eds.), *Policy-Making*, p. 43.

[8] M. Thatcher, 'European Regulation' in Richardson (ed.), *European Union*, pp. 304–7.

market programme has often helped to define appropriate policy responses and to take them forward.[9]

The technical mechanisms by which policy decisions are converted into law are also complex,[10] involving complicated voting requirements and what has been described as a 'maze of intricate legislative procedures'.[11] Law-making in the EU involves elements of diplomacy,[12] and the behind-the-scenes political bargaining between Member States that this inevitably entails results in some lack of transparency in the legislative processes.

This chapter examines the strengths and weaknesses of the EU regulatory process relating to securities laws and assesses the likely effectiveness of efforts that have been made to insulate the process from some of the difficulties that can arise. Section B outlines the emergence of the new process (which is generally known as the 'Lamfalussy process') and identifies its key features. Section C evaluates elements of the Lamfalussy process and the interaction of the various bodies and groups that are involved in it. Section D notes that the improvements that can be gained through the Lamfalussy process are subject to a powerful limitation because that process is not designed to override national protectionism or other deep-rooted influences that may lead Member States to oppose proposed new EU laws. Section E considers the more radical option than that represented by the Lamfalussy process: namely, the establishment of an EU-wide securities regulatory agency which has rule-making and supervisory powers. It suggests that the adoption of the regulatory agency model could create more problems than it solves and that it would be a premature step given securities market conditions across the EU. Section F draws the conclusion that, though not perfect, the Lamfalussy process is a step in the right direction. For the immediate future, the course of action that commends itself therefore is to concentrate on refining and upgrading the Lamfalussy process so as to enable it to work more efficiently and effectively rather than to pursue more radical and risky alternatives.

---

[9] A. R. Young and H. Wallace, 'The Single Market' in Wallace and Wallace (eds.), *Policy-Making*, pp. 98–102.

[10] A. Dashwood, 'The Constitution of the EU After Nice: Law-making Procedures' (2001) 26 *European Law Review* 215, 232: 'A high price is paid, in the coin of democratic accountability, for the increasing complexity of a process of making EU law that is unintelligible except to Brussels professionals.'

[11] G. de Búrca, 'The Institutional Development of the EU: A Constitutional Analysis' in P. Craig and G. de Búrca (eds.), *The Evolution of EU Law* (Oxford, Oxford University Press, 1999), p. 65.

[12] C. Harlow, *Accountability in the European Union* (Oxford, Oxford University Press, 2002), pp. 31–2.

B Recent refinement of the regulatory process – the Lamfalussy model

The path towards reform of the regulatory process

In July 2000 the Council (in its Economic and Finance ministers formation (ECOFIN)) appointed a Committee of 'Wise Men' under the chairmanship of Baron Alexandre Lamfalussy to conduct a broad examination
of the mechanisms for regulating and supervising EU securities markets.[13]
The Lamfalussy Committee published an initial report in November 2000
and a final report in February 2001.[14]

The Lamfalussy Committee's Reports were very critical of the established
regulatory process, finding it to be too slow, too rigid, complex and ill-adapted
to the pace of global financial market change. The Committee suggested a
new approach involving a four level structure: Level 1 (in essence primary
legislation decided upon by the Council and Parliament in accordance with
established law-making procedures); Level 2 (implementing measures, or more
detailed rules, decided upon by the Commission acting in accordance with
EU comitology procedures that had been developed in other fields but not
previously used in securities law-making); Level 3 (a drive towards consistent implementation and transposition of legislation at Member State
level); and Level 4 (greater emphasis on monitoring and enforcement). An
overview of the Lamfalussy process follows as Table 3.1. Detailed aspects of
the structure outlined in this table are considered throughout this chapter.

The Lamfalussy Committee's view of the inadequacies of the existing
regulatory process and its suggestions for change were speedily endorsed
at the highest political levels, by the Council[15] and the Heads of EU States

---

[13] The establishment of this Committee to look at radical options for the development of the
single securities market was the brainchild of Laurent Fabius, the French finance minister:
'A Ragbag of Reform', *Economist*, 3 March 2001, p. 93.

[14] *The Regulation of European Securities Markets: Final Report* (Brussels, 15 February 2001), in
which *The Regulation of European Securities Markets: Initial Report* (Brussels, 9 November
2000) appears as Annex 5, with the ECOFIN Council's terms of reference included as
Annex 1 to the *Initial Report*. The final report is referred to in this chapter as the '*Lamfalussy Report*' and the earlier one is referred to as the '*Lamfalussy Initial Report*'. The reports
are available via http://www.europa.eu.int/comm/internal_market/en/finances/general/
lamfalussyen.pdf (accessed May 2004).

[15] Results of the Council of Economics and Finance Ministers, March 2001, Stockholm, available
via http://europa.eu.int/comm/internal_market/en/finances/mobil/01-memo105.htm (accessed
May 2004). The Council's Resolution on More Effective Securities Market Regulation in

Table 3.1

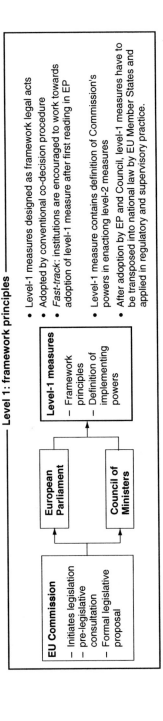

Level 1: framework principles

EU Commission
– Initiates legislation
– pre-legislative consultation
– Formal legislative proposal

European Parliament

Council of Ministers

Level-1 measures
– Framework principles
– Definition of implementing powers

- Level-1 measures designed as framework legal acts
- Adopted by conventional co-decision procedure
- *Fast-track*: institutions are encouraged to work towards adoption of level-1 measure after first reading in EP
- Level-1 measure contains definition of Commission's powers in enactiong level-2 measures
- After adoption by EP and Council, level-1 measures have to be transposed into national law by EU Member States and applied in regulatory and supervisory practice.

Table 3.1 (cont.)

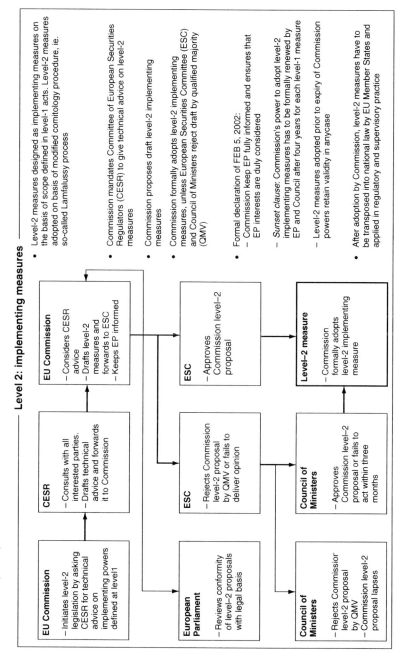

Level 2: implementing measures

EU Commission
- Initiates level-2 legislation by asking CESR for technical advice on implementing powers defined at level1

CESR
- Consults with all interested parties.
- Drafts technical advice and forwards it to Commission

EU Commission
- Considers CESR advice
- Drafts level-2 measures and forwards to ESC
- Keeps EP informed

European Parliament
- Reviews conformity of level-2 proposals with legal basis

ESC
- Rejects Commission level-2 proposal by QMV or fails to deliver opinion

ESC
- Approves Commission level-2 proposal

Council of Ministers
- Rejects Commission level-2 proposal by QMV
- Commission level-2 proposal lapses

Council of Ministers
- Approves Commission level-2 proposal or fails to act within three months

Level-2 measure
- Commission formally adopts level-2 implementing measure

- Level-2 measures designed as implementing measures on the basis of scope defined in level-1 acts. Level-2 measures adopted on basis of modified comitology procedure, ie. so-called Lamfalussy process

- Commission mandates Committee of European Securities Regulators (CESR) to give technical advice on level-2 measures

- Commission proposes draft level-2 implementing measures

- Commission formally adopts level-2 implementing measures, unless European Securities Committee (ESC) and Council of Ministers reject draft by qualified majority (QMV)

- Formal declaration of FEB 5, 2002:
  - Commission keep EP fully informed and ensures that EP interests are duly considered
  - *Sunset clause:* Commission's power to adopt level-2 implementing measures has to be formally renewed by EP and Council after four years for each level-1 measure
  - Level-2 measures adopted prior to expiry of Commission powers retain validity in anycase

- After adoption by Commission, level-2 measures have to be transposed into national law by EU Member States and applied in regulatory and supervisory practice

Table 3.1 *(cont.)*

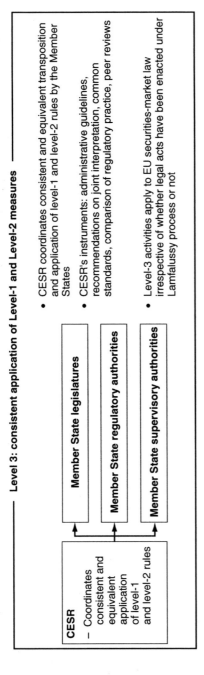

Level 3: consistent application of Level-1 and Level-2 measures

CESR
- Coordinates consistent and equivalent application of level-1 and level-2 rules

Member State legislatures

Member State regulatory authorities

Member State supervisory authorities

- CESR coordinates consistent and equivalent transposition and application of level-1 and level-2 rules by the Member States
- CESR's instruments: administrative guidelines, recommendations on joint interpretation, common standards, comparison of regulatory practice, peer reviews
- Level-3 activities apply to EU securities-market law irrespective of whether legal acts have been enacted under Lamfalussy process or not

Level 4: enforcement of Level-1 and Level-2 measures

EU Commission
- Monitors enforcement of EU securities-market law

Member States

- Commissions takes measures to enforce EU securities market law in case of infringement
- Level-4 activities apply to EU securities-market law irrespective of whether legal acts have been enacted under Lamfalussy process or not

Source: Deutsche Bank Research, 'Reform of EU Regulatory and Supervisory Structures: Progress Report' (2003) 4 *EU Monitor* (July 2003)

or Governments at their Summit Meeting in Stockholm in March 2001.[16] Then, with equal rapidity, the European Commission moved in June 2001 to give effect to the new approach recommended by the Lamfalussy Committee.[17]

Is there an explanation for such speed, remarkable because the EU is not usually noted for its swift reactions in institutional reform? In simple terms, the likely answer is that the Committee, under the chairmanship of 'a veteran of Brussels bureaucracy',[18] had done its homework well and was therefore able to make proposals that were informed by a good under-standing of what would be politically feasible. Key groundwork to ensure a favourable political reception by Member States for proposals designed to speed up the legislative process for a single financial market had been done at the highly-ambitious 'dotcom' Lisbon Summit Meeting in June 2000:[19] in Lisbon European leaders had set themselves the target of becoming the most competitive and dynamic knowledge-based economy in the world by 2010, with improvement of existing processes identified as being key to implementation of this strategic goal.[20] The European Heads called specifically for steps to ensure adoption by 2005 of the legislative measures set out in the European Commission's Financial Services Action Plan (FSAP).[21] For the European Commission, the Lamfalussy Commit-tee's identification of problems with the law-making process was more of an endorsement of its own long-held view than a new insight: there had been calls from the Commission stretching back many years for a more streamlined, flexible and faster legislative approach.[22]

---

the European Union (Stockholm 23 March 2001) ('Council Stockholm Resolution') is available via http://ue.eu.int/ueDocs/cms_Data/docs/pressData/en/ec/00100-r1.%20ann-r1.en1.html(accessed May 2004).

[16] *Presidency Conclusions*, Stockholm European Council, 23–24 March 2001, available via http://europa.eu.int/european_council/conclusions/index_en.htm (accessed May 2004).

[17] Commission Decision (2001/528/EC) Establishing the European Securities Committee [2001] OJ L191/45 ('ESC Decision') and Commission Decision (2001/527/EC) Establishing the Committee of European Securities Regulators [2001] OJ L191/43 ('CESR Decision').

[18] As he was described in 'How to Protect Investors', *Economist*, 27 April 2002, p. 81. Baron Lamfalussy was the one-time general manager of the Bank for International Settlements, and president of the European Monetary Institute, the forerunner of the European Central Bank.

[19] J. Gillingham, *European Integration 1965–2003* (Cambridge, Cambridge University Press, 2003), pp. 328–9.

[20] Presidency Conclusions, Lisbon European Council, 23–24 March 2000, available via http://europa.eu.int/european_council/conclusions/index_en.htm (accessed May 2004).

[21] Ibid. The Commission's FSAP proposal was contained in European Commission, *Finan-cial Services: Implementing the Framework for Financial Markets: Action Plan* (COM (1999) 232) ('*FSAP Action Plan*').

[22] E.g. European Commission, *Financial Services: Building a Framework for Action* (1998), available via http://www.europa.eu.int/comm/internal_market/en/finances/general/fsen.pdf (accessed May 2004). See further N. Moloney, *EC Securities Regulation* (Oxford, Oxford University Press, 2002), pp. 854–6.

The Member States, Council and Commission's rapid support for the Lamfulussy recommendations was in sharp contrast to the reaction of the European Parliament, which did not endorse the new process until February 2002.[23] The Parliament was concerned about potential dilution of its role in the regulatory process and the resultant loss of democratic safeguards.[24] It took considerable manoeuvring between the EU institutions, including a formal declaration by the President of the Commission assuring the Parliament that the implementation of the Lamfalussy proposals would mean no loss of democratic control and expressing Commission support for Treaty amendments to rationalise general EU comitology procedures so as to reflect properly Parliament's co-legislative role (an issue that goes far beyond securities law),[25] to overcome the considerable inter-institutional tensions.[26] Even then, Parliamentary support was guarded and provisional.[27] In particular it insisted upon the use of 'sunset'

---

[23] European Parliament Resolution on the Implementation of Financial Services Legislation (2001/2247(INI) P5_TA(2002)0035).

[24] The *Lamfalussy Report*, ch. II acknowledges the European Parliament's concerns about potential dilution of its role. Moloney, *EC Securities Regulation*, pp. 864–5 elaborates further.

[25] 'Comitology' is the process whereby technical, implementing rules are adopted by the European Commission. It usually requires proposals to be channelled through a comitology committee in accordance with procedures laid down in Council Decision 99/468/EC Laying Down the Procedures for the Exercise of Implementing Powers Conferred by the Commission [1999] OJ L184/23 ('Comitology Decision'). Article 202 of the EC Treaty provides the Treaty base for the Council to empower the Commission to exercise implementing powers. The Council can impose certain requirements on the exercise of implementing powers and it can reserve the right to exercise implementing powers directly in specific and exceptional cases. The special rights enjoyed by the Council in this respect sit very uneasily with the status of the Council and Parliament as co-legislators because Parliament's rights under comitology procedures are confined to being kept informed and being able to require the Commission to reconsider proposals if Parliament considers them to exceed the scope of implementing powers. Comitology procedures have attracted heavy academic attention because of concerns about lack of transparency and accountability: Harlow, *Accountability*, pp. 67–71; P. Craig, 'The Nature of the Community: Integration, Democracy, and Legitimacy' in Craig and de Búrca (eds.), *The Evolution of EU Law*, pp. 42–50; de Búrca, 'Institutional Development', pp. 71–5. Parliamentary suspicion of comitology is explored further in K. St Clair Bradley, 'The European Parliament and Comitology: On the Road to Nowhere' (1997) 3 *European Law Journal* 230. Generally on the Commission's commitment to reform of comitology: European Commission, *European Governance White Paper* (COM (2001) 428).

[26] The text of this declaration ('Prodi Declaration') is available via http://www.europarl. eu.int/comparl/econ/lamfalussy_process/ep_position/prodi_declaration.pdf (accessed May 2004).

[27] M. McKee, 'The Unpredictable Future of European Securities Regulation' (2003) 18 *Journal of International Banking Law and Regulation* 277.

clauses whereby any implementing powers afforded to the Commission would come to an end after four years.[28] The establishment of a more permanent settlement in place of this transitional arrangement is bound up with the wider debate on Treaty reform and an EU constitution.

Co-operation between the Commission, Council and European Parliament in the Lamfalussy process

The uneasy settlement between the Commission, Council and Parliament on securities law-making under the Lamfalussy process has two main strands. The first strand relates to ensuring effective co-operation between the three institutions through disclosure and consultation. Stipulations on openness and consultation range from high-level expressions of support for the need to involve all of the institutions throughout the regulatory process from its earliest stages,[29] through to specific statements about procedural matters such as entitlements to attend meetings and Internet publication of documentation.[30] As part of the delicate negotiations to secure Parliamentary support for the new process, the Commission has given the Parliament a formal promise of transparency in the regulatory process and specific undertakings to allow it time to comment on and examine measures that are subject to comitology procedures.[31] These specific stipulations reinforce general EU arrangements for transparency and dialogue that are intended to facilitate inter-institutional co-operation in the operation of comitology.[32]

Formal allocation of regulatory responsibilities as between the Commission, Council and European Parliament under the Lamfalussy process

The second strand concerns the formal allocation of legislative powers: the 'who does what?' On this, the European Commission's position as the initiator of new regulation is formally unchanged. On the actual making

---

[28] European Parliament Resolution.
[29] E.g. Council Stockholm Resolution, para. 2.
[30] E.g. European Parliament Resolution, para. 5.
[31] Prodi Declaration. The European Parliament has three months to comment on any proposed implementing measure that is formally submitted to the European Securities Committee and a further month for deliberations after the ESC has given its view.
[32] Considered generally in C. Joerges and E. Vos (eds.), *EU Committees: Social Regulation, Law and Politics* (Oxford, Hart Publishing, 1999).

of new laws, there is a major change in the distinction that is now drawn between framework principles (Level 1) and implementing measures (Level 2). The significance of the split is that only Level 1 principles go through the full legislative process of co-decision by Council and Parliament.[33] Level 2 measures are adopted by the Commission in accordance with comitology procedures. Decisions about where to draw the line between Level 1 and Level 2 are thus potentially very significant, particularly for the Parliament because it is on a lesser footing to the Council in matters dealt with via comitology. It is for the Commission to make suggestions on where the split should lie but the final decision is for the Council and Parliament 'on a case-by-case basis and in a clear and transparent way'.[34] Similarly, whilst the Commission must suggest the scope of the Level 2 implementing powers that should be permitted to it, the nature and extent of Level 2 implementing measures are ultimately for the Council and Parliament to determine.[35]

The Market Abuse Directive[36] was the first FSAP measure in which the Lamfalussy law-making process was employed and it can be used to illustrate its operation as regards timing and the way in which the Parliament and Council seek to retain control over the Level 2 process via the drafting of the Level 1 measure. In outline the Level 1 chronology of this Directive was as shown in Table 3.2.[37]

---

[33] There is more than one EU legislative procedure but the text concentrates on the co-decision procedure, in which the Council and European Parliament are co-lawmakers, because most securities laws are made in this way: Moloney, *EC Securities Regulation*, pp. 845–7.

[34] Council Stockholm Resolution, para. 3.

[35] ESC Decision and CESR Decision.

[36] Directive 2003/6/EC of the European Parliament and of the Council of 28 January 2003 on insider dealing and market manipulation (market abuse) OJ 2003 No. L96/16 ('Market Abuse Directive').

[37] A more detailed tabular account of the Level 1 process is provided in the Inter-Institutional Monitoring Group for Securities Markets ('IIMG') *First Interim Report Monitoring the New Process for Regulating Securities Markets in Europe (The Lamfalussy Process)* (Brussels, May 2003), Figure 3 which is available via http://europa.eu.int/comm/internal_market/en/finances/mobil/docs/lamfalussy/2003–05-monitoring_en.pdf?REQUEST = Seek-Deliver &COLLECTION=com&SERVICE=all&LANGUAGE=en&DOCID=502PC0460 (accessed May 2004).

The IIMG was established in 2002 and comprises representatives of the Commission, Council and European Parliament. The establishment of this group was recommended in the *Lamfalussy Report*, pp. 40–1. Its function is to produce half-yearly reports assessing the progress made on implementing the Lamfalussy process and identifying any possible emerging bottlenecks in this process. Its role is considered further later in this chapter.

Table 3.2

May 2001	Commission presents its proposal for a Directive
14 March 2002	European Parliament completes its First Reading and inserts amendments
7 May 2002	Council achieves political agreement on Common Position
19 July 2002	Council formally adopts Common Position
24 October 2002	European Parliament gives proposal its Second Reading and inserts further amendments
3 December 2002	Council agrees on the text approved by European Parliament at Second Reading
28 January 2003	Market Abuse Directive formally adopted by Parliament and Council
12 April 2003	Directive comes into force on publication in Official Journal; Member States given eighteen months in which to implement Directive in their national laws

Had the institutions agreed on the text at an earlier stage, the process could have been truncated. The *Lamfalussy Report* supported the idea in principle of 'fast tracking' Level 1 securities legislation, whereby measures would be adopted after a single reading in the European Parliament.[38] Initial reactions on this point were somewhat sceptical of the likelihood of widespread use of this facility save for uncontroversial or essentially procedural proposals.[39] These concerns may have been assuaged to some extent by experience with the Transparency Directive where, despite being a substantive measure with various controversial features, it was

---

[38] *Lamfalussy Report*, p. 21.
[39] Regulation (EC) No 1606/2002 of the European Parliament and of the Council of 19 July 2002 on the application of international accounting standards, OJ 2002 No. L243/1 (agreed after one reading) falls into this category because it established the procedural framework mechanism for the adoption of the standards, leaving the much more controversial issues arising in relation to actual adoption for a later stage. From Commission proposal (February 2001) to adoption (July 2002) this measure took seventeen months. Concerns about potentially limited use of the fast track facility are expressed in IIMG, *First Interim Report*, pp. 26–7.

passed in Spring 2004 with a single reading in the European Parliament.[40] However, the circumstances were a little unusual in this case because the looming enlargement of the EU on 1 May 2004 and forthcoming elections to the European Parliament in June 2004 created an environment in which there was particular pressure on all parties to come to agreement quickly.

Another, as yet untested, mechanism for making Level 1 securities laws effective more quickly is to pass them in the form of a Regulation rather than a Directive. Under EU law a Regulation takes effect directly in Member States on the date specified in it whereas a Directive's effectiveness is ordinarily dependent on its transposition into the national laws of Member States and Member States are given a grace period in which to make the necessary changes. The *Lamfalussy Report* called for more use to be made of Regulations, rather than Directives, in order to speed up the legislative process.[41] The establishment of the mechanism for the adoption of International Accounting Standards was effected by means of a Regulation but all of the Level 1 FSAP laws proposed or adopted in accordance with the Lamfalussy process have been in the form of Directives. The choice between a Directive or a Regulation has been more of a real issue at Level 2 where both have been used. Although a Regulation, once adopted, can take effect in Member States more quickly than a Directive, a counterbalancing consideration is that the process of adopting a Regulation may be slower than for a Directive because the inherent lack of flexibility in a Regulation may well complicate the process of securing Member States' agreement on issues that are politically contentious.

The use of Regulations raises some concerns with regard to the subsidiarity principle because, according to a Protocol on the Application of the Principles of Subsidiarity and Proportionality that is annexed to the EC

---

[40] The ECOFIN Council approved the text, as amended by Parliament, at its meeting on 11 May 2004. The Directive will not be published in the Official Journal until Autumn 2004, a delay that is related to the expanded translation burdens resulting from the enlargement of the EU on 1 May 2004. References to specific provisions of the Directive in this chapter are to an unofficial version available via http://europa.eu.int/comm/internal_market/en/ finances/mobil/transparency/directive-unofficial_en.pdf (accessed May 2004).

[41] *Lamfalussy Report*, p. 26 (and at p. 21 noting European Parliamentary support for the greater use of Regulations). The IIMG has recommended more frequent use of regulations at Level 2, although it notes that market participants and end-users are split on the issue: IIMG, *Second Interim Report Monitoring the Lamfalussy Process* (Brussels, December 2003), pp. 14–15, available via http://europa.eu.int/comm/internal_market/en/finances/mobil/ docs/lamfalussy/2003–12-monitoring_en.pdf?REQUEST = Seek-Deliver&COLLECTION = com& SERVICE = all&LANGUAGE = en&DOCID = 502PC0460(accessed May 2004).

Treaty, forms of legislation that leave the Member States the greatest room for manoeuvre are to be preferred to more restrictive forms of action.[42] This Protocol implies that there has to be a particularly good reason to opt for Regulations rather than Directives and that pace of implementation alone may not suffice. In areas where Regulations have been used in Level 2 securities laws the European Commission has made the case by emphasising 'legal certainty' and 'legal clarity' as justification for choosing this form of legal instrument.[43] Such justification relies less on the feature that Regulations can take effect more quickly than Directives than on the fact that direct application without transposition cuts down the scope for variation to creep in via differences in drafting at national level.

With regard to exerting control over the Commission in its exercise of Level 2 implementing powers, the Market Abuse Directive empowers the Commission to adopt implementing measures concerning the 'technical modalities' of various aspects of the Directive[44] but it expressly provides that implementing measures must not modify the essential elements of the Directive.[45] Additionally, the Directive specifies certain procedures[46] and the general principles that the Commission should respect in exercising implementing powers. The general principles are:[47]

- the need to ensure confidence in financial markets among investors by promoting high standards of transparency in financial markets;
- the need to provide investors with a wide range of competing investments and a level of disclosure and protection tailored to their circumstances;
- the need to ensure that independent regulatory authorities enforce the rules consistently, especially as regards the fight against economic crime;
- the need for high levels of transparency and consultation with all market participants and with the European Parliament and the Council;
- the need to encourage innovation in financial markets if they are to be dynamic and efficient;

---

[42] Protocol 30, para. 6.
[43] E.g. DG Internal Market Services, *Implementation of Article 8 of Directive 2003/6/EC (Market Abuse)* (Working Document ESC 14/2003), p. 4, available via http://www.europa.eu.int/comm/internal_market/en/finances/mobil/docs/marketabuse/esc-14–2003_en.pdf(accessed May 2004).
[44] Art. 10.
[45] Rec. 42 and art. 17.2.
[46] Rec. 7 (general comitology procedures) and rec. 9 (three-month period for Parliamentary scrutiny of draft implementing measures).
[47] Rec. 43.

- the need to ensure market integrity by close and reactive monitoring of financial innovation;
- the importance of reducing the cost of, and increasing access to, capital;
- the balance of costs and benefits to market participants on a long-term basis (including small and medium-sized businesses and small investors) in any implementing measures;
- the need to foster the international competitiveness of EU financial markets without prejudice to a much-needed extension of international cooperation;
- the need to achieve a level playing field for all market participants by establishing EU-wide regulations every time it is appropriate;
- the need to respect differences in national markets where these do not unduly impinge on the coherence of the single market; and
- the need to ensure coherence with other Community legislation in this area, as imbalances in information and a lack of transparency may jeopardise the operation of the markets and above all harm consumers and small investors.

Giving effect to the compromise deal between the Parliament and other EU institutions on the operation of the Lamfalussy process,[48] the Directive contains a sunset clause providing for the delegation of implementing powers to the Commission to come to an end after four years, although with the possibility of renewal.[49]

The approach adopted in the Market Abuse Directive for controlling Level 2 aspects of the securities law-making process – clear warnings that the Commission must act within the parameters and procedures set by the Level 1 measure, deadlines for stages in the Level 2 law-making process, recognition of the Parliament's entitlements under the political deal between itself and the other EU institutions, specification of principles within which the Commission must exercise its powers and a time-limit on the powers conferred on the Commission – has been followed and refined in subsequent securities law Directives to the point where it has now become largely standard form.[50]

---

[48] European Parliament Resolution; Prodi Declaration.

[49] Market Abuse Directive, art. 17.4.

[50] E.g., Directive 2003/71/EC of the European Parliament and of the Council of 4 November 2003 on the prospectus to be published when securities are offered to the public or admitted to trading and amending Directive 2001/34/EC, OJ 2003 No. L345/64 ('Prospectus Directive'), rec. 40 and art. 24 (compatibility with essential elements of the Level 1 measure and

The *Lamfalussy Report* endorsed calls for guiding principles covering all financial services legislation.[51] The idea of a clear set of principles against which particular pieces of legislation can be benchmarked has also been endorsed more recently by an independent group of securities market experts which was established by the European Commission to take stock of the FSAP.[52] Yet it is open to question whether such a long and diffuse list of general principles, as appears in the Market Abuse and later Directives, serves achieves much beyond a symbolic purpose. The overall scope is so broad that it is hard to envisage situations in which the Commission would struggle to justify its proposals by reference to one or more of the principles. There is no order of priority as between the various principles, a gap which leaves scope for them to be played off against each other. Furthermore, given the weak standards of judicial review applied by the European Court of Justice in areas of complex socio-economic policy choices, there is little chance of these principles forming the basis for a successful legal challenge of the Commission's decisions.

In addition to the controls over Level 2 that the Council and Parliament can impose in the empowering Level 1 measure, there are also further

with certain procedures), rec. 41 (guiding principles), rec. 42 (three-month time period for Parliamentary scrutiny of draft implementing measures) and art. 24 (sunset clause).

This model is also followed in the Transparency Directive which includes provisions on: rec. 22 (deadlines), rec. 24 (procedures), rec. 25 (three-month time period for Parliamentary scrutiny of draft implementing measures), rec. 26 and art. 23 (compatibility with essential elements of the Level 1 measure and with certain procedures), rec. 26a (guiding principles), and art. 23 (sunset clause).

The standard form recitals have also found their way into Directive 2004/39/EC of the European Parliament and of the Council of 21 April 2004 on markets in financial instruments amending Council Directives 85/611/EEC and 93/6/EEC and Directive 2000/12/EC of the European Parliament and of the Council and repealing Council Directive 93/22/EEC, OJ 2004 No. L145/1 ('Financial Instruments Markets Directive', also known as the revised Investment Services Directive or 'ISD2') and Directive 2002/87/EC of the European Parliament and of the Council of 16 December 2002 on the supplementary supervision of credit institutions, insurance undertakings and investment firms in a financial conglomerate and amending Council Directives 73/239/EEC, 79/267/EEC, 92/49/EEC, 92/96/EEC, 93/6/EEC and 93/22/EEC, and Directives 98/78/EC and 2000/12/EC of the European Parliament and of the Council, OJ 2003 No. L35/1 ('Financial Conglomerates Directive'): N. Reinhardt, *The Lamfalussy Process: A Guide and Evaluation* (Brussels, Houston Consulting Europe, April 2004), p. 11.

[51] *Lamfalussy Report*, pp. 12, 22.

[52] Securities Expert Group, *Financial Services Action Plan: Progress and Prospects* (Final Report, Brussels, May 2004), pp. 9–10. This report is available via http://www.europa.eu.int/comm/internal_market/en/finances/actionplan/docs/stocktaking/fasap-stocktaking-report-securities_ en.pdf (accessed May 2004).

institutional controls over the Level 2 process. Under the EC Treaty, the Council can amend or block comitology decisions and take implementing decisions itself (the 'call back' power).[53] The Parliament does not have an equivalent Treaty power, a difference that is rooted in the history of the EU but which is now anomalous because it fails properly to reflect the Parliament's status as a co-legislator with the Council.[54] However, under comitology procedures the Parliament can require the Commission to reconsider a proposal if it considers that it would exceed the scope of the implementing powers. Additionally, under the compromise deal that was entered into to secure the backing of the European Parliament for the Lamfalussy process, there is a specific undertaking from the Commission to 'take the utmost account of the Parliament's position if it considers that the Commission has exceeded its implementing powers'.[55] Although this is not a formal veto, it seems unlikely that the Commission and Council would seek to force through a measure in the face of opposition from the Parliament, not least because to do so would surely seriously undermine the chances of securing Parliamentary support for the continuance of the Lamfalussy process on a more permanent basis.

Yet, having noted that in practice the Parliament's position may not be as weak as constitutional formalities might suggest, it is undeniable that the Council is in a stronger position. As well as the formal differences in their Treaty powers, Council control over the Level 2 process is reinforced by a provision in the resolution of the Council endorsing the Lamfalussy process in which it was noted that the Commission had committed itself to 'avoid going against predominant views which might emerge within the Council, as to the appropriateness of such measures'.[56] Council control is also evident in the composition of the regulatory committee which assists the Commission in the adoption of Level 2 measures because this closely reflects the composition of the Council itself.

---

[53] EC Treaty, art. 202.
[54] Historically the European Parliament's involvement in the legislative process was slim but over the years, via various Treaty changes, it has acquired various co-legislative powers with the Council. M. Shackleton, 'The European Parliament' in J. Peterson and M. Shackleton (eds.), *The Institutions of the European Union* (Oxford, Oxford University Press, 2002), pp. 95–117 describes the evolution of the Parliament's legislative powers.
[55] Prodi Declaration.
[56] Council Stockholm Resolution, para. 5.

The establishment of new committees to assist the regulatory process

Existing committees and bodies that contribute to securities law-making

There is quite an array of EU committees and other bodies involved in the development of EU securities regulation. Some committees are part of the Council infrastructure, others the Parliament, whilst some are Treaty-based, self-standing organisations. Some of the most significant are as follows.

The Council's assessment of strategic policy concerns is informed by the Financial Services Committee (previously called the Financial Services Policy Group). The FSC, established in 1998, comprises personal representatives of the ECOFIN Council Ministers. It assisted the European Commission in drawing up the FSAP and continues to meet periodically with the Commission for fairly high-level discussions on issues of concern to Member States' finance ministries.[57] Since it focuses more on strategic policy issues than on the nitty-gritty of legislative proposals, the FSC is likely to play an important role in shaping the post-FSAP agenda, for the period from 2005 onwards.

When Commission legislative proposals reach the Council, in accordance with general EU procedures they go through the Committee of Permanent Representatives (Coreper) before they are considered at ministerial level.[58] Coreper is pivotal to EU decision-making because it is at or below this 'engine room' level that much of the work is done to strike compromises between divergent national interests and to reach solutions.[59] The Council's sectoral Economic and Financial Committee, which was established in 1999,[60] has begun to exert a powerful influence in financial matters[61]

---

[57] Brief notes of the meetings are available via http://www.europa.eu.int/comm/internal_market/en/finances/actionplan/fspg14_en.htm(accessed May 2004).

[58] A. M. Arnull, A. A. Dashwood, M. G. Ross and D. A. Wyatt, *Wyatt & Dashwood's European Union Law* (4th edn, London, Sweet & Maxwell, 2000), pp. 26–7.

[59] J. Lewis, 'National Interests: Coreper' in Peterson and Shackleton (eds.), *The Institutions of the European Union*, pp. 277–98.

[60] Nugent, *Government and Politics*, p. 151.

[61] The EFC is charged with keeping economic and financial conditions under review. As an illustration of its developing significance, it was an EFC report on financial regulation, supervision and stability in October 2002 that was the catalyst for the extension of the Lamfalussy process into banking and insurance: Economic and Financial Committee, *Report on Financial Regulation, Supervision and Stability* (Brussels, October 2002), available via http://europa.eu.int/comm/internal_market/en/finances/cross-sector/consultation/efc-eport_en.pdf(accessed May 2004). See also Economic and Financial Committee, *Report on*

but Coreper remains responsible for the development of legislation in this field.[62]

Within the European Parliament, the Standing Committee on Economic and Monetary Affairs (ECON or EMAC) has responsibility for financial services and does much of its detailed work in this area.[63] This Committee has worked hard to assert its claim for full involvement in the securities regulatory process and has secured specific undertakings from the European Commission with regard to transparency and to mechanisms for formal and informal dialogue between the two bodies.[64] The European Parliament's Legal Committee also plays a significant role.

A self-standing Treaty organisation with a role to play is the European Economic and Social Committee. This Committee was established by Treaty in 1957 as a separate EU institution.[65] It comprises representatives of socio-economic interests divided broadly into three groups: employers, workers and other public interests such as consumer groups. The Committee's opinion must be sought on financial services legislative proposals. However, the Committee's influence over the legislative proposals is weak because its opinions, which are often sought at quite a late stage in proceedings and under severe time constraints, carry no binding force.

The European Central Bank, another independent Treaty organisation,[66] tends to exert a more powerful role. The ECB has a Treaty entitlement to be consulted on any proposed Community act within its field of competence.[67] Proposed new securities laws fall into this category because they are measures to ensure the integrity of the Community's financial markets and to enhance investor confidence and financial

---

EU Financial Integration (ECFIN/194/02-EN) which sets out a series of steps for policy-makers to take in order to deliver the full benefits of financial integration.

[62] The relationship between Coreper and the EFC has been described as 'somewhat delicate': Arnull *et al.*, *Wyatt & Dashwood's European Union Law*, p. 26.

[63] The powers and responsibilities of this Committee are contained in the Rules of Procedure of the European Parliament and are available via http://www2.europarl.eu.int/omk/sipade2?PROG = RULES-EP&L = EN&REF = RESP-ECON (accessed May 2004).

[64] Letter (2 October 2001) from Frits Bolkestein, European Commissioner for the Internal Market, to Christina Randzio-Plath, Chair of the Economic and Monetary Affairs Committee, available via http://www.europarl.eu.int/comparl/econ/lamfalussy_process/ep_position/lt_bolkestein.pdf(accessed May 2004).

[65] Generally on the European Economic and Social Committee see Nugent, *Government and Politics*, pp. 279–85.

[66] On its establishment: Weatherill and Beaumont, *EU Law*, pp. 767–79.

[67] EC Treaty, art. 105.4.

stability.[68] The ECB's opinions cover the general effects of the proposed legislation, the impact on the ECB and national central banks, and any other points that the ECB chooses to raise.

As a result of the *Lamfalussy Report* two new important Committees have come onto the securities regulatory scene. These Committees play a key part in the development of Level 2 legislation, but their role is not confined to this dimension.

New committees under the Lamfalussy process (1): European Securities Committee

The first such body is the European Securities Committee (ESC) established in June 2001 by a decision of the European Commission.[69] The ESC plays a twofold role, acting in both advisory and regulatory capacities. In its advisory capacity the ESC advises the Commission on policy issues and draft legislation relating to securities markets. In this respect the ESC has assumed the functions of the High Level Securities Supervisors Committee, which was established by the Commission on an informal basis in 1985. The ESC also functions as a regulatory committee under comitology procedures. In essence this means that it has the right to deliver an opinion on draft Level 2 implementing measures before they can be adopted by the Commission.[70] If the Commission proposes measures that are not in accordance with the ESC's opinion or the ESC does not deliver an opinion, this stalls the process: the matter must go back to the Council, and the European Parliament must be informed.

The voting structure of the ESC is that a simple majority is required to approve a proposal from the Commission.[71] If ESC approval is not forthcoming, the Council can block the measure by a qualified majority vote. The requirement for a blocking, as opposed to a supporting, vote at

---

[68] The ECB's competence to give a view is stated in these terms in relevant opinions: see, e.g., European Central Bank, *Opinion of the European Central Bank on a proposal for a Directive on the prospectus to be published when securities are offered to the public or admitted to trading* (CON/2001/36), OJ 2001 No. C344/5, para. 2; and European Central Bank, *Opinion of the European Central Bank on a proposal for a Directive on the harmonisation of transparency requirements with regard to information about issuers whose securities are admitted to trading on a regulated market* (CON/2003/21) OJ 2003 No. C242/6, para. 2.

[69] ESC Decision.

[70] Comitology Decision.

[71] For differing views on the implications of these voting entitlements: G. Hertig and R. Lee, 'Four Predictions About the Future of EU Securities Regulation' [2003] *Journal of Corporate Law Studies* 359, 365; McKee, 'The Unpredictable Future'.

Council level dilutes the Council's control over the Level 2 process to some extent because so long as the Commission's proposal is supported by a qualified minority the measure will pass.

The ESC is comprised of a representative from each of the Member States under the chairmanship of a representative from the European Commission. Serving members of the ESC are usually senior officials from Member States' finance ministries. Full meetings of the Committee take place at roughly monthly intervals and a summary record of the proceedings at the meetings is made public.[72] In full meetings each member can be accompanied by only one expert.[73] As from May 2003 representatives from the ten countries that were to join the EU on 1 May 2004 began attending ESC meetings as observers.[74] Meetings and missions costs are met out of EU allocations.[75]

New committees under the Lamfalussy process (2): Committee of European Securities Regulators

The second new body is the Committee of European Securities Regulators (CESR), again formally established by the Commission in June 2001.[76] CESR, which comprises representatives from national regulators (in practice the Heads of the national securities regulator) of Member States plus Norway and Iceland, is responsible for advising the European Commission on the detailed implementing rules needed to give effect to framework securities laws. The countries that acceded to the EU on 1 May 2004 began to participate in CESR discussions as from 2003.[77] As a 'technical' adviser with regard to Level 2 measures, in public CESR can eschew any function with regard to political decision-making.[78] Yet given the regula-

---

[72] These Summary Records are available via http://europa.eu.int/comm/internal_market/en/finances/mobil/esc_en.htm (accessed May 2004).

[73] Summary Record of the Ninth Meeting of European Securities Committee/Alternates 30 January 2003 (ESC 9/2003), available via http://europa.eu.int/comm/internal_market/en/finances/mobil/docs/esc/meeting-01-2003-report_en1.pdf (accessed May 2004).

[74] Summary Record of the 11th Meeting of European Securities Committee / Alternates 23 May 2003 (ESC 21/2003), available via http://europa.eu.int/comm/internal_market/en/finances/mobil/docs/esc/meeting-05-2003-report_en.pdf (accessed May 2004).

[75] ESC Decision.

[76] CESR Decision.

[77] *Interim Report on the Activities of the Committee of European Securities Regulators to the European Commission and sent to: the European Parliament* (CESR/03–174b, 2003), available via http://www.cesr-eu.org (accessed May 2004).

[78] A. Docters van Leeuwen, 'Interview with CESR Chairman', (2002) 7(3) *The Financial Regulator* 20.

tory expertise of its members, it seems reasonable to assume that it plays a significant behind-the-scenes role in setting the pace for regulatory decision-making.

CESR traces its origins back to the Forum of European Securities Commissions, which was established on an informal basis in 1997. FESCO was an independent body operating outside the remit of the formal EU institutions. Although still independent of the EU institutions,[79] CESR has been brought inside the EU tent to the extent that it is accountable to the European Commission through the mechanism of an annual report. In its Charter CESR has also committed itself to submitting this report to the European Parliament and the Council, to reporting periodically to the Parliament, and to maintaining strong links with the ESC.[80]

CESR's role in providing technical advice to the European Commission on Level 2 implementing measures has been the primary focus of early attention because of the pressure of the FSAP deadlines but it is worth noting other CESR functions because these give an indication of just how influential this currently fledgling[81] body could eventually become. In the *Lamfalussy Report*, enhanced co-operation and networking amongst EU regulators to ensure consistent and equivalent transposition of Level 1 and Level 2 legislation were identified as necessary complementary aspects of the process, or, in Lamfalussy terms, its 'Level 3'.[82] CESR provides a forum that is conducive to the development of common EU-wide policies, practices and philosophies amongst regulatory authorities and to the establishment of an effective operational network to enhance day-to-day consistent supervision and enforcement.[83] As part of its Level 3 role, CESR performs a standard-setting function, i.e., it can issue standards, rules and guidance that are not binding EU rules but which, in a manner akin to the 'enforceability' of other forms of international 'soft law', are underpinned by loose commitments from CESR members to give effect to them in their national regulatory systems.[84] CESR also plays a peer review

---

[79] 'CESR is an independent Committee of European Securities Regulators', proclaims the opening sentence of its 2003 *Annual Report* to the EU institutions. This report is available via http://www.cesr-eu.org (accessed May 2004).

[80] CESR Charter, art. 6, available via http://www.cesr-eu.org (accessed May 2004). CESR's *Annual Reports* are also available here.

[81] McKee, 'The Unpredictable Future'.

[82] *Lamfalussy Report*, p. 37.

[83] McKee, 'The Unpredictable Future'.

[84] CESR Charter, art. 4. For example, the British regulatory regime for alternative trading systems is now based on Committee of European Securities Regulators, *Standards for Alternative*

role, monitoring regulatory practices within the single market.[85] It is envisaged that over time CESR's role in relation to peer review and peer pressure could bring about significant convergence in securities regulatory practices across Europe.[86] CESR is also charged with keeping an eye on global developments in securities regulation and considering their impact on the regulation of the single market for financial services.[87]

Despite this extensive range of functions, CESR's practical capabilities are limited by its rather modest resources. CESR is funded entirely by its members.[88] Its budget for 2003 was just €2 million. The full-time and seconded staff working for its secretariat by the end of 2003 numbered only around fifteen people.[89] In practice this means that much of CESR's work is effectively subsidised by its members through in-house devotion of resources at national level.

Full meetings of CESR take place around four times a year.[90] Most of the detailed work is done by Expert Groups that are established to deal with specific issues and then disbanded.[91] CESR has two permanent sub-groups, CESR-Fin, which deals with accounting issues, and CESR-Pol, which deals with surveillance and enforcement concerns.

Trading Systems (CESR/02–086b, 2002): Financial Services Authority, *Alternative Trading Systems: Policy Statement and Made Text* (London, FSA, 2003), paras. 1.3–1.9. The FSA notes that most CESR members are believed to have given effect to the CESR Standards: ibid., paras. 2.15–2.16.

[85] CESR Charter, art. 4.

[86] IIMG, *First Interim Report*, para. 1.5. C. Scott, 'The Governance of the European Union: The Potential for Multi-Level Control' (2002) 8 *European Law Journal* 59, 68 sees the emergence of CESR as the body responsible for implementation and application of EU securities law as 'displacing' the Commission from this role. However, as discussed later in this chapter, it is rather early to form any clear view on this.

[87] CESR Charter, art. 4.5.

[88] K. Alexander, 'Establishing a European Securities Regulator: Is the European Union an Optimal Economic Area for a Single Securities Regulator?' *Cambridge Endovment for Research in Finance* Working Paper No. 7 (December 2002) available via http://www.cerf.cam.ac.uk/publications/files/WP07-Kern%20Alexander2.prn.pdf (accessed May 2004).

[89] CESR, Interim Report.

[90] CESR, *Annual Report* 2003, Table 2 (Statistics on Meetings). A minimum of four meetings per year is required by the CESR Charter, art. 5.

[91] CESR, *Annual Report* 2003 provides details of the way in which the work of Expert Groups is structured, their arrangements for consultation, the frequency of their meetings and so forth.

In its Level 2 role, CESR makes decisions by qualified majority voting.[92] At Level 3 CESR makes decisions by consensus.[93]

The mechanics of Level 2 legislation

The Market Abuse Directive can be used to illustrate the operation of Level 2 of the process.[94] The chronology of the first Level 2 measures adopted under this Directive (these were also the first Level 2 measures adopted under the Lamfalussy process) was as shown in Table 3.3.

Table 3.3

December 2001	European Commission begins work on draft mandate to CESR.
March 2002	European Commission provisionally[95] requests CESR to provide technical advice on: • definitions of key terms ('inside information', 'market manipulation', 'financial instrument'); • technical methods and procedures for appropriate public disclosure of inside information and for fair presentation of research and other relevant information; and • technical conditions under which share buyback programmes and stabilisation should be allowed.
December 2002	After extensive consultation, CESR delivers technical advice to Commission.
March 2003	Commission publishes three working documents outlining its thinking on: • A Level 2 Directive defining key terms and dealing with information disclosure; • A Level 2 Directive on presentation of investment recommendations; and

[92] CESR Charter, art. 5.
[93] Ibid.
[94] IIMG *First Interim Report*, Figure 4 provides a more detailed tabular account of the Level 2 process.
[95] This request anticipated the adoption of the Level 1 Directive and its provisional status was necessary so as not to compromise the principle that it is for the Council and Parliament to define the split between Levels 1 and 2.

Table 3.3   (*cont.*)

	A Level 2 Regulation on share buybacks and stabilisation. These working documents were not formal Commission draft proposals but were issued so as to give the Parliament and other interested participants an opportunity to comment before the Commission began drawing up its formal proposals at the end of April 2003.
July 2003	Formal Commission drafts of two Level 2 Directives and one Level 2 Regulation published.
September 2003	First revised drafts of Directives and Regulation.
October 2003	Second revised drafts of Directives and Regulation.
29 October 2003	Final versions of Directives and Regulation agreed by the ESC
22 December 2003	Directives and Regulation published in the Official Journal.[96]

Role of the private sector and a new emphasis on transparency and consultation

In its Communication announcing the FSAP, the Commission acknowledged past failings rooted in a piecemeal and reactive approach to new regulatory needs.[97] It suggested that its strategic approach and also its selection of the best technical solutions could be improved, not only by closer co-operation with the Council and Parliament, but also by better dialogue with EU interest groups including market participants and consumers.[98] As with much else in the FSAP this was more of a reiteration of a long-held view than a radical new initiative.[99] A strong commitment to

---

[96] Commission Directive 2003/124/EC of 22 December 2003 implementing Directive 2003/6/EC as regards the definition and public disclosure of inside information and the definition of market manipulation OJ 2003 No. L339/70; Commission Directive 2003/125/EC of 22 December 2003 implementing Directive 2003/6/EC as regards the fair presentation of investment recommendations and the disclosure of conflicts of interest OJ 2003 No. L339/73; Commission Regulation (EC) No 2273/2003 of 22 December 2003 implementing Directive 2003/6/EC as regards exemptions for buy-back programmes and stabilisation of financial instruments OJ 2003 No. L336/33.
[97] European Commission, *FSAP Action Plan*, pp. 16–17.
[98] Ibid.
[99] It had, for example, been foreshadowed in European Commission, *Financial Services: Building* (1998).

openness in the securities regulatory process is consistent with the Commission's current thinking on its general approach to governance.[100] It is publicly committed to achieving a pervasive 'reinforced culture of consultation and dialogue' across its range of activities.[101]

The need to involve the private sector more effectively in the regulatory process is something on which all of the main EU institutions were able quickly to agree. The Lamfalussy Committee took a positive view of the role of the private sector in providing constructive input in the regulatory process, strongly recommending its early and institutionalised involvement.[102] In its Stockholm Resolution, the Council invited the Commission to make use of early, broad and systematic consultations with all interested parties in the securities area, in particular by strengthening its dialogue with consumers and market practitioners. The European Parliament also stressed the need for private sector involvement in the regulatory process and called specifically for the establishment of a market participants advisory committee.[103]

The Lamfalussy Committee gave specific content to its call for early involvement of the private sector in a recommendation that the Commission should consult with market participants and end-users 'in an open, transparent and systematic way' before it drew up any proposal for new Level 1 legislation, as well as iterative consultation throughout the legislative process. This call came too late for some of the measures in the FSAP because work on these had advanced beyond the policy formation stage by the time the Lamfalussy Committee reported. Pre-legislative consultation was, however, possible in respect of measures considered in the later stages of the FSAP, such as the Transparency Directive and the Financial Instruments Markets Directive (ISD2).

To facilitate dialogue with the private sector, the European Parliament's Economic and Monetary Affairs Committee has established its own advisory

---

[100] European Commission, *European Governance White Paper*, para. 3.1; and European Commission, *Action Plan 'Simplifying and Improving the Regulatory Environment'* (COM (2002) 278), para. 1.1. See further D. Wincott, 'Looking Forward or Harking Back? The Commission and the Reform of Governance in the EU' (2001) 39 *Journal of Common Market Studies* 897.

[101] European Commission, *European Governance White Paper*, para. 3.1 and European Commission, *Towards a Reinforced Culture of Consultation and Dialogue – General Principles and Minimum Standards for Consultation of Interested Parties by the Commission* (COM (2002) 704).

[102] *Lamfalussy Report*, p. 48.

[103] European Parliament Resolution.

panel of experts (Advisory Panel of Financial Services Experts (APFSE)). This Panel is composed of six market practitioners and four university professors. Its reports are only made available to the Committee.[104]

An emphasis on consultation has been passed down through the legislative process. In the decision establishing CESR, the Commission stipulated that it should 'consult extensively and at an early stage with market participants, consumers and end-users in an open and transparent manner',[105] and made provision for the establishment of working groups.[106] CESR responded with commitments in its Charter to openness, engagement in meaningful consultation and to the establishment of working consultative groups to facilitate dialogue with the private sector.[107] CESR also published its own public statement on consultation practices.[108]

CESR's consultative processes have three key elements.[109] Responding to the European Parliament's request for a standing advisory committee, CESR set up a Market Participants Consultative Panel in July 2002 to act as a 'sounding board' on CESR's work programme, major financial market evolutions and other matters.[110] Alongside this Panel, as the second element in the process CESR establishes ad hoc groups to provide specialist market expertise on particular areas. The third element is open public consultation.

C   Assessing the Lamfalussy process

The previous section identified the main bodies involved in the securities regulatory process in the EU and sketched out their functions, responsibilities and interaction. This section evaluates elements of the process. This evaluation is subject to a number of preliminary considerations.

First, the process heralded by the work of the Lamfalussy Committee is still relatively new and this inevitably limits what can credibly be said

---

[104] IIMG, *Second Interim Report*, p. 23.

[105] CESR Decision, art. 5.

[106] Ibid., art. 4.

[107] CESR Charter, art. 5.

[108] CESR/01–007c, December 2001, available via http://www.cesr-eu.org (accessed May 2004). CESR, *Annual Report* 2003, pp. 9 –10 provides an overview of CESR's views on the aims of consultation and on the processes that it adopts.

[109] B. Inel, 'Assessing the First Two Years of the New Regulatory Framework for Financial Markets in Europe' (2003) 18(9) *Journal of International Banking Law and Regulation* 363.

[110] CESR, *Annual Report* 2003, pp. 11–13 outlines the role of the Panel, its composition and its activities to date.

about it. It could be that a much more nimble and responsive regulatory system will emerge from the decision to devolve rule-making powers to the Commission and that CESR, supported by the private sector, will significantly assist the Commission in producing better-quality legislation. However, the short period during which the process has operated means that it would be premature to attempt any sort of definitive assessment.[111]

Secondly, it is important to bear in mind that there could be distortions in the process flowing from the fact that, as all the participants know, the design of the regulatory machine is unstable because of concerns about the European Parliament's ability to control the Commission's exercise of rule-making powers under the Lamfalussy process. A new settlement between the Commission, Council and Parliament as to their respective roles in the regulatory process could well change institutional patterns of behaviour and attitudes in ways that are hard to anticipate. This means that any currently discernible trends and practices may need to be viewed as transitional rather than as settled.

The third preliminary point is to note the broad contextual background against which issues concerning the EU's approach to the regulation of securities markets arise. Tensions between the Commission, Council and Parliament in the area of securities regulation are but a small part of much larger concerns about how the EU institutions operate and the new pressures on the institutional framework resulting from enlargement to a 25-Member Union. Reform of the institutional system is firmly on the EU agenda.[112] Although this chapter is focused on the interaction of the institutions in a relatively narrow, specialised field rather than bigger picture questions, such as the EU's democratic accountability and legitimacy and the general implications of enlargement, it is recognised that answers to the big questions that may emerge from wide-ranging deliberations on the constitutional future of the EU and the governance of EU institutions could have significant implications for the securities law-making process.

---

[111] This was also the view taken in IIMG, *First Interim Report*, introduction. In its *Second Interim Report*, p. 8 the IIMG went a little further with its 'interim' conclusion that the Lamfalussy process was proving to be a better device for securities market legislation than previous practice.

[112] The programme of internal reform of the European Commission under the Prodi Presidency is outlined in N. Nugent, 'The Commission's Services' in Peterson and Shackleton (eds.), *The Institutions of the European Union*, pp. 156–62. Inter-institutional issues are addressed in the Constitution for Europe. IIMG, *Second Interim Report*, pp. 15–16 discusses the overhaul of the EU's comitology infrastructure by a draft version of the EU Constitution and assesses its potential application to Level 2 securities laws.

Fourthly, what follows is a selective assessment of key issues arising in relation to recent developments in the EU securities law-making process rather than an exhaustive evaluation. This approach is appropriate given the potentially transient dimension of some aspects of the new process.[113]

Expansion of the Commission's role: empire-building or advancing towards a new model of collaborative governance?

As the initiator of securities regulatory proposals the Commission has always been in a very strong position. The Lamfalussy reforms appear to reinforce its dominant position by giving it new powers to write detailed regulatory rules.

Some observers of the Commission characterise it as a 'policy entrepreneur', by which is meant that it selects the policies that promote its own interests, presents these in ways that restrict the choices available to Member States and continually presses and negotiates until it gets its way.[114] However, others point to various limitations on the Commission's entrepreneurial role including the pervasive problem of lack of capacity.[115] Overall the Commission has a very small staff compared to the enormous range of policy areas for which it has responsibility. The problems of understaffing and overstretched resources are serious in financial services (of which securities is just one part), with the Commission having only around 100 people working in the area.[116] This suggests that simply coping with the demands that are put upon it is likely to be more of a priority for the Commission than pursuit of an empire-building agenda in which it positively seeks out and promotes ideas to build up its own power and influence. Seen in this light, the expansion of the Commission's role under Lamfalussy is not triumphal, institutional

---

[113] For example, the system of 'parallel working' – where CESR works on its advice regarding Level 2 implementing measures on the basis of provisional mandates at the same time as the Level 1 measures are proceeding through the co-decision process – may not be necessary once the burden of meeting deadlines that were adopted before the Lamfalussy process became effective is lifted: Barclays Bank, *Response to Inter-Institutional Group* (July 2003), available via http://europa.eu.int/comm/internal_market/en/finances/mobil/docs/lamfalussy/2003–07-comments-barclays_en.pdf (accessed May 2004).

[114] S. Hix, *The Political System of the European Union* (Basingstoke, Palgrave Macmillan, 1999), pp. 235–7.

[115] Wallace, 'The Institutional Setting', p. 15.

[116] 'A Ragbag'. The IIMG, *Second Interim Report*, pp. 16–17 highlights concerns about deficiencies in the Commission's resources.

self-aggrandisement. Rather it is a functional response to the need for a more streamlined regulatory process, and whatever new benefits flow to the Commission as a result of it are probably counterbalanced by plenty of additional burdens.

If there had been fears from market participants and others about the concentration of power in the European Commission, these would presumably have surfaced in response in the *Lamfalussy Report*. In fact, the *Lamfalussy Report* received a favourable reception from industry participants and from regulatory organisations,[117] as well as from the Council of Ministers and Heads of State or Government. Although the European Parliament had concerns, these related more to current weaknesses in the Parliament's constitutional powers to scrutinise the Commission's work rather than the basic principle that the Commission should play an expanded role in securities regulation.

Since its establishment, the operation of the Lamfalussy process has been kept under review by the Inter-Institutional Monitoring Group (IIMG) set up by the Commission, Council and European Parliament. The IIMG's reports have identified certain causes for concern about the Lamfalussy process but regulatory excess by the Commission has not featured prominently amongst them. Occasional references to the prospect of 'a flood of bureaucratic standards' aside,[118] the overall tone of responses to the IIMG's reports has tended to be supportive of the Commission's role but with an emphasis on the need for fine-tuning of certain aspects, particularly with regard to consultation.[119]

There are calls for an increase in the Commission's resources to work on financial markets matters in the May 2004 report from a group of securities market experts that was established to take stock of the FSAP.[120] Had the members of this group harboured serious concerns about an over-powerful Commission they had a powerful platform from which to express them; the absence of comments to such effect in their report is therefore significant.

---

[117] 'Labouring with Lamfalussy', *Economist*, 16 June 2001, p. 97.
[118] Federation of German Industries (BDI) *Lamfalussy Process – Statement on the First Interim Report of May 2003*, available via http://europa.eu.int/comm/internal_market/en/finances/mobil/docs/lamfalussy/2003–07-comments-bdi1_en.pdf (accessed May 2004).
[119] Responses are available via http://europa.eu.int/comm/internal_market/en/finances/mobil/lamfalussy-comments_en.htm (accessed May 2004).
[120] Securities Expert Group, *FSAP: Progress*, p. 8.

If the Commission's capacity is overstretched, this raises other potential concerns: the real centre of power could be elsewhere and the Commission could be at risk of being captured by interest groups pressing the case for legislation designed to protect their private interests.[121] Post-Lamfalussy, CESR is the obvious candidate for the role of power behind the throne but it is too early to say which is the dominant partner in the relationship between the Commission and CESR.[122] Signs thus far suggest that although the Commission draws heavily on CESR's work, it is prepared to depart from CESR's advice and does not simply rubber-stamp its recommendations.

The unfolding relationship between the Commission and CESR can be illustrated by looking at the process for the development of Level 2 implementing measures. As indicated in Table 3.1, the Commission starts the Level 2 process by issuing a formal request to CESR for technical advice. After consultation with market participants, CESR delivers its advice to the Commission. The Commission responds to this with the publication of a 'working document' containing a draft of the proposed implementing measures. After a further round of consultations, the Commission publishes its formal draft proposed legal text for consideration by the ESC and European Parliament. Once the approval of the ESC and European Parliament has been obtained, the Commission adopts the final version of the implementing measures.

Experience thus far indicates that the Commission will disagree with CESR on points of substance in proposed Level 2 measures where it considers it appropriate to do so.[123] The Commission is also prepared to make

---

[121] On regulatory capture: G. Stigler, 'The Theory of Economic Regulation' (1971) 6(2) *Bell Journal of Economics and Management Sciences* 3.

[122] P. Norman 'A Tiny Committee with Considerable Reach', *Financial Times*, 7 November 2002, p. 16.

[123] E.g. European Commission, *Main differences between the Commission draft regulation on draft implementing rules for the Prospectus Directive and the CESR advice* (ESC / 42/2003-rev2), which indicates the Commission's changes of substance in the implementing measure for the Prospectus Directive.

The Commission did not issue an explanatory memorandum of this sort on the early implementing measures for the Market Abuse Directive (where it did disagree with the substance of some of CESR's advice, particularly as regards the position of rating agencies). The change of approach in relation to the Prospectus Directive has been welcomed as a helpful innovation: Securities Expert Group, *FSAP: Progress*, p. 14.

detailed, technical changes to drafting.[124] The Commission's propensity to redraft CESR's advice has raised concerns. Level 2 measures operate at a technical level and, so, seemingly minor differences in wording could well have significant practical implications.[125] For the Commission to rely more heavily on the form of CESR's advice would be a way of speeding up the Level 2 process that could reduce the risks of last-minute mistakes creeping in unnoticed because of subtle drafting changes.[126] It could also avoid duplicative consultation and/or disillusionment by those consulted by CESR as to the usefulness of participation in that exercise. On the other hand, inter-institutional sensitivities and concerns about democratic accountability make it particularly important to ensure that the process of writing implementing measures is a genuine exercise involving the Commission, with input from the Council via the ESC and from the Parliament, and not merely a rubber-stamp. There are issues, too, about the location of the appropriate expertise and capacity – CESR's very limited resources and the Commission's long experience in writing rules that are suitable for pan-European application are compelling factors in favour of looking to it to draft the legal text. So long as it is plain to participants in CESR's consultations that CESR's advice is just that, they should have no legitimate grounds for disillusionment when they see the text of the advice redrafted by the Commission. Industry concerns about the possibility of late drafting changes resulting in unintended changes of substance can be (and, to an extent, have been)[127] alleviated through the provision of a late round of public consultations on the Commission's working documents.

[124] B. Inel, 'Implementing the Market Abuse Directive' (2003) (8) *European Financial Services Regulation* 10 looks generally at the Commission's proposals and how they compare to the CESR advice.
[125] This point is made in various responses to Commission working documents outlining Level 2 rules in draft form – see, e.g., the response by the International Primary Market Association, 22 April 2003. Public responses to Commission working documents are available via http://europa.eu.int/comm/internal_market/en/finances/mobil/market-abuse_en.htm (accessed May 2004).
[126] In its response to the IIMG, *First Interim Report*, the French Association of Investment Firms calls for CESR to be given formal responsibility for the form and content of Level 2 measures under the oversight of the Commission. This response is available via http://www.europa.eu.int/comm/internal_market/en/finances/mobil/docs/lamfalussy/2003–07-comments-afei_en.pdf (accessed May 2004). Inel, 'Implementing', 11 notes generally that 'rare' critics have pointed out that the process would be speedier if CESR produced legal drafts.
[127] Inel, 'Implementing', 11–12.

There is admittedly something rather cumbersome about a model in which CESR provides carefully worded and heavily consulted-upon advice and then the Commission, assisted by further rounds of consultations, redrafts it in the form of legal text. In principle the system would be far smoother if the departures from CESR's text were limited to areas where there are policy issues that CESR is unable to resolve or where the Commission feels absolutely compelled to depart from the CESR view. It seems likely that, as the system beds down, some streamlining will be possible whilst still respecting the formal allocation of responsibilities as between the various bodies – for example the gap between the form of CESR's advice and what is suitable for adoption as legal text could narrow[128] – and there is certainly scope for improvement in the management of related consultation exercises, as discussed later in this chapter. It is possible to see evidence of a degree of refinement of the process already taking place in the Commission's provisional request to CESR for technical advice on implementing measures for the Financial Instruments Markets Directive (ISD2). The Commission included a new passage in its mandate letter to the effect that the technical advice given by CESR to the Commission would not take the form of a legal text but that CESR should follow a 'structured approach', by which it meant that CESR should 'provide the Commission with an "articulated" text in a language which is easily understandable and respects current legal terminology used in the field of financial securities law'.[129] However, care needs to be taken not to allow law-making power to shift too far in CESR's direction because this could undermine positive features of the model that has emerged in which this power is shared between the Commission, the ESC, the European Parliament and CESR.

Recent theoretical analysis of regulation in complex fields such as financial services emphasises the fragmentation of regulatory resources as between State and private actors.[130] The existence of informational

---

[128] The IIMG, *Second Interim Report*, p. 28 recommends that 'CESR formulates technical advice as concretely and clearly as possible – thus contributing to the drafting of Level 2 implementing measures.'

[129] European Commission, 'Provisional Mandate to CESR for Technical Advice on Possible Implementing Measures Concerning the Future Directive on Financial Instruments Markets' (MARKT/G2 D(2003)), available via http://europa.eu.int/comm/internal_market/en/finances/mobil/isd/docs/esc37-mandate_en.pdf (accessed May 2004).

[130] C. Scott, 'Analysing Regulatory Space: Fragmented Resources and Institutional Design' [2001] *Public Law* 329; J. Black, 'Mapping the Contours of Contemporary Financial Services Regulation' [2002] *Journal of Corporate Law Studies* 253; J. Black, 'Decentring Regulation: Understanding the Role of Regulation and Self Regulation in a "Post-Regulatory" World' (2001) 54 *Current Legal Problems* 103.

asymmetries as between regulated firms and specialist securities regulators and, in turn, as between specialist regulators and government legislators is an obvious example of such fragmentation. Decentralised analysis of regulation has implications for its institutional design because it suggests that designers should pay careful attention to how they can best capitalise on fragmented resources and draw them all into the regulatory process.[131] One good design strategy would be explicitly to recognise that regulation is the product of interaction between numerous actors and to build networks accordingly.[132] It is possible to regard the collaborative arrangements between the Commission, ESC, European Parliament and CESR as an attempt to do this. The arrangement can be characterised as one that seeks to establish interdependence between the various bodies, with each of them providing their own internal checks and balances on the others' activities thereby giving rise to an accountability-enhancing system of multiple control.[133] On the one hand, the burden of turning technical advice into legal text can be viewed as a helpful discipline that forces the Commission, ESC and European Parliament to scrutinise CESR's work very closely. If CESR had the qualitatively different role of providing draft legal text for endorsement by the Commission, ESC and European Parliament, arguably the limits of CESR's role would be more blurred and the discipline would be de facto relaxed. This could leave more scope for CESR to engage in surreptitious illegitimate policy-making in the guise of draft rules, and could result in the production of rules that reflect the narrow preoccupations of one group (regulators) rather than broader economic considerations. On the other hand, a consensus on technical needs that is established by CESR in close consultation with market experts should act as a discipline on the Commission and the ESC, since departures from it are likely to attract attention from the European Parliament and other parties.[134]

---

[131] Scott, 'Analysing', 347.

[132] Comitology has been described 'as a network of European and national actors within which the Commission acts as co-ordinator': C. Joerges, '"Good Governance" Through Comitology' in Joerges and Vos (eds.), *EU Committees*, p. 318.

[133] G. Majone, 'Regulatory Legitimacy' in Majone (ed.), *Regulating Europe*, p. 300 concludes that multiple control systems, in which no one controls but the system is 'under control' provide a solution to the problem of regulatory legitimacy.

[134] McKee, 'The Unpredictable Future'.

Consultation and transparency by the Commission and CESR: the development and management of dialogic webs[135]

The operation of the new consultative processes prompts a number of lines of inquiry. Two important questions are whether their use is making a positive difference to the quality of EU securities law and whether they are enhancing the overall legitimacy and accountability of the regulatory system. Adopting Francis Snyder's definitions, 'legitimacy' is used here to mean 'the belief that a specific institution is widely recognized or at least accepted as being the appropriate institution to exercise specific powers', and 'accountability' means that 'the institution is, or is deemed to be, more or less responsive, directly or indirectly, to the people who are affected by its decisions'.[136] A subsidiary question, which can be considered alongside the quality assessment, is whether the mechanics are working well or are in need of fine-tuning.

Consultation and transparency as quality-enhancing devices

Quality is hard to measure and causal links between elements of a process and the outcomes of that process are hard to pinpoint authoritatively. Nonetheless, there are some indications that changes in the Level 1 pre-legislative consultation process are producing beneficial results with regard to the quality of legislation. The Commission's first drafts of the Market Abuse Directive and the Prospectus Directive, published in May 2001, did not have the benefit of open pre-legislative consultation,[137] a move that the Commission sought to justify on grounds of urgency and by reference to 'extensive' (but non-specific) informal consultations it had carried out with Member State Governments, regulators and supervisors, industry and other interested parties.[138] This proved to be a serious misjudgment.

---

[135] J. Braithwaite and P. Drahos, *Global Business Regulation* (Cambridge, Cambridge University Press, 2000), pp. 550–63 explores webs of dialogue and webs of reward and coercion. The authors identify a strongly positive role for dialogic webs as mechanisms for, amongst a range of matters, defining problematic issues and motivating agreement and compliance.

[136] F. Snyder, 'EMU Revisited: Are We Making a Constitution? What Constitution Are We Making?' in Craig and de Búrca (eds.), *The Evolution of EU Law*, p. 463.

[137] Inel, 'Assessing', describes the omission of any formal prior public consultation as a violation of the spirit of the Lamfalussy process.

[138] European Commission, *Proposal for a Directive of the European Parliament and of the Council on insider dealing and market manipulation (market abuse)* (COM (2001) 281), explanatory memorandum, p. 5 and European Commission, *Proposal for a Directive of the European Parliament and of the Council on the prospectus to be published when securities are offered to the public or admitted to trading* (COM (2001) 280), explanatory memorandum, p. 2.

As *The Economist* noted, the drafts were greeted with 'howls of protest from practitioners, and even from some national regulators' that 'the proposals were half-baked'.[139] For example, it was claimed that the first version of the Prospectus Directive, reputedly drafted by a Commission official with no experience of wholesale capital markets, threatened to dismantle parts of the European international capital market.[140] It took a concerted lobbying effort by groups such as the European Banking Federation,[141] British Bankers Association and International Primary Market Association,[142] and pressure from Members of the European Parliament[143] to secure amendments designed to preserve most of the flexibility on which the success of that market had been built.

The Commission's initial proposal to revise the Investment Services Directive[144] got a warmer reception, with the difference in quality being widely attributed to the fact that the Commission had gone through two rounds of open consultations before publishing the first draft of the revised Directive.[145] However, the journey from proposal to new legislation (Financial Instruments Market Directive or ISD2) provides a telling illustration of the limits of pre-legislative open consultation as a mechanism for improving the quality of draft legislation because the text of the draft that was finally published by the Commission departed in certain key respects from the tenor of the ideas consulted upon. One of the most controversial provisions in the draft (on pre-trade transparency) had not

---

[139] 'A Ragbag'.

[140] F. Guerrera and P. Norman, 'European Leaders Invested Heavily in Building a Single Capital Market to Rival the US', *Financial Times*, 4 December 2002, p. 17.

[141] The Financial Markets Adviser for the EBF (Burçak Inel) received an award from the Compliance Monitor for her lobbying campaign on the Prospectus Directive, which was considered to have contributed to a key improvement of the original draft, as noted in: B. Inel, 'Impact of Enlargement on the Wholesale Banking Markets' (2004) 14 *European Financial Services Regulation* 3.

[142] Links to IPMA's work on the Prospectus Directive are available via http://www.ipma.org.uk/cu_index.asp.

[143] D. Dombey and A. Skorecki, 'MEPs Clear Way For Deal on Borrowing', *Financial Times*, 27 June 2003, p. 8.

[144] European Commission, *Proposal for a Directive of the European Parliament and of the Council on investment services and regulated markets, and amending Council Directives 85/611/EEC, Council Directive 93/6/EEC and European Parliament and Council Directive 2000/12/EC* (COM (2002) 625). The market reception to this proposal is noted in 'A Ragbag'.

[145] Reinhardt, *The Lamfalussy Process*, p. 13. The main elements of the Commission's approach to pre-legislative consultation are available via http://www.europa.eu.int/comm/ internal_market/en/finances/mobil/isd/index.htm (accessed May 2004).

been exposed to pre-legislative open consultation.[146] A consequence of the late insertion of this provision by the Commission was that diluting its potentially damaging impact unavoidably became a major preoccupation during the legislative process.[147]

The proposal went through these rather secretive changes prior to its publication essentially for reasons connected with national protectionism by certain Member States.[148] The key point at issue in the dispute over pre-trade transparency was whether banks and investment firms should be permitted on a Euro-wide basis to 'internalise' client orders to buy and sell equities rather than putting them through regulated markets. The established position, sanctioned by the old ISD, left it to Member States to choose whether to permit internalisation: some, such as the UK, did but others, including France and Italy, maintained a requirement for the concentration of orders on exchanges. The dispute essentially focused on the conditions governing internalisation, with States that wanted to protect a favourable position for formal exchanges arguing for restrictions and limitations on internationalisation that, argued the UK, threatened to destroy the ability of banks and investment houses to compete effectively with exchanges. The eventual outcome in the final version of the Financial Instruments Markets Directive (ISD2)[149] requires pre-trade transparency (i.e. publication of firm quotes in shares) and, to this extent, it represents a victory for the opponents of internalisation; however, this disclosure obligation only applies under certain conditions,[150] and the limitations on its scope go some way towards meeting the concerns of the banks and investment houses.[151] It is too early to say whether this will prove to be a workable and satisfactory compromise but what does emerge clearly from the experience is a simple political reality: open and early consultation by the Commission can improve the quality of legislative proposals but it is

---

[146] Reinhardt, *The Lamfalussy Process*, p. 15.

[147] T. Villiers, 'Where Next for the ISD?' (3 November 2003) *The Parliament Magazine* 23.

[148] Lex Column, 'The Prodi Plot', *Financial Times*, 19 November 2002, p. 20 outlines the chain of events: last-minute lobbying from French and Italian stock exchanges prompted the Commission President, Romano Prodi, to intervene personally to have the pre-trade transparency requirement inserted into the text.

[149] Art. 27.

[150] It applies to firms that are 'systematic internalisers' in shares admitted to trading on a regulated market and for which there is a liquid market. However, it only applies to systematic internalisers when dealing for sizes up to standard market size.

[151] A. Skorecki and T. Buck, 'Banks in EU Set for Share Trading Shake-up', *FT.com*, 24 February 2004.

likely to be insufficiently robust to insulate the legislative process from political distortions.

In theory there is less likelihood of the benefits of consultation on Level 2 measures being undermined by political machinations between Member States because issues touching upon national sensitivities should have been resolved at Level 1. Early signs are that Member States are making some use of the ESC to amend proposed Level 2 measures in their own interests[152] but the extent to which this has happened has not been so great as to derail or disrupt seriously the legislative programme.

Consultation and transparency processes: the functioning of the machinery

Experience relating to the development of Level 2 measures has thrown up some difficulties with the mechanical aspects of the consultative processes. Foremost amongst these has been the pressure of short consultation deadlines set by CESR in respect of its draft advice.[153] To an extent, this problem is linked to the superimposition of the Lamfalussy process onto a pre-existing legislative agenda, the FSAP, in which the timetable was already fixed. The problem should therefore recede as the Lamfalussy process becomes embedded in the securities law-making machinery since this should mean that in future the need to structure the legislative timetable so as to allow sufficient time for proper consultation will be clear from the outset.

Teething trouble in the way that CESR approached the task of consulting market participants was always likely. In its early days CESR made itself a target for criticism by issuing poorly constructed, excessively detailed consultation papers that were insufficiently attuned to established market practices.[154] This undermined the credibility of claims that the new approach was more in touch with the markets. CESR was also criticised for not talking to the right people, with the absence of any representative

---

[152] Inel, 'Implementing', 17.

[153] The IIMG *Second Interim Report*, p. 26 notes widespread agreement among market participants on inadequate time for responses on Level 2 issues.

A response to the IIMG by the European Savings Banks Group provides a valuable commentary on experience with CESR consultation practices and the impracticability of the deadlines that applied in relation to implementing measures for the Market Abuse Directive and Prospectus Directive. The response is available via http://www.europa.eu.int/comm/internal_market/en/finances/mobil/docs/lamfalussy/2003–07-comments-esbg_en.pdf (accessed May 2004).

[154] S. Revell, 'The Prospectus Directive' (2003) 14 *Practical Law for Companies* 14.

from the country with the largest capital market in the world outside the US (i.e. the UK) on CESR's Consultative Working Group for the Prospectus Directive used to illustrate the point.[155] Examples such as this could be taken to suggest that CESR is vulnerable to distortions because considerations other than the location of the appropriate expertise may influence choices about the composition of the committees and working groups that do the bulk of its work. Yet, as time has gone on, criticism of CESR's consultative practices has begun to die down, and there are no current indications of major disquiet.[156]

Consultation and transparency as mechanisms for improving accountability and legitimacy

In a world where regulatory capabilities are fragmented and knowledge is unevenly distributed between different actors, the development of dialogic webs between epistemic communities is both essential and inevitable.[157] Legitimacy and accountability considerations make it important to pay attention to the institutional management of such dialogue. Commission and CESR officials might, arguably, be able to inform themselves quite well on the appropriate regulatory response to issues through private, informal conversations with selected market experts. However, this type of behind-the-scenes consultation could well create the impression of bias towards certain groups on the inside track of the regulatory process. An organised process of public consultation mitigates this concern. Furthermore, widespread involvement in the process of rule-formulation through open consultation should reinforce the propensity towards compliance, on the basis that public respect for the legitimacy of rules is likely to be increased where those affected by them feel that they have had a say in their development.

The opportunities to enhance the legitimacy of regulation through public participation and due processes do not stop at the point where policy is decided upon and rules are made. It is inevitable that those who are sufficiently engaged in a process to respond to consultation papers and

---

[155] Ibid.

[156] IIMG *Second Interim Report*, pp. 21–9 provides an extensive review of the practical operation of consultation mechanisms under the Lamfalussy Process.

[157] P. M. Haas, 'Introduction: Epistemic Communities and International Policy Co-ordination' (1992) 46 *International Organization* 1, 3 defines epistemic communities as networks 'of professionals with recognized expertise and competence in a particular domain and an authoritative claim to policy-relevant knowledge within that domain or issue-area.'

to engage in dialogue will often have a particular underlying interest that they want to project. This means that rather than helpfully illuminating the appropriate way forward, consultation exercises may instead produce a heap of contradictory advice from lobbyists, each of whom is motivated more by a desire to promote particular business and/or national interests than a detached concern for the development of good regulation.[158] What matters, then, is how this mass of information is distilled and evaluated.[159] At the evaluation stage, a requirement for the recipient of the information to give reasons for its choices can therefore perform an important legitimacy and accountability-enhancing function. Feedback can be a powerful discipline because a requirement to explain fully and openly what has been done with expert input should limit the scope for perverse choices (i.e. where the selector favours the expert advice that is most consistent with its own preconceptions) or poor choices (e.g., where the selector goes along with a proposal simply because a numerical majority of the respondents are in favour of it).[160]

Overall the signs are fairly positive for the legitimacy and accountability-enhancing effects of the improvements in consultation and transparency under the Lamfalussy process. The weakest spot is lack of transparency when regulatory decisions depart from the clear results of consultation. Here CESR has led the way at Level 2 by issuing feedback statements explaining how it has arrives at Level 2 advice proffered to the Commission, although there is some suggestion that the quality of such feedback could be improved.[161] The Commission attracted criticism for not providing similar feedback on its decision to depart from CESR advice on implementing measures for the Market Abuse Directive;[162] but its feedback statement on implementing measures for the Prospectus Directive indicates that this gap is closing.[163] It is at Level 1 where substantial

---

[158] R. Baldwin and M. Cave, *Understanding Regulation* (Oxford, Oxford University Press, 1999), p. 157.

[159] A. M. Slaughter, 'Global Government Networks, Global Information Agencies, and Disaggregated Democracy' (2003) 24 *Michigan Journal of International Law* 1041, 1057–8.

[160] Majone, 'Regulatory Legitimacy', p. 292: 'The simplest and most effective way of improving transparency and accountability is to require regulators to give reasons for their decisions.'

[161] This point is made in several of the responses to the IIMG *First Interim Report*. The responses are available via http://www.europa.eu.int/comm/internal_market/en/finances/mobil/lamfalussy-comments_en.htm (accessed May 2004).

[162] Possibly this was a short-term problem caused by deadline pressures rather than a deliberate policy decision by the Commission not to provide feedback: Inel, 'Implementing', 12.

[163] European Commission, *Main differences*.

problems still remain. Unexplained departures from consultation results, as occurred with the Financial Instruments Markets Directive (ISD2), are unhelpful,[164] as too are assertions from the Commission that legislative proposals remain broadly intact despite significant and controversial changes made by the Parliament and/or Council during the legislative process, as again occurred in relation to that Directive.[165] No doubt the Commission's language in such situations is finely judged so as not to exacerbate inter-institutional tensions but the impression it creates can be quite misleading.

Consultation and transparency: can there be too much of a good thing?

Thus far this section has concentrated on the potential for consultation and transparency to deliver the entwined benefits of better-quality regulation produced by a process that is widely regarded as being legitimate and safeguarded by appropriate mechanisms of accountability. However, to leave the discussion at this point would risk giving an unbalanced picture. Large-scale public consultation takes time and its management is likely to absorb potentially scarce personnel and other resources. The provision of post-consultation feedback presents the same dilemma: although legitimacy and accountability-enhancing, it also puts an additional burden on strained resources. Further, excessive use of consultation risks generating 'consultation fatigue' which could impair its effectiveness as an evidence-gathering technique. Worse still, it could arouse suspicion that the over-use is a deliberate ploy designed to cloak proposals in a shroud of consultation-based legitimacy when in fact no one has had the time and resources to consider them properly. As the Lamfalussy process moves from infancy into a more mature stage, one key issue will be how well the Commission

---

[164] Criticism of the last-minute changes to the draft proposal that were done at the political level just prior to its publication are voiced in particular in the following two responses to the IIMG *First Interim Report*: Federation of European Securities Exchanges, Futures & Options Association, International Swaps and Derivatives Association, International Primary Market Association, International Securities Market Association, London Investment Banking Association, Swedish Securities Dealers Association and European Banking Federation, *Joint Response to the Inter-Institutional Monitoring Group First Interim Report* (June 2003), available via http://www.europa.eu.int/comm/internal_market/en/finances/ mobil/docs/lamfalussy/2003–07-comments-bdb_en.pdf (accessed May 2004) and British Bankers Association, *BBA Comments on the Lamfalussy Process*, available via http:// www.europa.eu.int/comm/internal_market/en/finances/mobil/docs/lamfalussy/2003–07-comments-bba_en.pdf

[165] E.g. European Commission, 'Investment Services Directive: Council Agreement is Major Step Towards Integrated EU Equities Market', Commission Press Release, 7 October 2003.

and CESR deal with the challenges of reconciling these competing considerations.[166] The trick will be to find a balance that satisfies legitimacy and accountability concerns without compromising the system's ability to deliver procedural and substantive efficiencies in the form of good regulation produced cost-effectively and in a timely fashion. To pull this off, a range of consultation and feedback strategies is needed; deciding which ones are appropriate to which circumstances will be an exercise requiring sensitive and expert judgment.

Boundaries between levels of regulation within the Lamfalussy process

Level 1 and Level 2

Level 1 legislation should contain only framework principles, described by the *Lamfalussy Report* in these terms:[167]

> The framework principles are the core political principles, the essential elements of each proposal. They reflect the key political choices to be taken by the European Parliament and the Council of Ministers on the basis of a proposal by the European Commission. They determine the political direction and orientation, the fundamentals of each decision.

'Essential elements' is not a precise legal concept in EU jurisprudence.[168] Where the line between Level 1 and Level 2 is drawn will thus reflect political choices made on a case-by-case basis rather than being the outcome of the application of a predetermined system of legal classification.[169] Some unevenness and inconsistency is therefore inevitable, and is already apparent: some quite detailed provisions appear in Level 1 legislation because the main EU institutions did not want to cede direct control over the issue in question.[170] This feature undermines the overall coherence of Level 1 legislation. Over time it could result in the emergence of a very muddled regulatory structure that is inexplicable except to those who can still

---

[166] Recognition of the need for balanced use of consultation has started to emerge: IIMG, *Second Interim Report*, p. 28.

[167] *Lamfalussy Report*, pp. 22–3.

[168] Y. V. Avgerinos, 'Essential and Non-essential Measures: Delegation of Powers in EU Securities Regulation' (2002) 8 *European Law Journal* 269, 271–83 ('the delegation of powers under Community law and the distinction between essential rules and implementing measures like so many things, is more a political problem than a point of law' (at 282)).

[169] IIMG *First Interim Report*, p. 27.

[170] IIMG, *Second Interim Report*, pp. 13–14.

recall the stale political battles of the past that dictated the allocation of each regulatory matter to a particular legislative Level.

Although this feature of the Lamfalussy process is not ideal, realistically it does seem to be the only practically feasible way of reconciling the various tensions arising in relation to EU legislative functions. The most optimistic prognosis is that a pro-Level 2 momentum will develop from experience in using the procedures. One of the factors on which this potential development is obviously dependent is a satisfactory resolution of the European Parliament's general concerns in relation to comitology.

Level 2 and Level 3 – a new 'boundaries' issue that could become increasingly significant

As Table 3.1 indicates, Level 3 of the Lamfalussy process embraces a range of activities, some of which have more to do with supervisory functions than with regulation in its narrow, rule-making sense.[171] Nonetheless it is important to note that there is a regulatory component at Level 3 in the form of non-binding rules, standards and guidelines agreed by CESR members. Although there is already some Level 3 activity,[172] the potential importance of Level 3 regulation was not fully appreciated while the pressure was on to complete the FSAP agenda because that tended to focus attention on Level 1 and Level 2 laws. As the distorting effect of the FSAP disappears, the regulatory convergence possibilities at Level 3 will move more into the foreground.[173]

There are in principle two broad areas in which there is room for the operation of Level 3 regulation: first, to add further detail to matters that are covered by binding Level 1 and Level 2 law; and second, to address issues that are not explicitly covered in binding EU law and for which formal Community legislative competence, as determined by the EC Treaty, may not even exist. If Level 3 CESR-driven regulation were to move into areas where Community legislative competence is lacking, this would be a

---

[171] CESR has said that Level 3 covers three areas: co-ordinated implementation; regulatory convergence (which is the aspect considered in the text); and supervisory convergence: CESR, *The Role of CESR At 'Level 3' Under the Lamfalussy Process* (CESR/04–104b, 2004), p. 5.

[172] IIMG, *Second Interim Report*, pp. 31–2, noting various CESR initiatives, including the development of recommendations/ standards on clearing and settlement by a CESR–ESCB Working Group. CESR has also produced common standards on Investor Protection and on Alternative Trading Systems and is working on standards connected to the Market Abuse Directive and the Prospectus Directive: Reinhardt, *The Lamfalussy Process*, p. 26.

[173] That attention is turning in this direction is evident from CESR, *The Role of CESR at 'Level 3'*.

further example of the 'competence creep' through the use of non-binding standards ('soft law') that is evident across EU governance as a whole.[174]

In areas where there is scope for Level 1 and Level 2 law, the potential for Level 3 intervention necessarily depends on whatever decisions have been made at the higher levels by the various EU institutions. In practice this is likely to include CESR because its regulatory expertise should give it a strong voice in policy deliberations notwithstanding that its formal status is that of technical adviser. Clear criteria for drawing the line between Level 2 and Level 3 have yet to be established.[175] One suggestion is that issues might be relegated down to Level 3 where it is impossible to secure political agreement at Level 1 or Level 2.[176] However, whilst it is possible to envisage occasional circumstances where it might be useful for Level 3 regulation to perform this default role, it could be dangerous to treat this as its main function because that might encourage disagreement designed cynically to manipulate the Lamfalussy process so as to insulate established, divergent local practices from mandatory change. Level 3 regulation would be better seen as a positive policy choice that can avoid the rigidity of Level 1 and Level 2 law but with the potential to bring about a helpful degree of regulatory convergence more quickly than could be expected to emerge from a process of regulatory competition between Member States. The previous chapter in this book argued for a mixed strategy for securities market regulation, which embraces both harmonised law and regulatory competition. Advocating a positive role for non-binding standards and best practices agreed by national regulatory bodies is consistent with this argument because it is a further option that adds to the mix and which may be appropriate in some circumstances.[177]

CESR has quickly developed a positive reputation for fostering co-operation and constructive dialogue between European regulators amongst themselves and also between regulators and the European financial services industry.[178] Based on current trends, CESR thus looks well positioned to become a force for regulatory convergence across Europe

---

[174] J. Scott and D. M. Trubek, 'Mind the Gap: Law and the New Approaches to Governance in the European Union' (2002) 8 *European Law Journal* 1, 7.

[175] IIMG, *Second Interim Report*, pp. 33–4.

[176] Ibid.

[177] Securities Expert Group, *FSAP: Progress*, p. 11 advocates non-binding solutions, including CESR standards, as potentially offering faster and more flexible responses to market developments, thus allowing more room for innovation.

[178] Guerrera and Norman, 'European Leaders Invested Heavily'.

through the mechanism of Level 3 standards and guidance. This prospect is not entirely problem-free, however, because CESR could develop into a strong European regulatory 'club' whose members are tempted to engage in rent-seeking behaviour resulting in excessive regulatory intervention across Europe. This prospect implies a need for robust accountability mechanisms to rein in any tendencies towards bureaucratic excess within CESR.

CESR's relations with the Commission and with interest groups: legitimacy and accountability concerns

Evaluating CESR's role presents a particularly tricky challenge because of the relatively short period for which it has been in operation and the limited amount of evidence about how it works that is publicly available. Early indications from the process of developing Level 2 implementing measures do not suggest that CESR has yet moved into a dominant role vis-à-vis the Commission, and its ability to do so in the future is likely to be somewhat constrained by its modest resources. Yet the potential for CESR to dominate the Commission (another overstretched, resource-constrained institution) in the regulatory process is clearly present because CESR can draw upon its superior understanding of regulatory issues based on its members' day-to-day experience of grappling with the operation of financial markets.[179]

One specific suggestion that has been made is that CESR, in its Level 3 role, may displace the Commission as the key body for monitoring uniformity in the implementation of regulation across the EU.[180] However, thus far, CESR has been at pains to emphasise that it is the Commission which is the 'Guardian of the Treaty' and that its role is to *complement* the Commission in ensuring that Member States meet their obligations to give effect to EU securities laws.[181] It will take time and experience to see whether words and deeds coincide.

A natural assumption is that Commission officials would want to keep CESR in check so as to resist encroachments on their own power and prestige but it is possible to envisage a scenario in which the forces pushing for a shift in the balance of power towards CESR become practically irresistible. In that event the Commission could be at risk of capture by CESR because ambitious Commission officials could well decide that it is within

---

[179] Norman, 'A Tiny Committee'.
[180] Scott, 'The Governance of the European Union', 68.
[181] CESR, *The Role of CESR at 'Level 3'*, pp. 6–7.

CESR that the best opportunities for career progression will be found.[182] However, no doubt many varied personal preferences and interests underlie the career aspirations of Commission officials and it would seem unwise over-readily to assume that they would be attracted to (or necessarily have the requisite skills for) a career within a more narrowly defined regulatory organisation.

However things progress, there can be no doubt that CESR is a powerful body, and that its influence is likely to increase over time. It is therefore necessary to pay close attention to its accountability and legitimacy. It is doubtful whether the present system of control, which rests on commitments to openness and consultation, and requirements to report periodically to the EU institutions, will prove adequate in the longer term, particularly with regard to CESR's potentially highly significant Level 3 functions. Level 3 activity could take CESR into areas that technically fall outside Community competence thus giving rise to some quite tricky questions about the standing of EU institutions to review them. At worst, this could be characterised as a structure that is deliberately designed so as to evade accountability via EU organs.[183] CESR members are, to be sure, accountable within their national regulatory systems but the mechanisms that operate at that level could be focused more on domestic issues than on agencies' supranational activities; and such mechanisms are also subject to all of the vagaries that may affect different accountability structures within the Member States. There is a risk that the effectiveness of national accountability mechanisms could be threatened by agencies' involvement in CESR – for example, where an agency participates in a CESR decision to develop a controversial new regulatory standard but then clings to the moral high ground of needing to be a 'good European partner' to justify imposing that standard in the face of strong, national opposition.

National protectionism leading to dispute and division between CESR members would act as a practical brake on the development of its power, particularly at Level 3 where consensus is required. However, that would be an unhealthy type of control. CESR's role in eroding the national biases and preoccupations of regulatory agencies should therefore be welcomed and encouraged as part of an overall system that accommodates some

---

[182] G. Majone, 'Delegation of Regulatory Powers in a Mixed Polity' (2002) 8 *European Law Journal* 319, 329–30 puts forwards this type of argument generally, not specifically in relation to securities regulation. Also G. Majone, 'Functional Interests: European Agencies' in Peterson and Shackleton (eds.), *The Institutions of the European Union*, p. 323.

[183] Harlow, *Accountability*, 76.

commonality and some diversity. Whatever problems of concentration of power that this process could engender should be addressed directly.

Fears about CESR developing into a body with immense, inadequately controlled powers over the operation of European securities markets lead into concerns about the powers behind CESR itself. It is only to be expected that, as CESR's power and influence grows, it will attract increasing attention from lobbyists. There is a longstanding tradition of interest group involvement in EU processes.[184] This can take a variety of forms embracing both indirect lobbying via national governments and direct lobbying of EU institutions. Firms may lobby individually or in coalitions. A standard pattern is that the intensity of Euro-orientated lobbying increases broadly in tandem with the growth of EU policy responsibilities in any area.

The European Commission has a reputation for being particularly open to lobbyists, a phenomenon that is associated with the twin pressures of the large and often highly complex range of issues with which it must deal and its thin internal resources. This has both advantages, in terms of enabling the Commission to make better-informed, evidence-based decisions about appropriate regulatory responses, and drawbacks, in terms of the Commission's susceptibility to the views of the best-organised, most well-resourced interest groups. CESR's position is not dissimilar to that of the Commission – it is a relatively new bureaucracy that must engage in dialogue with market participants if it is to have any real hope of working out sensible solutions to highly complex questions arising in relation to securities markets. By sharing the regulatory burden with market participants in this way it can reduce the pressure on its own tiny resources. At the same time, however, there is an ever-present risk that CESR will cross the line between drawing upon expert input constructively and being in thrall to it.

Overall, there is insufficient empirical data publicly available to assess authoritatively the role that interest groups have played in influencing the development of EU securities regulation.[185] Anecdotally, however, there are various indications that the establishment of CESR and the Lamfalussy process more generally have (unsurprisingly) triggered a growth in

---

[184] A general review of the literature is provided by S. Mazey, and J. Richardson, 'Interest Groups and EU Policy-making' in Richardson (ed.), *European Union*, 217–37.

[185] G. Hertig, 'Regulatory Competition for EU Financial Services' in D. C. Esty and D. Geradin, *Regulatory Competition and Economic Integration* (Oxford, Oxford University Press, 2001), p. 218.

euro-lobbying.[186] The multinational firms that, for obvious reasons, were ahead of the game in lobbying for securities market opening measures are increasingly being joined by financial trade associations and other industry groups that historically concentrated their lobbying efforts at the domestic level. Looking, for example, at the responses to the IIMG's interim reviews of the Lamfalussy process, these reveal the formation of powerful coalitions that are likely to be well equipped to mobilise for desired regulatory outcomes.[187] The opening of offices by national bodies in European regulatory centres is a further physical sign of the growing awareness of the importance of developing and maintaining good connections with European policy-makers. The Secretary-General of the Federation of European Stock Exchanges has drawn attention to this trend: 'The FSAP has dramatically and definitively shifted the centre of legislation for the internal market in financial products to Brussels. By way of illustration, even the City Corporation of London is now opening an office in the European capital.'[188]

Some groups have lagged behind others in developing EU-orientated lobbying capabilities. There is some evidence that issuers, insurance companies and asset managers feel that their interests have been underrepresented.[189] However, the group that is most conspicuous by its absence is retail investors. The IIMG has noted the lack of responses to its work from investor groups and consumers.[190] Retail investor groups traditionally lag behind industry groups in engagement in lobbying on European issues. There are various possible explanations for this imbalance. Some are rooted in general considerations that tend to put retail consumers and public interest groups at a disadvantage to business groups in lobbying efforts, such as diffusion of interests, poorer organisational capabilities and thinner resources. Securities market conditions, in particular the

---

[186] Guerrera and Norman, 'European Leaders Invested Heavily'.

[187] See joint submissions from groups including the Federation of European Securities Exchanges, Futures & Options Association, International Swaps & Derivatives Association, International Primary Market Association, International Securities Market Association, London Investment Banking Association, Swedish Securities Dealers Association and European Banking Federation. Responses to the IIMG Reports are available via http://www.europa.eu.int/comm/internal_market/en/finances/mobil/lamfalussy-comments_en.htm (accessed May 2004).

[188] P. Arlman, Speech by FESE Secretary General, at Globalisation 5, a FEAS/FESE Conference, Prague, 25 February 2004 The text of this speech is available via http://www.fese.be/initiatives/speeches/2004/arlman_25feb2004.htm (accessed May 2004).

[189] IIMG, *Second Interim Report*, p. 29.

[190] Ibid.

continuing fragmentation of retail investment in Europe along national lines, may also play a part because these may mean that retail investors have not yet felt the full implications of the Europeanisation of regulatory power.

The experience with the FSAP suggests that EU policy-makers (which will increasingly include CESR) need to develop a better understanding of retail investor issues if they are to make successful policy choices in this area. Although broadly wholesale market-orientated (a justifiable bias taking the view that regulatory strategy should be against intervention in areas where there is a strong likelihood of poorly-informed decisions because of deficiencies in information-gathering mechanisms), the FSAP has taken the EU regulatory programme further into retail investor territory than ever before, particularly in the Financial Instruments Markets Directive (ISD2) which contains a raft of measures intended to ensure investor protection.[191] The treatment of 'execution only' dealings in the original version of this Directive, as proposed by the Commission, provided an example of shaky judgment on how best to deliver effective and efficient investor protection in the interests of retail investors. Had the Commission's original draft been adopted, its impact could have been very damaging to retail investors because, by imposing costly obligations on firms to gauge the suitability of investments for clients, it potentially jeopardised the continued viability of low-cost, execution-only securities trading business.[192]

Under the Lamfalussy model, it is CESR that will be expected to provide technical advice on the appropriate regulatory response to retail investor issues. For example, CESR is likely to have to get to grips with many retail investor-related issues in its work on implementing measures for the Financial Instruments Markets Directive (ISD2). As yet, however, CESR does not appear to have engaged significantly in dialogue with retail investor groups. As Moloney has noted, its Market Participants Group, which is a core element of its Level 2 consultation mechanism, is dominated by wholesale market interests.[193]

---

[191] N. Moloney, 'Confidence and Competence: the Conundrum of EC Capital Markets Law' [2004] *Journal of Corporate Law Studies* 1 considers the increasing reliance on promotion of investor confidence as the rationale for securities regulation within the EU. Moloney identifies revision of the ISD as signalling a shift in emphasis in regulatory policy towards prioritising the protection of investors: ibid., 12.

[192] R. Carr, 'EU Investment Services Directive Could Kill Off Execution-only Share Trading', *Investors Chronicle*, 25 April 2003, p. 13. The issue was addressed by means of amendments to the text inserted by the European Parliament and Council.

[193] Moloney, 'Confidence', 42.

Admittedly CESR members should be in touch with retail investor concerns through their domestic activities[194] but this may not be sufficient to ensure that such concerns receive due attention at the EU level. Furthermore, this sort of indirect representation of retail investor concerns at EU level arguably fails from a legitimacy perspective. Failure to seek out direct input from diffused and poorly organised groups, such as retail investors are likely to be, could undermine regulatory legitimacy and create at least a perception of industry capture. The Commission has recognised that there is a gap in the input that is offered to it by lobbyists: 'The Commission already receives much valuable input into its policy initiatives from the financial services industry but recognises the need for a closer dialogue with users of retail financial services.'[195] To close this gap it has established 'FIN-USE', which is a forum of twelve financial services experts, who will formulate policy recommendations to the Commission on EU financial services initiatives, with particular focus on problems encountered by users (retail consumers and small and medium-sized businesses).[196] It is too early to assess the usefulness of this Group but it does represent a positive attempt to give a formal voice within the system to interests whose views might not otherwise be heard. There is a case for CESR to consider a similar initiative to bring (and to be seen to bring) retail investor issues more directly into the mainstream of its activities.

The role of the European Securities Committee (ESC)

It has been said of the ESC that it is simply the Council 'writ small' and a prediction that has been drawn from this is that political disputes will slow up and impair Level 2 of the Lamfalussy process in just the same way as they can impede the progress of legislation that passes through the full (or, in Lamfalussy terms, Level 1) EU legislative channels.[197] Although it is not quite formally correct to see the ESC as a mini-Council because it operates on the basis of a different voting structure,[198] it is undeniable that the ESC could be a venue for time-consuming arguments rooted in national

---

[194] IIMG, *Second Interim Report*, p. 29 notes that it has been suggested that national regulators take particular responsibility for retail investor issues.

[195] European Commission, 'Financial Services: Commission to set up Expert Forum to Look at Policies from Users' Point of View (FIN-USE)', Commission Press Release, 25 July 2003.

[196] Ibid.

[197] Hertig and Lee, 'Four Predictions'.

[198] McKee, 'The Unpredictable Future'.

protectionism and for messy compromises. How much weight should be attached to the fact that the Commission could ultimately push through a measure that is not supported by the ESC so long as it has the qualified minority support of the Council is questionable given that to do so would surely provoke major inter-institutional tensions and a likely backlash in the form of opposition by the Council to any further use of the Lamfalussy process.[199] Moreover, the existence of the 'Aerosol' clause – obscure EU terminology[200] to describe the Commission's commitment to 'avoid going against predominant views which might emerge within the Council' – though replete with uncertainty,[201] suggests that measures to which there is substantial opposition should not even reach the point of being put to the vote in any event. However, even though the mechanism might never be tested in practice, it is possible that the mere existence of favourable voting requirements at Council level could strengthen the hand of Commission officials in discussions with the ESC members and thus affect the dynamics of their meetings.

Whilst the potential for the ESC to undermine the realisation of a smooth-running legislative machinery clearly exists, in its favour stands the, admittedly small, body of evidence of how it has actually operated. To date, there is no indication that work on implementing measures has been significantly slowed up by political manoeuvring,[202] nor that the quality of such measures has been seriously compromised by late insertions into legislative texts to protect national interests. To be sure, the ESC's constructive stance could be a temporary phenomenon flowing from goodwill

---

[199] Hertig and Lee, 'Four Predictions', 365–6.

[200] The name is derived from the first use of this method of blocking the adoption of implementing rules in the 1970s in relation to EU legislation on chlorofluorocarbon emissions from spray cans: IIMG *First Interim Report*, fn 17.

[201] IIMG, *First Interim Report*, p. 39. Reinhardt, *The Lamfalussy Process*, p. 9 interprets this to mean that a simple majority in Council or even possibly the opposition of one or two larger Member States would require the Commission to review its position.

[202] Thus experience thus far does not bear out the suggestion that the existence of Level 2 could delay rather than speed up the legislative process: Y. V. Avgerinos, 'EU Financial Market Supervision Revisited: The European Securities Regulator', *Jean Monnet* Working Paper 7/03, available via http://www.jeanmonnetprogram.org/papers/03/030701.pdf (accessed May 2004). Arguments on the superiority of the single regulator model are developed further in Y. V. Avgerinos, *Regulating and Supervising Investment Services in the European Union* (Basingstoke, Palgrave Macmillan, 2003).

It is impossible to be sure whether the Directives passed under the Lamfalussy process would have proceeded more or less slowly had that process not been available but the history of EC securities regulation (noted in the *Lamfalussy Report*, p. 14) strongly suggests that progress would have been much slower.

towards the new system and a shared willingness to give it a fair chance. It could though be a sign of a more permanent positive development in the evolution of an efficient EU securities regulatory process. A key feature of the Lamfalussy process is that politically sensitive issues are meant to be separated off from technical concerns but in practice a watertight distinction will be hard to maintain. The ESC provides a mechanism for the resolution of minor political skirmishes without invoking the full panoply of Level 1 and it has at least the potential to operate more flexibly and quickly than might be possible within the formalities of the Council.[203]

Although most of the focus of attention on the ESC has been with regard to its potentially malign influence on the regulatory process, it is also worthwhile to consider its potential for good.[204] In principle it is possible to envisage the ESC making a positive contribution to the development of high-quality legislation by acting as a route through which the expertise and experience of national finance ministries in the drafting of technical securities legislation can be fed directly into the process. However, it is unclear yet whether the ESC will wish to develop significantly its technical contribution. Thus far its role appears to have been largely confined to acting as a political mechanism to secure a measure of Member State control over the Level 2 regulatory process.

The role of the European Parliament

In its handling of FSAP Level 1 measures the European Parliament has developed a strong reputation for correcting market-insensitive aspects of legislative proposals.[205] Amongst its significant contributions were amendments to the Prospectus Directive that alleviated the regulatory burden on smaller companies and preserved flexibility within international bond markets. Most of the success was attributed to the individual MEPs who acted as rapporteurs in respect of specific measures and, as such, steered the legislative proposals through the Economic and Monetary

---

[203] This prediction is consistent with evidence of the usually consensual nature of the work done by regulatory committees across the range of EU activities: R. Dehousse, 'Towards a Regulation of Transitional Governance? Citizens' Rights and the Reform of Comitology Procedures' in Joerges and Vos (eds.), *EU Committees*, pp. 110–12.

[204] Hertig and Lee present a caricature of the ESC's role as being 'either futile or useless': 'Four Predictions', 366.

[205] 'Scrapping Over the Pieces – Laborious Efforts Towards a Single Market', *Economist*, 9 March 2002, p. 85.

Affairs Committee of the Parliament and through voting by the Parliament in plenary session.[206]

Like the other EU institutions the European Parliament can usually draw from a deep pool of expert advice proffered to it by lobbyists.[207] Although the work of the Economic and Monetary Committee's Advisory Panel of Financial Services Experts (APFSE) is not in the public domain, some of the Parliament's success in contributing helpful amendments to draft legislation has been attributed to its access to the advice of market experts.[208] This Committee has also made some effort to include retail investor representatives directly in discussions.[209]

The European Parliament is not immune to making decisions that are distorted by protectionist national considerations. The starkest recent example of this in the securities field was provided by the July 2001 tied (and therefore unsuccessful) European Parliament vote on the proposed Takeover Directive. Almost all German MEPs voted against the measure, which was opposed by a coalition of conservative German business interests and by trade union federations.[210] However, overall the European Parliament has made a positive contribution to the development of recent securities laws. This assessment casts its concerns about the inter-institutional implications of the Lamfalussy process into a favourable light. EU securities law passed before the European Parliament acquired significant legislative powers (i.e. the bulk of the pre-FSAP legislative framework) was hardly a beacon of success. Although it is impossible to make firm predictions on how FSAP measures will fare in the longer term, broadly speaking Parliamentary interventions do seem to have anticipated and addressed at least some of the potential problems that might well have been encountered had measures been adopted in their original form. This suggests that it is important to ensure that the

[206] E.g. G. Trefgarne, 'MEP Wins AIM Concessions', *Daily Telegraph*, 27 February 2002, p. 39 (commending the work of Christopher Huhne MEP as rapporteur to the Prospectus Directive).

[207] Mazey and Richardson, 'Interest Groups', pp. 229–30.

[208] Reinhardt, *The Lamfalussy Process*, p. 15.

[209] E.g. Public Hearing on Revision of Investment Services Directive, 18 February 2003, which included a presentation from ProShare, a UK private shareholder representative organisation. Details and papers available via http://www.europarl.eu.int/hearings/20030218/econ/hay.pdf (accessed May 2004).

[210] D. Dombey, 'EU Rejects Chance to Set Cross-border Takeover Rules', *Financial Times*, 5 July 2001, p. 1.

Parliament's role is not emasculated through excessive or inadequately-controlled reliance upon comitology processes.

D   The limitations of processes

There is no doubt that over the last twenty-five years the locus of decision-making power for the regulation of securities markets in Europe has shifted significantly in favour of the EU. This trend intensified with the FSAP. Whereas some of the early initiatives were fairly modest in their reach, a much broader regime has begun to emerge. The old system, characterised by harmonisation only to the extent needed to establish a sufficient level of trust in each other's standards to enable mutual recognition to operate (minimum harmonisation), is giving way to a more aggressive approach in which the power of Member States to impose their own additional requirements over and above the harmonised core is being limited. The new approach also moves significantly beyond regulation in the strict sense of rule-writing with the establishment of the CESR infrastructure for closer co-operation and co-ordination between national supervisory bodies and with a new focus on ensuring consistency in supervision and enforcement across the EU via CESR and also the European Commission.

The rather technocratic nature of older EU securities laws may well have been a factor explaining why they came into being and were not blocked by coalitions of Member States intent on preserving their own national interests. Furthermore, with supervision and enforcement responsibilities remaining firmly rooted in fragmented national systems, there was scope for Member States to go along with the adoption of new EU laws whilst quietly leaving room for themselves to apply them in ways best suited to meeting perceived national interests.[211] And, in any case, Member States could usually postpone the day when they needed to think about the practical, operational impact of new EU laws because such laws usually only took effect after they had been implemented into national laws, a process over which Member States could drag their feet.[212]

---

[211] 'A Ragbag'.

[212] As of 1997, it was estimated that Germany had failed to implement more than one in nine Directives: 'Thatcherites in Brussels (Really)', *Economist*, 15 March 1997, p. 25. By 2003, France and Italy were topping the table for foot-dragging: 'Actions Speak Louder than Words', *Economist Global Agenda*, 7 May 2003, via www.economist.com (accessed June 2004).

The current significant expansion in the scope and depth of the EU securities regulatory regime, the upgraded efforts by the European Commission to pursue countries that fail on timely implementation,[213] and the development of peer review processes via CESR, combine to shatter the argument that the Europeanisation of securities market regulation is attributable simply to the fact that it is all too technically rarefied and remote for anyone to care enough about it to engage in serious blocking efforts.[214] Yet the dreary character of early measures could have been crucial in that their adoption helped establish the principle that regulation of securities markets was something that could appropriately be done at the European level, and thus provided a platform for the incremental development of more ambitious forms of regulatory intervention.

It is easy to see that Member States will be willing to support EU regulatory intervention where the advantages of collective action are judged to outweigh any disadvantages involved in pooling sovereignty. But this begs the question: what are the possible advantages offered by a collective approach that might encourage States to engage in intergovernmental bargaining? In addressing this question, it needs to be kept in mind that a well-known feature of EU policy development is that Member States can often agree on the need for a European approach whilst at the same time having quite different perceptions of its potential advantages.[215]

Self-interest in capturing the projected macroeconomic benefits associated with the establishment of a truly integrated financial market will lead States to give broad support to proposals that can be credibly associated with the realisation of that goal. Officially the European 'line' tends to be that such benefits will apply across Europe as a whole and that, by coming together internally, the overall ability of Europe to compete with the US, Japan and China will be enhanced. Reading between the lines, however, it is often possible to find a different story in which British and German agreement on the benefits of a single financial market masks an

---

[213] 'Actions Speak'.

[214] Though as late as 2002 the British Prime Minister was quoted in the press as having described a European Summit Meeting on which financial services regulatory reform featured prominently on the agenda as being mainly concerned with 'nerdy' issues of interest only to 'anoraks': J. Hartley Brewer, 'PM Allows His Frustration to Show at the European Summit As the Day's Business is "Strictly for Anoraks"', *Sunday Express*, 17 March 2002, p. 11.

[215] L. Tsoukalis, 'Economic and Monetary Union', in Wallace and Wallace (eds.), *Policy-Making*, pp. 164–5, 176 (discussing how fear about its ability to compete with Germany drove France's support for monetary union whilst for Germany the motivations were more to do with embedding the economy and State within a wider European framework).

underlying fierce competition between them on whether its centre of power is to be London or Frankfurt, whilst France waits in the wings as the 'ideal' compromise choice for the location of the business of regulating the pan-European financial industry.[216]

The application of the auditor oversight provisions of the Sarbanes-Oxley Act[217] to foreign auditors of US listed firms provided an opportunity to test the theory that the collective weight of Member States, acting through the European Commission, would be a more effective counterbalance to US power in the operation of securities markets than the efforts of Member States acting individually. The 'extra-territoriality' of Sarbanes-Oxley provoked a furious transatlantic row, including loosely-veiled threats of reciprocation, such as the possibility of an EU Directive on the consolidated supervision of financial conglomerates being applied so as to put an additional regulatory burden on US firms.[218] A compromise on auditor oversight, brokered by the European Commission in negotiations with the US regulatory agencies,[219] eventually emerged, whereby there will be certain changes to EU laws on auditors and reciprocal registration requirements will apply.[220] Although it is impossible to say whether Member States, acting individually, could have made their own deals with the US authorities, the fact that EU finance ministers made specific requests to the Commission for it to act as their voice[221] suggests that some advantages in a collective approach were recognised on the European side. According to some reports, the US Public Company Accounting Oversight Board (PCAOB) did not want to do bilateral deals with individual Member States,[222] and the EU's strength as a trading bloc was identified as a reason why the PCAOB paid particular attention to its

---

[216] 'Scrapping Over the Pieces'.

[217] Formally the Public Company Accounting Reform and Investor Protection Act of 2002.

[218] 'A Bit of Give and Take: Another Transatlantic Row Over Financial Regulation', *Economist*, 19 October 2002, p. 99.

[219] D. Dombey and D. Sevastopulo, 'No Accord Yet Over European Auditors', *Financial Times*, 16 October 2003, p. 8.

[220] The outline of this compromise solution was announced during a visit to Brussels in March 2004 by William McDonough, Chairman of the PCAOB: D. Dombey, 'Sarbanes-Oxley and Europe – US Legislation Finds a Friend Across the Water', *Financial Times*, 23 April 2004, Understanding Corporate Governance Supplement, p. 9.

[221] European Commission, 'EU Concerned About US Audit Registration Step', Commission Press Release, 24 April 2003.

[222] 'Bolkestein Sees EU–US Audit Firm Deal by Year End', Forbes.com, quoting Frits Bolkestein, European Internal Market Commission http://www.forbes.com/personalfinance/retirement/newswire/2003/10/09/rtr1103943.html.

concerns.[223] Yet it is open to question who really will benefit most from the EU's collective approach on this matter. The US authorities presumably welcomed the convenience of dealing with a single EU 'voice', though it appears that they will continue to deal individually with certain EU Member States too.[224] Arguably it is the European Commission that is worst off because it now faces the hard task of conducting delicate political negotiations to secure Council and European Parliament support for changes to EU laws on auditing that could appear to amount to caving in to US demands for a Sarbanes-Oxley mimicking auditor oversight regime within the EU.[225]

Externality considerations are also influential as a reason for Member States to support collective action at EU level. Countries that already have sophisticated securities laws have an incentive to support the extension of high standards across the EU to avoid being dragged down by association with poorer-quality regulatory regimes elsewhere in the EU. Equally, States with less-developed regimes may welcome European intervention because it relieves them of the burden of having to invest in national law reform exercises to upgrade their rules to more acceptable international standards.

The prospect of having 'its' high standards adopted across Europe carries with it the related benefit for a country that its firms may gain a competitive advantage through their established familiarity with the rules and their avoidance of significant adaptation costs.[226] This motivation can be described as a form of 'regulatory imperialism'.[227] It can also be seen as a defensive action designed to reduce incentives for firms to relocate to other European countries with laxer regulatory regimes.[228]

---

[223] Dombey, 'US Legislation Finds a Friend'.

[224] Ibid., reporting that until the EU system is up and running (estimated to be four years after it has been through the EU legislative process (which in itself could be time-consuming), the PCAOB will step up collaboration with individual jurisdictions such as the UK, France and Germany. Under the Final Rules Relating to the Oversight of Non-US Public Accounting Firms (PCAOB Release No. 2004–005, June 2004), there is a 'sliding scale' regulatory procedure for non-US auditors, which is intended to be less stringent in those countries where audit control is closest to the US.

[225] See further ch. 6.

[226] A. Heritier, 'The Accommodation of Diversity in European Policy-making and Its Outcomes: Regulatory Policy as Patchwork' (1996) 3 *Journal of European Public Policy* 149.

[227] J. Macey, 'Regulatory Globalization as a Response to Regulatory Competition' (2003) *Emory Law Journal* 1353.

[228] Baldwin and Cave, *Understanding Regulation*, pp. 173–5.

Another motivation that sometimes underpins international (including EU) consensus-formation is that this can be designed indirectly to break down entrenched national opposition: an unpopular measure can acquire an enhanced legitimacy through having been agreed at international level or, where it is part of a package, it may be possible to present it as a trade-off that was pragmatically necessary in order to secure other benefits.[229]

Support for European regulatory expansion in relation to securities markets can also be seen as a response to globalisation. Securities markets facilitate the international flow of capital unimpeded by national borders but they also present challenges that national regulatory regimes struggle to meet on their own. The challenges are multidirectional. From a public interest perspective, we can envisage States coming together in order to devise regulation that enables legitimate international business and investment to take place cost-effectively and, at the same time, limits the opportunities for international financial fraud and market manipulation. From a public choice viewpoint, however, regulatory co-ordination by States can look rather more like 'cartelisation' so as to prevent national regimes becoming powerless in the face of the opportunities for regulatory arbitrage that globalised markets make available to firms.[230] The pooling of sovereignty to deal with the opportunities and risks presented by globalisation is a regulatory technique that is not exclusive to Europe[231] but the institutional structure and legal system of the EU enable it to operate in a particularly developed form.[232]

The fundamental freedoms enshrined in the EC Treaty provide a further, if somewhat attenuated, incentive for Member States to engage with the harmonisation programme.[233] Simply by becoming a Member State of the EU, a country is, in effect, pre-committing itself to support the integration process.[234] Under ECJ jurisprudence, protectionist Member State legislation is liable to be struck down if it impedes the efforts of firms to rely on Treaty freedoms to carry on cross-border financial services

---

[229] Slaughter, 'Global Government Networks', 1054.

[230] Macey, 'Regulatory Globalization'.

[231] J. Stiglitz, *Globalization and its Discontents* (London, Penguin, 2002), pp. 222–4 notes that globalisation has increased awareness of the need for global collective action in arenas where impacts are global.

[232] Hertig, 'Regulatory Competition', p. 229.

[233] M. Andenas, 'The Financial Market and the Commission as Legislator' (1998) 19 *Company Lawyer* 98.

[234] Majone, 'Delegation', 324.

business.[235] Harmonised legislation introduced in place of divergent national rules provides Member States with a mechanism to maintain regulatory control over an area without infringing Treaty freedoms.[236] However, the ECJ has not been particularly aggressive in outlawing national laws covering the area of financial services,[237] which means therefore that Treaty considerations cannot be viewed as a particularly strong force underlying the trend towards Europeanisation of securities regulation.

There are also counter-considerations that will lead Member States sometimes to oppose securities laws proposals or to offer only conditional support for them. The reasons for Member States' opposition can vary and the consequences can be unpredictable. Sometimes the opposition may be rooted in Member States' concerns about the preservation of important national principles or institutions. On other occasions opposition may be a tactical step in intergovernmental bargaining across a range of different issues. The sorry tale of the Takeover Directive[238] provides examples of various motivations at work and serves as a graphic illustration of their potentially destructive impact. The Directive's progress was significantly impeded at key stages by Members States' substantive concerns about its potential impact on national arrangements (including British concerns about the potential threat to the self-regulatory status of its Takeover Panel, German concerns about the risk of the non-reciprocal opening up of German business to foreign ownership and the implications for employee involvement in corporate governance,[239] and Nordic country concerns about the threat to dual-class share structures that were used to keep the ownership of the largest Nordic listed firms concentrated in the hands of a few families and banks).[240]

Unrelated issues that got thrown into the mix as States sought to strike bargains to protect their national preferences with regard to takeovers

---

[235] Moloney, *EC Securities Regulation*, pp. 311–35; D. O'Keefe and N. Carey, 'The Internal Market and Investor Protection' in G. Ferrarini, K. J. Hopt and E. Wymeersch (eds.), *Capital Markets in the Age of the Euro* (London, Kluwer Law International, 2002), pp. 1–16.

[236] Generally on harmonisation legislation as a 'lawful barrier': A. McGee and S. Weatherill, 'The Evolution of the Single Market – Harmonisation or Liberalisation' (1990) 53 *Modern Law Review* 578.

[237] Moloney, *EC Securities Regulation*, pp. 335–6.

[238] Directive 2004/25/EC of the European Parliament and of the Council of 21 April 2004 on takeover bids, OJ 2004 No. L142/12.

[239] M. Becht, 'Reciprocity in Takeovers', *European Corporate Governance Institute* Law Working Paper No. 14/2003, ssrn abstractid = 463003.

[240] P. Hogfeldt, 'The History and Politics of Corporate Ownership in Sweden', *European Corporate Governance Institute* Finance Working Paper No30/2003, ssrn abstractid = 449460.

included the status of Gibraltar (Spain's support for a version of the Directive approved by the British at one stage becoming a pawn in complex Anglo-Spanish negotiations over the former colony's fate),[241] a Commission proposal on the rights of temporary agency workers (in a classic instance of horse-trading, a British–German deal was struck whereby Germany agreed to lend the UK its support in blocking the temporary workers proposal and in return the UK agreed to support the blocking of a version of the Takeover Directive that was objectionable to Germany[242]), and the EU Common Agricultural Plan (in another deal Germany softened its opposition to reform of the CAP to secure French support for its objections to the Takeover Directive[243]). The end result of these long periods of national intransigence followed by messy compromises was a severely emasculated measure characterised by multi-tiered optionality in respect of important provisions.[244] The deal to achieve this result was brokered by Member States in the Council of Ministers and was secured in spite of strong opposition from the European Commission.

The Takeover Directive in its final form is an embarrassment for the EU: so much time and effort spent to achieve so little. It manifestly fails to open up the market for corporate control by making the ownership of European companies more contestable.[245] As such it represents a victory for national protectionism. Furthermore, in the delicate power play between the various EU institutions, it is a sign of the Council's growing

---

[241] J. Wolf and D. Atkinson, ' 'Spain Rocks Takeover Pact', *Guardian*, 22 June 1999, p. 20.

[242] D. Rudnick, 'Big Guns Voice Concern at Takeover Directive Amendments', *Daily Telegraph*, 6 November 2003, p. 15.

[243] A. Evans-Pritchard, 'EC Fury at Franco-German Backroom Deal', *Daily Telegraph*, 13 June 2003, p. 34.

[244] Member States have the option of opting into the provision requiring shareholder approval for defensive measures by a target's board (art. 9) and the 'breakthrough provision' whereby any restrictions on voting rights and on transfer can be ignored in certain circumstances, for example by the bidder following a takeover (art. 11). In Member States that do not opt in, individual companies will be allowed to opt in, but they will be free to opt out again when faced with a bidder that does not apply the same provisions.

[245] Becht, 'Reciprocity', comments on the emphasis on reciprocity that, 'in view of the history of the Takeover Directive one could not fail to suspect a Machiavellian plot most foul; by asking for everything, the politicians pressing for reciprocity hoped to get nothing. To the extent that this is true, the plotters must be pleased with the result.'

ascendancy over the Commission, a pattern that has also been evident elsewhere in the EU's activities.[246]

Does the Takeover Directive represent a failure for the Lamfalussy process? A simple answer to this question is 'no' because the Takeover Directive was not dealt with under the Lamfalussy process: indeed its origins long pre-dated the emergence of that process. And even it had been handled under the Lamfalussy process, strictly it would not have been a 'failure' because that process was not designed to override Member States' political objections to proposed new laws (had it been, the proposal to introduce it would surely have been a political non-starter).[247] At the same time, it is indisputable that the Takeover Directive debacle has damaged the credibility of the Lamfalussy process because, in line with some predictions,[248] it has been tainted by association.[249] If Member States repeat the pattern of the Takeover Directive and, within the Lamfalussy process, regularly use their Level 1 powers to dilute or distort measures to the point where they are deprived of significant practical effect it is likely that the process will indeed become 'an ingenious but largely irrelevant footnote in history'.[250] But the Takeover Directive could be the outlier, distinctive in part because of its convoluted legislative history and in part because of special deep sensitivities about the desirability of pushing Continental European countries towards the Anglo-American model of widely-held corporate ownership.[251] The contribution made by the Lamfalussy process in moving forward other, more 'core' securities law proposals in the FSAP suggests that there remains room for optimism about its long-term significance.

---

[246] The Commission has been on the back foot since 1999 when, under the Presidency of Jacques Santer, the College of Commissioners, its political arm appointed by Member States, was forced to resign amid charges of fraud and mismanagement within the Commission's operations: J. Peterson, 'The College of Commissioners' in Peterson and Shackleton (eds.), *The Institutions of the European Union*, pp. 71–94.

[247] McKee, 'The Unpredictable Future'.

[248] Hertig and Lee, 'Four Predictions', 369.

[249] Leader Column, 'Concerns About the Lamfalussy Approach', *Financial Times*, 1 December 2003, p. 18 lambasts the Takeover Directive as 'craven'.

[250] Ibid.

[251] Becht, 'Reciprocity'.

E   An alternative model: a pan-European securities regulatory (and supervisory) agency

An alternative model for securities rule-making and supervision within the EU would be to abandon the Lamfalussy process in favour of the establishment by the EU of a securities regulatory agency with regulatory and supervisory functions. Arguments for a central regulatory agency are that this would establish a machinery for the production of better laws more quickly, assist with the uniform implementation of rules on a pan-European basis, facilitate exploitation of scale economies, provide a one-stop shop for investor complaints and concerns, diminish the risk of regulatory capture and provide at least the potential for improved transparency and accountability.[252]

There are counter-arguments. Whatever its other deficiencies, the evidence to date strongly supports the claim that the Lamfalussy process has speeded up the legislative process. Advocates of the regulatory agency model who suggest that Lamfalussy might have the opposite effect,[253] are not on strong ground. True, there remain some politically sensitive issues that can slow up the process considerably, particularly at Level 1, but it is unclear that Member States would even countenance delegating rule-making power in respect of the most controversial issues, such as take-overs, to a regulatory agency. Implementation takes place within a system, and crucial parts of the European system, particularly with regard to enforcement, remain fragmented along national lines. A single regulatory agency would thus face the quite daunting task of having to work with some twenty-five different judicial infrastructures, most of which would at any given time inevitably be unfamiliar to the single regulator's staff. It is not self-evident that this would lead to more uniform implementation of rules than is potentially achievable under Level 3 of the Lamfalussy process. Industry participants and consumers would still have to invest resources in understanding the different enforcement mechanisms available across the EU, so cost savings in that area might not be great. A supranational agency might indeed be less vulnerable to capture by national interest groups, but it does not follow that the risk of capture necessarily would be lower because supranational regulators would be susceptible to similar temptations to take advantage of blandishments proffered

---

[252] Avgerinos, 'EU Financial Market Supervision Revisited', provides a review of the issues.
[253] Ibid.

by supranationally-active lobbyists. Even if it were true that a supranational agency would be less prone to capture because of its greater
distance from regulated entities than a national agency, this could have
harmful implications in another direction because its remoteness could
make it less market sensitive and less able to engage constructively with
market participants in mutual problem-solving. That a regulatory
agency would deliver improvements in transparency and accountability
is not assured.[254]

The arguments for and against an EU securities regulatory agency are
not new[255] but they have recently begun to attract considerable attention
in academic and policy circles, and also amongst market participants.[256]
Superficially, views appear to split along national grounds, with the
French leading the proponents[257] and the British leading the opponents.[258] However, closer examination suggests that reported French
enthusiasm for a securities regulatory agency could be overstated.[259]

The European Commission has traditionally been opposed to the
establishment of regulatory agencies, understandably so since this could
entail an encroachment on its powers, but there are suggestions that blows
to the Commission's prestige and influence in recent years are producing
a change of attitude as ambitious Commission technocrats look to the
possibility of rechanneling their careers into independent agencies.[260]
In relation to securities market regulation, such a sea-change in the
Commission's attitude is not yet apparent. Although the Commission has

---

[254] Harlow, *Accountability*, pp. 75–8.

[255] See, e.g., K. J. Hopt, 'The Necessity of Co-ordinating or Approximating Economic Legislation, or of Supplementing or Replacing it by Community Law – A Report' (1976) 13
Common Market Law Review 245.

[256] See, e.g., Deutsche Bank Research, 'Reform of EU Regulatory and Supervisory Structures:
Progress Report' (2003) 4 *EU Monitor* (July 2003) (Financial Markets Special) 10, which
strongly endorses the case for a single EU regulatory and supervisory authority.

[257] P. Norman, 'EU Urged to Mull Single Financial Watchdog', *Financial Times*, 27 November 2002, p. 3 reporting results of a survey by the Paris-based Eurofi 2000 Association
(Eurofi, *An Integrated European Financial Market* (Survey, November 2002)) and British
reaction to it.

[258] 'A Ragbag'; 'Trojan Horses', *Economist*, 15 February 2003, p. 77. See also D. Green,
'Enhanced Co-operation among Regulators and the Role of National Regulators in a
Global Market' (2000) 2 *Journal of International Financial Markets* 7; R. M. Lastra, 'The
Governance Structure for Financial Regulation and Supervision in Europe' (2003) 10
Columbia Journal of Economic Law 49, 54–5.

[259] Parliamentary Select Committee on the European Union, *Towards a Single Market for
Finance: the Financial Services Action Plan* (45th Report, London, TSO, 2003) para. 91.

[260] Majone, 'Delegation', 329–30; Majone, 'Functional Interests', p. 323.

acknowledged that the option of a single authority to oversee securities markets supervision may eventually emerge as a meaningful proposition in the light of changing market reality,[261] for the moment it remains committed to the 'network'-based approach of the Lamfalussy process and has actively supported its extension into banking and insurance regulation.[262] A network approach to regulation, in which regulatory decisions are made on the basis of inputs from a range of sources rather than by a single, centralized body, is evident too elsewhere across the range of the Commission's policy-making activities.[263]

There are serious legal and practical obstacles in the path towards the establishment of an EU securities regulatory agency because this would probably require a Treaty change (although there is some difference of views on this point).[264] Whether or not a Treaty change is needed, were the idea of a pan-European securities regulatory agency to move up to the top of the policy agenda, the strong difference of views in Member States on its desirability would undoubtedly lead to long-running heated political debate and negotiations. For European policy-makers to risk getting sucked into a debate on an issue of such legal complexity and political tortuousness just at a time when the EU has established a workable alternative model for securities regulation and supervision could prove to be a serious mistake.

The timing is also wrong for another fundamentally important reason. The now conventional thinking that underpins the concentration of regulatory and supervisory authority in a single agency is that this is economically efficient and effective because it achieves a neat match between regulatory infrastructure and market conditions. In the context of bringing together responsibility for different parts of the financial services industry, this argument is framed in terms of the blurring of sectoral distinctions that renders sectorally fragmented regulation inappropriate. Blurring of sectoral boundaries is not an issue that is directly relevant to the European debate about a securities regulatory agency because, for the moment, EU regulation is still organised on a sectoral basis but the core of

---

[261] European Commission, *FSAP Action Plan*, p. 14.

[262] European Commission, *Financial Services: The FSAP Enters the Home Strait* (9th FSAP Progress Report, November 2003).

[263] O'Keefe and Carey, 'The Internal Market', p. 15. See further R. Dehousse, 'Regulation by Networks in the European Community: The Role of European Agencies' (1997) 4 *Journal of European Public Policy* 246.

[264] Avgerinos 'EU Financial Market Supervision Revisited'.

the thinking about unitary models of regulation – that regulatory systems should match the markets they are designed to regulate – is useful. It implies that a good starting point in thinking about whether an EU securities regulatory agency is appropriate is to ask whether the EU actually does have a single securities market. We do not find this in current European market conditions: wholesale financial markets are integrating and infrastructure providers such as exchanges are increasingly gearing up to operate transnationally but there is clear evidence that retail financial services in the EU are still fragmented along largely national lines.[265] Prospects for the immediate future are that fragmentation is likely to increase rather than diminish with the enlargement of the EU in May 2004 to include formerly Communist Eastern European and Baltic countries where securities market activity lags far behind the EU-15. From an economic perspective, therefore, it looks distinctly premature to push the case for a single regulatory agency when lack of market integration means that the expanding EU does not constitute a optimal area, in terms of its economic development, for its application.[266] Regulatory intervention ahead of the market is always fraught with difficulty. In this particular situation, the uncertain benefits flowing from the establishment of a single securities regulatory agency do not warrant the very considerable risks of mistakes in infrastructure planning that could significantly impede progress towards a properly integrated securities market.

F   Conclusions

This chapter has sought to consider whether post-Lamfalussy, the EU has in place a well-functioning securities regulatory machinery that is suitably designed for the delivery of high-quality legislation. Devising a regulatory system that is simultaneously efficient in substance (i.e. it delivers good rules), efficient in process (i.e. it works cost-effectively and promptly), legitimate and properly accountable raises major challenges whatever the legal environment. There are particular difficulties in a transnational context, such as that of the EU, because of strong perceptions of lack of legitimacy and poor accountability.

---

[265] See further ch. 2.
[266] Alexander, 'Establishing a European Securities Regulator'.

The broad conclusion is that, though not perfect, the Lamfalussy process is a step in the right direction. For the immediate future, the course of action that commends itself therefore is to concentrate on refining and upgrading the Lamfalussy process so as to enable it to work more efficiently and effectively. The Lamfalussy process has been openly described as one in which people are 'learning by doing' and CESR's Chairman has publicly said that it is just 'a good beginning'.[267] Gathering more evidence on existing practices and approaches in Member States before legislative proposals are brought forward and using this evidence to conduct regulatory impact analysis have been suggested as disciplines that could enhance the operation of the Lamfalussy process.[268] Incremental improvements of this sort seem more likely to advance the cause of good regulation than more radical alternatives. The establishment of an independent regulatory agency in place of the Lamfalussy process would not guarantee the correction of the known deficiencies. Moreover, consideration of the agency model looks distinctly premature in the light of prevailing economic market conditions across the expanding EU.

The Lamfalussy process is best seen as a pragmatic solution to a multi-dimensional, difficult problem. The regulatory challenge presented by the mismatch between slow-moving legislative machinery and dynamic securities markets is well known to securities market specialists. This challenge is encountered in an acute form in the EU because of the particularly cumbersome nature of its traditional legislative processes. Also familiar to securities market specialists is the fact that the issues that arise in relation to the regulation of technically sophisticated securities markets often require solutions that legislators, many steps removed from the markets, are not well-equipped to deliver. This issue, too, acquires a distinctive flavour when considered in the broad context of the EU. Across the board new collaborative methods of governance,[269] embracing dialogue and co-ordinated efforts at mutual problem-solving between the central institutions, national bodies, technical experts and other parties, are emerging in order to deal with the increasing complexity of the issues on the EU's

---

[267] A. Docters van Leeuwen, Speech by Chairman of CESR, 'A Network of Regulators to Meet the Challenges of Regulating European Capital Markets' (Ref.: CESR/03–055), Guildhall, London, 6 March 2003, text available via http://www.cesr-eu.org (accessed May 2004).

[268] Securities Expert Group, *FSAP: Progress*, pp. 10–11.

[269] 'Governance' in the EU context tends to be used to denote how the EU exercises its powers: Scott, 'The Governance of the European Union', 60–1 (criticising the partial nature of the EU's governance debate).

policy agenda.[270] At the same time, however, major policy questions are arising about the legitimacy of these new approaches,[271] as well as political battles over the position of the main EU institutions in emerging new governance structures. Against this background, the mere fact that a process that addresses the key, specialist problems – namely the need for a speedier and more technically sophisticated method of making regulation for securities markets – has gained a foothold rather than being submerged under a welter of policy concerns or bogged down in an inter-institutional power struggle can be counted as a significant achievement.

Giving a broad welcome to the Lamfalussy process implies not judging its deficiencies too harshly but, at the same time, it does not mean uncritical acceptance of how it operates. Foremost amongst its positive features is the establishment of a split between Level 1 and Level 2 legislation. In most fields of regulation there is a need for some form of executive, delegated rule-making machinery to fine-tune the regime and keep it broadly up to date; the need is acute in relation to securities markets because of their complexity and dynamism. The structure for controlling decisions about where to draw the line between Level 1 and Level 2 reflects political realities. As such, it seems inevitable that the line will sometimes be put in the 'wrong' place if judged from a detached, theoretical perspective but the system should be sufficiently robust to withstand some degree of misplacement. An optimistic prognosis is that misplacement problems will diminish as time goes on, as the Council and European Parliament become less wary of dropping matters down to Level 2 (and also to Level 3), and as CESR develops the capabilities to deal effectively with the resulting large workload.

The evidence to date suggests that separating 'technical' details from 'essential' elements has helped to speed up the initial rule-making process. Some speed/quality arbitrage has been spotted[272] but the root cause of this has been more to do with the FSAP deadlines (which pre-dated the Lamfalussy process) than with the process itself. Similarly, blame for poor-quality rules that were a fudged compromise concocted to satisfy sectarian national interests of Member States cannot strictly be laid at the feet of the Lamfalussy process, though it is unlikely to avoid becoming tainted by association.

---

[270] Scott, and Trubek, 'Mind the Gap'.
[271] Ibid.
[272] Select Committee, *Towards a Single Market*, paras. 43–5; P. Norman, 'EU Tries to Balance Quality and Haste', *FT.com*, 6 April 2003.

A system that makes it easier to write and amend rules could also be a system that lends itself to the production of a regime that is of poor quality because it is overly prescriptive and legalistic. Although concerns have been voiced about this, the few Level 2 measures passed to date do not support claims that the emerging post-FSAP regime is already too detailed. Yet the potential is clearly present for regulatory excess, particularly at Level 2 and Level 3 of the Lamfalussy process. Whether this potential is kept in check depends of a range of variables, such as how well informed those who have power to make the rules are about regulatory needs and how disciplined they are (or are required to be) in taking heed of the information at their disposal. It is therefore appropriate to emphasise the need for evidence-based law-making, regulatory impact assessments and feedback statements, although the strain that such requirements may place on already stretched resources does need to be recognised and addressed.

The effective operation of a network-based approach to rule-making, where regulatory decisions are informed by evidence and expert advice, depends on openness and dialogue between all interested parties. The Lamfalussy process has brought more openness into the securities law-making process and has engendered more systematic use of consultation mechanisms. Refinements are needed, but the early signs as regards procedural fairness are broadly encouraging. A potential weakness is the unevenness of representation in the policy and rule formation processes of investor groups as compared to industry lobbies. If left unchecked, in the longer term this could make the law-making process appear haphazard, if not unfairly selective.

The ties that bind the participants in the Lamfalussy process form a complex and delicate web. The interdependence of the various actors and the mechanisms by which they hold each other in check are still evolving. Indeed the whole Lamfalussy edifice presently rests on a shaky, temporary inter-institutional compromise over their respective involvement in the process and the mechanisms whereby they can control each other. The long term future may eventually be secured under the new EU Constitution but, in the meantime, the extension of the Lamfalussy process into banking and insurance regulation suggests that the controversy is dying down and that its place is becoming more secure on a de facto basis.

Within its specialist field, the Lamfalussy process can thus be seen as an ongoing attempt to reduce the tensions between the need for an efficient regulatory system characterised by speed, expertise and adaptability and the need for a system that is legitimate and properly accountable. The Lamfalussy process seeks to address some of the concerns about regulatory techniques that are expert-driven (such as the informality of networks and the lack of transparency about how they operate that can generate a sense of complexity and yield results that can appear arbitrary or tainted by self-interest).[273] As such, its operation over time could usefully inform more wide-ranging assessments of possible solutions to contemporary problems of regulatory legitimacy and accountability.

---

[273] S. Picciotto, 'Networks in International Economic Integration: Fragmented States and the Dilemmas of Neo-liberalism' (1997) 17 *Northwestern Journal of International Law and Business* 1014.

4

The centrality of disclosure as a regulatory strategy

A Scope of chapter

This chapter serves as an introduction to the remaining chapters, which examine the emerging new EU framework for the regulation and institutional oversight of issuer disclosure. This chapter explains why issuer disclosure merits particular attention and establishes the scope of the inquiry.

Disclosure as the first-choice regulatory strategy generally, and for issuers in particular

Disclosure philosophy has been described variously as the 'bedrock'[1] and as 'a – if not the – defining characteristic'[2] of US securities law. The EU has adopted a similar philosophical stance with disclosure being a fundamental tenet of its approach to the regulation of securities markets.[3] Disclosure occupies a central position in the EU's efforts to build the regulatory framework for an integrated pan-European securities market, and issuer disclosure is an important component of this overall strategy.

Functions that issuer disclosure regimes can perform

In principle issuer disclosure requirements can perform two key functions: to improve the accuracy of securities prices;[4] and to address corporate

---

[1] J. R. Macey, 'A Pox on Both Your Houses: Enron, Sarbanes-Oxley and the Debate Concerning the Relative Efficacy of Mandatory Versus Enabling Rules' (2003) 81 *Washington University Law Quarterly* 329, 330.

[2] S. M. Bainbridge, 'Mandatory Disclosure: A Behavioral Analysis' (2000) 68 *University of Cincinnati Law Review* 1023.

[3] K. Lannoo and A. Khachaturyan, *Disclosure Regulation in the EU: The Emerging Framework* (Brussels, Centre for European Policy Studies Task Force Report No. 48, October 2003) 1.

[4] M. B. Fox, A. Durnev, R. Morck and B. Yeung, 'Law, Share Price Accuracy and Economic Performance: The New Evidence', working paper (2003), ssrn abstract = 437662; E. Kitch, 'The Theory and Practice of Securities Disclosure' (1995) 61 *Brooklyn Law Review* 763.

governance agency problems.[5] These functions can overlap but they are also distinguishable.

Securities markets are driven by information and, according to the predominant theory explaining the efficiency of their operation, market prices rationally reflect publicly-available information.[6] Where information is not properly reflected in prices, prices can be inaccurate in the sense that they are misaligned to the fundamental value of securities.[7] Inaccurate prices can adversely affect investment decisions in primary and secondary capital markets thereby undermining the efficiency with which investment resources are allocated to competing projects to the detriment of the real economy.[8]

Inaccurate prices affect corporate governance by undermining the disciplining effect of markets on corporate management.[9] Systems of corporate governance where share ownership is dispersed rely on the market to exert a restraining influence on the exercise of managerial discretion. The theory is that managers should be incentivised or deterred by the knowledge that performance failures will be likely to affect adversely the value of their share-based remuneration and their chances of further reputationally-enhanced personal career progression, as well as their ability to raise new corporate finance on favourable terms. Further, where there is an active takeover market, there should be an additional corporate governance discipline in that poor managerial performance should increase vulnerability to hostile bids. However, where the share price flatters the management, the operation of these competitive market mechanisms is liable to be distorted because they rely on share prices as indicators of

[5] P. Mahoney, 'Mandatory Disclosure as a Solution to Agency Problems' (1995) 62 *University of Chicago Law Review* 1047.

[6] E. Fama, 'Efficient Capital Markets: A Review of the Theory and Empirical Work' (1970) 25 *Journal of Finance* 383.

[7] L. A. Stout, 'The Mechanics of Market Inefficiency: An Introduction to the New Finance' (2003) 28 *Journal of Corporation Law* 635, 640 defines 'fundamental' market efficiency as being where 'market prices mirror the best possible estimates, in light of all available information, of the actual economic values of securities in terms of their expected risks and returns'. See also on the meaning of 'market efficiency' J. D. Cox, R. W. Hillman and D. C. Langevoort, *Securities Regulation Cases and Materials* (3rd edn, New York, Aspen, 2001), pp. 28–31.

[8] M. B. Fox, 'Securities Disclosure in a Globalizing Market: Who Should Regulate Whom' (1997) 95 *Michigan Law Review* 2498, 2544–50; Fox, Durnev, Morck and Yeung, 'Law, Share Price Accuracy'.

[9] Fox, 'Securities Disclosure', 2544–50; and Fox, Durnev, Morck and Yeung, 'Law, Share Price Accuracy'.

current managerial performance. Equivalent distortive effects are also likely where securities are undervalued.[10]

Whilst there are corporate governance benefits in better pricing accuracy, it is possible also to identify a narrower corporate governance-orientated role for disclosure. Corporate governance agency problems exist between insiders (directors and/or controlling shareholders) and outside shareholders in that insiders may seek to run a company and use its assets for their own personal benefit rather than those of its general body of shareholders. Information asymmetries mean that shareholders face considerable difficulties in detecting and monitoring such abuse. Suitably tailored disclosure requirements can go some way towards redressing the balance by putting information about controllers' personal interests into the hands of shareholders. Armed with such disclosures, shareholders should be able to hold controllers more effectively to account.[11]

The policy choice, and how the EU has chosen to exercise it

A disclosure regime based primarily on the policy of seeking to resolve a narrowly defined range of agency problems would have a more manageable focus than one that attempted the more ambitious task of trying generally to promote the accuracy of securities prices.[12] There stems from this insight a view that designers of issuer disclosure regimes might do better to confine their efforts to finding solutions to defined agency problems than to attempt to grapple with potentially intractable problems concerning the identification of precisely those matters on which mandatory disclosure would be likely cost-effectively to improve pricing accuracy.[13] This argument reflects wider underlying uncertainty on the extent to which it is possible to justify regulatory intervention in the form of disclosure requirements as a desirable strategy based on the ability of such requirements efficiently to correct market failures in information-gathering

---

[10] Fox, Durnev, Morck and Yeung, 'Law, Share Price Accuracy'.

[11] M. B. Fox, 'Required Disclosure and Corporate Governance' (1999) 62 *Law and Contemporary Problems* 113.

[12] Disclosures relating to agency issues would be relevant to pricing and to that extent the distinction outlined has little significance: D. C. Langevoort, 'Managing the "Expectations Gap" in Investor Protection: the SEC and the Post-Enron Reform Agenda' (2003) 48 *Villanova Law Review* 1139, 1152. However it is meaningful the other way round – that is, the range of information relevant to price extends far beyond principal–agent related concerns and embraces the issuer and its prospects more generally.

[13] See Mahoney, 'Mandatory Disclosure'.

processes.[14] However, approaches advocating slimmed-down, agency problem-orientated mandatory disclosure regimes are normative suggestions rather than an accurate description of current regulatory practice around the world.[15]

The EU issuer disclosure regime conforms to the international norm because it is largely designed with a view to improving the accuracy of securities prices in the interests of investor protection and market efficiency.[16] This basic policy choice has resulted in a large disclosure regime for issuers with publicly traded securities, whereby they are subject to wide-ranging obligations to disclose information about their business operations, financial affairs, and prospects when they come to market, at periodic intervals thereafter and in response to certain events whose occurrence may move securities prices. In fact, it is only relatively recently that the EU has started explicitly to address corporate governance disclosures, such as in the area of directors' remuneration. Regulatory initiatives in the corporate governance field are intended to add to existing pricing accuracy-orientated disclosure requirements and they do not signal a policy shift in a new, more narrowly focused, direction.

---

[14] J. C. Coffee, 'Market Failure and the Economic Case for a Mandatory Disclosure System' (1984) 70 *Virginia Law Review* 717 provides the classic statement of the case for a mandatory disclosure system based on market failures. The issues remain contestable but for recent empirical evidence suggesting that mandatory disclosure can effectively contribute towards the accuracy of securities prices, see Fox, Durnev, Morck and Yeung, 'Law, Share Price Accuracy'.

[15] Mahoney, 'Mandatory Disclosure', 1049 argues that historically the principal purpose of issuer disclosure requirements in US securities law was to address certain agency problems arising between corporate promoters and investors, and between corporate managers and shareholders. He accepts that the accuracy-enhancement model later moved into the ascendancy in the US, thereby resulting in a modern regime which reflects shifting theoretical approaches.

[16] E.g. Directive 2003/71/EC of the European Parliament and of the Council of 4 November 2003 on the prospectus to be published when securities are offered to the public or admitted to trading and amending Directive 2001/34/EC, OJ 2003 No. L345/64 (Prospectus Directive), rec. 10 notes that the Directive aims to ensure investor protection and market efficiency. The European Central Bank noted that the Directive should 'ultimately ... enhance the capability of issuers to raise capital on an EU-wide basis by reducing the cost of financing and *improving the efficiency of the allocation of resources across the euro area*' (emphasis added): European Central Bank, *Opinion of the European Central Bank on a proposal for a Directive on the prospectus to be published when securities are offered to the public or admitted to trading* (CON/2001/36) OJ 2001 No. C344/5), para. 4.

How well does the EU manage the high risk of making regulatory mistakes? Analysing issuer disclosure provides an opportunity to test the Lamfalussy process for securities law-making

The existence of a large and ambitious issuer disclosure regime could suggest that EU rule-makers (like their counterparts elsewhere) are (over?)[17] - confident of their ability to come up with disclosure rules that will contribute on a cost-effective basis to more accurate securities prices or suggest that assessments of the difficulties involved in this selection process could be overstated. Alternatively, from a public choice perspective it could be taken to indicate the continuing effectiveness of the influence exerted by the lawyers, accountants, investment bankers and other powerful interests in the securities industry and the professions for whom an elaborate, vast disclosure regime through which issuers will need to be expertly navigated represents a lucrative business opportunity.[18]

Chapter 3 examined the EU's process for the making of securities laws and concluded that the system that is now in place (the 'Lamfalussy process'), though not perfect, is reasonably well-designed for the delivery of regulation that is sensitive to market needs and for holding in check regulatory tendencies towards bureaucratic excess or bias towards certain interest groups. Close examination of the new EU issuer disclosure rules that have been adopted pursuant to the Lamfalussy process (that is, the Prospectus Directive, Transparency Directive[19] and Market Abuse Directive[20]) provides an opportunity to test whether the quality of the rules that have emerged in a substantive area of central importance supports this assessment of the regulatory process. This examination is provided by

---

[17] Behavioural finance scholarship identifies over-optimism and over-confidence as cognitive biases that may contribute towards irrationality in securities markets: see, e.g. L. A. Cunningham, 'Behavioral Finance and Investor Governance' (2002) 59 *Washington & Lee Law Review* 767 and R. Prentice, 'Whither Securities Regulation? Some Behavioral Observations Regarding Proposals for its Future' (2001) 51 *Duke Law Journal* 1397. Investor irrationality tends to attract particular attention but, as various commentators have noted, regulatory agencies and other rule-makers are also vulnerable to over-confidence and other biases that could distort their decisions: Bainbridge, 'Mandatory Disclosure'; S. J. Choi and A. C. Pritchard, 'Behavioral Economics and the SEC' (2003) 56 *Stanford Law Review* 1.

[18] On disclosure as a form of over-regulation desired by the securities industry see J. R. Macey, 'Administrative Agency Obsolescence and Interest Group Formation: A Case Study of the SEC at Sixty' (1994) 15 *Cardozo Law Review* 909.

[19] Political agreement on the text of this Directive was secured in spring 2004 but it is not expected to be published in the Official Journal until autumn 2004.

[20] Directive 2003/6/EC of the European Parliament and of the Council of 28 January 2003 on insider dealing and market manipulation (market abuse), OJ 2003 No. L96/16.

chapter 5. The conclusions drawn in that chapter are not particularly encouraging: although certain aspects of the new regime represent an improvement on what was in place before, others, such as the treatment of non-EU issuers and of some specialist segments of market activity, appear ill-adapted to market conditions and could be counterproductive.

The importance of credible disclosure; and what the EU is doing about it by way of organisation of supervisory oversight of issuer disclosure

It is axiomatic that the practical utility of disclosure requirements is heavily dependent on the quality of compliance. Thus it would be a mistake to concentrate on the selection of those matters on which disclosure is to be mandated at the expense of paying attention to the mechanisms for ensuring the quality of issuer compliance. In principle there are numerous policy options for ensuring that rules are credible in the sense of being set within a system that contains enough incentives and deterrents to deliver adequate levels of full and frank disclosure. However, the existence of different legal traditions within the Member States of the EU and strong national sensitivities about their preservation precludes extensive reliance by EU policy-makers on one of the compliance-inducing options that national rule-makers ordinarily have at their disposal: detailed specification of legal sanctions for breach of disclosure obligations.[21] Instead the quality of the institutional oversight of issuer disclosure, and how it can be improved, are issues that occupy a more central position within EU policy debate.

This debate now recognises the systemic position of harmonised rules and that they must be supported by a greater degree of consistency in implementation and enforcement than has been the case within the EU historically if they are to become regarded as being genuinely pan-European. Chapter 6 reviews the policy steps that have been taken to promote supervisory convergence across the EU and identifies their limitations. It exposes a dilemma for EU Member States that flows from unevenness in supervision across the EU – although it may sometimes be advantageous for Member States to present a united, and hence stronger, front to the rest of the world, this runs the risk that other countries may treat the EU as a block for the purposes of supervisory reciprocity which is an outcome that could penalise those EU countries whose supervisory regimes are towards the top end of the EU quality spectrum.

---

[21] This issue is considered further in ch. 5.

The role of stock exchanges in the regulation and supervision of issuers within the EU

New EU issuer disclosure laws leave little room for exchanges to play a role in the regulation and supervision of issuers. The diminution of their role was partly driven by the argument that the number and diversity of organisations involved in regulation and supervision within the EU were impediments to convergence. In part it also reflected the EU's response to international debate about the continued appropriateness of relying on exchanges to perform public interest functions in an increasingly competitive market environment.

Chapter 7 questions whether the EU has gone too far in its exclusion of stock exchanges from the regulatory scene. International comparison indicates that the changing commercial position of exchanges need not be regarded as leading inevitably and inexorably to the conclusion that they must be stripped of all regulatory and supervisory functions. Furthermore, it is not clear that attainment of the goal of genuine EU market integration would be fatally undermined if stock exchanges were to be permitted to play a larger role under the supervision of independent regulatory agencies.

Issuer disclosure

A Scope of chapter

This chapter focuses on the new securities law disclosure regime for issuers.[1] The framework for these aspects of issuer disclosure within the EU is provided by the Prospectus Directive,[2] the Transparency Directive,[3] and the Market Abuse Directive.[4] These Directives are supplemented by implementing measures (in EU language, 'Level 2' legislation) that contain more detailed, technical rules to amplify the basic concepts provided for in the primary (or 'Level 1') legislation.

The Prospectus and Transparency Directives establish the regime for initial disclosure when securities are offered to the public or admitted to trading on a securities market, and for periodic financial disclosures by listed issuers. As complementary measures, they reflect broadly the same basic ideas and concepts, and provide similar responses on some controversial issues.

---

[1] Disclosure obligations on persons other than issuers, such as the requirement for persons offering securities or seeking admission of securities to trading to produce a prospectus, are therefore outside the scope of this chapter.

[2] Directive 2003/71/EC of the European Parliament and of the Council of 4 November 2003 on the prospectus to be published when securities are offered to the public or admitted to trading and amending Directive 2001/34/EC, OJ 2003 No. L345/64 ('Prospectus Directive' or 'PD' in these notes).

[3] Final political agreement on this Directive was secured in May 2004 but the text is not expected to be formally published in the Official Journal until autumn 2004. Translating the text into the numerous official languages of the expanded EU is a cause for delay. References to this Directive ('Transparency Directive' or 'TD') are to an unofficial version of the Directive which is available via http://europa.eu.int/comm/internal_market/en/finances/mobil/transparency/directive-unofficial_en.pdf (accessed May 2004).

    The Transparency Directive also revises Community law on the disclosure of interests in shares and makes provision for the dissemination of certain corporate governance information to shareholders and holders of debt securities, such as information about company meetings and proxy voting arrangements. This chapter concentrates on securities law disclosures.

[4] Directive 2003/6/EC of the European Parliament and of the Council of 28 January 2003 on insider dealing and market manipulation (market abuse), OJ 2003 No. L96/16 ('Market Abuse Directive' or 'MAD').

The Market Abuse Directive deals with timely disclosure of price sensitive information by issuers, as well as with insider dealing and market manipulation more generally. The Market Abuse Directive stands a little apart from the Prospectus and Transparency Directives in its conceptual approach, and it raises its own distinct concerns.

The approach adopted in this chapter is first to examine the Prospectus and Transparency Directives together, starting with some brief background (section B) and then focusing on potentially troubling features of the regime they establish. These are: high levels of prescription from the centre with little room for competition between Member States (section C); a policy on language standardisation (especially financial language) that could be damaging, particularly to the ability of EU markets to attract business from foreign issuers (section D); a special regime for specialist debt securities that is intended to preserve the lightly-regulated character of relevant markets but which could be sub-optimal because of the location of the threshold for the application of the regime (section E); arguably, too much weight to the informational needs of retail investors at the expense of wholesale market segments (section F); mixed messages on whether smaller and younger companies, and stock markets that cater for them, merit special treatment (section G); only tentative steps, but understandably so, into the sensitive area of harmonisation of liabilities and sanctions (section H); and, also, a cautious approach with regard to the promotion of centralised data collection and dissemination mechanisms (section I). Then section J adds remaining important pieces of the issuer disclosure jigsaw by providing a brief review of the timely disclosure requirement for issuers under the Market Abuse Directive. Section K concludes with some general reflections.

B   Prospectus and periodic disclosure: the legislative background and the emerging new regime

Regulation of issuer disclosure is a regulatory strategy that the EU has used for some time. Its first foray into this field under its programme of regulation for securities markets was a Directive relating to admission to official listing, which was adopted in 1979.[5] Incremental expansion of the securities laws on issuer disclosure took place at various intervals during

---

[5] Council Directive 79/279/EEC of 5 March 1979 coordinating the conditions for the admission of securities to official stock exchange listing, OJ 1979 No. L66/21 ('Admission Directive').

the 1980s, most notably with Directives regulating disclosures in public offer and admission to trading prospectuses and a Directive relating to the periodic disclosure obligations of issuers with officially listed shares.[6]

Various deficiencies in the EU prospectus and periodic disclosure regime emerged during the 1990s. In some respects the shortcomings were inherent in the original design[7] but there were also some problems stemming from the passage of time, whereby changes in market conditions had undermined certain of the assumptions that were part of its original foundations.[8] Thus, the old EU issuer disclosure rules provide a good illustration of the twin difficulties that policy-makers face in attempting to regulate securities markets: of devising good rules at the outset, and maintaining their quality in the face of often dynamic changes in market circumstances. Since the old regime is in the process of being dismantled and replaced, it is unnecessary at this point to dwell long on its various failings. Some of the issues that caused the most significant problems historically will emerge from the examination of the new regime. The new approach can be seen, at least in part, as an attempt to learn from the mistakes of the past.

The move towards a new regime for prospectuses and periodic disclosures began with a formal proposal for a new Directive on prospectuses, which was published by the Commission in 2001.[9] After considerable negotiation

---

[6] Chronologically, the disclosure requirements for admission to official stock exchange listing were addressed first: Council Directive 80/390/EEC of 17 March 1980 coordinating the requirements for the drawing up, scrutiny and distribution of the listing particulars to be published for the admission of securities to official stock exchange listing, OJ 1980 No. L100/1 ('Listing Particulars Directive'). Next came the regulation of ongoing disclosures by issuers of officially listed shares: Council Directive 82/121/EEC of 15 February 1982 on information to be published on a regular basis by companies the shares of which have been admitted to official stock exchange listing, OJ 1982 No. L48/26 ('Interim Reports Directive'). A later Directive extended disclosure requirements beyond the listed segment by imposing a general prospectus requirement in respect of all offers of securities to the public: Council Directive 89/298/EEC of 17 April 1989 coordinating the requirements for the drawing-up, scrutiny and distribution of the prospectus to be published when transferable securities are offered to the public, OJ 1989 No. L124/8 ('Public Offers Directive').

[7] The passporting regime, discussed in this chapter, is an example of inherently flawed design.

[8] Such as the outmoded distinction between the officially listed and other market segments, as discussed in this chapter. See also G. Ferrarini, 'Securities Regulation and the Rise of Pan-European Securities Markets: An Overview' in G. Ferrarini, K. J. Hopt and E. Wymeersch (eds.), *Capital Markets in the Age of the Euro* (London, Kluwer Law International, 2002), p. 272.

[9] European Commission, *Proposal for a Directive of the European Parliament and of the Council on the prospectus to be published when securities are offered to the public or admitted to trading* (COM (2001) 280).

(but not the protracted battles that characterised some earlier EU securities law initiatives), a Directive was finally adopted in November 2003 and published in the Official Journal on 31 December 2003. Member States must implement the Directive into their national law by 1 July 2005 and it is on transposition that the new regime will become effective as a matter of national law for EU issuers.[10] A rather curious feature of the Directive is that for non-EU issuers some aspects of the regime kicked into operation on publication in the Official Journal, that is on 31 December 2003.[11]

The Prospectus Directive is intended to facilitate 'the widest possible access to investment capital on a Community-wide basis, including for small and medium-sized enterprises (SMEs) and start-ups'.[12] It aims to 'ensure investor protection and market efficiency, in accordance with high regulatory standards adopted in the relevant international fora'.[13]

In March 2003 the Commission published its formal proposal to overhaul the periodic financial disclosure regime for listed issuers through the adoption of a Transparency Directive.[14] This Directive imposes obligations on issuers with securities admitted to trading on certain stock markets to publish audited annual financial information drawn up according to International Accounting Standards (IAS) (or, latterly, International Financial Reporting Standards or IFRS) or an equivalent set of accounting

---

[10] PD, art. 29.

[11] PD, art. 1(m)(iii) (determination of EU 'home' Member State). The implications of this timing issue are explored further in this chapter.

[12] PD, rec. 4.

[13] PD, rec. 10.

[14] European Commission, *Proposal for a Directive of the European Parliament and of the Council on the harmonisation of transparency requirements with regard to information about issuers whose securities are admitted to trading on a regulated market and amending Directive 2001/34/EC* (COM (2003) 138).

The Prospectus Directive also contains an annual updating requirement for issuers admitted to trading on a regulated market. They must provide a document containing or referring to all information published or made available over the preceding twelve months in compliance with securities laws and regulations: PD, art. 10. This document must be filed with the home State competent authority. Since this obligation involves gathering together already published information into one source (a website publication with hyperlinks to the original documents and stating that the original information may be out of date should suffice: Commission Regulation (EC) No. 809/2004 of 29 April 2004 implementing Directive 2003/71/EC of the European Parliament and of the Council as regards information contained in prospectuses as well as the format, incorporation by reference and publication of such prospectuses and dissemination of advertisements, OJ 2004 No. L149/1 ('Commission Prospectus Regulation'), art. 27), it is more of an administrative chore than an additional obligation of substance.

standards.[15] The Directive also requires such issuers to publish semi-annual financial information, similarly drawn up but with no mandatory requirement for auditing.[16] This Directive originally also proposed mandatory quarterly reporting but that proposal was downgraded during the legislative process.[17]

The Transparency Directive secured final political agreement in May 2004. This chapter is based on the agreed final text but makes some reference to earlier draft versions to indicate how thinking evolved during the legislative process.

The Transparency Directive echoes the policy aspirations of the Prospectus Directive with regard to the building of sustained investor confidence and enhanced market efficiency.[18]

C Building a comprehensive, standardised disclosure regime at the expense of loss of opportunities for competition between Member States – a move in the right direction?

Prospectus disclosure requirements – a new world of 'maximum harmonisation'

The Prospectus Directive seeks to impose an exhaustive disclosure regime that applies uniformly across the whole of the EU and leaves no room for Member States to impose additional requirements on issuers. Standardisation of information within a sophisticated market necessarily means having multiple sets of disclosure requirements to cater for varying investor informational needs in different market segments. The EU has certainly attempted to provide an appropriate degree of calibration within its issuer disclosure regime. As a consequence, its rules on the content of prospectuses have been drafted to a level of detail that is unprecedented in EU securities disclosure laws.[19]

---

[15] TD, art. 4.

[16] TD, art. 5.

[17] TD, art. 6. In its final form this requires issuers that do not publish quarterly financial reports to publish interim management statements explaining material events and transactions and giving a general description of their financial position and performance during the relevant period.

[18] TD, rec. 1.

[19] The Listing Particulars Directive was the most detailed previous attempt. Its three schedules provided layouts for listing particulars relating to shares, debt securities and certificates

There is a mandatory general duty of disclosure imposed by the Prospectus Directive itself[20] and detailed disclosure requirements contained in a lengthy Regulation adopted by the Commission.[21] The Commission Prospectus Regulation is a Level 2 implementing measure under the Lamfalussy process.[22] The use of a Regulation as the form of legal instrument for the specification of the detailed disclosure requirements is significant from a standardisation perspective because, unlike Directives, Regulations apply directly in Member States and thus there is no opportunity for subtle differences in the interpretation of the rules to creep in through the process of national transposition.

The approach taken in the Commission Prospectus Regulation is to provide a series of schedules and building blocks containing additional information that issuers must combine in order to draft their prospectus.[23] The combination required in any case depends on the type of issuer and security concerned. Three main dividing lines in the schedules are between those that relate to shares,[24] those that relate to debt and derivative securities with a denomination per unit of less than €50,000,[25] and those that relate to debt and derivative securities with a denomination per unit of at least €50,000.[26] There are also separate schedules for specialist types of securities, such as asset-backed securities,[27] and for certain types of issuer, such as banks,[28] States[29] and other public bodies.[30] The building blocks

---

representing shares. However, this Directive did not attempt fully to get to grips with the complexities of different types of issuers and sophisticated sub-categories of equity, debt and hybrid securities. It did not need to because, unlike the Prospectus Directive, which is meant to be exhaustive, the Listing Particulars Directive was a minimum harmonisation measure that allowed Member States to add their own additional requirements.

[20] PD, art. 5.1.

[21] Commission Prospectus Regulation or 'CPR' in these notes.

[22] Ch. 3 considers the Lamfalussy process.

[23] CPR, arts. 3 and 21.

[24] CPR, art. 4 and Annex 1 (share registration document schedule); art. 6 and Annex III (share securities note schedule).

[25] CPR, art. 7 and Annex IV (securities registration document schedule); art. 8 and Annex V (securities note schedule); art. 15 and Annex XII (derivative securities note schedule). Where, as in the case of derivative securities, there is no individual denomination, the dividing line is based on whether the minimum subscription price is below or at least €50,000.

[26] CPR, art. 12 and Annex IX (securities registration document schedule); art. 16 and Annex XIII (securities note schedule); art. 15 and Annex XII (derivative securities note schedule).

[27] CPR, art. 10 and Annex VII. There is also an asset-backed securities building block: art. 11 and Annex VIII.

[28] CPR, art. 14 and Annex XI.

[29] CPR, art. 19 and Annex XVI.

[30] CPR, art. 19 and Annex XVI; art. 20 and Annex XVII.

include one for pro-forma financial information required for certain major transactions,[31] and one for guarantees.[32]

The detailed disclosure requirements are based on the IOSCO international disclosure standards for share issues[33] and also build upon the disclosure requirements that applied under previous Directives.[34] The EU has moved towards the IOSCO Standards in a conscious effort to simplify the procedure for Community issuers wishing to raise cross-border capital.[35] As well as facilitating cross-border issuance within the EU, the move towards IOSCO standards should be helpful for EU issuers that want to make offerings into the US because it should position them to take advantage of SEC dispensations in respect of foreign issuers' disclosures.[36]

For certain types of issuer, including start-up companies, the Commission Prospectus Regulation is not wholly prescriptive. Instead it delegates authority to the competent authorities in Member States to adapt the information that is required, taking into consideration the specific nature of the activities involved.[37] Reflecting evident European Commission unease about encroachments upon the intended exhaustive nature of the specific disclosure requirements, the Commission has sought to highlight the restrictive character of this derogation.[38]

The same unease underlies the approach to the treatment of new securities not fitting within the established schedules and building blocks. Market ingenuity and creativity mean that the emergence of such securities is a

---

[31] CPR, art. 5 and Annex II (pro-forma financial information building block). Pro-forma financial information is usually required where a transaction will change the situation of an issuer by more than 25 per cent relative to one or more indicators of its size: CPR, rec. 9.

[32] CPR, art. 9 and Annex VI (guarantees building block).

[33] International Organization of Securities Commissions, *International Disclosure Standards for Cross-Border Offerings and Initial Listings by Foreign Issuers* (IOSCO, 1998), available via http://www.iosco.org/pubdocs/pdf/IOSCOPD81.pdf (accessed June 2004).

[34] Committee of European Securities Regulators, *Advice on Level 2 Implementing Measures for the Prospectus Directive* (CESR/03–208, 2003), para. 22.

[35] PD, rec. 22.

[36] J. D. Cox, R. W. Hillman and D. C. Langevoort, *Securities Regulation Cases and Materials* (3rd edn, New York, Aspen, 2001), pp. 326–8.

[37] CPR, art. 23 and Annex XIX.

[38] CPR, rec. 22 provides that adapted information should be appropriate and proportionate to the type of business involved. See also European Commission, *Main differences between the Commission draft regulation on draft implementing rules for the prospectus Directive and the CESR advice* (ESC / 42/2003-rev2) where the Commission lays out its justification for rejecting a broader power that had been recommended by CESR. This document is available via http://www.europa.eu.int/comm/internal_market/securities/prospectus/index_en.htm (accessed June 2004).

highly likely occurrence, and the Commission has had to bow to the near inevitability of the detailed regulatory framework sometimes lagging behind market developments. The solution adopted is that national competent authorities have some discretion with regard to the disclosure rules they apply to new types of securities[39] but, at the same time, they are obliged to find similarities and make as much use as possible of the existing schedules.[40]

Subject to restricted derogations such as these, the disclosure requirements are comprehensively prescribed and cannot be added to by any Member State.[41] In 'Eurospeak' the Prospectus Directive has for this reason become known as a 'maximum harmonisation' Directive. The exhaustive approach is in sharp contrast to the previous EU prospectus disclosure regime, which set minimum disclosure requirements but left room for Member States to add their own additional disclosure requirements. An aspect of that old regime, which was rooted in the minimum harmonisation approach, had proved to be an impediment to the use of prospectuses on a cross-border basis within the EU. However, maximum harmonisation, as now employed, is open to the criticism of being an over-reaction to the problems that had arisen.

Under the old regime, it was theoretically possible to use a prospectus that had been approved in one Member State for issuance or listing activity in other Member States. However, in practice issuers found that obtaining approval from one State was not in fact sufficient because other relevant Member States would ask for additional information tailored to their national market. This was permitted under the old regime so long as the additional information requested related to local income tax, paying agency arrangements or the mechanisms for publishing notices to investors. Compliance with additional local disclosure requirements of host Member States added to the overall costs of cross-border activity and, combined with translation burdens, served to act as a considerable disincentive to use of the prospectus passport mechanism.[42]

---

[39] CPR, art. 23.3.

[40] CPR, rec. 23.

[41] PD, recs. 15 and 20 (though the point is not especially obvious). There is provision for competent authorities on a case-by-case basis as part of the prospectus approval process to require supplementary information to be included in a prospectus if necessary for investor protection: PD, art. 21.3(a); however, generally applicable additional requirements are not permitted.

[42] For an early, influential discussion of this problem see Forum of European Securities Commissions, A 'European Passport' for Issuers: Consultation Paper (FESCO/99-098e, 2000) which is available via http://www.cesr-eu.org (accessed May 2004).

A simple solution to the specific problem encountered in practice would have been to have removed the possibility for Member States to impose additional disclosure requirements on issuers whose prospectuses had satisfied the requirements for approval in another Member State. The Prospectus Directive does this,[43] but it goes further by also banning the approving Member State from imposing its own disclosure requirements beyond those mandated by, or under, the Directive. Thus even for purely single-State offers or listings that have no cross-border dimension, the disclosure rules are fixed at EU level and there is no scope for the exercise of national discretion to impose additional requirements. So far as cross-border access for issuers is concerned, a prohibition on host Member States imposing additional disclosure requirements beyond those required by the approving Member State would have been sufficient to open up the market; maximum harmonisation goes beyond what is needed for this purpose and is thus arguably a disproportionate response.[44]

Why did the EU opt for comprehensive maximum harmonisation? Background documentation leaves the impression that the case for it was based more on intuition and aspiration regarding the perceived benefits of standardisation than on the establishment of a clear need to solve an immediate practical problem.[45] For instance the Commission simply asserted that: 'adequate and equivalent disclosure standards should be in place in all European Member States when securities are offered to the public or traded on regulated markets. This implies that the existing disclosure standards need to be aligned in order to introduce the same standards for the public offer of securities and admission to trading

---

[43] PD, arts. 17–18: a prospectus which is approved by the issuer's home State is valid throughout the EU subject only to the host State receiving notification from the home State that the prospectus has been drawn up in accordance with the Directive and a copy of the prospectus.

[44] It has been argued that maximum harmonisation is needed to prevent Member States from blocking the sale to their investors of a bond or share issue that has been approved in another EU country: Letter to the *Financial Times* by Christopher Huhne MEP, published 4 September 2002. This argument appears to conflate two distinct issues: (i) whether the approving State should be constrained from imposing additional disclosure requirements; and (ii) whether other Member States, apart from the approving State, should be so constrained.

On the disproportionate nature of maximum harmonisation: K. Lannoo, 'The Emerging Framework for Disclosure in the EU' [2003] *Journal of Corporate Law Studies* 329, 345.

[45] J. D. Cox, 'Regulatory Duopoly in US Securities Markets' (1999) 99 *Columbia Law Review* 1200, 1251 notes that there are few truths in formulating disclosure policy and that intuition, experience and culture are important factors.

throughout the Union, in accordance with the principle of maximum harmonisation.'[46]

Standardisation of prospectus information through maximum harmonisation certainly could be beneficial. Having exactly the same rules applying across the entirety of the EU could help to erode national biases in investment decisions by simplifying the comparability of prospectus information.[47] Gains in terms of clarity and simplicity of pan-European information[48] could facilitate the smooth flow of savings to the most deserving investment projects across the entirety of the EU market.[49] Although maximum harmonisation is not strictly essential to the operation of the issuer passport, the passport's usefulness in practice could be enhanced by it because of its impact on investor behaviour – the practical benefits of a prospectus that is valid across borders are liable to disappear if investors are disinclined to consider the offer because of the complexities of evaluating information by comparative reference to prospectus information with which they are familiar in their home market.

Yet standardisation through maximum harmonisation comes at the expense of the potentially beneficial contribution of Member States' initiatives to the development of prospectus disclosure requirements. The process for making securities laws in the EU has improved considerably in recent years[50] but, however optimistically it is regarded, it is clearly still vulnerable to political compromises and other adverse influences that may detract from the quality of the legal rules it produces. Furthermore, the ability of the improved law-making process to act quickly to update rules that have fallen behind the market is untested. Even if the law-making process works as well as can be reasonably expected of it, it is

---

[46] European Commission, *Amended proposal for a Directive of the European Parliament and of the Council on the prospectus to be published when securities are offered to the public or admitted to trading and amending Directive 2001/34/EC* (COM (2002) 460), explanatory memorandum, p. 3. See also, Forum of European Securities Commissions, *A European Passport for Issuers: Report* (FESCO/00–138b, 2000), para. 7.2.

[47] N. Moloney, 'Confidence and Competence: The Conundrum of EC Capital Markets Law' [2004] *Journal of Corporate Law Studies* 1.

[48] Financial Services Authority, *Review of the Listing Regime* (Consultation Paper No. 203, 2003), para. 5.7

[49] Cox, 'Regulatory Duopoly', pp. 1211–17; J. C. Coffee, 'Racing Towards the Top? The Impact of Cross-Listings and Stock Market Competition on International Corporate Governance' (2002) 102 *Columbia Law Review* 1757, 1827–8. Compare S. J. Choi, 'Assessing Regulatory Responses to Securities Market Globalization' (2001) 2 *Theoretical Inquiries in Law* 613, 632–5 (for a more sceptical assessment of the benefits of standardisation).

[50] See ch. 3.

unlikely to produce disclosure rules that are, and are always maintained at, the highest standards expected by the international investment community. So what? It is the fate of all regulatory regimes to lag behind dynamic markets; and all law-making processes are vulnerable to distortions flowing from the preferences and underlying agenda of the individuals and bodies involved in them, so it would be unfair to single out the EU for criticism on these grounds alone. However, the point here is that, by imposing maximum harmonisation, the EU has deliberately forgone a mechanism that could have alleviated deficiencies in its laws, namely intervention by Member States to exceed the general EU-wide standards.

Maximum harmonisation was not the only option. As noted previously, the EU authorities could have improved the passport regime by banning the imposition of additional host State requirements on approved prospectuses but left room for approving Member States to require additional disclosures as preconditions to the granting of prospectus approval. EU policy-makers could have taken the view that the better formulated the general regime the less incentive there would be for Member States to seek to exceed it and thus concentrated on doing their best, within the limitations of the legislative process available to them, to upgrade the prospectus disclosure regime to a good international standard. That done, they could then have reasoned that allowing approving Member States some discretion to add their own additional disclosure requirements was a useful sideline that would not seriously undermine the standardisation principle because, realistically, it would only be used in limited circumstances: to plug gaps in the EU regime (possibly as a precursor to EU-wide change); or where, on the basis of (presumably) a finely judged balancing exercise, a particular Member State concluded that, notwithstanding the quality of the general regime, the potential advantages of providing prospectus disclosure rules tougher than the norm outweighed the potential unattractiveness to issuers of a regime exceeding the EU requirements.[51]

This, though, is to argue for a system that is unlikely to be adopted in the foreseeable future. Having adopted maximum harmonisation so recently and so emphatically, it seems unrealistic to expect a rapid change of direction in EU regulatory policy with regard to prospectuses. Although the high level of prescription from the centre that is inherent in maximum harmonisation sits uneasily with EU concepts of subsidiarity

---

[51] On the use of high standards as a regulatory strategy to attract business: Coffee, 'Racing'.

and proportionality, constitutional challenges on these grounds are hard to sustain.[52]

There may be some scope for Member States to side step the maximum harmonisation effect of the Prospectus Directive by recasting disclosure requirements that are outside the Directive in the form of substantive criteria that must be satisfied by issuers seeking admission to trading on a regulated market.[53] There is some EU-wide control over admission criteria but this is in minimum harmonisation form and does not pre-clude tougher national standards.[54] For Member States to have to resort to this sort of stratagem could be regarded as signalling a flaw within the basic regulatory framework, yet it is doubtful whether it would be sufficiently controversial to spark a momentum for change.

But compare the Transparency Directive

It is striking that, although they are in many respects parts of a single package, the Transparency Directive does not adopt the same maximal approach as the Prospectus Directive. Instead this Directive provides that home Member States may impose requirements that are more stringent than the Directive but host Member States may not.[55] This difference prompts the obvious question: why not a maximal approach?

Maximum harmonisation promotes information standardisation but at the expense of national intervention that could improve the flow of information to investors. This suggests that the non-maximal character of the Transparency Directive could have been the result of a careful weighing of the benefits of standardisation of periodic information against the costs inherent in the rigidity of maximum harmonisation. It is doubtful, how-ever, whether the Transparency Directive's character reflects this sort of assessment. A more compelling explanation for the difference between the Prospectus Directive and the Transparency Directive in this respect is that it was a pragmatic response to the political impossibility of eliminating

---

[52] T. Tridimas, *The General Principles of EC Law* (Oxford, Oxford University Press, 1999), pp. 118–23.

[53] The freedom to do this is expressly acknowledged in PD, rec. 15. However, this provides that admission requirements may not directly or indirectly restrict the drawing up, content and dissemination of a prospectus. It is conceivable that this proviso might be used to strike down too-obvious attempts to evade the intended maximum harmonisation effect of the Prospectus Directive.

[54] Admission Directive, later consolidated into Directive 2001/34/EC of the European Parliament and of the Council of 28 May 2001 on the admission of securities to official stock exchange listing and on information to be published on those securities, OJ 2001 No. L184/1 ('CARD').

[55] TD, art. 3.

the quite significant differences in established periodic disclosure regimes in EU Member States. The UK *Listing Rules*, for example, impose significant periodic disclosure obligations above the level set by the Transparency Directive.[56] In theory the European Commission could have proposed a maximum harmonisation measure either to impose UK-style periodic disclosure requirements across the EU as a whole or to realign the UK's regime with that in other Member States; either way it seems likely that any such proposal would have been killed off under an avalanche of criticism and controversy.

If it is correct to view the non-maximal character of the Transparency Directive as having been driven more by pragmatism than by principle, this suggests that the position could be temporary and that the periodic disclosure aspects of the issuer disclosure regime within the EU might eventually also be switched over onto a maximal basis.[57] Despite the scepticism about maximum harmonisation expressed thus far in this chapter, it has to be acknowledged that the arguments for its extension to periodic disclosure obligations would become harder to resist if, in the coming years, there is de facto convergence around the Directive's disclosure requirements and Member States do not choose to exploit the freedom to impose additional requirements.[58] In assessing this possibility, it is important to pay close attention to the true scope of this freedom. Since it is a freedom enjoyed only by 'home' Member States, the rules on how

---

[56] See, generally, Financial Services Authority, *Review* (Consultation Paper), pp. 37–41. Currently the most stringent rules apply to UK issuers. There are some relaxations for foreign issuers with a primary listing in the UK (on disclosure: accounts can be in local GAAP; no obligation to provide a comply or explain statement in respect of the Combined Code on Corporate Governance); and the regime is further relaxed for foreign issuers with a secondary listing in the UK.

[57] There are already indications that in some quarters the Transparency Directive's different approach is regarded as a staging-post pending the emergence of a political climate favourable to the extension of maximum harmonisation. See, e.g., European Economic and Social Committee, *Opinion on the Proposal for a Directive of the European Parliament and of the Council on the harmonisation of transparency requirements with regard to information about issuers whose securities are admitted to trading on a regulated market and amending Directive 2001/34/EC*, OJ 2004 No. C80/128 (arguing that minimum harmonisation in the Transparency Directive is one stage in the process but that the goal should continue to be maximum harmonisation).

[58] Rather than simply relying on collective memory to ensure that such an important strategic issue is properly evaluated on an ad hoc basis, attention might usefully be given by EU policy-makers to a suggestion on the drafting of general conditions under which the use of maximum harmonisation would be justifiable: M. Levin, *EU Financial Regulation and Supervision Beyond 2005: An Agenda for the New Commission* (Brussels, Centre for European Policy Studies, 2004).

issuers' home States are determined necessarily come to the foreground in this discussion.

In principle, Member States might see some potential advantages in pursuing a competitive strategy of attempting to attract business from issuers and investors through high periodic disclosure requirements.[59] However, the degree of enthusiasm for such a strategy is obviously likely to be strongly affected by the extent to which disclosure requirements can act as a magnet for listing business from issuers. If, or to the extent that, issuers are not free to choose a high disclosure country as their home State, the strategy loses appeal. In fact, the Transparency Directive does reduce the scope for issuer choice with respect to the selection of home States for the purposes of EU securities disclosure laws. This feature could make it less likely that Member States will wish to impose higher disclosure standards on their home issuers and thus lead to de facto convergence around the Directive.

This point requires elaboration by way of an excursion into the rules for the determination of 'home' States. This excursion first takes us back to the Prospectus Directive because this measure establishes the scheme which is then followed in the Transparency Directive too.

Allocation of regulatory and supervisory responsibilities for issuers amongst the competent authorities of EU Member States

Prospectus Directive – identification of home State is important for supervisory rather than regulatory purposes (because the rules are the same)

A lively debate has recently raged in US law journals over radical proposals to shake up securities regulation by allowing issuers freedom to choose the disclosure regime applicable to their securities offerings.[60] At first glance,

---

[59] Coffee, 'Racing', develops the bonding thesis explanation for cross-listing – that a motivation for some issuers to migrate to particular exchanges is that by voluntarily subjecting themselves to higher disclosure standards and greater threat of enforcement in that jurisdiction, they may compensate for weaknesses in their domestic regulatory environment and thereby achieve a higher market valuation.

[60] R. Romano, 'Empowering Investors: A Market Approach to Securities Regulation' (1998) 107 *Yale Law Journal* 2359 (advocating issuer choice for US and foreign issuers over the legal regime governing transactions in their securities); R. Romano, 'The Need for Competition in International Securities Regulation' (2001) 2 *Theoretical Inquiries in Law* 387 (developing the case for issuer choice in an international context); S. J. Choi and A. T. Guzman, 'Portable Reciprocity: Rethinking The International Reach of Securities Regulation'

this debate looks somewhat removed from recent developments within the European Union with regard to prospectus disclosure. As already noted, the new Prospectus Directive represents a reinvigorated effort by the EU finally to achieve the goal of having uniform disclosure rules across the region. Issuer choice, so far as choosing between the prospectus disclosure regimes of Member States of the EU is concerned, looks like an irrelevance because, thanks to maximum harmonisation, the disclosure rules are the same in any event.

However, the issuer choice debate found an echo in the EU debate on the new prospectus disclosure regime with regard to questions about the national identity of competent authorities responsible for supervising prospectus disclosure, including pre-publication approval of prospectuses. In the absence of a pan-European securities regulatory authority, supervisory responsibilities within the EU must necessarily be devolved down to national authorities. There are varying levels of expertise and experience in dealing with prospectuses, particularly those relating to specialist securities, amongst EU national securities regulators. In principle, issuers might want to be able to associate themselves with the

---

(1998) 71 *Southern California Law Review* 903 (advocating a system of portable reciprocity whereby issuers could select the regulatory regime that will govern their securities. Once the regime is selected and the issuer has complied with its requirements, securities transactions may commence in any location. The firm, therefore, is able to select a regime and have the regime 'travel' with the securities it issues. For this reason, its authors term the regime 'portable' reciprocity). The Choi & Guzman and Romano proposals share some common ground but are not identical (see S. J. Choi, 'Assessing Regulatory Responses to Securities Market Globalization' (2001) 2 *Theoretical Inquiries in Law* 613, fn. 7). A different proposal is that securities law should follow issuer nationality: M. B. Fox, 'Securities Disclosure in a Globalizing Market: Who Should Regulate Whom' (1997) 95 *Michigan Law Review* 2498 and M. B. Fox, 'The Political Economy of Statutory Reach: US Disclosure Rules in a Globalizing Market for Securities' (1998) 97 *Michigan Law Review* 696; M. B. Fox, 'Retaining Mandatory Securities Disclosure: Why Issuer Choice is Not Investor Empowerment' (1999) 85 *Virginia Law Review* 1335, 1414–17.

Doubts about enforcement represent the Achilles heel of issuer choice theories: how can officials of State X overcome major political and international law barriers to enforcing State X's standards in State Y in respect of issuers that have chosen State X's law; even assuming such difficulties can be overcome, would authorities in State X be willing to expend scarce resources on enforcement in respect of activity that has no substantial connection to State X; would officials of State Y have appropriate political incentives to engage in rigorous enforcement of State X's standards; and, even if they are willing, would State Y's officials be good enforcers of State X's standards given their likely unfamiliarity with them? On these and related questions: Cox, 'Regulatory Duopoly', 1239–44; B. S. Black, 'The Legal and Institutional Preconditions for Strong Securities Markets' (2001) 48 *UCLA Law Review* 781, 843–5; J. C. Coffee, 'Law and Regulatory Competition: Can They Co-exist?' (2002) 80 *Texas Law Review* 1729, 1733–4.

high (or low) reputation of a particular national regulator by choosing it as their prospectus supervisor. Whether they should be allowed such freedom was heavily debated during the passage of the Prospectus Directive into law.

Identifying an issuer's EU home State for the Prospectus Directive

Under the old EU rules on prospectuses, issuers were tied to the State of their registered office for supervisory purposes only where they were listing or offering their securities in that State. Where they were not, they could choose their supervisory authority from amongst the regulatory authorities in the States where they were applying for listing or making their offer.[61] The basic rule in the new Prospectus Directive is more rigid: permanent home State control which, for EU-incorporated issuers, means the Member State where their registered office is situated.[62] For non-EU issuers, in broad terms there is a one-off opportunity to choose their EU home State but they are then tied permanently and irrevocably to whichever State they have chosen.[63] The rules are modified for issues of debt securities with a minimum denomination of €1,000 but the discussion in this section is confined to the basic situation.[64]

Where the Prospectus Directive led, the Transparency Directive (broadly) followed

In the interests of consistency, the rules adopted in the Prospectus Directive on the identification of issuers' home States were then broadly incorporated into the Transparency Directive without much debate on the desirability in principle of issuer choice as regards associating with particular national periodic disclosure regimes.[65] So, for an EU issuer that has shares or low-denomination (in this case less than €1,000) debt securities admitted to

---

[61] Listing Particulars Directive, art. 15 (CARD, art. 37); Public Offers Directive, art. 20 (but regulatory approval of unlisted public offer prospectuses was only required in those (rare) cases where issuers sought to rely on the passport in cross-border offers). See further E. Pan, 'Harmonization of US–EU Securities Regulation: The Case for a Single European Securities Regulator' (2003) 34 *Law and Policy in International Business* 499, 507.

[62] PD, art. 2.1(m)(i). Host States can take precautionary measures against incoming issuers to protect investors: PD, art. 23.

[63] PD, art. 2.1(m)(iii).

[64] The relaxation of the basic rules for debt securities with a minimum denomination of €1,000 is discussed further later in this chapter.

[65] TD, art. 2.1(i). Host States can take precautionary measures against incoming issuers to protect investors: TD, art. 22.

trading on a regulated market anywhere in the EU, the applicable periodic disclosure requirements and associated supervisory regime are thus those of its State of incorporation (based on the location of its registered office), not its State(s) of trading. For a non-EU issuer, the relevant periodic disclosure requirements and accompanying supervisory regime are that of the EU Member State which it has designated as its home State for the purposes of the Prospectus Directive. The trading States, i.e., the host States, are forbidden from imposing their own additional disclosure requirements[66] because this would undermine the passport concept – cross-border listing within the EU would likely remain unattractive if the principle of having to comply with just one set of standards were confined to initial disclosure because the prospect of having to satisfy multiple different sets of periodic disclosure requirements thereafter would act as a significant deterrent.

Concerns about the rigidity of the rules on the determination of home States

Consistency in the allocation of supervisory responsibilities for initial and ongoing securities disclosures makes sense. However, an underlying problem with the rules adopted in the Prospectus Directive, and applying consequentially for the Transparency Directive too, is the questionable assumption that achievement of this goal necessarily requires EU issuers to be tied rigidly to the State of their registered office and non-EU issuers to be permanently tied to a designated EU Member State.

The official justification for this reduction of issuer mobility is that States are assumed to be in the best position to regulate and supervise those issuers that have their registered office within their jurisdiction.[67] However, specific empirical evidence supporting the assertion of State of registered office superiority in this respect is difficult to find. On the contrary, it can be argued that EU experience under the old regime, whereby issuers were linked for prospectus approval purposes either to their registered-office State or to the State of the offer/admission of securities, in fact undercuts the claim: regulatory authorities seem to have managed for many years to assume supervisory responsibilities in respect of issuers from other Member States or third countries without any notable difficulty.[68]

---

[66] Member States are not prohibited from imposing more stringent standards on incoming issuers otherwise than in the area of disclosure.

[67] PD, rec. 14.

[68] European Economic and Social Committee, *Opinion on the Proposal for a Directive on the harmonisation of transparency requirements*, sec. 4.

Tying EU issuers in this way means that, in effect, national regulators are shielded from competition by their monopoly with regard to their home issuers. They will thus have little incentive to improve their efficiency and effectiveness.[69] Rigid adherence to the registered-office State principle also gives rises to technical difficulties in relation to multiple issuer programmes since, if those issuers have their registered offices in different EU Member States, this raises the spectre of cumulative approval being required by several competent authorities.[70] There is an obvious inconsistency as between EU issuers (that have the choice of best-placed supervisory authority made for them) and non-EU issuers (that at least have a one-off opportunity to make the choice for themselves).

Combining the rigid rules on home States with the language scheme established by the Directives reveals results that are not necessarily conducive to the achievement of high standards in the quality of issuer information. Take, for example, an issuer incorporated in Member State A which wants to make an offer of its shares only in Member State B. For the sake of argument only, let us say that State A is Greece and that State B is the UK, to which the issuer is attracted because of its deeper capital market. Under the language scheme mandated by the Prospectus Directive, there is every likelihood that the prospectus will be drawn up in English,[71] thus presenting the Greek authority with the problem of having to grapple with a complex, technical document written in a language which is unlikely to be the mother-tongue of the officials who are dealing with it. The Greek authority may well know more about the issuer and its operations than its counterpart in the UK (though not necessarily so if the bulk of the issuer's activities is located outside Greece) but, even if it does, it cannot be assumed that its superior background knowledge of the issuer will outweigh the language difficulties.[72]

---

[69] Ibid.

[70] Ibid.

[71] PD, art. 19.2 provides that in this situation for the purpose of the scrutiny by the Greek authorities, the prospectus must be drawn up in a language acceptable to the Greek authorities or a language customary in the sphere of international finance, at the option of the issuer. For the general purposes of satisfying the Directive, the prospectus must be in a language accepted by the UK authority or a language customary in the sphere of international finance, again at the issuer's option. On all counts, the odds are surely overwhelmingly in favour of the issuer choosing to write its prospectus in English.

[72] PD, art. 13.5 provides for the competent authority of the home State to transfer the approval of a prospectus to the competent authority of another Member State. It is possible that use might be made of this power in this type of case; but it is not yet clear exactly how regulators will use this power in practice.

A further point can also be made: will officials of State A have appropriate incentives to care sufficiently about the information in a prospectus relating to an issue that will be made only to investors in State B to do a good job in discharging supervisory responsibilities in relation to it; might they not prefer to concentrate their likely scarce resources on prospectuses for issues that will be made directly into their own market? The risk that foreign issuance activity by State A's issuers could distort the allocation of resources to the most deserving projects to the detriment of State A's local real economy is a reason to care.[73] So too is State A's interest in maintaining a reputation for professionalism and reliability amongst fellow EU-regulators within CESR.[74] If CESR works effectively, it should foster a sense amongst regulatory agencies that they are engaged in a common endeavour and are mutually dependent on each other in the quest for effective cross-border supervision and enforcement. Yet, the regulatory officials of State B also have incentives to protect their home market from the distortive effects of substandard information, incentives that can be thought of as being stronger in the European context than they would be in other cross-border securities transactions because of the underlying agenda to integrate EU Member States' real economies. Whilst State A officials might have a superior understanding of the legal framework (especially corporate and employment law) and cultural and social influences within which State A's issuers operate, the CESR-generated network should, if it is effective, facilitate sharing of that expert knowledge with officials from State B.

Thus there are strong arguments against rigid rules tying issuers to the securities supervisory regime of the State in which they have their registered office. In one sense the rigidity of the new approach can be regarded as an admission of underachievement in the EU single securities market project: if there were a truly integrated market, backed up by an effective pan-European supervisory network, the arguments for restricting issuer choice as regards selecting a supervisory regime located anywhere within the EU would surely fall away. At a less lofty level, if there were in place at least a suitable architecture for the pan-European dissemination of information, another argument that is sometimes used in this context – that issuers need to be linked to their State of incorporation so that people

---

[73] Fox, 'Political Economy'; Fox, 'Retaining', 1415–16.
[74] See ch. 3 for discussion of CESR's role generally.

know where to look to find out information about them[75] – would lose whatever force it may currently enjoy.

It is not the intention here to criticise EU bodies for an outbreak of modesty and realism in regulatory design, save to note that the argument for linking issuers to the State of their registered office in order to make it easier for investors to know where to look for information is a weak one given the way in which electronic technology has eroded the significance of territorial connections. If information-finding difficulties persist, these should be addressed directly by promoting the development of better mechanisms for pan-European dissemination of information rather than by imposing a rigid rule on the allocation of supervisory responsibilities.[76] Instead, the main focus for criticism here is that the EU appears to have taken a backward step, imposing rigidity where there was previously an element of flexibility, and replacing a system that was not burdened with significant problems with one that offers at best uncertain net benefits. The extent to which this step was grounded in a principled assessment of the optimal supervisory arrangements is open to question. At least some of the motivation for moving in this direction seems to have come from behind-the-scenes political machinations rooted in a desire by certain countries to protect their national regulators against loss of business from issuers registered in their jurisdiction.[77]

Potential implications for EU issuers

Under the new regime, EU issuers are stuck with the supervisory regime of the State in which they have their registered office and, it follows, with its periodic disclosure requirements. This is so, irrespective of where within the EU an issuer offers its shares or has them admitted to trading on a regulated market. So far as the equity market is concerned, the adverse practical ramifications of this rigidity are diluted by the fact that most

---

[75] L. Burn, 'The EU Prospectus and Transparency Directives' *Practising Law Institute, Corporate Law and Practice Course Handbook Series 1400 PLI/Corp* (December 2003) 15 notes this argument.

[76] Policy choices for improving the mechanisms for the dissemination of information are considered further later in this chapter.

[77] 'Spoilt Choice: Horse-trading on EU-wide Prospectus Rules Could Have a Perverse Outcome', *Economist*, 9 November 2002, p. 101. A general study of capital formation practices of European corporate issuers in 1999 supports the existence of this strong home bias: H. E. Jackson and E. J. Pan, 'Regulatory Competition in International Securities Markets: Evidence from Europe in 1999 – Part I' (2001) 56 *Business Lawyer* 653.

companies first list their shares on a market in the State where they have their registered office anyway.[78] The significance of this practice for the purposes of this discussion it that it indicates a lack of market demand from issuers to exploit the freedom that was previously available to avoid the supervisory regime and additional regulatory requirements of their State of incorporation by engaging in issuance or listing activity only in other Member States. This data, it could be contended, makes concerns about the rigidity of the new regime seem rather theoretical – why worry about tying issuers rigidly to their home States when the evidence suggests that this is the arrangement that they tend to opt for anyway even when they have a choice? Yet, this is a troubling stance from the perspective of the broader EU market integration project in that the acceptability of the regime seems to be premised on a state of affairs that would be expected to fade away as integration intensifies, namely issuer home (i.e., registered office) State bias in primary equity listings. Furthermore, assumptions about issuers' preference for their State of incorporation as the location for primary listing presuppose the existence of suitable securities market trading facilities located within the country in question. Recent research has however raised the prospect that the relatively new exchanges in EU accession countries could fail to survive thereby leaving domestic issuers without a home exchange.[79]

There is a possibility that, if standards of supervisory skill and competence across the EU do not even out, issuers incorporated in States where the securities regulators have a relatively poor reputation might take flight and reincorporate themselves in States with stronger reputations for securities regulation. Equally, if periodic disclosure obligations that exceed the Transparency Directive persist in some Member States, it is conceivable that a desire to 'bond' with particular high-standard periodic disclosure regimes could become relevant to decisions on where to locate or relocate registered offices. There are numerous factors militating for and against issuer mobility within the EU, but it is at least plausible to suggest that association with a good-quality securities regulatory or supervisory regime could become a consideration that some issuers will

---

[78] International Primary Market Association, *The International Capital Markets 2000* (London, IPMA, 2000), p. 24; 'Spoilt Choice'.

[79] S. Claessens, R. Lee and J. Zechner, *The Future of Stock Exchanges in European Union Accession Countries* (London, Corporation of London, Centre for European Policy Research, May 2003), available via http://www.cepr.org/pubs/fse/fse.pdf (accessed May 2004).

take into account in weighing the pros and cons of such a move.[80] Presumably EU planners did not intend to create something that could distort the market for incorporations. However the fact that the risk of things turning out this way could easily have been avoided by retaining the possibility for issuers to 'bond' with a particular supervisory regime by offering securities or listing in that jurisdiction,[81] gives credence to suggestions that the outcome was largely the result of a political fudge rooted in national protectionism.

Potential implications for non-EU issuers

Issuer choice (on a one-off basis) on the applicable supervisory and periodic disclosure regime still applies for non-EU incorporated issuers. So long as such issuers take care to choose a competent authority that they feel able to live with indefinitely, superficially the rigidity may not seem too bad. However, there is a risk that being locked into a particular home State could become a factor that might eventually drive some non-EU issuers out of the EU securities market, such as where changes in an issuer's own position or in the quality of the supervision provided by a particular national regulator have undermined the appropriateness of the choice made possibly many years before. To acquire a new competent authority a non-EU issuer could conduct its new securities market activity through a subsidiary or connected company that does not yet have a designated EU-home State. Yet, whilst professional advisers could no doubt construct such schemes, these would involve transaction costs that could well render them commercially unattractive.

In the short term, that is until the new regime heralded by the Prospectus and Transparency Directives becomes embedded at national level and

---

[80] European Economic and Social Committee, *Opinion on the Proposal for a Directive on the harmonisation of transparency requirements*, sec. 4 (noting that the fact that issuers are tied to their home country (in perpetuity) may affect the choice of country of incorporation for newly established companies). As the barriers to issuer mobility for established companies erode, this could become more of an issue also for them. The European Commission is consulting on a proposed 14th Company Law Directive to facilitate issuer mobility by providing a harmonised procedure for transfers of registered offices around the Community: European Commission, *Public Consultation on the Transfer of the Registered Office of Limited Companies* (2004), available via http://www.europa.eu.int/comm/internal_market/company/seat-transfer/index_en.htm#consult (accessed May 2004).

[81] For instance, the original FESCO (later CESR) proposals on the European passport for prospectuses suggested that the home State should be either the State or incorporation or the State of primary listing: FESCO, *A European Passport for Issuers: Report*.

it becomes possible to gauge its practical operation, there is a risk that non-EU issuers may be disinclined to engage in securities market activity within the EU for fear that locking into a home State would, in time, expose them to undesired periodic disclosure requirements that exceed the Transparency Directive or to a supervisory regime that fails to rise to the challenges of the new regulatory environment.[82] Market disruption as a consequence of this uncertainty could be a transitional problem,[83] but it is possible that the damage could be more enduring and that the EU market could struggle to re-establish itself with non-EU issuers in the longer term.

Are Member States likely to exceed the Transparency Directive – or is de facto convergence on periodic disclosure requirements a more likely prospect?

The rules on the determination of home States have important implications for Member States with regard to potential exercise of the discretion to exceed the Transparency Directive's periodic disclosure requirements for home issuers. Member States have a monopoly over issuers whose registered offices are located in their jurisdiction, though if they impose tough requirements that are out of line with market preferences, they risk triggering issuer mobility within the EU or driving their issuers into securities markets outside the EU altogether. Member States have no power to require incoming EU issuers, with registered offices in other Member States, to adhere to their domestic super-equivalent (i.e. above the Transparency Directive) periodic disclosure requirements; to this extent, Member States lose control over securities trading on regulated markets in their jurisdiction. In respect of foreign (non-EU) issuers, it is still possible for Member States to seek to use super-equivalent periodic disclosure standards as a mechanism for attracting European business from that sector. However, for foreign (non-EU) issuers that are motivated by

---

[82] Time for fixing the home States of non-EU issuers started to run on 31 December 2003 when the Directive was published in the Official Journal: PD, art. 2.1(m)(iii).

[83] Federation of European Stock Exchanges, *Comments on the Commission Proposals for a Transparency Directive*, reports considerable confusion in the markets about the position of foreign (non-EU) issuers and cautions that drainage of admissions away from markets within the EU to other markets was imminent if clarity was not provided quickly. This paper is available at http://www.fese.be/initiatives/european_representation/2003/transparency_ Directive_position.htm.

reasons other than bonding with high standards,[84] such as issuers that are incorporated in high-quality regulatory jurisdictions that want to list in the EU in order to tap into liquidity pools or to raise their international profile with investors and/or business customers, opting for an EU home State that has disclosure standards at just the Directive level and then passporting into other Member States (including those where the domestic disclosure standards are tougher) may appeal instead. Clearly the stringency of the national periodic disclosure regime is only one of the factors likely to be considered by a non-EU issuer that is looking for an EU 'home' State supervisor and it could well be outweighed by other factors, such as the supervisor's reputation for professionalism and efficiency. Yet it is plausible to suppose that it could tip the balance in a marginal case.

It would be premature to attempt to give firm predictions on Member States' practice with regard to framing their national periodic disclosure requirements after the Transparency Directive comes fully in effect. However, some possible clues on whether Member States are likely to exercise the freedom to impose super-equivalent periodic disclosure requirements are available in the UK where regulators and market participants are already grappling with the challenge of reconfiguring the listing regime in the light of the FSAP Directives. The Financial Services Authority (FSA) has raised the question whether super-equivalent provisions should be retained for UK-incorporated issuers and for foreign (non-EU) issuers (that is, only those that designate the UK as their home State).[85] Such

---

[84] Generally on motivations for cross-listing: M. Pagano, A. A. Röell and J. Zechner, 'The Geography of Equity Listing: Why Do Companies List Abroad?' (2002) 57 *Journal of Finance* 2651. The authors explore the following as reasons for cross-listing: to reduce barriers for foreign investors (regulatory barriers, transaction costs and informational frictions); to capitalise on product market reputation; to expose themselves to foreign expertise, such as specialist investment analysts; to commit to high regulatory standards (i.e. bonding); to enhance liquidity; to exploit relative mispricing of their securities in different international markets; to strengthen their output market; and to secure low listing costs relative to benefits.

[85] Including, for UK issuers, disclosures relating to class tests and a 'comply or explain' disclosure as regards the Combined Code on Corporate Governance: Financial Services Authority, *Review* (Consultation Paper), pp. 30–2 (tabular comparison between FSAP Directives and existing UK requirements). For overseas issuers with a primary listing in the UK, current disclosure rules are similar to those for UK issuers but with certain key exceptions: use of issuers' local GAAP is permitted; and there is no obligation to provide a 'comply or explain' statement as regards the Combined Code: Financial Services Authority, *Review* (Consultation Paper), p. 38. 'Primary listing' is currently defined as meaning a listing by virtue of which the issuer is, as respects that security, subject to the full requirements applicable to listing of the relevant listing authority.

requirements will necessarily have to go as regards foreign (EU-incorporated and non-EU incorporated with an EU home State other than the UK) issuers, although non-disclosure-based standards can be retained.

Thus far into the review, although it has acknowledged the difficulty of the balancing exercise, the FSA appears to be in favour of retaining super-equivalent disclosure provisions for UK issuers and, in some respects, intensifying their stringency for non-EU issuers seeking a primary listing for their shares in the UK.[86] Investor bodies seem broadly to agree with this strategy: the Association of British Insurers, a major trade body for institutional investors, has supported the proposal to increase the regulatory burden on foreign (non-EU) issuers seeking a primary listing in the UK, on the basis that issuers in this position should comply with the full UK standards expected by UK investors;[87] and the Investment Management Association, the UK trade body for the professional investment management industry, has expressed a similar view.[88] Other groups are less sure. The British Bankers Association, the leading UK trade association in the banking and financial services industry, considers that super-equivalent requirements for UK-incorporated issuers enhance the integrity of London markets and provide useful information for investors. However, it is more equivocal about the proposals to intensify the regulatory burden on foreign issuers.[89] Some reservations about the merits of increasing the regulatory burden on foreign issuers are also expressed by the Law Society's Company Law Committee, a powerful committee of technical experts drawn from both sides of the legal profession.[90]

The current disclosure requirements for overseas issuers with a secondary listing in the UK are below Transparency Directive level: Financial Services Authority, *Review* (Consultation Paper), p. 40.

[86] Including to require 'comply or explain' statements in respect of the Combined Code. There are also proposals regarding reconciliation of financial statements prepared otherwise than on the basis of IAS/IFRS. These are considered further later in this chapter.

[87] Association of British Insurers, *Review of the Listing Regime – ABI Response to FSA Consultation Paper 203* (2004), available via http://www.abi.org.uk/Display/File/39/FSACP203.doc (accessed May 2004).

[88] Investment Management Association, *Review of the Listing Regime – Responses to Specific Questions Raised*, available via http://www.investmentfunds.org.uk/investmentuk/publications/Responses/cp203–02.pdf (accessed May 2004).

[89] British Bankers Association, *BBA Response to CP203: Review of the Listing Regime*, available via http://www.bba.org.uk/bba/jsp/polopoly.jsp?d=155&a=1784 (accessed May 2004).

[90] Law Society Company Law Committee, *Review of the Listing Regime* (Committee Paper No. 472, 2004).

It is important not to read too much into this evidence. Current industry and FSA views on the merits of super-equivalence have been formed against the background of an unsettled and unfamiliar new EU regime, which is untested by practical experience. Such views are liable to change once the market adapts to the practical realities of the FSA having lost control over the periodic disclosure regime applicable to issuers from else-where in the EU[91] that are listed in the UK, and the UK corporate sector absorbs fully the fact that it cannot opt out of tougher UK standards by listing elsewhere in the EU. Exactly how these changing dynamics will affect perceptions is impossible to anticipate. Yet tentatively the signs seem to be that, notwithstanding the changes wrought by the Prospectus and Transparency Directives, the FSA's benefit-burden assessment will still come out in favour of the imposition of some super-equivalent periodic disclosure requirements, at least for UK-incorporated issuers and possibly for foreign (non-EU) issuers, and that there will not be total convergence around the Transparency Directive's standards.

Assessment – moving in the right direction?

Maximum harmonisation in the Prospectus Directive reduces the scope for EU Member States to compete on disclosure standards. Although the Transparency Directive is a bit more flexible on disclosure standards, the room it leaves for competition between States on periodic disclosure requirements is, in effect, curtailed by the rigid rules on the identification of home States because it is only home States that are permitted to exceed the Directive. The rigidity of the home State rules also has potential adverse ramifications for the quality of issuer supervision across the EU because it gives national regulators a monopoly over their home issuers and thereby reduces the discipline of competition in that context too.

The strongest potential justifications for these features of the new issuer disclosure regime appear to lie in the achievement of more standard, and therefore more easily comparable, information relevant to investment decisions, and the establishment of a coherent system for issuer supervision in a complex environment containing a multiplicity of regulatory bodies spread across the EU.

Whatever benefits there are in promoting the standardisation of informa-tion, they should always be considered in conjunction with the various costs that are implicit in the establishment of a common standard. On this basis, it

---

[91] Including non-EU issuers that have another Member State as their EU home State.

is not clear that the EU has in fact paid the right price for improvements in information-standardisation. Had some freedom to exceed common prospectus standards been allowed to them, Member States would have been constrained against using it excessively by the risk that this could provoke negative market reactions and issuer flight to less burdensome regulatory environments. The UK's weighing of the pros and cons of super-equivalent periodic disclosures gives an indication of the sort of debate that could have taken place on prospectus disclosures too. It does not suggest that Member States would have exploited a more flexible prospectus regime in a manner that would have been liable seriously to erode the benefits of standardisation.

On supervision, consistency considerations do seem broadly to militate in favour of requiring issuers to have the same supervisor for their prospectuses and their periodic disclosures. Beyond this degree of standardisation, the level of centralised control that is appropriate depends on the view that one takes on the merits of the issuer choice debate. A free issuer choice system could be vulnerable to exploitation by issuers anxious to evade proper supervision and enforcement and it is questionable whether market mechanisms would necessarily ensure the accurate reflection of such exploitative practices in securities prices. This points towards intervention to link issuers to supervisory regimes that are equipped with the appropriate incentives and expertise to supervise them properly. In fact that seems to have been achieved under the old EU system of constrained issuer choice whereby there was scope for issuers to choose to be supervised by the State of trading rather than the State of incorporation. Removing that choice looks like a backward step that is strangely inconsistent with developments elsewhere in the EU market integration project: the establishment of CESR, and the improvements in information-sharing and general supervisory co-operation that this network is meant to foster should make national regulators better able to supervise EU issuers irrespective of the territorial location of their registered offices within the EU, so why move to a system that restricts their opportunity to do so?

D   Demolishing the tower of Babel – standardising the language of financial and other information

Financial information in prospectuses and periodic disclosures – treatment of foreign issuers

The new prospectus and periodic disclosure regime contained in the Prospectus and Transparency Directives is not, in fact, as committed to the promotion of information standardisation as the discussion thus far into this chapter might appear to suggest. This is because both Directives make provision for non-EU issuers to use financial statements prepared otherwise than in accordance with IAS/IFRS provided the accounting standards under which they have been drawn up have been deemed 'equivalent' by the EU.[92] Foreign issuers provide a significant component of securities market activity within the EU.[93] Thus, depending on how the mechanisms for determining that other financial reporting systems are equivalent to IAS/IFRS and are therefore acceptable for EU purposes will actually operate (the details of this are not yet entirely clear), a large number of issuers could be allowed to report their financial results otherwise than in IAS/IFRS, thereby significantly compromising the quest for standardisation.[94]

---

[92] CPR, Annex 1, para 20.1 and TD, art. 19 (subject to transitional arrangements: CPR, art. 35 and TD, art. 26). The derogation power in respect of foreign issuers is not confined to financial information: Member States can exempt foreign issuers generally from the EU requirements if there are equivalent provisions in the third country. It is the scope for exemption in respect of financial information that attracts most attention however.

Subject to certain transitional arrangements (CPR, art. 35 and TD, art. 26), the basic requirement for EU issuers is for use of IAS/IFRS: CPR, Annex I, para 20.1 and TD, arts. 4–5.

[93] For instance, as of December 2003, 381 international companies (roughly 20 per cent of total listings), with a market capitalisation of nearly £2,000 bn, were listed on the LSE's main market: London Stock Exchange, *Statistics*, available via http://www.londonstockexchange.com/cmsattach/2834.pdf (accessed May 2004).

As at March 2004, there were 339 foreign companies out of a total of 1379 in the Euronext, across all four exchanges (Amsterdam, Brussels, Lisbon and Paris), but within the Euronext 150 only two were foreign: Corus (UK), Gemplus (Luxembourg), (source: World Federation of Exchanges statistics and Datastream).

In 2002 there were 219 foreign listings on the Deutsche Börse, representing around 23 per cent of total listings: H. Skeete, *Key Trends in the Market Data Sphere* (Presentation by the Head of Exchange Strategy, Reuters plc), available via http://www.afma.com.au/afmawr/pdf/fmc_herbie_skeete.pdf (accessed May 2004).

Generally on foreign listings on EU exchanges at various points during the 1990s: Pagano, Röell and Zechner, *The Geography of Equity Listing*, Table 2.

According to one estimate from a leading expert in the international capital markets field, two-thirds of the issuers in the European market come from outside the EU: C. Dammers, 'Life under the Prospectus Directive', Presentation to European Parliament, available at http://www.europarl.eu.int/hearings/20021002/econ/dammers.pdf (accessed May 2004).

More detailed formal data on the countries of origin of issuers in the European capital market can be found in International Primary Market Association, *The International Capital Markets 2000*, table 11.

[94] Cox, 'Regulatory Duopoly' (arguing that special dispensations for the ADR and Rules 144A markets do not constitute significant encrochments on the comparability principle in US securities regulation but considering the potentially greater challenge to this principle presented by possible SEC relaxation of its insistence on US GAAP in favour of IAS/IFRS).

Formally, the Directives leave the decision on equivalence in the hands of individual competent authorities but provide for the Commission to adopt implementing measures to ensure uniform application.[95] The Commission is committed to establishing an EU equivalence determination mechanism by 2007.[96] There is strong pressure on the European Commission from market participants to operate the equivalence mechanism in a manner that is accommodating of variations in financial reporting systems around the world (in particular to recognise US GAAP). Participants in the international bond markets are particularly concerned that the Commission should resolve equivalence issues quickly: only high-denomination (minimum €50,000) debt securities are outside the periodic reporting requirements and there is concern that the possibility of having to reconcile financial information to IAS/IFRS could drive away foreign issuers of lower denominated debt. That would impact severely on a market where at least 50 per cent of all issuers are estimated to come from outside the EU; as of January 2004, on the Luxembourg bourse alone there were 490 US issuers listing more than 3,100 separate bonds issues.[97]

Arguments such as these and also the fact that current practice in Member States is overwhelmingly in favour of accepting US GAAP[98] demonstrate well that markets do not value standard information above all else, and send a powerful message to regulatory policy-makers about the importance of weighing its benefits against competing considerations. Whether foreign issuers should be allowed to use financial statements drawn up otherwise than on the basis of IAS/IFRS is a question that properly depends on balancing the need for EU investors to receive full, reliable and easily comparable financial information against the need to maintain the attractiveness of the EU for foreign issuers.

---

[95] PD, art. 20.3 and TD, art. 19.3.

[96] CPR, art. 35 provides for the establishment of an equivalence mechanism by the Commission before 1 January 2007. TD, art. 19.3 makes the establishment of equivalence mechanism a mandatory obligation on the Commission and commits it to making equivalence decisions within five years from implementation of the Directive.

[97] Data drawn from D. G. Strongin, 'EU Transparency Obligations Directive' 13 January 2004 (letter from the Securities Industry Association to the European Commission), available via http://www.sia.com/international/pdf/SIALuxembourgTOD.pdf (accessed May 2004). Participants in other market segments are also concerned: see, e.g., Federation of European Stock Exchanges, *Comments*.

[98] Committee of European Securities Regulators, *Summary of the Answers to the Questionnaire on Factual Information on the Legislation and Practices of Member States Regarding the Treatment of Third Country Issuers with Respect to the Drawing up and Approval of Prospectuses (Article 20 of the Prospectus Directive)* (CESR/03–496, 2003).

Yet, despite pressure from market participants for a quick resolution of equivalence concerns, there is a distinct risk that this issue could become bogged down in political arguments between the EU and the US on the acceptability of each other's accounting standards, underlying which is a strong element of competition between supporters of US GAAP and supporters of IAS/IFRS for the prize of becoming the global language of financial statements.[99] This sort of continuing uncertainty could be very damaging to EU securities markets in that it could repel foreign issuers.

It is unclear whether, once the equivalence mechanism is fully operational, there will be any room for individual Member States to make their own decisions on equivalence – either to add additional sets of standards that they regard as equivalent on a case-by-case basis or to narrow things down by insisting upon the reconciliation of financial statements notwithstanding that they were drawn up under standards that have been deemed equivalent by the European Commission. The former option would enhance flexibility but the notion that Member States could simply make their own additions to the list of equivalent financial standards sits rather uncomfortably with the general harmonisation agenda and the emphasis on consistent EU-wide implementation. The idea of Member States taking a narrower view than the Commission on equivalence is easier to square with the harmonisation agenda (at least in relation to its non-maximal form in the Transparency Directive) because this could be regarded as a super-equivalent national requirement. That a Member State might want to take a narrower view than the Commission with regard to equivalence might seem rather theoretically fanciful because of its potentially damaging impact on that State's ability to compete for foreign listings but the discussion in the UK on the imposition of super-equivalent periodic disclosure requirements indicates that it may not be: apparently independently of whatever position might be taken at EU level on equivalence, the FSA has suggested that foreign issuers with shares listed in the UK might be required to reconcile to IAS/IFRS or US GAAP. This suggestion has received a mixed reception.[100] For an individual Member State to take a narrower view than the Commission on equivalence could seriously damage its attractiveness to foreign issuers; this could well become a factor that could strongly influence foreign issuers' choice of EU

---

[99] R. Bruce, 'Global Harmony Hangs in the Balance', *Financial Times*, 23 February 2004, FT Special Report, *International Accountancy*, p. 1.

[100] See, e.g., Law Society Company Law Committee, *Review*.

home State. Thus the arguments for not converging around the common standard in this respect would need to be very strong indeed.

The language(s) of non-financial information

The multilingual character of the EU presents another challenge to the standardisation principle and creates a need for a compromise that is attuned to reasonable investor and issuer needs, and also to the political sensitivities of Member States about their official languages. The old regime undoubtedly got the balance wrong, and the imbalance was a major reason why the prospectus passport it provided became practically defunct. Language was a significant barrier to the use of passports in cross-border offers because Member States could insist upon the translation of the entire prospectus into their local language. Compliance with such requests would have necessitated time-consuming, intensive cross-checking and verification exercises to counter the risk of inaccuracies creeping into disclosure via the translation process, hence adding to the overall transaction costs.

In broad terms the Prospectus and Transparency Directives seem to offer a better compromise response to the various competing considerations and sensitivities. This assessment can only be tentative, however, because the success of the scheme is partially dependent on the as yet unknown attitude that Member States will adopt where they have some say over permissible languages.

The language scheme for prospectuses is shown in Table 5.1.[101]

Table 5.1

Location of offer/application for admission to trading on a regulated market	Language requirement for prospectus
Offer/application in home State only (of equity, or non-equity securities with denominations below €50,000)	In a language accepted by the home State's regulator
Offer/application in more than one Member State including the home State (of equity securities or non-equity securities with denominations below €50,000)	(i) In a language accepted by the home State's regulator, and (ii) In a language accepted by the host States' regulators or, at the issuer's option,

---

[101] PD, art. 19.

	In a language customary in the sphere of international finance
Offer/application in one or more Member States excluding the home State	In a language accepted by the host States' regulators or, at the issuer's option, In a language customary in the sphere of international finance
Any application in respect of non-equity securities with a minimum denomination of €50,000[102]	In a language accepted by the home and host States' regulators or, at the issuer's option, In a language customary in the sphere of international finance

The equivalent scheme for periodic disclosures is shown in Table 5.2[103]

Where issuers have the choice of using a language customary in the sphere of international finance, they will presumably exercise it so as to avoid costly translation obligations. This formula neatly sidesteps the political minefield that could have been encountered had the Directive sought to prescribe specifically which European languages would be acceptable. In theory there could be disputes ahead on which languages fall within the formula; in practice, however, this approach surely reinforces the dominance of English as the language for international securities market documentation.[104]

The practical impact of the schemes where they lock issuers into making disclosures in a language accepted by their home State depends on the attitude of national regulators. They could, but they are not obliged to, insist upon disclosures in their official language(s). For a national regulator to take a narrow rigid stance on which languages it regards as acceptable would be risky, because this could prompt EU-incorporated issuers to avoid their home markets in issuance or listing activity and could be unattractive for foreign issuers looking for an EU home State.

---

[102] Offers of non-equity securities with a minimum denomination of €50,000 are exempt from the requirement to produce a prospectus except where there is also an application for admission to listing.

[103] TD, art. 16. For securities (including equity securities) with a minimum denomination of €50,000, the regime is modified to one of issuer choice between a language customary in the sphere of international finance or a language accepted by home and host States.

[104] E. Wymeersch, 'Company Law in Turmoil and the Way to Global Company Practice' [2003] *Journal of Corporate Law Studies* 283, 288 noting the de facto emergence of English as the internationally accepted business language.

Table 5.2

Location of admission to trading	Language requirement
Home Member State only	In a language accepted by the home State's regulator
More than one Member State including the home State	In a language accepted by the home State's regulator and In a language accepted by the host States' regulators or, at the issuer's option, A language customary in the sphere of international finance
One or more Member States not including the home State	In a language accepted by the host States' regulators or, at the issuer's option, In a language customary in the sphere of international finance And The home State regulator may require disclosure either in a language accepted by its regulator or, at the issuer's option In a language customary in the sphere of international finance

Translations of prospectus summaries

Prospectuses aimed at the retail securities market must include a short summary in non-technical language.[105] Where a prospectus has been drawn up under another language in accordance with the scheme just outlined, it is only the summary that host Member States can require to be translated into their official language (and they have no power to require it to be translated into any other language).[106] Summary translation has costs implications but these should be considerably less than would have been involved in full prospectus translation under the old regime. For issues of shares or straightforward debt securities that are genuinely aimed

---

[105] PD, art. 5.2. The summary should not normally exceed 2,500 words in the language in which the prospectus was originally drawn up: PD, rec. 21.

[106] PD, arts. 19.2 and 19.3.

at retail investors in various countries (these are a rarity to date but may become more common in future), translating the summary could be a step that issuers would wish to take in any event as part of the marketing exercise; for such issuers, living with the costs of mandatory translation of summaries should not therefore be particularly burdensome. Where the costs of translation summary could weigh more significantly is in relation to more complex, low-denominated debt securities or other specialist securities that, in commercial terms, are aimed at the wholesale market but which cannot take advantage of the Prospectus Directive's special regime for wholesale securities because that is generally restricted to securities with a minimum denomination of €50,000. In such cases it is possible that summary translation costs could sometimes tip the balance away from a cross-border prospectus offer towards instead either structuring the issue as an unlisted offer to qualified investors that does not require a prospectus[107] or making it outside EU regulated markets.

Prospectuses relating to wholesale securities (that is, non-equity securities with a minimum denomination of €50,000) do not need to contain summaries, understandably so since they are not targeted at the retail market. A rather curious sentence in the Prospectus Directive states that, in respect of wholesale securities for which admission to trading is sought: 'Member States may choose to require in their national legislation that a summary be drawn up in their official language.'[108] This option must surely be an irrelevance so far as the mainstream English-language wholesale market is concerned. This market is concentrated in London, where the option is obviously meaningless, and in Luxembourg, where participants are long since accustomed to operating in English and where the regulator is highly unlikely to want to damage a major economic success story by imposing costly summary and translation requirements that would undermine Luxembourg's competitive position vis-à-vis London.

E   Adapting the prospectus and periodic disclosure regime for specialist debt securities markets

The ideas are simple: the different risk–reward profiles of equity and debt securities mean that likely investors' informational needs have different focuses; and, wholesale securities markets are dominated by professional

---

[107] As discussed in the next section of this chapter.
[108] PD, art. 19.4.

investors and thus do not need to be burdened with disclosure requirements that are designed to help retail investors. So there may be good reason to exempt certain market segments from regulation altogether or at least to impose a lighter regulatory regime.[109] However, to put these ideas into practice it is necessary to set boundaries, a process that raises broad policy concerns about where lines should be drawn and also technical complexities in matching the regulatory regime appropriately to a sophisticated market which contains a myriad and dynamic array of exotic securities combining features of debt and equity. The EU has been struggling with numerous technical complexities, for example in figuring out the appropriate prospectus disclosure regimes for convertible securities and for derivatives.[110] It would be unrealistic to suppose that it has got the detail exactly right in every respect but how much concern should be attached to this issue depends on the as-yet untested ability of the law-making machinery to step in quickly to rectify regulatory mistakes before they can cause significant damage to the market. Technical problems that arise because the rules prove to be a poor fit in relation to some arcane types of securities would be best discussed in the light of experience of practical operation of the new regime. Therefore this discussion abstracts from detailed, technical problems and concentrates instead on broader policy concerns and the way in which the constructors of the new regime have responded to them.

---

[109] On the need to modify the general regime in relation to specialist securities: European Commission, *Amended proposal*, explanatory memorandum, p. 4.

[110] Burn, 'The EU Prospectus and Transparency Directives', notes problems with regard to the application of the equity/shares disclosure regime to convertibles, and also various difficulties with regard to derivatives. Derivatives presented a particular difficulty because the Prospectus Directive's instructions to the Commission on the drafting of the detailed disclosure rules referred only to denomination by unit (art. 7.2(b)) but derivatives do not necessarily have a denomination. Despite this, the Commission and CESR managed to satisfy themselves that it was permissible within the scope of the Directive to make the wholesale disclosure regime available in respect of derivative securities with a price per unit of at least €50,000: Committee of European Securities Regulators, *Prospectus Consultation Feedback Statement* (CESR/03–301, 2003) paras. 70–3). This can be seen as an example of 'fudging' by the Commission and CESR to arrive at a commercially acceptable outcome, yet it also illustrates the dangers of attempting to regulate appropriately for highly complex, sophisticated markets. It is not necessarily the case that there will always be room for unobtrusive 'interpretation' of the regime in ways that accommodate specialist considerations that may not have been appreciated properly when the relevant rules were drawn up.

Exemptions from the requirement to produce a prospectus

Under the Prospectus Directive, the requirement to publish a prospectus does not apply to certain offers (assuming the securities are not also being admitted to trading on a regulated market).[111] The category of excluded unlisted offers includes offers to 'qualified investors',[112] offers to fewer than 100 people per Member State (other than qualified investors),[113] offers of large denominated securities (minimum €50,000)[114] and offers with high minimum subscriptions (minimum €50,000 per investor).[115] It is anticipated that the qualified investors, minimum investment and minimum denomination exemptions will henceforth do the bulk of the work of carving out from the scope of mandatory prospectus law the marketing of specialised securities to wholesale investors.[116] However, exemption from the prospectus requirement does not take wholesale public offers completely outside the Directive because certain controls on advertising will still apply.[117]

Excluding certain sorts of offer from the mandatory prospectus requirement is not a new concept in EU securities law but the exemptions are now set out in more specific language than that used in predecessor Directives. For instance, the exemption for offers to fewer than 100 people per Member State replaces an old exemption for offers to a 'restricted circle of persons'.[118] The exemption for offers addressed solely to qualified

---

[111] Art. 3.2.

[112] Defined in art. 2.1(e). The exemption is provided by art. 3.2(a). Qualified investors include financial industry firms, governments and central banks, and large corporates; Member States have the option to treat certain sophisticated individuals and also certain SMEs as qualified investors if they so request: art. 2.1(e) and (f) and art. 2.2.

[113] Art. 3.2(b).

[114] Art. 3.2(c).

[115] Art. 3.2(d).

[116] The 100 persons per Member State exclusion is also theoretically available though in the view of the European Parliament's Economic and Monetary Affairs Committee (which pressed for 150 rather than 100) the ceiling is too low to be of much practical relevance: Economic and Monetary Affairs Committee, *Recommendation for second reading on the common position adopted by the Council with a view to adopting a European Parliament and Council Directive on the prospectus to be published when securities are offered to the public or admitted to trading* (A5–0218/2003, 13 June 2003).

[117] Art. 15. The applicable control prohibits selective disclosure: any information disclosed to some qualified investors or special categories of investors must be disclosed to all qualified investors or special categories of investors to whom the offer is exclusively addressed. The competent authority of the home Member State is empowered to exercise control over compliance with this requirement.

[118] Public Offers Directive, art. 2.1(b).

investors replaces a vaguely drawn exemption for offers to persons 'in the context of their trades, professional or occupations.'[119] An old exemption for euro-securities, which was notoriously uncertain,[120] is not carried forward into the new Prospectus Directive in any form.

The greater precision attaching to the exemptions should reduce the room for Member States to interpret them in different ways. Cross-border exempt institutional offerings and private placements are already an established and important part of securities market activity in the EU (far more so than cross-border prospectus offers which are rare).[121] Whereas under the current regime it is necessary for those involved in this type of cross-border issuance activity to check on the precise scope of the exemptions as interpreted from State to State,[122] in future the process of establishing whether a proposed issue fits within exemptions should be simplified and therefore less costly. The improved drafting of the exemptions could prove to be one of the most beneficial aspects of the new Prospectus Directive. Although standardisation has its dangers, even critics of harmonisation would presumably see little to trouble them in a set of rules that gives issuers greater certainty on when mandatory prospectus disclosure rules do *not* apply, and thus facilitates issuance on the basis of alternative, market-driven disclosure standards.[123]

Modified disclosure requirements for prospectuses relating to wholesale securities that are to be admitted to trading on regulated markets

Under the old rules for prospectus disclosure in respect of listed securities, there were no special disclosure requirements specifically for wholesale securities. However, that disclosure regime applied on a minimum harmonisation basis, which left plenty of scope for national regulators to

---

[119] Public Offers Directive, art. 2.1(a). In the UK this was interpreted as the 'professionals' exemption.

[120] For a brief discussion of the different ways in which this exemption was interpreted in various Member States: H. S. Scott, 'Internationalization of Primary Public Securities Markets' (2000) 63 *Law and Contemporary Problems* 71, 83–3. In the UK the scope of the exemption was generally felt to be so uncertain as to make it unsafe to rely on it: ibid.

[121] Jackson and Pan, 'Regulatory Competition'.

[122] European Economic and Social Committee, *Opinion on the Proposal for a Directive of the European Parliament and of the Council on the prospectus to be published when securities are offered to the public or admitted to trading*, OJ 2002 No. C80/52.

[123] Jackson and Pan, 'Regulatory Competition', considers the operation of the professionals market within the EU.

mould their requirements appropriately to the needs of markets in specialist securities. Maximum harmonisation removes the room for manoeuvre thereby making it necessary for EU policy-makers to confront the issues head on.

Under the Prospectus Directive, the key difference[124] between the general rules on the matters that issuers have to disclose and the special rules for wholesale securities is that non-EU issuers of specialist securities do not need to produce financial information drawn up under IAS/IFRS or an equivalent set of accounting standards. Foreign issuers can instead use accounts based on other accounting standards so long as the prospectus contains an appropriate warning and provides a narrative description of the differences between the standards in question and IAS/IFRS.[125]

These modified disclosure requirements apply to large denominated securities (minimum €50,000) of a certain type (non-equity).[126] Major questions here are – why have an approach that is based on minimum denominations, and why alight upon €50,000 as the relevant threshold amount? An explanation for the use of a monetary threshold is revealed by a statement from the European Commission: 'Since wholesale and retail investors have free access to these stockmarkets, an objective criterion based on a high nominal value for the securities to be traded has been introduced, in order to create an effective distinction between markets for professionals and the general public.'[127] Why €50,000? This figure parallels the threshold for one-off exemptions in respect of unlisted offers, an exemption which is itself a modern version of an old unlisted offers exemption suitably updated for the adoption of the Euro and for the effects of inflation.[128] This consistency has a superficial attractiveness[129] yet reflection quickly exposes a problem: the requirement creates a rigidity in relation to securities that are to be admitted to a regulated market that does not exist in relation to offers of securities outside regulated markets

---

[124] There is also the more modest difference that the requirement for prospectus summaries does not apply (justifiable on the basis that the people with such large amounts of money can be expected to read and evaluate full information): PD, art. 5.2.

[125] CPR, Annex IX, para. 11.1.

[126] PD, art. 7.2(b). On the definitions of equity and non-equity securities: PD, art. 2.1(b) and (c).

[127] European Commission, *Amended proposal*, explanatory memorandum, p. 4.

[128] The Euro replaced the ECU on a one-for-one basis: Council Regulation (EC) No 1103/97 of 17 June 1997 on certain provisions relating to the introduction of the euro, OJ 1997 No. L162/1.

[129] European Economic and Social Committee, *Opinion on the prospectus*, para. 3 (making the case for an exemption equivalent to that for unlisted offers).

because, in the latter case, offers of lower-denominated securities can still be made without a full retail prospectus (indeed without any mandatory prospectus at all) so long as they are still within the exemption for offers to qualified investors.

A requirement for minimum denominations of €50,000 does not reflect existing market practice within the EU, which instead is for wholesale issues to be in smaller denominations so as to facilitate portfolio diversification and management.[130] For instance, one study of the European bond market in the first half of 2002 found that over 77 per cent of issues had a denomination of less than €5,000.[131] So what appears to have occurred is that the EU has adopted a policy stance that is geared more towards protecting retail investors by de facto keeping them out of nominally open segments of regulated markets[132] than preserving a flourishing and highly successful segment of market activity. This could be thought perverse. Admittedly, the regulatory regime is unlikely to kill off the market entirely, particularly since unlisted offers can still be structured to take advantage of the qualified investors exemption, yet it could well have a significant impact on some aspects of EU securities market activity. For example, it could drive away institutional investors whose investment mandates restrict them to securities admitted to trading on certain markets and for which high-denominated securities are unattractive from a portfolio management perspective. It could also conceivably drive away some foreign issuers that want to tap into markets for listed, low-denomination debt securities but do not want to assume the costly burden of restating their accounts to IAS/IFRS.[133] Whether foreign issuers of low-denomination debt securities will take flight from Europe depends crucially on the stance that is yet to be taken on the 'equivalence' of financial

---

[130] Freshfields Bruckhaus Deringer, *The Prospectus Directive* (Client Publication, 2003), available via http://www.freshfields.com/practice/corporate/publications/pdfs/4968.pdf (accessed May 2004).

[131] International Primary Market Association and European Banking Federation, 'Banking Sector Satisfied with Progress on Prospectus Directive', Joint Press Release, 5 November 2002, available via http://www.ipma.org.uk.

[132] That the intention is investor protection is clear: European Commission, *Amended proposal*, explanatory memorandum, p. 4 ('Thus the more flexible arrangements envisaged [for wholesale markets] cannot be put into effect to the detriment of retail investors.').

[133] Whether this occurs is tied up with the arrangements for determination of the 'equivalence' of financial information prepared otherwise than on the basis of IAS/IFRS. According to one estimate the costs of reconciliation to IAS/IFRS for a Japanese issuer would be in the region of €10 million, compared to costs of between US $500,00 and US $1 million to reconcile the accounts with US. GAAP: Dammers, C, 'Life'.

information prepared otherwise than on the basis of IAS/IFRS. Transitional uncertainty could disrupt the market, and that, in turn, could undermine the longer-term competitiveness of the EU securities market in attracting business from international issuers.

Periodic disclosure requirements and specialist securities

Problems stemming from the fact that the minimum denomination threshold for the application of special disclosure rules is higher than is consistent with market practices are not confined to prospectuses. The Transparency Directive's periodic disclosure requirements for issuers with securities admitted to trading on regulated markets do not apply to specialist securities but the minimum denomination threshold for this disapplication is again €50,000. Thus all listed issuers of low-denomination debt securities are now caught by new obligations to publish periodic financial information, and foreign (non-EU) issuers are in a state of limbo pending resolution of equivalence issues. This extended disclosure obligation risks repelling issuers of low-denomination debt securities from seeking a listing on EU regulated markets.

But a different threshold for a special regime on the allocation of supervisory responsibilities

The principal centres for bond issuance activity in the EU are London and Luxembourg and there is a concentration of supervisory expertise in respect of both EU and foreign issuers in these locations. A requirement linking issuers to the State of their registered office for supervisory purposes would thus have threatened to disrupt a highly successful and economically significant market by undermining the quality of the supervisory process, putting this in the hands of potentially very inexperienced national regulators. This issue received considerable attention during the passage of the Prospectus Directive and a solution was eventually devised that seeks to preserve established practices in the bond market.

For issues of non-equity securities denominated in units of least €1,000, and also certain derivatives, the alternative rule for the determination of the 'home' State under the Prospectus Directive is broadly one of issuer choice as between the Member State(s) where the issuer has its registered office and the Member State where the securities are offered to the public or admitted to trading on a regulated market.[134] For Transparency Directive purposes, an issuer that just has non-equity securities with a minimum denomination of €1,000 admitted to trading can choose between its registered office State and those Member States which have admitted its securities to dealings on regulated markets.[135]

Why this adaptation? Why in particular is there a departure from the usual €50,000 minimum denomination threshold for the application of a more relaxed regime? It is possible to construct a theoretical case for relaxing in relation to bond issues the rule tying an issuer to its State of incorporation on the basis that bond issues do not raise the sort of internal, shareholder/director corporate governance issues that could arise in equity issues and for which, it can be argued, that a proper vetting of the relevant disclosures might require quite intimate knowledge of the incorporation State's corporate law.[136] This argument would point, however, to a general relaxation of the rule, not a qualified adaptation at or above a certain threshold. It is also possible to argue that a more relaxed rule may be appropriate for wholesale markets on the grounds that, whatever risks are entailed in more flexibility, these will be absorbed quickly by the market and accurately reflected in securities prices.[137] In the EU context, however, that reasoning would seem to point towards a €50,000 threshold consistent with the rest of wholesale regime rather than the €1,000 threshold that in fact applies.

The explanations for the existence of a threshold at all and for it being set at a much lower level than applies for the wholesale regime generally lie in the nitty-gritty realities of practical politics rather than in abstract principle. The €1,000 threshold represents a success for lobbying groups that fought hard to whittle down the €50,000 threshold set originally by the Commission.[138] No threshold at all would have been the preferred outcome for many;[139] its survival, but in a minor

---

[134] Art. 2.1(m)(ii).

[135] TD, art. 2.1(i)(ii). This choice must remain valid for at least three years unless the issuer's securities are no longer admitted to trading on any regulated market in the EU.

[136] Romano, 'Empowering', 2410.

[137] S. J. Choi, 'Promoting Issuer Choice in Securities Regulation' (2001) 41 *Virginia Journal of International Law* 815 acknowledges that the effectiveness of the 'portable reciprocity' version of issuer choice turns on the sophistication of the investors associated with a particular issuer.

[138] Various key stages in the battle garnered press attention: e.g. Leader Column, 'Uncommon Market: Senseless Decision on Bonds must be Reversed', *Financial Times*, 6 May 2003, p. 20.

[139] IPMA and EBF, 'Banking Sector Satisfied', contends that: 'There is no logical connection whatsoever between issuer choice and minimum denomination.'

form,[140] may perhaps be best regarded as a face-saving compromise for those who had originally pressed for it to be set at a much higher level.

F Tailoring prospectus and periodic disclosure requirements to cater for retail investors

There exists a political agenda to encourage retail investors into the securities market on an EU-wide basis. This agenda is supported by economic data estimating that an effective pan-European retail market would boost EU GDP by some 0.5–0.7 per cent.[141] The same study also claimed that the benefits of international portfolio diversification could be largely captured through Europe-wide diversification. Yet, despite its current popularity, a policy of encouraging retail investors into securities markets is not without potentially problematic side-effects that deserve attention from policy-makers.

One concern is that a policy of stimulating retail investor activity could[142] expose the market to more and more investors whose trading strategies are likely to be distorted by irrational psychological impulses and cognitive weaknesses.[143] Influences that are liable to distort the accuracy of securities prices are worrying from a policy standpoint because inaccurate prices threaten the socially important function of securities markets as mechanisms for the allocation of scarce investment resources

---

[140] It is estimated that freedom of choice will be available in around 95 per cent of bond issues despite the threshold: Brussels Bureau, 'Brussels Agenda: Bonds Foreign and Financial', *FT.com*, 1 July 2003.

[141] F. Heinemann and M. Jopp, *The Benefits of a Working European Retail Market for Financial Services* (Bonn, Europa Union Verlag GmbH, 2002), p. 12.

[142] This statement rests on an assumption that laws can stimulate investment activity but as is discussed elsewhere in this book (see ch. 2), there is no certainty on law's catalytic role.

[143] Behavioural finance, which draws upon insights from behavioural science to understand the gap between the empirical reality of stock market behaviour and orthodox theoretical expectations of investor rationality and homogeneous preferences, is a burgeoning area for scholarship. D. C. Langevoort, 'Taming the Animal Spirits of the Stock Markets: a Behavioral Approach to Securities Regulation' (2002) 97 *Northwestern University Law Review* 135 reviews the main strands of the current debate. Two leading book length treatments of behavioural finance are: A. Shleifer, *Inefficient Markets: An Introduction to Behavioral Finance* (Oxford, Oxford University Press, 2000) and R. J. Shiller, *Irrational Exuberance* (Princeton, N.J.; Princeton University Press, 2000).

On the application of insights from behavioural finance to the EU's agenda for the promotion of retail securities market activity: N. Moloney, 'Confidence'.

to the most deserving projects.[144] Taken to its limits, this line of thinking could point towards a sharp reversal of the policy that currently enjoys political favour within the EU because it suggest that the emphasis should be on devising regulatory strategies to keep retail investors out of the securities markets rather than to attract them in.[145] Such a reversal looks unlikely on political grounds because of the powerful pull of the vision of a single, open market[146] but, in any event, the current policy is defensible. The jury is still out on the impact of investors' cognitive biases and weaknesses on the accuracy of securities prices and hence on the seriousness of any resulting problems with regard to allocative efficiency. Although it is undeniable that assumptions of investor rationality and homogeneous preferences do not match up to empirical reality, there is still force in the view that the problems are not systemic, that trades based on a range of different distorting influences should net off against each other and also that such trades are likely to be countered by professional arbitrage activity.[147] The potential for

---

[144] M. B. Fox, 'Shelf Registration, Integrated Disclosure and Underwriter Due Diligence: An Economic Analysis' (1984) 70 *Virginia Law Review* 1005, 1018–22; M. B. Fox, 'Securities Disclosure in a Globalizing Market: Who Should Regulate Whom' (1997) 95 *Michigan Law Review* 2498, 2544–50. But contesting the strength of the links between accurate prices and the ability of a securities market to structure the efficient allocation of scarce resources: L. A. Stout, 'The Unimportance of Being Efficient: An Economic Analysis of Market Pricing and Securities Regulation' (1988) 87 *Michigan Law Review* 613; L. A. Stout, 'Are Stock Markets Costly Casinos? Disagreement, Market Failure, and Securities Regulation' (1995) 81 *Virginia Law Review* 611, 677–82.

[145] Such strategies might include imposing new taxes on securities trading (Stout, 'Are Stock Markets Costly Casinos?', 699–702) or restricting unsophisticated investors to low-risk collective investment schemes (S. Choi, 'Regulating Investors not Issuers: a Market-based Proposal' (2000) 88 *California Law Review* 279, 300–2).

[146] European Commission, *Amended proposal*, explanatory memorandum, p. 4. However, note the Directive's special regime for wholesale securities. This regime applies to securities denominated at €50,000 or above which in effect should operate so as to create a retail investor exclusion zone: ibid.

[147] A special symposium issue of the *Journal of Corporation Law* (Summer, 2003) reveals the current state of play. L. A. Stout, 'The Mechanics of Market Inefficiency: An Introduction to the New Finance' (2003) 28 *Journal of Corporation Law* 635 argues that a new intellectual framework is developing on which to build a more powerful working model of securities markets, a framework which is informed by recognition of the significance of investors' heterogeneous expectations and irrationalities, and of limits to arbitrage as a mechanism for ensuring pricing accuracy. R. J. Gilson and R. Kraakman, 'The Mechanisms of Market Efficiency Twenty Years Later: The Hindsight Bias' (2003) *Journal of Corporation Law* 715 acknowledge that we are in the early stages of quite a different framework for evaluating stock markets but they remain sceptical about the sustained, as opposed to episodic, impact of investor irrationality on the accuracy of securities prices because of indeterminancy concerning the incidence and

harm to the securities market as a result of a growing retail presence is thus too speculative for it to undercut the legitimacy of the EU policy choice, rooted in established notions of laissez-faire markets that are basically open to all comers, to regard retail securities market activity as socially beneficial and to take steps to encourage its development.[148]

Whereas investor exclusion for market-protection reasons is a drastic option, disclosure has a ready appeal as a more modest strategy that could protect the market by lessening the incidence of investor irrationality.[149] The idea of tailoring disclosure to the needs of retail investors can be viewed positively from a behavioural perspective on the grounds that it accords with the idea that investors are not homogeneous and specifically tries to promote rationality amongst less sophisticated investors by providing them with information in a comprehensible form.[150] However, a fair degree of scepticism about disclosure's potential contribution to the protection of the market from irrational, poorly-informed trading is in

---

interaction of the variety of cognitive biases. They emphasise the importance of the arbitrage mechanism and argue for the removal of legal and institutional barriers to arbitrage.

[148] There is support for the view that regulators should proceed with caution in using behavioural finance insights as a guide to public policy: e.g. Langevoort, 'Taming', 138: 'positive strategies for regulation are hard to craft precisely because the alternative behavioral theories in the literature are so tentative'. For similar caution about basing regulatory policy-making on insights from behavioural finance see Gilson and Kraakman, 'The Mechanisms of Market Efficiency Twenty Years Later'.

In relation to the potential for retail investors to damage EU markets, Moloney, 'Confidence', 25 notes: 'Further evidence is needed, however, as to whether particular groups of investors are more affected by over-confidence and whether particular investment decisions are prone to over-confidence, before radical policy decisions can be made' and 'considerably greater understanding of how investors make decisions is needed before radical policy decisions can be made.'

[149] The discussion in the text throughout this section is based on the premise that the primary function of disclosure is promotion of efficiency in the real economy rather than investor protection. Disclosure's role as a mechanism for the protection of investors (particularly retail investors) is limited. There is a compelling view that official policies to promote retail stock market investing should also address the deficiencies of disclosure as a mechanism for making retail investors aware of the dangers inherent in securities investment: H. E. Jackson, 'To What Extent Should Individual Investors Rely on the Mechanisms of Market Efficiency: A Preliminary Investigation of Dispersion in Investor Returns' (2003) 28 *Journal of Corporation Law* 671; H. T. C. Hu, 'Faith and Magic: Investor Beliefs and Government Neutrality' (2000) 78 *Texas Law Review* 777. Investor education is an obvious way forward on this but, in the EU context, this provokes questions about the appropriate level – national or regional – for the development of such programmes: Moloney, 'Confidence', 33–7.

[150] Stout, 'Costly Casinos', 687. Behavioural financial analysis tends to assume that professional investors are less prone to irrationality than non-professionals: Langevoort, 'Taming', fn 159.

order.[151] Investor over-confidence is a significant distortive bias[152] and it is plain that disclosure can only ever play a limited role in countering its effects since cocksure investors are likely to ignore the warning signs that cold assessment of public information would reveal.[153] There is even a risk that summary or simplified disclosure could feed over-confidence by giving unskilled investors a false sense of security about their understanding of the risks involved in trading activities and about their ability to compete on equal terms with more sophisticated investors.[154] The potential for information overload also serves to limit the likely protective effect of disclosure: even where information is presented in accessible language or in summary form, the time and effort involved in evaluation may still be simply too much for some unskilled retail investors.[155] These observations suggest that, although there may be some value in mandatory disclosure as a counterweight to retail investor irrationality, the policy orientation should still be towards restraint in the development of disclosure rules specifically for the benefit of less sophisticated investors because intervention will generate additional costs in return for only limited and uncertain benefits.[156]

In relation specifically to the EU, where levels of retail activity in securities markets are low,[157] lack of certainty about the power of the law to change investment behaviour[158] serves as a further general factor militating against the development of a disclosure regime that is heavily weighted towards the interests of retail investors. The prospect of the EU adopting a regulatory strategy that burdens issuers with heavy additional disclosure

---

[151] S. M. Bainbridge, 'Mandatory Disclosure: A Behavioral Analysis' (2000) 68 *University of Cincinnati Law Review* 1023 suggests that, in relation to US capital markets, behavioural analysis offers little or no support for the mandatory disclosure regime.

[152] Langevoort, 'Taming', 145–7.

[153] The ability of the market (sophisticated and unsophisticated investors) to ignore the writing on the wall has recently attracted considerable scholarly attention in the aftermath of the spectacular fall from grace of companies such as Enron: e.g. J. N. Gordon, 'What Enron Means for the Management and Control of the Modern Business Corporation: Some Initial Reflections' (2002) 69 *University of Chicago Law Review* 1233.

[154] Langevoort, 'Taming', 175.

[155] Moloney, 'Confidence', 28–9.

[156] Extra compliance costs for issuers are an obvious additional burden. There would also be costs for retail investors if tailored disclosure did operate so as to feed over-confidence since this could lead to excessive trading activity and unprofitable investment of time and resources: Langevoort, 'Taming', 175.

[157] See further ch. 2.

[158] Ibid.

requirements for the benefit of a small, stagnant pool of retail investors has only to be mentioned to see the obvious dangers.

With these reservations about the value of tailored disclosure in mind, how does the new prospectus and periodic disclosure regime shape up? The Prospectus Directive in particular has a number of features that can be regarded as retail-investor orientated. The requirements for the use of accessible language,[159] due prominence for risk factors,[160] and non-technical summaries[161] have a modest and largely uncontroversial feel. Maximum harmonisation is more troubling. As discussed earlier in this chapter, maximum harmonisation is aimed at facilitating pan-European comparability of information by investors. In theory, retail investors should benefit most from it because, as compared to professional investors, they can be assumed broadly to lack the evaluative skills and resources needed to make sense of the differences in prospectuses that could occur under a more flexible regime. However, that maximum harmonisation is a worthwhile regulatory strategy to pursue because it is helpful to the promotion of pan-European trading strategies by retail investors is a proposition that can only ring true by making certain heroic assumptions: that there will be growth in retail securities market activity in the EU; that retail investors' investment strategies will move away from a home bias and will be conducted on a pan-European basis; and that, in making investment decisions, retail investors will plough through prospectuses in their entirety and thus benefit from the enhanced comparability that maximum harmonisation of the whole prospectus (i.e. not just the summary) is intended to provide. Given how far removed from reality these assumptions are, the retail investor case for maximum harmonisation is unconvincing.

G   The impact of the new regime for prospectuses and periodic disclosures on smaller/younger issuers and on second-tier market infrastructure providers

Another EU political aspiration is to widen access to investment capital for smaller and younger issuers and to tailor the regulatory requirements appropriately to their needs whilst maintaining adequate levels of investor

---

[159] PD, art. 5.1.
[160] PCR, arts. 25–6 and Annex 1.
[161] PD, art. 5.2. The summary should not normally exceed 2,500 words in the language in which the prospectus was originally drawn up: PD, rec. 21.

protection.[162] The new disclosure regime contains a number of features that are linked to these objectives. However, there are evidently two competing philosophies at work in the European debate, one inclining to the view that smaller and younger companies tend to have smaller capital requirements and that therefore the 'default' disclosure regime, framed by reference to larger companies, should be lightened so as not to burden them disproportionately with compliance costs, the other being that such companies represent more risky investment opportunities and that therefore the full weight of regulation should apply to them so as to protect the interests of investors.[163] The fluctuating fortunes of these competing views during the legislative process have resulted in a disclosure regime that is inconsistent and verging on uncertainty in some important respects.

SMEs and start-ups as a deserving case for a lighter touch – only limited success for this argument in the Prospectus Directive

There is a small issues exclusion from the Prospectus Directive. Securities included in an offer with a total consideration of less than €2.5 million calculated over twelve months fall entirely outside the scope of the Directive.[164] There is also an exemption from the requirement for a prospectus (but not other aspects of the Prospectus Directive) for unlisted offers of securities that have a total consideration of less than €100,000 calculated over a twelve-month period.[165] These limitations on the scope of the prospectus regime can be viewed as being broadly equivalent to the small offer exemptions available under US federal securities law.[166] Monetary thresholds are always vulnerable to the criticism that, depending on the context, they are too low or too high.[167] It is not clear exactly how

---

[162] PD, rec. 4 and art. 7.2(e).

[163] For the view that SMEs should not be allowed to disclose less information because this would undermine quality: K. Lannoo and A. Khachaturyan, *Disclosure Regulation in the EU: The Emerging Framework* (Brussels, Centre for European Policy Studies Task Force Report No. 48, October 2003), p. 18. The authors discount cost concerns arguing that these are counterbalanced by the fact that better disclosure would attract more investors.

[164] Art. 1.2(h).

[165] Art. 3.2(e).

[166] By virtue of Regulation D and Regulation A, as discussed in Cox, Hillman Langevoort, *Securities Regulation*, pp. 400–51.

[167] E.g. S. R. Cohn, 'The Impact of Securities Laws on Developing Companies: Would the Wright Brothers Have Gotten Off the Ground?' (1999) *Journal of Small & Emerging Business Law* 315 discussing whether the limit in Regulation A is too low to be workable.

the Prospectus Directive's thresholds were determined[168] but they are obviously very low, thereby limiting the likely practical utility of the exemptions.

With regard to the content of prospectus disclosure requirements, the Prospectus Directive contains a specific instruction to the Commission in respect of implementing measures that these should take account of the various activities and size of issuers, in particular SMEs.[169] Given this background, it is initially surprising not to find in the Commission Prospectus Regulation a special schedule or building block relating specifically to SMEs. An explanation for this omission lies in the consultation exercises that CESR conducted in order to advise the Commission on the drafting of the implementing measures. Consultation revealed that there was no meaningful backing for having special provisions for SMEs, a finding that was in line with CESR's initial assessment of the appropriate way forward,[170] and also with the Commission's own original views on the point.[171] Specifically, consultation found no real support for reducing for SMEs the number of years of required historical financial information from three to two.[172]

On start-ups, CESR did originally propose a series of specialist building blocks for certain issuers including start-ups. However, this approach did not find favour on consultation and it was therefore dropped and replaced with a limited derogation whereby competent authorities are permitted to adapt the disclosure requirements applicable to such issuers.[173]

Whether this approach to SMEs and start-ups will suffice to create a regime that successfully balances investor protection considerations against the need to avoid imposing a disproportionate regulatory compliance cost burden on issuers seeking smaller amounts of capital can only be a matter for speculation at this stage. Although the fact that the approach

---

[168] For instance, the €2.5 million threshold first formally appeared in the second version of the Directive proposed by the Commission (European Commission, *Amended proposal*) but the accompanying explanatory memorandum does not make clear how the figure was selected.

[169] PD, art. 7.2(e).

[170] Committee of European Securities Regulators, *Prospectus Consultation Draft Feedback Statement* (CESR/03–129, 2003), paras. 78–9.

[171] In the Impact Assessment Form annexed to European Commission, *Proposal for a Directive on the prospectus*, the Commission stated its belief that that there should not be any difference in disclosure standards due to the size of issuers.

[172] CESR, *Prospectus Consultation Draft Feedback*, paras. 78–9.

[173] CPR, rec. 22, art. 23 and Annex XIX. European Commission, *Main differences*, outlines the way in which CESR and the Commission's thinking on this issue evolved.

is based on evidence obtained through consultation provides some grounds for optimism about how it will work, this optimism needs to be qualified by acknowledging imperfections in the consultation process that could have compromised the quality of the data obtained. It is, for instance, possible to interpret the omission of any special treatment for SMEs as an indication of the relative strength of the representation of securities market experts (who would be expected broadly to favour high disclosure) over issuer groups (that would be expected broadly to favour disclosure obligations proportionate to the amounts of capital being sought) in the consultative processes.[174] That the position on SMEs has, in effect, reverted to what the Commission thought it should be in the first place provide an interesting insight on the manoeuvring that can take place between EU institutions.[175] The outcome suggests that efforts by the Council and European Parliament to rein in the Commission in the exercise of Level 2 implementing powers may not be entirely effective.

The derogation power could be significant as a mechanism for relieving the regulatory burden on certain issuers including start-ups. However, the extent to which this power will be available for this purpose is uncertain. Wording in the Commission Prospectus Regulation suggests that it is actually intended to perform the opposite function: that is, rather than being a mechanism for lightening the regulatory load, its real purpose is to empower competent authorities to ask for additional information going beyond the requirements of the applicable schedules and building blocks.[176]

But more success in the Transparency Directive

The original draft Transparency Directive published by the European Commission controversially proposed a mandatory quarterly reporting obligation for issuers with shares admitted to trading on regulated

---

[174] Inter-Institutional Monitoring Group, *Second Interim Report Monitoring the Lamfalussy Process* (Brussels, December 2003) p. 29 notes some concern that issuer interests might not have been as well represented in the consultation processes as the interests of securities market experts. Generally on the Lamfalussy consultation process see further ch. 3.

[175] That the Commission is liable to be swayed more by arguments *for* regulation to address the risks inherent in SME investment than by arguments *against* regulation so as not to burden disproportionately SMEs with disclosure compliance costs is evident in its justifications for the proposal to impose mandatory quarterly reporting in the Transparency Directive: *Proposal for a Directive on the harmonisation of transparency requirements*, p. 16.

[176] CPR, art. 23.1. European Commission, *Main differences*.

markets.[177] The Commission contended that mandatory quarterly financial reporting would provide better investor protection, and that the availability of more-structured and reliable information would increase market competition and efficiency.[178] It argued that comparable, publicly available information would help investors to judge companies. It noted the lack of empirical evidence pointing towards a link between mandatory quarterly reporting and stock market volatility. Further, it cited evidence of widespread adoption of quarterly reporting requirements at Member State level, either in State law or stock exchange rules, and of the number of publicly traded European companies already engaging in quarterly reporting, to demonstrate that the Community's existing disclosure regime was lagging behind best practice and was outdated. In an open acknowledgement of the agenda to attract international investment capital into Europe, the Commission also referred to the longstanding US requirement for quarterly reporting as a strong influence.

The content of the mandatory quarterly reporting requirement, as set out in the original draft Transparency Directive proposed by the Commission, was for three-monthly consolidated figures indicating net turnover and profit or loss before or after tax, together with an explanation. This proposal set the disclosure obligation at a level below the highest existing national standards on quarterly reporting.[179] It was also lighter than the Commission had had in mind when the idea of a new Transparency Directive was first mooted. That the Commission retreated from its more onerous original ideas can be seen as illustrating the value of pre-legislative consultation,[180] though it is also open to the more cynical interpretation that the Commission might have knowingly put forward unpalatable proposals at the outset with a view to a later compromise. As justification for its stance in the draft Transparency Directive, the Commission argued that regularly updated turnover and profit and loss figures were data that companies should maintain for operating purposes in any event, and that

---

[177] European Commission, *Proposal for a Directive on the harmonisation of transparency requirements*, draft Directive, art. 6.

[178] The Commission's views are set out in European Commission, *Proposal for a Directive on the harmonisation of transparency requirements*, explanatory memorandum, pp. 13–17.

[179] European Commission, *Proposal for a Directive on the harmonisation of transparency requirements*, explanatory memorandum, p. 17.

[180] The Commission conducted two rounds of open, public consultation before publishing its draft: European Commission, *Proposal for a Directive on the harmonisation of transparency requirements*, explanatory memorandum, p. 4.

therefore the administrative cost burden involved in complying with the proposed mandatory disclosure obligation would not be significant.[181]

Despite the Commission's concessions over the content of the quarterly disclosure requirement and its attempts to justify the proposal, this part of the draft Directive did not receive a warm reception. Opponents of quarterly reporting argued that a mandatory EU-wide obligation applying to all regulated markets would create additional administrative costs for only limited incremental benefits and could lead to undue emphasis on short-term considerations at the expense of issuers' longer-term objectives.[182] They pointed out that data used by the Commission to build the argument that quarterly reporting was becoming common practice could also be used against it: for instance, the Commission's argument for quarterly reporting on the basis that about 1,100 out of 6,000 publicly traded European companies already provided quarterly reports drawn up according to national GAAP, IAS/IFRS or US GAAP could be taken either way. More generally, the fact that the proposal for quarterly reporting provoked such mixed reactions amongst market participants undermined any attempt to present it as an essentially 'housekeeping' exercise to bring the law into line with converged market practice. The Commission's argument that its proposal only required issuers to disclose information they would be likely to have anyway and so would not be costly ignored the fact that prudent managers would be likely to be concerned about the liability risks inherent in publication and might therefore incur quite significant additional costs in audit fees as a safeguard.[183]

---

[181] European Commission, *Proposal for a Directive on the harmonisation of transparency requirements*, explanatory memorandum, pp. 16–17.

[182] European Economic and Social Committee, *Opinion on the Proposal for a Directive on the harmonisation of transparency requirements*, sec. 3.1 notes the concerns. They are developed further in a Position Paper on *News Dissemination and the EU Transparency Directive* (October 2003) to which the signatories were a powerful group including the London Stock Exchange, PR Newswire, Investor Relations Society, Association of British Insurers, Confederation of British Industry, Waymaker, Quoted Companies Alliance, National Association of Pension Funds, Association of Private Client Investment Managers and Stockbrokers, London Investment Banking Association, Institute of Chartered Secretaries and Administrators, British Bankers Association and The Association of Corporate Treasurers. The paper is available at http://www.treasurers.org/technical/papers/resources/positionpaper2003.pdf (accessed May 2004).

The arguments voiced in the EU debate over quarterly reporting have received attention in the past in the US: B. A. Mann, 'Reexamining the Merits of Mandatory Quarterly Reporting' (1992) 6(4) *Insights* 3.

[183] European Parliamentary Financial Services Forum, *Transparency Obligations Directive* (September 2003), available via http://www.epfsf.org/meetings/2003/briefings/briefing_10sep 2003.pdf (accessed May 2004).

The eventual result was that the Council and the European Parliament combined to throw out the proposal for mandatory quarterly reporting.[184] Given the genuine disagreement and uncertainty amongst market participants on the merits of a generally applicable quarterly reporting requirement,[185] it is highly questionable whether the time was ripe for this issue to appear on the harmonisation agenda at all, so an outcome that leaves it outside central control looks like the right result.

The benefits of the retreat from mandatory EU-wide quarterly reporting will not be felt only in junior market segments. Indeed, some junior segments of EU markets – typically those targeted at young, potentially high-growth venture businesses – will benefit less from it than more senior segments because these already operate subject to quarterly reporting requirements imposed by Member States or stock exchanges.[186] Yet, amongst ordinary commercial companies, it should be smaller companies with modest capital requirements that are especially assisted by the decision to drop the proposal for a mandatory EU-wide quarterly reporting requirement because of the likelihood that they would have been disproportionately affected by the burden of the compliance costs this would have entailed.

Implications for second-tier stock markets

The Prospectus and Transparency Directives impose requirements for a prospectus and for periodic disclosures when securities are admitted to trading on a regulated market. 'Regulated market' here means a market to

---

[184] At its meeting in November 2003 the ECOFIN Council approved a proposal to amend the draft by dropping the mandatory quarterly reporting obligation and replacing it with either quarterly reporting or a periodic obligation to explain material events and transactions and their impact on the financial position of the issuer during the relevant period, and to provide a general description of the financial position and performance of the issuer during the relevant period: D. Dombey, 'EU Drops Plan for Mandatory Profit, Loss Data', *Financial Times*, 26 November 2003, p. 28. This revised approach was accepted by the European Parliament and is reflected in the TD, art. 6.

[185] E.g. S. Tucker, 'Quarter Reports Gain Support', *Financial Times*, 11 February 2004, p. 24 noting the inconsistent results of two surveys. One, commissioned by the Association for Investment Management and Research, found that nearly half of respondents believed that quarterly reporting would improve information quality 'significantly', while a further 36 per cent said it would improve the quality of information 'somewhat'. The other, commissioned just a few months earlier by Mori, indicated that support for quarterly reporting among UK fund managers and investment analysts was waning, with nearly 60 per cent disagreeing with the statement that it would be 'very useful'.

[186] European Commission, *Proposal for a Directive on the harmonisation of transparency requirements*, explanatory memorandum, p. 14.

which the rules in the Investment Services Directive[187] or its replacement, the Financial Instruments Markets Directive (ISD2),[188] on access and operating requirements apply and which benefits from the liberalisation provisions in those Directives.[189] The category of ISD/ISD2[190] regulated market embraces second-tier markets, and as of June 2004 included the Second Marché and the Nouveau Marché in Paris, the Alternative Investment Market (AIM) in London, the Mercato Ristretto in Milan, the Nuevo Mercado in Spain and the Nouveau Marché in Belgium.[191]

Early forms of EU intervention had imposed disclosure requirements that were limited in scope to the officially listed segment of the market.[192] Broadly speaking, 'official listing' denoted the senior, most prestigious sector of a securities market, although the term was not legally defined.[193] The upgrading of disclosure requirements to a consistent level across all ISD/ISD2 regulated markets reflects the way in which the policy under-pinning the development of securities laws within the EU has adapted to changing market conditions, in particular to the emergence of increasingly significant second-tier markets.[194] Regulatory policy has moved firmly away from the old distinction between listed and unlisted securities because it is regarded as outmoded. Early legislative measures concentrated on the officially-listed sector because those were the markets that were known at that time. Since then, second-tier markets have become much more significant economic actors. Contemporary policy, shaped by reference to current market conditions, is that, in the interests of efficiency, market

---

[187] Council Directive 93/22/EEC of 10 May 1993 on investment services in the securities field, OJ 1993 No. L141/27.

[188] Directive 2004/39/EC of the European Parliament and of the Council of 21 April 2004 on markets in financial instruments amending Council Directives 85/611/EEC and 93/6/EEC and Directive 2000/12/EC of the European Parliament and of the Council and repealing Council Directive 93/22/EEC, OJ 2004 No. L145/1.

[189] Moloney, *EC Securities Regulation*, pp. 655–7.

[190] It is unclear yet whether market practice will change to refer to 'FIMD' markets instead of 'ISD' markets. The text assumes that the established practice will persist.

[191] European Commission, *Proposal for a Directive on the harmonisation of transparency requirements*, explanatory memorandum, p. 5, fn 7. A full list of ISD/ISD2 regulated markets is available via http://www.europa.eu.int/comm/internal_market/en/finances/mobil/isd/docs/isd–regulated–market_en.pdf (accessed May 2004).

[192] Listing Particulars Directive, later consolidated into CARD; Interim Reports Directive, later consolidated into CARD.

[193] Moloney, *EC Securities Regulation*, pp. 98–9.

[194] G. Ferrarini, 'Securities Regulation and the Rise of Pan-European Securities Markets: An Overview' in G. Ferrarini, K. J. Hopt and E. Wymeersch (eds.), *Capital Markets in the Age of the Euro* (London, Kluwer Law International, 2002), p. 272.

confidence and investor protection, the same rules should generally apply.[195]

Given that the policy has moved away from regulating different market segments on a different basis, it might be supposed that the new regime is comprehensive, applying to all market infrastructure providers. However, this is not the case and gaps remain. It is possible for a securities market to sit outside the category of ISD/ISD2 regulated market: in the UK, OFEX is an example of a market that has chosen to do so.[196] The admission of securities to a market which is not ISD/ISD2-regulated falls outside the Prospectus and Transparency Directives. Thus, so far as EU securities law is concerned, there is no requirement for a prospectus at the time of admission of an issuer's securities to such a market (assuming there is no public offer of the securities), nor do periodic disclosure requirements apply thereafter.

The different regulatory burdens for issuers depending on whether their securities are admitted to trading on an ISD/ISD2 regulated market or an unregulated market, provoke strategic questions for operators of securities markets on the choice of regulatory status that will best enable them to compete for business, particularly from smaller issuers that could be disproportionately burdened by heavy disclosure requirements. Some infrastructure providers, such as AIM, which has been the UK's ISD regulated market for smaller issuers, have historically carved out a niche for themselves in a competitive market by providing a lighter regulatory regime for smaller issuers.

There are suggestions that the extension of the prospectus scrutiny requirements[197] and periodic disclosure regime beyond the officially-listed segment could drive smaller issuers into securities trading facilities within the EU that do not have ISD/ISD2 regulated market status or into overseas exchanges that are outside the reach of the EU. The possibility of some regulated markets choosing to opt out of that status in order to escape the

---

[195] PD, rec. 12.

[196] OFEX, *About Ofex plc*, available via www.ofex.com (accessed May 2004). Another example is that the *Freiverkehr* segment at German exchanges (including, for derivatives issuers, the EUWAX at the Stuttgart exchange) is not a regulated market: Shearman & Sterling, *The EU Prospectus Directive – Home Member State for Non-EU-Issuers* (Client Publication, November 2003) available at http://www.shearman.com/documents/CM_1103.pdf (accessed May 2004).

[197] Under the old regime, prospectuses relating to securities outside the officially listed segment were subject to institutional oversight only if they were to be used cross-border but such usage of prospectuses was rare.

burdensome impact of the disclosure Directives has also been mooted.[198] This possibility became a reality in the UK when, in May 2004, the London Stock Exchange confirmed its intention to relinquish AIM's status as an EU regulated market with effect from October 2004.[199]

The operators of a regulated market who are considering the option of changing status would need to weigh the benefits of a lighter regulatory environment against the costs involved in ceasing to be a regulated market, in particular the risk that this could lower the market's status in the eyes of issuers and investors (some of whom may be subject to investment constraints that require them to invest only in securities trading on regulated markets) and thus result in a loss of business.[200] However, it is significant to note that the LSE's decision in respect of AIM's status was made notwithstanding evidence of AIM's recent success in attracting new business, as compared to OFEX, and some suggestions that the difference in performance was linked to their different regulatory status.[201] The LSE's decision in respect of AIM, which was in direct response to the increasing regulatory burden attaching to regulated markets under the new Directives, is powerful evidence that the strength of the benefits of that status as against countervailing considerations can no longer be lightly assumed.

H   Ensuring candid and careful compliance with prospectus and periodic disclosure requirements

Recent failures in the operation of disclosure regimes have provided a sharp reminder of the importance of paying attention not just to the content of disclosure obligations but also to the mechanisms for ensuring that those responsible for making disclosures do so candidly and carefully. As

---

[198] E.g. A. Skorecki, 'AIM Chiefs Query EU Prospectus Proposals', *Financial Times*, 29 May 2003, p. 24, reporting that the London Stock Exchange, AIM's owner, was considering making it an unregulated market to put it outside the scope of Directives relating to regulated markets.

[199] London Stock Exchange, 'London Stock Exchange Confirms Change to AIM's Regulatory Status', LSE Press Release, 18 May 2004. AIM will instead be an exchange-regulated market under the supervision of the FSA: ibid.

[200] D. Blackwell, 'OFEX Left on Blocks as AIM Sprints Away', *Financial Times*, 15 March 2004, p. 28, reporting that Loyalward, an OFEX company with significant interests in the Crete tourist resort development industry, was considering a move onto AIM in order to enhance the marketability of its shares to Greek institutional investors.

[201] In 2003, AIM attracted sixty IPOs whereas only fifteen issuers joined OFEX: Blackwell, 'OFEX Left on Blocks'. In January and February 2004, there were seven IPOs on AIM whereas OFEX had none: ibid.

is obvious, good disclosure rules on the statute books are practically meaningless if they are not matched by good-quality compliance. According to one study, laws facilitating private enforcement through disclosure and liability rules are distinctly beneficial to the development of stock markets.[202]

A strategy for promoting compliance that was employed in the old prospectus disclosure regime and which is maintained in the Prospectus Directive is a requirement for Member States to ensure that responsibility for prospectus information is clearly assumed. Member States must ensure that, at a minimum, the issuer, or its administrative, management or supervisory body, takes responsibility for prospectus information.[203] Responsible persons must make declarations about the accuracy and completeness of the prospectus information.[204] A new feature of EU law on prospectuses is that the Directive now expressly requires Member States to underpin such declarations with civil liability under national law.[205]

The Transparency Directive, in its original form, appeared to be trying to replicate in the periodic disclosure regime a responsibility and liability position equivalent to that for prospectuses. The Commission's commentary on the draft Directive left no doubt that the decision so to extend the regime was strongly influenced by 'pace-setting' developments in US securities regulation.[206] However, the draft Directive's original stipulations for Member States to prescribe mandatory assumption of responsibility requirements underpinned by civil liability and to require certification of annual and half-yearly financial statements[207] were changed during the legislative process to the extent of requiring Member States to impose 'appropriate' rather than 'civil' liability.[208] Thus, it appears that it would be possible for Member States to satisfy the Directive by imposing criminal

---

[202] R. La Porta, F. Lopez-de-Silanes and A. Shleifer, 'What Works in Securities Laws?' *National Bureau of Economic Research* Working Paper 9882 (July 2003).

[203] PD, art. 6.1.

[204] PD, art. 6.

[205] PD, art. 6.2.

[206] European Commission, *Proposal for a Directive on the harmonisation of transparency requirements*, explanatory memorandum, pp. 8–9.

[207] TD, art. 4.2 (annual financial reports); art. 5.2 (half-yearly financial reports). There is no requirement for express certification in respect of interim management statements under TD, art. 6 but, as with annual and half-yearly disclosures, Member States must ensure that the issuer or its administrative, management or supervisory body, assumes responsibility for these statements and that provisions on liability apply: TD, art. 7.

[208] TD, rec. 10 and art. 7.

sanctions for inaccurate periodic disclosures. This flexibility with regard to the type of legal sanctions applied may sit more easily with established legal traditions in some EU Member States than the original proposal.[209] However, criminal sanctions could be a poor choice if viewed from the perspective of research that suggests that civil sanctions and private enforcement are especially associated with the growth of securities markets.

Additionally, the scope of the responsibility required to be assumed was narrowed down between the original draft and later versions. As originally drafted, the Transparency Directive largely followed the Prospectus Directive by requiring responsibility statements to the effect that the information was in accordance with the facts and made no omission likely to affect its import. This was later replaced by a requirement for assumptions of responsibility on financial statements giving a true and fair view and on management reports providing a fair review of the matters covered. This narrower form of responsibility statement could be significant in legal systems where civil liability turns on precisely what the maker of a statement has assumed responsibility for.[210] Also added to the Directive during its passage was a statement that Member States would remain free to determine the extent of the liability.[211] This may be intended to allow Member States to limit the category of persons entitled to sue in respect of false reports.[212]

Concerns about intensified legal risk lay behind these changes to the liability provisions in the Transparency Directive.[213] The Transparency Directive sparked this concern more than the Prospectus Directive because of their different provisions on the publication of information:

---

[209] Wymeersch, 'Company Law', 296–7 suggests substantial equivalence between the Sarbanes-Oxley certification requirements and the European tradition whereby the accounts are the prime responsibility of the board and are signed by them, and there are strict criminal sanctions for drawing up false accounts.

[210] On assumption of responsibility as an element triggering liability for negligent misstatement: *Hedley Byrne & Co. Ltd* v. *Heller & Partners Ltd* [1964] AC 465; *Henderson* v. *Merrett Syndicates Ltd* [1995] 2 AC 145; and generally W. V. H. Rogers, *Winfield & Jolowicz on Tort* (16th edn, London, Sweet & Maxwell, 2002) paras. 5.27–5.30.

[211] TD, rec. 10.

[212] E.g. to limit liability to existing shareholders as is the position in respect of accounts under current English law, as established by *Caparo Industries plc* v. *Dickman* [1990] 2 AC 605.

[213] These concerns are discussed in a paper published by the UK Financial Markets Law Committee (a body comprising senior lawyers, representatives of financial markets participants, regulatory authorities, trade associations and similar bodies), *Issue 76 – Transparency Obligations Directive* (January 2004), available via www.fmlc.org (accessed May 2004).

the Prospectus Directive broadly requires publication to be concentrated in the State(s) where an offer is made or admission to listing is sought,[214] and, as such, it is plausible to suggest that the risk of litigation in respect of prospectus inaccuracies could be largely confined to those States. However, the Transparency Directive requires the dissemination of information throughout the EU,[215] thus broadening the purpose of the communication and thereby potentially widening the scope for multi-jurisdictional liability and for forum shopping. During the passage of the Transparency Directive a move was made specifically to address the concerns about the potential for multi-jurisdictional litigation by the proposed inclusion of a provision limiting determination of liability to the issuer's home State.[216] This was not taken up by the political institutions of the EU in the Transparency Directive but it may, and arguably more appropriately, receive attention in the context of a broader EU initiative to harmonise Member States' conflict of laws rules regarding non-contractual obligations.[217] It is not necessarily the case that confining liability determination to the issuer's home State would represent the most desirable policy choice from a securities market-building perspective: the threat of multi-jurisdictional liability could make civil litigation a more powerful mechanism for ensuring the credibility of securities law disclosures within the EU, a potential benefit that would need to be weighed carefully against the additional burdens and costs for issuers that this approach would entail.

Both Directives also contain loosely-worded provisions requiring Member States to impose 'effective, proportionate and dissuasive' administrative measures or sanctions for non-compliance with provisions adopted in implementation of the Directives.[218] Again the relatively low level of prescription in these provisions has to be understood in the context of the distinctive, non-federal structure of the EU: sanctions and the procedural rules governing their enforcement remain essentially unharmonised Member State responsibilities. However, in this case the Directives do deal with the possibility of multiple actions by regulators by concentrating supervisory and enforcement authority in home States and

---

[214] PD, art. 14.

[215] TD, art. 17.

[216] This suggestion is made in Financial Markets Law Committee, *Issue 76*.

[217] European Commission, *Proposal for a Regulation of the European Parliament and the Council on the Law Applicable to Non-contractual Obligations ('Rome II')* (COM (2003) 427).

[218] PD, art. 25 and TD, art. 24.

by regulating the minimum range of investigative tools that national securities regulators must have at their disposal.[219]

Post-Enron discussion of company law and corporate governance within the EU has resulted in a proposal for the introduction on a pan-European basis of a directors' disqualification sanction for misleading disclosures.[220] The details of this proposal – such as precisely which disclosures it would cover,[221] whether it would be an administrative or judicial sanction and, if administrative, which agencies would be responsible for its administration[222] – remain to be fleshed out. Pending further detail, an initial reaction to this proposal is that constitutional sensitivities about EU intervention in the area of sanctions mean that, even if such a rule were to be introduced, it would be likely to be in a form that would leave plenty of room for Member States to apply it differently within their national systems.[223] Thus, it is possible that such a step could create a veneer of standardisation whereas, in fact, persistent differences in the administrative and judicial systems of Member States would make a broad measure of pan-European consistency in the operation of a disqualification sanction realistically unachievable.[224] Arguably, policy attention would be better concentrated for now on promoting convergence in supervisory

---

[219] However, under the PD (art. 23) and TD (art. 22). there is scope for 'precautionary measures' – a host State can take action directly in respect of infringements/irregularities when it has first referred its findings to the home Member State and, despite the home State intervention or because its intervention proves inadequate, the problems persist. The home Member State has to be informed prior to the host State's action and the Commission has to be informed as soon as possible.

[220] High Level Group of Company Law Experts, *A Modern Regulatory Framework for Company Law in Europe* (Brussels, European Commission, November 2002) (report by a group of experts who were commissioned by the European Commission to make recommendations on the modernisation of company law within the EU).

[221] The High Level Group suggested that it should apply at least for misleading financial and key non-financial disclosures: ibid.

[222] Although institutional responsibilities for the oversight of securities law disclosures are now to be concentrated in securities regulators, the oversight arrangements for financial and corporate governance disclosures are still characterised by diversity (see ch. 6). Such diversity could feed into the institutional arrangements for the administration of any disqualification sanction.

[223] K. J. Hopt, 'Modern Company and Capital Market Problems: Improving European Corporate Governance after Enron' [2003] *Journal of Corporate Law Studies* 221, 246–7. Hopt is a proponent of the adoption of a disqualification sanction but he accepts that its details should be left to the Member States and that they might approach it quite differently.

[224] E. Ferran, 'The Role of the Shareholder in Internal Corporate Governance: Enabling Shareholders to Make Better-Informed Decisions' (2003) 4 *European Business Organization Law Review* 491.

and enforcement practices amongst national regulators, and for detailed standardisation of the sanctions available to them to follow later, once an appropriate degree of convergence in practice has emerged.

I   Dissemination of information

The technical processes whereby market participants gain access to information matter because how widely and how quickly investors become aware of new disclosures can influence the speed with which information becomes impounded into securities prices. This means that it is appropriate for regulatory policy-makers to pay attention to the mechanics of information dissemination. This is an area where it makes sense to consider the issues on a pan-European basis: seamless provision to EU investors of information on issuers whose securities are trading on EU markets is exactly the sort of practical step that could bring closer to reality the vision of a single pan-European securities market in which old-fashioned national biases in issuance and investment activity have disappeared.

Paying attention to information dissemination mechanisms does not necessarily mean that Member States should themselves assume the role of constructing and maintaining data access points. The UK provides an example of an alternative approach. After it became the regulator of listed companies, the FSA conducted a detailed inquiry into the mechanisms it ought to put in place to ensure proper dissemination of issuers' regulatory announcements.[225] The end result of this review was the establishment of a competitive system whereby a number of media organisations have been authorised by the FSA to act as primary distributors of regulatory announcements.[226] The FSA was satisfied that investors' needs for a single source of full-text regulatory information would be satisfied by news agencies that would collate all the regulatory information from the various

---

[225] Financial Services Authority, *Review of the UK Mechanism for Disseminating Regulatory Information by Listed Companies* (London, FSA, Consultation Paper 92, 2001).

[226] Financial Services Authority, *Proposed Changes to the UK Mechanism for Disseminating Regulatory Information by Listed Companies* (London, FSA, Policy Statement, November 2001). As of March 2004, the primary information providers recognised by the FSA were: Business Wire Regulatory Disclosure provided by Business Wire; FirstSight provided by Waymaker; Hugin Announce provided by Hugin ASA; Newslink Financial provided by Newslink; PimsWire provided by Pims; PR Newswire Disclose provided by PR Newswire; and RNS provided by the London Stock Exchange (UK Listing Authority, *Listing Rules*, sch. 12).

primary distributors and make it available on their systems at no extra cost to their customers.[227] The FSA considered further that market forces would ensure that a real-time aggregated regulatory information source would remain available, for free or at a low cost, for retail investors, though it held in reserve the possibility of a freely accessible FSA website to act as such a source.[228]

Introducing competition between commercial news providers into the process for the dissemination of regulatory information offers various potential benefits, such as lower costs and rapid embrace of technological advances. There are risks that competition between providers could lead to fragmentation and that the principle of non-discriminatory access to information could be impaired. However, the FSA's investigations provide reassurance on the seriousness of these risks and/or suggest that it may be enough for regulators to maintain a watching brief in respect of them.

The involvement of commercial companies in the dissemination of regulatory information is also potentially beneficial from a cross-border perspective, in that private actors are not constrained by national boundaries and jurisdictions in the way that national regulators are. News dissemination providers that operate internationally are positioned to challenge old rigidities, whereby issuers made their disclosures to a national public or quasi public organisation and distribution of such information was largely confined to the home market.[229]

Thus, it would seem sensible for EU policy-makers to examine closely the potential role for commercial operators in the development of effective pan-European mechanisms for the dissemination of information, and to consider the forms of supervisory oversight that would best galvanise such operators to maintain high standards in the quality and reliability of their

[227] FSA, *Review of the UK Mechanism*, paras. 5.11 and 5.26.

The FSA lists (at http://www.fsa.gov.uk/ukla/ukla_faq.html (accessed May 2004)) the following news organisations as providers of aggregated information services to institutional investors: AFX News; Bloomberg; Perfect Information; Reuters; Thomson Financial (who provide ICV and TOPIC products); and Track Data Corporation. For retail investors the listed providers of aggregated information services were: Financial Express-UK Wire; Hemscott.net; Ample, and the London Stock Exchange's website.

[228] FSA, *Review of the UK Mechanism*, pp. 27 and 30. This suggests that the costs involved in the development and maintenance of any such website should be borne by the market and that the FSA would recover them through the annual listing fees paid by listed companies.

[229] E.g. Hugin, which is authorised by the FSA in the UK and also has regulatory dissemination experience in the German, Swedish, Swiss, Austrian and Norwegian markets. Information available: Hugin, *About Us*, via www.hugincorporate.com (accessed May 2004).

distribution channels and mechanisms. However, EU policy-makers have been slow to move in this direction, possibly because of the historical entrenched position of the State in Continental European capital markets[230] and possibly also because of recent transitional concerns relating to the enlargement of the EU.[231] Even a measure as recent as the Prospectus Directive reflects a traditional approach in that it designates national regulators as the central prospectus data point in each country. Under this Directive, primary responsibility for prospectus disclosure lies with issuers. They have a choice of publication mechanisms, including options that have a rather old-fashioned feel to them, such as insertion in newspapers circulating in the Member States where the offer to the public is made or admission to trading is being sought, or collection in physical form from designated addresses.[232] Central access to prospectus information is to be achieved through a requirement for national securities regulators to publish electronically all prospectuses they have approved over a period of twelve months or at least a list of such prospectuses with applicable hyperlinks.[233] This requirement is largely administrative in nature and, as such, the compliance cost burden on the State should be modest. Yet the relative benefits of lists of approved prospectuses maintained on a fragmented basis by national regulators are also likely to be fairly limited.

Controversy sparked by the Transparency Directive finally brought the potential for market mechanisms to assist in the development of effective pan-European information dissemination to the foreground of policy debate. The Commission's proposal for a new Transparency Directive contained a suggestion that issuers should be required to disseminate information through their own websites, supplemented by an 'efficient e-mail alert mechanism' set up by issuers 'to inform all interested parties on a real-time basis of any changes to information' so presented.[234] This proposal deservedly attracted strong criticism, with informed market participants making the point that 'constantly monitoring thousands of individual websites for company news is practically impossible even for global investment banks let alone the individual private investor'.[235]

---

[230] Lannoo and Khachaturyan, *Disclosure Regulation*, p. 21.
[231] Federation of European Stock Exchanges, *Comments*, suggests that enlargement presented a challenge to the Europe-wide introduction of innovative IT-based solutions.
[232] PD, art. 14.2. But Member States can in addition require publication in electronic form.
[233] PD, art. 14 and CPR, art. 32.
[234] European Commission, *Proposal for a Directive on the harmonisation of transparency requirements*, explanatory memorandum, p. 7.
[235] London Stock Exchange *et al.*, *News Dissemination*.

Differences in the accessibility and quality of individual corporate websites is a further powerful ground against relying on issuers' websites for the publication of regulatory information.[236]

The proposal for mandatory issuer website publication was dropped as the draft Directive made its way through the legislative process. The final version of the Directive instead contains a requirement for home Member States to require issuers to use such media as can be relied upon for the effective dissemination of information to the public throughout the EU and to ensure that there is at least one officially appointed mechanism for the central storage of regulated information.[237] Implementing measures will focus on minimum standards for information dissemination and central storage.[238] A recital in the Directive notes that: 'Issuers should benefit from free competition when choosing the media or operators for disseminating information.'[239] Although much is still dependent on the details and practical arrangements that will be worked out in implementing measures and through co-operation between Member States in the context of CESR, things seem to be evolving towards a more flexible position that would permit reliance on supervised commercial news organisations for information dissemination. This evolving flexibility represents a positive development. Market solutions may not be appropriate for the entirety of the EU because of varying levels of market development, including coverage from competing commercial news organisations, across the different regional segments of the EU securities market, yet for the regulatory framework to be sufficiently flexible as to permit States to withdraw from direct responsibility for information dissemination in favour of a more indirect supervisory role whenever suitable local market conditions are in place, looks like a sensible strategy.

As noted in Section H, the emphasis in the Transparency Directive on EU-wide dissemination of information brings to the foreground concerns about potential concomitant EU-wide expansion of civil liability. However, such concerns do not constitute a good reason to shy away from the policy of promoting better mechanisms for the pan-European dissemination of investment information. The performance of securities markets is crucially dependent on information so whatever problems flow from improving information dissemination mechanics should be addressed

---

[236] Financial Services Authority, *Review of the UK Mechanism*, pp. 30–1.
[237] TD, art 17.
[238] TD, art. 17.3.
[239] TD, rec. 15.

directly rather than compromising the policy strategy of ensuring better EU-wide non-discriminatory investor access to information.

J   The Market Abuse Directive and issuer disclosure

The Market Abuse Directive was adopted by the European Council and European Parliament on 28 January 2003. It is due to be implemented into the national law of Member States by 12 October 2004. The Market Abuse Directive replaces a previous Directive on insider dealing and significantly expands the scope of EU regulatory intervention to embrace market manipulation as well as insider dealing.

So far as issuer disclosure is concerned, the Market Abuse Directive provides an important missing piece of the jigsaw by requiring prompt disclosure of inside information.[240] Inside information is defined by the Directive as: 'information of a precise nature which has not been made public, relating, directly or indirectly, to one or more issuers of financial instruments or to one or more financial instruments and which, if it were made public, would be likely to have a significant effect on the prices of those financial instruments or on the price of related derivative financial instruments'.[241] Aspects of this definition are further elaborated in a Level 2 implementing measure adopted under the Directive.[242] One key element of the definition in the implementing measure is that information that 'would have a significant effect on price' is defined as 'information a reasonable investor would be likely to use as part of the basis of his investment decisions'. There are concerns that this broadens the disclosure obligation to an excessive degree beyond the old position,[243] which was that disclosure was required only of developments that might lead to substantial movements

---

[240] MAD, art. 6.1.

[241] MAD, art. 1.1. The definition is expanded further in relation to derivatives on commodities and for intermediaries charged with the execution of orders concerning financial information: ibid

[242] Commission Directive 2003/124/EC of 22 December 2003 implementing Directive 2003/ 6/EC as regards the definition and public disclosure of inside information and the definition of market manipulation, OJ 2003 No. L339/70, art. 1 (on the 'precise nature' of information, and importing a reasonable investor test into determining when information, if made public, would be likely to affect price). On potential problems with some of this drafting: J. Coffey, 'The Market Abuse Directive – The First Use of the Lamfalussy Process' (2003) 18(9) *Journal of International Banking Law and Regulation* 370.

[243] Herbert Smith, *Market Abuse: Key Implementation Issues* (Corporate Briefing, April 2004).

in the price of an issuer's shares[244] or significantly affect its ability to meet its commitments.[245]

As with the Prospectus and Transparency Directives, this disclosure obligation is broadly confined to issuers with securities admitted to trading on an ISD/ISD2 regulated market.[246] The broad scope of the disclosure obligation could be a factor militating against having securities admitted to trading on a regulated market and could thus serve to foster the growth of alternative trade execution mechanisms.[247] For non-EU issuers that are interested in EU markets for reasons other than bonding with high standards, the prospect of a broad ongoing disclosure obligation that may be more onerous than that imposed by their home jurisdiction could be a powerful repellent.[248]

Issuers are required to make information public 'as soon as possible'.[249] They can delay disclosure so as not to prejudice their legitimate interests only where this would not be likely to mislead the public and where confidentiality can be maintained.[250] This qualification, which did not exist in explicit form in the predecessor law, could be a source of considerable uncertainty in practice: when can issuers safely assume that delayed disclosure is unlikely to mislead the public? Selective disclosure of information is prohibited except in circumstances covered by duties of

---

[244] CARD, art. 68 (for issuers with shares admitted to official listing). By virtue of the Insider Dealing Directive (Council Directive 89/592/EEC of 13 November 1989 coordinating regulations on insider dealing, OJ 1989 No. L334/30), this obligation was extended to companies with shares admitted to trading on ISD regulated markets.

[245] CARD, art. 81 (for issuers with debt securities admitted to official listing). This obligation was likewise extended to issuers with debt securities admitted to trading on ISD regulated markets.

[246] MAD, art. 9.

[247] Most secondary bond trading activity in the EU already takes place outside traditional exchanges, but bonds are usually formally listed in either London or Luxembourg. Alternative mechanisms account for only 1 per cent of equity trading volumes but the financial trading landscape is changing: European Commission, *Proposal for a Directive of the European Parliament and of the Council on investment services and regulated markets, and amending Council Directives 85/611/EEC, Council Directive 93/6/EEC and European Parliament and Council Directive 2000/12/EC* (COM(2002) 625), explanatory memorandum, p. 8.

[248] However, for a more optimistic assessment of the impact of this disclosure obligation: J. lau Hansen, 'MAD in a Hurry: The Swift and Promising Adoption of the EU Market Abuse Directive' [2004] *European Business Law Review* 183.

[249] MAD, art. 6.1.

[250] MAD, art. 6.2. The Level 2 Directive 2003/124/EC, art. 3 provides a non-exhaustive list of legitimate reasons for delaying public disclosure. This article also regulates the arrangements that issuers are required to have in place to ensure the confidentiality of information.

confidentiality. Whenever in the ordinary course of business there is an intentional disclosure of information to a party who does not owe a duty of confidentiality, this must be accompanied by simultaneous public disclosure.[251] If the selective disclosure is unintentional, the public disclosure must be made promptly.[252]

The mandatory dissemination mechanism for issuers' disclosures under this Directive is posting on issuers' websites.[253] The arguments previously considered in Section I against regarding issuers' websites as an adequate mechanism for ensuring that information that is relevant to investment decisions comes to the attention of the EU-wide investment community apply here too. If the worst fears about the scope of the disclosure obligation on issuers that is imposed by this Directive come true, there may be some pragmatic advantages in regulatory news services not being flooded by a constant stream of issuer announcements. However, this would be far from an ideal position.

The Market Abuse Directive does not explicitly link issuers to designated home States for supervisory purposes. Instead it is primarily territorial in its approach, requiring each Member State to apply the Directive to actions carried out in its territory, but there is also a secondary requirement for Member States to apply it to actions abroad concerning financial instruments that are admitted to trading on a regulated market within their jurisdiction.[254] This approach raises the prospect of more than one national regulator being competent to act in certain circumstances, for example against issuers with multiple listings within the EU. It is conceivable, too, that overlapping competencies could arise because of the difference in approach on supervisory jurisdictional matters between this Directive and the Prospectus and Transparency Directives, for example where an EU issuer which is accused of making disclosures that infringe the Market Abuse Directive as well as one of the other Directives has its securities admitted to trading on a regulated market outside its home (registered-office) State. The increased risk of having to answer to more than one national regulator possibly could serve to discourage cross-border admission to trading activity; but how much weight issuers in fact attach to this concern is likely to depend on how well national regulators respond to the

---

[251] MAD, art. 6.3.

[252] MAD, art. 6.3.

[253] MAD, art. 6.1. Additional detailed requirements are specified in the Level 2 Directive 2003/124/EC, art. 2.

[254] MAD, art. 10.

challenge of developing effective and efficient systems for consultation and co-operation on matters of mutual concern.

K   Concluding remarks – moving closer to a genuine single securities market?

The Prospectus, Transparency and Market Abuse Directives have a common underlying purpose: they are designed to promote the development of an integrated, efficient EU securities market that will foster growth and job creation by improving the allocation of capital and reducing costs.[255] It is market participants rather than laws that make markets, so questions that can usefully be asked here relate to whether the new rules considered in this chapter are likely to promote more cross-border activity by issuers and help erode a home bias in investment behaviour. Before looking at these questions, however, it is worth noting that issuers and investors can also connect with each other on a cross-border basis through secondary market linkages between exchanges located in different Member States. Such linkages make it possible for investors to trade in securities listed on markets located in other Member States via their local brokers. As such, they reduce the need for issuers to maintain multiple listings in order to reach out to geographically dispersed pools of investors.[256] Improved rules on multi-State offers and multiple listings are thus not absolutely essential to EU securities market integration but they could make a positive impact by adding to the range of structures that can be utilised in transnational securities market activity.

The new rules should facilitate exempt offers of unlisted securities to the wholesale markets

To date, cross-border unlisted issuance activity within the EU has been orientated towards the wholesale market and has relied heavily on exemptions from the requirement to produce a prospectus. This segment of market activity could receive a boost from the new rules because they clarify the exemptions and reduce the scope for inconsistent interpretation in different Member States, improvements that should yield savings in the professional advisory fees associated with exempt cross-border offerings. Preventing

---

[255] PD, rec. 4; TD, rec. 1; MAD, recs. 1 and 2.
[256] Jackson and Pan, 'Regulatory Competition', 677–8.

seepage from wholesale to retail markets through resales of securities that were offered originally on an exempt basis remains an issue that EU policy-makers appear disinclined to address vigorously.[257] Thus it is possible that if there is a growth in wholesale offerings activity this could indirectly boost levels of secondary retail trading in international securities.

Cross-border offers/multiple listings making use of the passport are likely to remain rare

The new rules certainly improve the passport mechanism and this could encourage EU issuers to consider the possibility of applying to have their securities admitted to trading on a number of regulated markets within the EU as an alternative to relying on secondary market linkages to reach scattered pools of retail, as well as wholesale, investors. However it is not clear that there is a real commercial demand for this facility. Thus far, informed market opinion suggests that retail equity offerings that make use of the passport are likely to remain rare.[258]

Whilst it must be correct that better-quality rules alone will not lead to greater passport usage, it is still worthwhile to ask whether the passport rules are as good as they could be or whether there are still areas in which they are likely to prove deficient. Language was a barrier to passport usage historically and, despite significant improvements, it is possible that it could still be so to some extent. Under the language regimes for prospectuses and periodic disclosures, an issuer could find itself having to make disclosures in two languages – the language required by its national regulator and also a language customary in the sphere of international finance. It may be that national regulators will be flexible with regard to the languages

---

[257] Under the new regime, resales of securities that were the subject of an exempt offering will trigger a requirement for the offeror to produce a prospectus where the resale offer is itself not covered by an exemption: PD, art. 3.2. Each resale is to be regarded as a separate offer: ibid. Thus, for example, a resale offer addressed to fewer than 100 persons, whatever their status, would fall outside the prospectus requirement for resales. Some practical problems in the operation of this scheme are envisaged. For example it is unclear how on-exchange resales could be effected where, as is usual in the EU, the exchange operates as an anonymous dealers' market and it is not possible to determine if the ultimate purchasers are qualified purchasers or if there are less than 100 of them in any Member State: Cleary Gottlieb, *The EU Prospectus Directive – Impact on European Capital Markets* (Alert Memorandum, January 2004), available via http://www.cgsh.com/files/tbl_s5096AlertMemoranda/FileUpload5741/154/20-2004.pdf (accessed May 2004).

[258] International Financial Law Review, *European Financial Services Forum* (21 April 2004), Panel Discussion on the Prospectus and Transparency Directives.

that they are prepared to accept so as to minimise the burden on issuers, but there is at least short-term uncertainty on this aspect of the new rules. Depending on how things work out, language burdens could remain a factor militating against issuers seeking multiple listings within the EU.

One way of escaping the burden of translation costs if national regulators prove inflexible would be for an issuer to avoid its home State and maintain multiple listings on regulated markets in other Member States. Under the language schemes, issuers in this position would be free to make their disclosures only in a customary language of international finance. However, the benefits of a more favourable language regime may not be sufficient to persuade issuers to shun their home market as their location of primary listing.

The new regime does not seek to address the home State bias in primary equity listings and may have only limited impact on home bias in investment portfolios

An erosion of home State bias in primary equity listings would be one indicator of EU securities market activity maturing into a truly integrated Continental business rather than being an amalgam of different national securities markets. Although issuers are tied to their home (i.e. State of incorporation) State for supervisory and super-equivalent regulatory purposes, they are in principle free to offer their securities or have them admitted to trading wherever they like within the EU. Yet the rules connecting issuers to their State of incorporation for supervisory and regulatory purposes could in practice also influence their choices on where to locate their primary venue for securities trading activity and hence reinforce home (State of incorporation) biases. Certainly, the rigidity of the new approach to the determination of home States for supervisory and regulatory purposes is a feature that is not well designed to inculcate a sense amongst EU issuers that securities markets are genuinely pan-European and can be utilised by them in whatever way works best to meet their personal preferences.

For investors, asymmetric information with respect to domestic and foreign equity is recognised by economists as a possible explanation for the home bias in investors' equity portfolios.[259] Thus, to the extent

---

[259] K. K. Lewis, 'Trying to Explain Home Bias in Equities and Consumption' (1999) 37 *Journal of Economic Literature* 571; M. J. Brennan and H. H. Cao, 'International Portfolio Investment Flows' (1997) 52 *Journal of Finance* 1858; K. Jeske, 'Equity Home Bias: Can Information Cost Explain the Puzzle?' (2001) 3 *Federal Reserve Bank of Atlanta Economic*

that the new disclosure regime standardises investment information across the EU and improves non-discriminatory access to it, there is the potential for the legal changes to spark modifications in investing practices. Yet there are also many other possible explanations for home biases in portfolios,[260] so even if improvements in information standardisation and access do somehow matter, the benefits may not be sufficient to outweigh the countervailing costs that are inherent in standardisation.

As the debate on the proposal on mandatory quarterly reporting in the original draft of Transparency Directive demonstrated, the mere fact that a regulatory idea is designed to standardise information does not guarantee it unanimous support from the investment community. In advocating quarterly reporting the Commission misjudged the sentiment of many in the investment community because post-Enron (where US quarterly reporting requirements had not helped to expose problems quickly) priorities had moved away from a desire for more standard-format information published at fixed intervals and towards a new emphasis on the need for timely reporting of price-sensitive information and for information of reliable quality.[261] The debate provoked by the proposal provides a good illustration of the way in which regulators' perceptions of the regulatory steps that they ought to take in order to stimulate market activity can be wide of the mark because

Review 31; J.-K. Kang and R. M. Stulz, 'Why is There a Home Bias? An Analysis of Foreign Portfolio Equity Ownership in Japan' (1997) 46 *Journal of Financial Economics* 3.

[260] G. Fellner and B. Maciejovsky, 'The Equity Home Bias: Contrasting an Institutional with a Behavioral Explanation' *Max Planck Institute for Research into Economic Systems* Papers on Strategic Interaction No. 3–2003, ssrn abstractid = 390100, provides a review of the theoretical and empirical data. As well as information asymmetries, other institutional explanations for home bias in equity portfolios that the authors identify are investors' concerns for hedging possibilities against domestic risk and barriers to capital flow (such as transaction costs, taxes, market frictions and restrictions on capital holdings by foreigners). The authors note previous behavioural approaches to the equity home bias that refer to familiarity of companies, overly optimistic performance predictions of domestic firms, and subjective competence in the home market as possible explanations for the equity home bias. The authors add to the literature by testing the psychological theory of social identity (broadly that group affiliation leads to more favourable and positive evaluations of one's own group) as a further possible behavioural explanation.

[261] *Financial Times*, 4 November 2003, Letter to the Editor by Christine Farnish, Chief Executive, National Association of Pension Funds, Peter J. C. Borgdorff, Directeur, Dutch Association of Industry-wide Pension Funds, and Nora Finn, Chief Executive, Irish Association of Pension Funds.

they rest on over-simplistic and/or outdated assumptions about investor preferences.

The different approaches to the mechanisms for information dissemination in the various Directives suggest that EU policy in this area is still unsettled. The mechanical channels and systems whereby information becomes available to investors may be more to do with the plumbing of a market building project than its grand design,[262] but they are no less important for that. Given the obvious potential advantages that could flow from a well-judged, centrally co-ordinated strategy for the development of effective pan-European information dissemination mechanisms, and also the fact that it is not an area where deep national political sensitivities are likely to arise, this issue has occupied a surprisingly low place on the recent EU policy agenda. The Financial Services Action Plan (FSAP) was a grand design phase: in the words of the European Commission, it was 'one of the most important adjuncts to the introduction of the single currency' and 'one of the driving forces behind profound changes in the European financial landscape'.[263] The post-FSAP phase is likely to be less ambitious[264] but that may be no bad thing if it enables attention to turn to less glamorous areas, such as information dissemination channels, from which investors could reap practical benefits if the right solutions are found.

---

[262] This phraseology is borrowed from debate on the development of the international financial architecture: S. Fischer, 'Reforming the International Financial System' (1999) 109 *Economic Journal* F557. On the need for policy attention to shift more onto information dissemmination mechanisms: B. M. McCall, 'Why Europe Needs a Data Source Like Edgar' (June 2004) *International Financial Law Review* 17.

[263] European Commission, *Financial Services: The FSAP Enters the Home Strait* (FSAP, 9th Progress Report, November 2003), available via http://www.europa.eu.int/comm/internal_market/en/finances/actionplan/progress9_en.pdf (accessed May 2004).

[264] In announcing the establishment of expert groups of market practitioners to take stock of the FSAP and to look to the future, the Commission expressly acknowledged that this was not the prelude to a comprehensive new legislative programme along the lines of the FSAP: European Commission, 'Financial Services: Commission Sets Up Specialist Groups to Take Stock of Action Plan and Look to The Future', Commission Press Release, 27 October 2003, available at http://www.europa.eu.int/rapid/start/cgi/guesten.ksh?p_action.gettx = gt&doc = IP/03/1458/0/RAPID&lg = EN&display = (accessed May 2004). Also, P. Norman, 'Credit Due to Brussels' Achievement', *Financial Times*, 19 April 2004, Fund Management Supplement, 8 (noting that it is clear that there will be no FSAP II and that the future emphasis will be on a case-by-case approach to new laws).

Regulatory 'humility' for the future was also a theme emphasised by Internal Market Commissioner Bolkestein in a speech on the lessons from the FSAP: F. Bolkestein, 'Learning the Lessons of the Financial Services Action Plan' Speech/04/50, text available via http://europa.eu.int/rapid/start/cgi/guesten.ksh?p_action.gettxt = SPEECH/04/50/0/RAPID&LG = EN.

The interests of non-EU issuers have received insufficient attention and this could have adverse long-term consequences

The position of foreign (non-EU) issuers is shrouded in some uncertainty at the time of writing but the fact that such uncertainty has been allowed to take hold is significant. Foreign issuers provide a large and economically valuable component of international activity in European securities markets and it is therefore reasonable to suppose that EU policy-makers might have given special attention to not needlessly damaging the attractiveness of EU markets to foreign issuers. Yet events rather belie this expectation. Not giving rapid guidance on the acceptability of financial statements compiled otherwise than in accordance with IAS/IFRS exposes EU officials to the charge of behaving in an inappropriately cavalier manner on an issue of major significance. Similarly, the omission of 'grandfathering' provisions in the first draft of the Transparency Directive so as to shield existing listed issuers from new regulatory requirements. True the uncertainty over the need for reconciliation of financial statements may only be temporary, and grandfathering arrangements were added to the Transparency Directive during its passage; but incidents such as these send out signals about regulatory priorities that could have adverse implications in the longer term.

It is hard to see the justification for requiring foreign issuers to designate their EU-home State for prospectuses and periodic disclosures before those disclosure regimes come generally into effect and while important aspects are still shifting. This might have been a drafting error or the product of an inability by EU institutions to agree on the appropriate course rather than a deliberate policy choice. But, whatever the explanation, the outcome is hardly likely to instil confidence amongst foreign issuers that their interests are safe in the hands of EU policy and law-makers.

Furthermore, the EU strategy in favour of a very stringent continuous disclosure regime in the Market Abuse Directive arguably has been formed without due attention to the risk that this could harm the EU's ability to compete with other markets for business from international issuers.

Overall, therefore, the pessimistic but seemingly inescapable conclusion is that there is a real risk that the new disclosure regime could be counterproductive in its application to foreign issuers. Rather than helping to build an international market, it could in fact damage

the very segment of it that was already the most international in its
orientation.[265]

*Non-ISD/ISD2 regulated markets and alternative trade execution
mechanisms could benefit at the expense of ISD/ISD2 regulated markets*

The Transparency and Market Abuse Directives apply to issuers whose
securities are admitted to trading on an ISD/ISD2 regulated market. An
obvious escape route from whatever regulatory mistakes are inherent in
these Directives is for issuers to avoid markets with that status and to seek
out other markets or alternative trading mechanisms.[266] This possibility
has been mooted with regard to smaller issuers for which the costs of
compliance with the full panopoly of EU disclosure requirements for
regulated markets could prove disproportionate. It has become a reality in
the UK where AIM, the London Stock Exchange's second-tier market, is
to relinquish that status as from October 2004. It could also become an
actively explored option for other segments of market activity, such as the
specialist debt securities market, where sophisticated market participants
will surely invest heavily in developing ingenious structures to maintain
the EU's competitive position as against other international markets and
to shield a highly successful market from the damaging consequences of
regulatory error. Current normal practice is for most secondary trading of
bonds to take place through alternative trading systems but bonds are still
usually formally listed, in either London and Luxembourg, in order to
enhance their marketability particularly to institutional investors that
may be subject to restrictions on permissible investments. As the disclosure
burden associated with listing on a regulated market increases, market
participants may look for alternatives to admission to a regulated market
to satisfy investor requirements or preferences for a 'quality mark'. It is
conceivable that a market such as AIM, which has the alternative, market-
based 'quality mark' of being run by an operation with a strong, international

---

[265] C. Pretzlik, 'European Directives "Could Undermine Plans for More Efficient Capital
Markets"', *Financial Times*, 27 January 2004, p. 7 reporting a speech by Dick Thornburgh,
Chairman of the Securities Industry Association in which he outlined potential major
damage to European capital markets that could result from the Transparency Directive –
'diminished liquidity, reduced investor choice and less appeal to non-EU country issuers'.
Even if those comments were tinged by hyperbole, they still deserve close attention.
[266] The Prospectus Directive is less easy to evade because it applies generally to public offers
too (though the requirement for an annual summary of published information (art. 10)
only applies to issuers with securities admitted to trading on a regulated market).

commercial reputation under the general supervisory oversight of the UK's financial regulator, could position themselves so as to meet this need. Significant movement of issuer business away from regulated markets might eventually trigger some reassessment of the scope of the EU regulatory regime but this could take some time. The time lag between market developments and the regulatory response might well be sufficient to allow significant changes to become embedded within the EU financial landscape.

There is precedent for new forms of securities market activity to develop in Europe as an ingenious response to regulatory mistakes.[267] Thus, it would be no real surprise if history were to repeat itself. That outcome would also be consistent with doubts expressed throughout this book about the ability of regulatory policy-makers to make the best strategic choices to build markets.

---

[267] The introduction in 1963 of US Interest Equalisation Tax, which increased the cost of raising funds in the US capital market for foreign borrowers, is usually singled out as the development that gave the initial impetus to the development of the Eurobond market in Europe: P. Krijgsman, *Brief History: IPMA's Role in Harmonising International Capital Markets 1984–1994* (London, International Primary Market Association, 2000), p. 5.

6

Institutional supervision of issuer disclosure within the EU

A Scope of chapter

This chapter is concerned with the institutional supervision of issuer disclosure within the EU. This issue is important because the credibility of the EU-wide regulatory regime is crucially dependent on whether it is effectively supported by a system of institutional oversight that can deliver consistent standards of supervision across the EU. Fragmented and institutionally diverse oversight arrangements have the potential to undermine the EU securities market integration project. Mixed competencies and different responsibilities amongst oversight bodies are liable to impede the quest for EU-wide consistency in supervision and enforcement.[1] Institutionally diverse organisations are likely to struggle more to find common ground on which to develop shared policies and philosophies than networks comprised of organisations that share basic internal organisational characteristics.

Institutional responsibility for the oversight of issuer disclosure under the Prospectus,[2] Transparency[3] and Market Abuse[4] Directives ('core' securities laws disclosures for the purposes of this chapter) has now been concentrated in national securities regulators. These Directives contain provisions that oblige Member States to give their national securities regulators the same

---

[1] Lamfalussy Committee, *The Regulation of European Securities Markets: Final Report* (Brussels, February 2001) ('*Lamfalussy Report*'), p. 15.

[2] Directive 2003/71/EC of the European Parliament and of the Council of 4 November 2003 on the prospectus to be published when securities are offered to the public or admitted to trading and amending Directive 2001/34/EC, OJ 2003 No. L345/64.

[3] This Directive secured final political agreement in May 2004. The Directive will not be published in the Official Journal until autumn 2004, a delay that is related to the expanded translation burdens resulting from the enlargement of the EU on 1 May 2004. References to specific provisions of the Directive in this chapter are to an unofficial version available via http://europa.eu.int/comm/internal_market/en/finances/mobil/transparency/directive-unofficial_en.pdf (accessed May 2004).

[4] Directive 2003/6/EC of the European Parliament and of the Council of 28 January 2003 on insider dealing and market manipulation (market abuse), OJ 2003 No. L96/16.

minimum set of supervisory and investigatory powers, and they also oblige the regulators to co-operate with each other and to share information. A pan-European network has been put in place to bring national regulators together (the Committee of European Securities Regulators or CESR) and to facilitate the development of common supervisory standards, practices and philosophical approaches.[5]

Whether this approach will deliver an adequate degree of pan-European supervisory consistency in relation to core securities law disclosures by issuers is necessarily a matter for the future because the Directives are not yet implemented in Member States and the accompanying supervisory regime is still in its infancy. However, it is at least possible to say that a serious attempt has been made to provide the sort of institutional under-pinning that seems apt to promote the development of pan-European supervisory consistency.

The oversight arrangements for core securities law disclosures do not extend directly to financial disclosures. The content of financial disclos-ures for listed companies in the EU is governed by the Regulation on the application of international accounting standards (IAS Regulation),[6] a measure which, though part of FSAP, was developed under a process distinct from that which is now employed for the making of core securities laws. The IAS Regulation does not follow the pattern of the core securities law in the sense of laying down a model for the institutional oversight of the accuracy of financial statements that Member States are obliged to follow.

Corporate governance disclosures are the subject of separate initiatives in corporate, rather than securities, law. These initiatives are still at an early stage of development but current indications are that Member States will continue to enjoy considerable latitude to make their own arrangements for the institutional oversight of compliance with corporate governance disclosure obligations.

The lighter-touch approach to the organisation of institutional oversight of financial and corporate governance disclosures reflects traditional

---

[5] On CESR see further ch. 3.

[6] Regulation (EC) No 1606/2002 of the European Parliament and of the Council of 19 July 2002 on the application of international accounting standards, OJ 2002 No. L243/1. IAS denotes financial standards adopted by the International Accounting Standards Committee from 1973 to 2000. After an institutional reorganisation the International Accounting Standards Committee was replaced by the International Accounting Standards Board in 2001. International Financial Reporting Standards (IFRS) are the new pronouncements being issued by the IASB.

deference by central EU institutions to Member States' discretion in respect of supervision.[7] Brussels is not Washington in the sense that it is not a federal regulator that can easily step in to override national arrangements.[8] Its powers of intervention are subject to legal restrictions in that any exercise of legislative power must be grounded in a Treaty base and there are Treaty restrictions, such as the subsidiarity principle, that restrict the options that are available to it.[9] Moreover there are practical constraints flowing from the fact that Member States are directly involved in the EU law-making process through the Council of Ministers. Whilst individual national preferences may be diluted by compromises and horse-trading, and may sometimes be overridden by the mechanism of qualified majority voting, EU law is nevertheless still strongly shaped by Member States, and is not simply imposed on them by an exogenous process.

Yet if the EU is serious about building a supervisory regime to support a single market, central policy-makers cannot afford to ignore questions about the organisation of supervision. They face a major problem in examining such questions because their assessment of the degree of rationalisation of oversight arrangements that in principle is needed to fulfil the demands of the market integration project may well go beyond what Member States are prepared to countenance. Resolution of this problem may require compromises and 'second-best' policy choices. The progressively lighter touch to the oversight of disclosures depending on their classification (securities, financial or corporate governance) is understandable in these terms: not ideal in principle perhaps, but representing a realistic political compromise that brings about some rationalisation but, at the same time, respects Member States' sensitivities and local preferences.

Since the European Commission cannot easily force Member States to move their national supervisory structures in ways that do not accord with national preferences, the spotlight must inevitably turn to factors that are likely to drive change at the national level. US regulatory requirements have recently been a powerful catalyst for institutional remodelling in EU Member States. The experience of Member States converging around similar institutional models for auditor oversight in response to US

---

[7] As noted in European Commission, *FSAP Action Plan*, p. 14.

[8] M. J. Roe, 'Delaware's Competition' (2003) 117 *Harvard Law Review* 588 (arguing that the reality of American corporate law-making is that the United States has never had a pure interstate race because on important issues federal authorities can step in to override US States, or threaten to do so).

[9] N. Moloney, *EC Securities Regulation* (Oxford, Oxford University Press, 2002), pp. 888–9.

regulatory pressures gives credence to suggestions that the EU could end up with the sort of supervisory convergence that is needed within a single market but that it might get there more by dint of Member States' responses to external influences than by central diktat.[10]

Persistent lack of uniformity in supervision across the EU could be a source of difficulty in external relations with the rest of the world. Presenting a unified front internationally can strengthen the voice of EU Member States in international dialogue on the regulation of securities markets. However, a collective approach also carries the risk that other countries could increasingly view the EU as a single block and assess its supervisory capabilities and competencies on that basis, to the detriment of Member States with systems of supervision that are at the top end of the EU quality spectrum. There is no hard evidence to suggest that this risk has become a reality yet but it is sufficiently serious to warrant close and continuing attention.

This chapter is organised as follows. Section B outlines the recent development of EU law on the content of financial disclosures, and proposals for new EU rules on corporate governance disclosures. This section is largely by way of background: it fills in some of the detail of the substantive disclosure requirements to provide a basis from which to consider the arrangements for the organisation of institutional oversight. It is not necessary to include the substantive content of core securities law disclosure obligations for issuers in this discussion because those obligations are considered fully in chapter 5. Section C compares the EU's interventionist approach to the institutional organisation of supervision of core securities law disclosures with its considerably lighter touch as regards the institutional supervision of financial and corporate governance disclosures. It suggests that the differences in approach are not the product of a fundamental decision in principle that different categories of disclosure merit different supervisory arrangements but, rather, reflect political realities within the EU. Section D examines the remodelling of institutional arrangements for the public oversight of auditors within the EU to demonstrate the powerful influence of US regulation as a catalyst for change. Section E concludes with an examination of the risk that high-quality segments of supervisory activity within the EU could suffer internationally because of association with lower-quality elements.

---

[10] D. Dombey, 'Parmalat: A Scandal "Made in the EU"', *FT.com*, 20 January 2004.

B Issuer disclosure obligations outside core securities law

Financial disclosures

The FSAP identified comparable, transparent and reliable financial information as being fundamental for an efficient and integrated capital market.[11] It recognised that solutions to enhance comparability within the EU market would need to mirror international developments and, to that end, identified International Accounting Standards (IAS or, latterly, International Financial Reporting Standards (IFRS)) as the most appropriate benchmark.

This was followed in 2001 by a formal proposal from the European Commission for new legislation requiring all EU companies admitted to trading on regulated markets (commonly referred to in this context as listed companies) to prepare their consolidated accounts in accordance with IAS/IFRS.[12] The Commission put forward the proposal on the basis that the adoption of uniform, high-quality financial reporting rules in EU capital markets would enhance overall market efficiency, thereby reducing the cost of capital for companies.[13] The European Commission indicated that it had considered the option of giving EU-listed issuers a choice between using US GAAP and IAS/IFRS and then leaving it to market forces to identify the preferred set but had ruled it out on three grounds: that the process of market convergence would move too slowly; that IAS/IFRS were preferable because they were drawn up with an international perspective rather than being tailored to the complex US environment; and that the EU had no influence in the development of US GAAP.[14]

---

[11] European Commission, *FSAP Action Plan*, p. 7. As with much else in the FSAP this was not an entirely new departure for the EU: see, e.g., European Commission, *Accounting harmonisation: a new strategy vis-à-vis international harmonisation* (COM (1995) 508) in which the Commission advocated the use of IAS to facilitate access by European issuers to international capital markets. Overall the FSAP was, to a large extent, an exercise in gathering together ideas that had been mooted previously and setting them together within a more comprehensive and cohesive framework.

[12] European Commission, *Proposal for a Regulation of the European Parliament and of the Council on the application of international accounting standards* (COM (2001) 80).

[13] European Commission, *Proposal for a Regulation*, explanatory memorandum, p. 2.

[14] European Commission, *EU Financial Reporting Strategy: The Way Forward* (COM (2000) 359), p. 6. The Commission's bias towards IAS/IFRS had already been evident in earlier communications: Moloney, EC *Securities Regulation*, pp. 236–7.

With reference to the third ground, later events have tested the EU's ability to influence the development of IAS: A. Parker and C. Pretzlik, 'French Call IASB to Account', *Financial Times*, 2 February 2004, p. 28 detailing the dispute between French and EU authorities on the one side and the International Accounting Standards Board on the other over IAS 32 and IAS 39 on a proposed IASB accounting treatment of derivatives which was based on US standards.

In making its proposal the Commission would have been confident of securing broad political backing from Member States because it fitted with the aspirations they had expressed at the Lisbon Summit Meeting in March 2001. In a mood of rhetorical exuberance that reflected the prevailing mood in relation to stock market investment, the political leaders attending this 'dotcom' Summit had adopted a grand vision for the EU as the world's leading knowledge-based economy by 2010.[15] The proposal also enjoyed wide support in the European corporate sector.[16]

The lack of controversy surrounding the proposed adoption of IAS/IFRS for listed companies helped the process from proposal to new legislation to proceed smoothly and remarkably quickly (judged by the standards of some previous EU efforts to pass new laws relating to securities markets): the IAS Regulation was adopted in July 2002 in accordance with a 'fast-track' legislative process that involved a single reading by the European Parliament.[17] The use of a Regulation rather than a Directive, which is the form of legal instrument more commonly used for measures relating to the regulation of securities market activity, is significant. A Regulation is directly applicable in Member States whereas Directives require some step to be taken at national level in Member States to transpose the new laws into their domestic law and thereby make them effective. The transposition stage both slows down the process whereby new EU laws acquire 'bite' and provides an opportunity for national variations in interpretation of the rules contained in the EU measure to creep in, thereby undermining the quest for consistency and uniformity across all Member States. Eliminating these opportunities by opting for the use of a Regulation therefore has certain advantages but precisely because there is less flexibility it can be difficult to secure Member States' support for their use.

Closer examination of what the IAS Regulation actually does sheds light on why legislation in the form of a Regulation was acceptable on this occasion to Member States. The IAS Regulation does not directly and unconditionally make mandatory the use of IAS/IFRS by listed companies. Instead, the Regulation provides a procedure for Community endorsement

---

[15] The political background to the proposal is outlined in European Commission, *EU Financial Reporting Strategy*.

[16] European Commission, *Proposal for a Regulation*, explanatory memorandum, p. 2, cites a survey of 700 EU listed companies that revealed that 79 per cent of Chief Financial Officers supported the European Commission's recommendation that IAS/IFRS should be mandatory for listed companies by 2005.

[17] The 'fast track' legislative process is considered further in ch. 3.

of IAS/IFRS and obliges listed companies to draw up their consolidated accounts in accordance only with those IAS/IFRS as have been so endorsed. The endorsement mechanism thus provides for EU oversight and control over the application of IAS. Although the European Commission has said that the role of the mechanism is not to reformulate or replace IAS/IFRS, but to oversee the adoption of new standards and interpretations, intervening only when these contain material deficiencies or have failed to cater for features specific to the EU environment,[18] there are some concerns that the endorsement mechanism provides scope for the EU to tamper with IAS/IFRS in ways that could impede broader international efforts to establish common standards.[19] Such concerns acquired a practical focus in 2003–4 in a controversy over the accounting treatment of derivatives and other complex financial instruments: the European Commission's efforts to secure changes to the relevant IAS/IFRS (which it had not yet endorsed) were seen by US regulators as potentially jeopardising efforts to achieve convergence between IAS/IFRS and US GAAP.[20]

A dedicated infrastructure has developed to support the endorsement mechanism. This infrastructure has some superficial resemblance to the Lamfalussy process for securities law-making[21] in that it comprises two Committees, one of which ensures that Member States retain some political control over the Commission's actions, and the other of which provides technical advice. The Accounting Regulatory Committee comprises political representatives from Member States and its function is to assist the Commission under established EU comitology procedures in the process of endorsing IAS/IFRS for use by EU companies.[22] The Accounting Technical Committee provides technical input. The composition of this Committee provides an immediate contrast with the position in core securities law: whereas the technical adviser in securities law is CESR, a body comprised of public officials from Member States' securities regulatory agencies, the Accounting Technical Committee is a private-sector initiative

---

[18] European Commission, *EU Financial Reporting Strategy*, p. 7.

[19] Moloney, *EC Securities Regulation*, p. 240.

[20] A. Michaels and A. Parker, 'US Warns Europe on Accounting Rules', *Financial Times*, 2 February 2004, p. 1.

[21] Considered in detail in ch. 3.

[22] The legal basis for the establishment of the ARC is provided by the IAS Regulation, art. 6. Details of the Committee's membership and rules of procedure and minutes of its minutes can be found on the Commission's website, via http://www.europa.eu.int/comm/internal_market/accounting/committees_en.htm (accessed May 2004).

that involves representatives from companies, financial analysts, stock exchanges, the accounting profession and national standard-setters.[23] The differences go further: CESR, whose members are the bodies that are responsible at national level for supervision of compliance with core disclosure laws, has a responsibility for developing supervisory convergence across the EU but the Accounting Technical Committee does not have formal responsibility for the promotion of supervisory convergence.

No post-Enron reassessment of EU policy choices on the content of financial disclosure obligations

There is a marked tendency for reform of financial and securities regulation to be driven by corporate frauds and stock market collapses that expose failings in existing regulatory regimes.[24] The FSAP, at its inception, was distinctively different from the norm because it was deficiencies of another sort – the failings of the regulatory regime to promote a fully integrated pan-European securities market – that principally drove change. The period during which the regulatory ideas that were formalised in the FSAP were under development was one of considerable buoyancy in global securities markets and it was that economic background, and the desire to equip EU players to exploit its opportunities more effectively, that informed the process of policy agenda formation.

The market downturn in the early 2000s and the spectacular collapse of various major companies, as symbolised by the failure of the Enron Corporation,[25] refocused policy-makers' attention.[26] The regulatory lessons

---

[23] European Commission, 'Financial Reporting: Commission Welcomes Creation of European Technical Expert Group', Commission Press Release, 26 June 2001, available via http://www.europa.eu.int/rapid/start/cgi/guesten.ksh?p_action.gettxt = gt&doc = IP/01/899|0|AGED&lg = EN&display = (accessed May 2004).

[24] S. Banner, 'What Causes New Securities Regulation? 300 Years of Evidence' (1997) 75 *Washington University Law Quarterly* 849; F. Partnoy, 'Why Markets Crash and What Law Can Do About It' (2000) 61 *University of Pittsburgh Law Review* 741; B. A. K. Rider, 'The Control of Insider Trading – Smoke and Mirrors!' (2000) 19 *Dickinson Journal of International Law* 1, 31–5; E. Ferran, 'Examining the United Kingdom's Experience in Adopting the Single Financial Regulator Model' (2003) 28 *Brooklyn Journal of International Law* 257.

[25] For an overview of Enron and other high profile corporate collapses, see: L. E. Ribstein, 'Market v Regulatory Responses to Corporate Fraud: A Critique of the Sarbanes-Oxley Act of 2002' (2003) 28 *Journal of Corporation Law* 1, 4–7.

[26] The UK FSA noted the refocusing of attention in these words: 'International attention was drawn to the issue of conflicts of interest in the production of investment research by the events in the US, where the most obvious manifestations occurred.' Financial Services Authority, *Conflicts of Interest: Investment Research and Issues of Securities* (London, FSA, Consultation Paper 205, 2003), Annex 5, para. 7.

to be learnt from the market abuses that the economic downturn helped
to expose can be debated endlessly.[27] The European Commission's interpretation of events was that there were a number of issues that had major
significance for the EU in the context of creating its efficient and competitive capital market,[28] and it launched various initiatives in response to
them.[29] The language used to explain and justify existing proposals also
shifted, with the emphasis on EU market integration objectives that had

---

[27] From the huge amount of literature discussing the issues arising from Enron and similar
scandals, certain interpretations seem to stand out: that the problems were more to do
with compliance failures than the content of existing disclosure requirements (Ribstein,
'Market v Regulatory Responses', 16 and K. Lannoo and A. Khachaturyan, Disclosure
Regulation in the EU: The Emerging Framework (Brussels, Centre for European Policy
Studies Task Force Report No. 48, October 2003), p. 7); that, as well as failures on the
supply side, there were also problems on the demand side in that securities analysts, rating
agencies and other finance professionals did a poor job of decoding disclosures and
evaluating their proper significance (J. R. Macey, 'A Pox on Both Your Houses: Enron,
Sarbanes-Oxley and the Debate Concerning the Relative Efficacy of Mandatory Versus
Enabling Rules' (2003) 81 *Washington University Law Quarterly* 329); that 'gatekeeper'
failures on both the supply and demand side, that is failure by issuers' accountants, lawyers
and investment bankers to perform proper verification of information prior to its disclosure and failure by securities analysts and other financial professionals to detect problems
in information that had been disclosed, were systemic failures rooted in conflicts of
interest (J. C. Coffee, 'Understanding Enron: "It's About the Gatekeepers, Stupid"' (2002)
57 *Business Lawyer* 1403 and J. C. Coffee, 'What Caused Enron? A Capsule Social and
Economic History of the 1990s' (2004) 89 *Cornell Law Review* 269); and that the events
provided powerful new evidence of irrationality by investors (J. N. Gordon, 'What Enron
Means for the Management and Control of the Modern Business Corporation: Some
Initial Reflections' (2002) 69 *University of Chicago Law Review* 1233, 1235) and also by
corporate officers (R. Prentice, 'Enron: A Brief Behavioral Autopsy' (2003) *American
Business Law Journal* 417).

[28] The Commission's views were set out in a note which it prepared for a meeting of the
Council of Ministers (ECOFIN) at Oviedo on 12 and 13 April 2002: European Commission, *Analysis of Repercussions of the Enron Collapse: A First EU Response to Enron Related
Policy Issues* (April 2002), available via http://www.europa.eu.int/comm/internal_market/
accounting/otherdocs_en.htm (accessed May 2004).

[29] The European Commission instigated its own investigation into the role of financial analysts. The Forum Group of experts established by the Commission to conduct this investigation produced a report setting out proposed best practices for financial analysts: Forum
Group, *Financial Analysts: Best practices in an integrated European financial market*
(Brussels, European Commission, September 2003), which is available via http://www.europa.
eu.int/comm/internal_market/en/finances/mobil/finanalysts/docs/fin-analysts-report_en.pdf
(accessed May 2004).

   On the wider international front, the issues have also been considered by IOSCO and it
has produced its own *Statement of Principles for Addressing Sell-side Securities Analyst Conflicts of Interest* (Madrid, IOSCO, 2003) http://www.iosco.org/pubdocs/pdf/IOSCOPD150.pdf
(accessed May 2004).

characterised pre-Enron pronouncements to some extent giving way to the new priorities of protecting investors and market integrity.[30]

However, the content of financial disclosures was not an area where the Commission felt that unfolding events signalled a need for a radical change of direction in regulatory policy. If anything, the events reinforced the confidence of EU authorities in the merits of the 'principles-based' IAS/IFRS model over the 'rule-based' approach of US GAAP and thus enabled them to conclude that there was no reason to change the fundamental financial reporting strategy.[31] Not changing its basic strategy was a fair decision by the EU authorities, though the language used sometimes struck a hubristically sanctimonious tone as to supposed less European vulnerability to the kinds of financial reporting problems that had been exposed in various major US corporations.[32]

---

[30] E.g., whereas European Commission, *FSAP Action Plan*, p. 7 had emphasised the need for information comparability so as to facilitate cross-border investment, by the time that the specific case for the Transparency Directive came to be made by the European Commission in 2003, the proposed overhaul of the requirements for annual and interim reporting was presented as an appropriate response to developments in the US, as well as being designed to achieve EU integration objectives: European Commission, *Proposal for a Directive of the European Parliament and of the Council on the harmonisation of transparency requirements with regard to information about issuers whose securities are admitted to trading on a regulated market and amending Directive 2001/34/EC* (COM (2003) 138), p. 3. Similarly, *FSAP Action Plan*, pp. 5–6 made the case for a revision of the Investment Services Directive mainly by reference to paving the way for effective cross-border provision of investment services, the needs of an integrated securities market and new regulatory issues such as the emergence of alternative trading systems. This contrasts with the later formal proposal for a revising Directive in which the protection of investors and market integrity were identified as the key elements of the first over-arching regulatory objective: European Commission, *Proposal for a Directive of the European Parliament and of the Council on investment services and regulated markets, and amending Council Directives 85/611/EEC, Council Directive 93/6/EEC and European Parliament and Council Directive 2000/12/EC* (COM (2002) 625), pp. 7–8.

[31] European Commission, *Analysis of Repercussions*, sec. 1.

[32] 'Holier Than Thou: European Sanctimony Over American Accounting Scandals is Misplaced', *Economist*, 8 February 2003, p. 85. Events in Europe soon invalidated any suggestion that the financial disclosure problems typified by Enron were somehow an exclusively US concern: 'Europe's Enron', *Economist*, 1 March 2003, p. 63 (detailing the collapse of Royal-Ahold, a Dutch retailer); 'The Pause After Parmalat: Europe's Enron Calls for a Measured but More Determined Response', *Economist*, 17 January 2004, p. 13 (detailing the collapse of Parmalat, an Italian dairy-products group, and the exposure of major accounting irregularities); Dombey, 'Parmalat: A Scandal'.

Generally on the lessons for Europe from Enron: K. J. Hopt, 'Modern Company and Capital Market Problems: Improving European Corporate Governance after Enron' [2003] *Journal of Corporate Law Studies* 221.

Corporate governance disclosures

The corporate collapses and scandals that were uncovered during the market downturn of the early 2000s dramatically revised interest at EU level in company law and corporate governance. Although there had been quite a large programme of company law initiatives during the 1960s and 1970s, things had stagnated by the 1990s.[33]

Corporate governance merited a brief mention in the original FSAP but, at that point in time, the Commission's view was against strong EU intervention with respect to national arrangements that were grounded in long-standing legal and socio-economic traditions.[34] However, in its initial response to Enron the Commission identified corporate governance as a key issue demanding attention.[35] This led to an examination by an expert group[36] and eventually to the announcement by the European Commission of an Action Plan for Company Law.[37] The European Commission explicitly acknowledged that, in developing the Company Law Action Plan, it shared the same broad objectives and principles as underpinned the US Sarbanes-Oxley Act.[38]

The Company Law Action Plan contains several proposals for new pan-European disclosure requirements to strengthen corporate governance. One is a proposed new obligation on listed companies to include in their annual report and accounts a coherent and descriptive statement covering the key elements of their corporate governance structure and practices, including a 'comply or explain' obligation in respect of any applicable corporate governance code of best practice.[39] Another is a proposal for disclosure of information relating to directors' remuneration.[40] In a departure from the usual reluctance to tie the hand of Member States with regard to sanctions, the Company Law Action Plan suggests that there

---

[33] W. F. Ebke, 'Company Law and the European Union: Centralized Versus Decentralized Law-making' (1997) 31 *International Lawyer* 961, 963; K. J. Hopt, 'Company Law in the European Union: Harmonisation and/or Subsidiarity' (1999) 1 *International and Comparative Corporate Law Journal* 41.

[34] European Commission, *FSAP Action Plan*, p. 15.

[35] European Commission, *Analysis of Repercussions*, sec. 3.

[36] High Level Group of Company Law Experts, *A Modern Regulatory Framework for Company Law in Europe* (Brussels, European Commission, November 2002).

[37] European Commission, *Modernising Company Law and Enhancing Corporate Governance in the European Union – A Plan to Move Forward* (COM (2003) 284).

[38] Ibid., p. 5.

[39] Ibid., pp. 12–13.

[40] Ibid., p. 16.

may be a case for the imposition of directors' disqualification across the EU as a sanction for misleading disclosure.[41] The Commission has issued a variety of consultation documents outlining its plans for taking forward these proposals,[42] but discussions are still at a fairly early stage.

C   Supervision of issuer disclosure

In the absence of a central EU supervisor for securities market activity (which is ruled out elsewhere in this book as a step too far for the EU at this juncture[43]), supervision and enforcement responsibilities in respect of EU laws must remain located with national agencies. It would be unrealistic to look for total uniformity in the way in which supervision is delivered across the EU's twenty-five Member States because the agencies involved in the supervisory process are inevitably conditioned by deep-rooted cultural and social differences, have widely differing levels of past experience in dealing with securities market activity depending on whether they are based in countries where securities market financing is historically strong (as in the UK) or in countries where bank-based financing dominates (as in most of the rest of the EU), and are often dependent on unharmonised elements of their national systems (in particular their legal system) in carrying out their functions. So a degree of supervisory diversity is inevitable, and could be beneficial as a means of avoiding compromising high-quality supervision where that exists and of facilitating some constructive competition between agencies. On the other hand, too much supervisory diversity would threaten the credibility of the integration project. The issue is thus one of balance: establishing an adequate level of supervisory convergence, and finding the best policy tools to promote its further development.

Within core securities law, a twin strategy has been adopted by EU policy-makers. The first element involves intervention to standardise the nature, status and powers of the agencies that are responsible for supervision at national level. The second element involves the establishment of

---

[41] Ibid., p. 16.

[42] European Commission, *Fostering an Appropriate Regime for the Remuneration of Directors* (MARKT/23.02.2004); European Commission, Online Consultation on *Board Responsibilities and Improving Financial and Corporate Governance Information* (April 2004), available via http://www.europa.eu.int/comm/internal_market/accounting/board/index_en.htm (accessed May 2004).

[43] See ch. 3.

a pan-European institutional structure to bring those agencies closer together.

The first element is given effect in the core securities law Directives which expressly recognise that a variety of supervisory authorities in Member States having different responsibilities may create confusion among economic actors and increase costs.[44] To address this, they impose an obligation on Member States to designate administrative authorities to assume the supervisory responsibilities relating to the Directives, and also international collaboration.[45] These competent authorities must be independent of economic actors and of conflicts of interest.[46] The Directives impose tight restrictions on the delegation of supervisory responsibilities by competent authorities, a rigid and arguably excessive feature of the regime.[47] The Directives contain provisions that are intended to standardise the supervisory and investigatory powers available to competent authorities.[48] Competent authorities are subject to obligations under the Directives to co-operate with other each, and the supervisory arrangements in each Member State should not hinder such co-operation.[49] More tentatively, but still significant because of historical deference by the EU to Member States in this regard, these Directives also try to steer Member States towards greater uniformity in sanctions by specifying in broad terms the minimum nature of the sanctions that should be imposed for breach of the Directives[50] and reminding Member States to be alert to the need to ensure a degree of uniformity of regulation from State to State.[51]

---

[44] Market Abuse Directive, rec. 36; Prospectus Directive, rec. 37.

[45] Market Abuse Directive, rec. 36 and art. 11; Prospectus Directive, rec. 37 and art. 21; Transparency Directive, rec. 18 and art. 20.

[46] Market Abuse Directive, rec. 36; Prospectus Directive, rec. 37; Transparency Directive, rec. 18.

[47] This argument is developed further in relation to stock exchanges in ch. 7.

[48] Market Abuse Directive, art. 12; Prospectus Directive, rec. 38 and art. 21; Transparency Directive, rec. 18 and art. 20. A fuller comparative review of the provisions in various recent Directives on co-operation and coordination between national securities regulators can be found in Committee of European Securities Regulators, *The Role of CESR At 'Level 3' Under the Lamfalussy Process* (CESR/04–104b, 2004), Annex 4.

[49] Market Abuse Directive, rec. 40 and art. 16; Prospectus Directive, rec. 39 and art. 22; Transparency Directive, rec. 18 and art. 21.

[50] Market Abuse Directive, art. 14 (administrative sanctions that must be effective, proportionate and dissuasive); Prospectus Directive, rec. 43 and art. 25 (administrative sanctions that are effective, proportionate and dissuasive, and measures to ensure that sanctions are actually applied); Transparency Directive, rec. 27 and art. 24 (appropriate administrative measures or civil sanctions; measures to be effective, proportionate and dissuasive).

[51] Market Abuse Directive, rec. 39.

Whether high-minded Directive exhortations on supervisory convergence acquire meaningful practical effect is likely to depend heavily on the effectiveness of CESR as a forum for the pooling of supervisory practices and policies amongst securities regulatory agencies and for the sharing of information. On this, it is still early days but the signs are fairly positive.[52]

The arguments for rationalising institutional oversight arrangements so as to promote supervisory convergence can be applied to the oversight of the accuracy of financial disclosures as much as to any other sort of disclosure that issuers may be called upon to make to the securities markets. Financial disclosures are not immune from the problem that achieving consistency in supervision and enforcement is hard when the institutional responsibility for these functions is spread between numerous national agencies which have different characteristics and powers.

According to one major European study of Member States, which was published in 2001, the institutional oversight system for the enforcement of accounting standards in the consolidated accounts of listed companies differed from country to country and did not exist in all countries.[53] Where financial disclosure oversight arrangements were in place, responsibilities lay variously with public regulatory agencies, government departments, review panels (that were sometimes self-regulatory in composition) and stock exchanges.[54] Institutional diversity continues: in 2003, CESR noted that 'in the EU Member States various organizational models of the enforcement systems are in place, including enforcement conducted by securities regulators, stock exchanges and review panels'.[55]

Despite the fact that the challenges are the same as those in core securities law, the EU has not attacked the problem of institutional diversity in relation to agency oversight of financial disclosures by way of Directives that are binding on Member States. Although the European Commission has expressed the view that securities supervisors have a critical role in ensuring that listed companies comply with financial reporting requirements,[56] EU law does not impose this sort of organisational arrangement on Member

---

[52] Ch. 3 discusses CESR's performance thus far.

[53] European Federation of Accountants, *Enforcement Mechanisms in Europe: A Preliminary Investigation of Oversight Systems* (April 2001), available via http://www.fee.be/publications/main.htm (accessed May 2004).

[54] European Federation of Accountants, *Enforcement Mechanisms in Europe*.

[55] Committee of European Securities Regulators, *Standard No.1 on Financial Information. Enforcement of Standards on Financial Information in Europe* (CESR/03–073, 2003), p. 5.

[56] European Commission, *EU Financial Reporting Strategy*, p. 9.

States. Instead, the IAS Regulation simply provides for the European Commission to liaise with Member States, notably through CESR, to develop a common approach to the enforcement of financial disclosures.[57]

CESR has produced a number of *Standards on Financial Information*.[58] Awareness of the difficulties involved in reconciling the need for supervisory convergence with due deference to the individual national preferences of Member States runs through CESR's commentary on the Principles in the first of these *Standards*. On the one hand, CESR argues that 'harmonization of enforcement mechanisms in Europe is needed in order to contribute to the creation of an efficient single capital market in Europe within the context of the evolving EU legislation',[59] and that 'the integration of European security markets requires that the national models operate on the basis of harmonized concepts and comparable techniques';[60] on the other, that 'differences in corporate governance legislations as well as other companies regulations in the European Member States ask for the organization of the institutional oversight at national level according to the different legal environments'.[61]

CESR resolves this dilemma by specifying that ultimate responsibility for enforcement of compliance with financial disclosures should lie with independent administrative authorities set up by Member States but with wide scope for delegation to other bodies.[62] These administrative authorities should have adequate independence from Government and market participants, possess the necessary powers and have sufficient resources.[63] The necessary powers should at least include power to monitor financial information, require supplementary information from issuers and auditors, and take measures consistent with the purposes of enforcement.[64] In order to promote harmonisation of enforcement practices and to ensure a consistent approach, the CESR *Standard No. 1* also advocates co-ordination of enforcement decisions.[65]

---

[57] IAS Regulation, rec. 16.
[58] Committee of European Securities Regulators, *Standard No. 1*; Committee of European Securities Regulators, *Standard No. 2 on Financial Information. Coordination of Enforcement Activities* (CESR/03–317c, 2004).
[59] Committee of European Securities Regulators, *Standard No. 1*, p. 4.
[60] Ibid., p. 5.
[61] Ibid., p. 5.
[62] Ibid., p. 5, Principle 3.
[63] Ibid., p. 5, Principle 6.
[64] Ibid., p. 5, Principle 7.
[65] Ibid., p. 10, Principle 20.

Standard No 1 committed CESR to establishing a mechanism to bring together CESR members and oversight bodies that are not CESR members in a forum for discussion to promote pan-European co-ordination and convergence. The basis for this mechanism is put in place by Principle 4 of *Standard No. 2*.[66] This Principle provides for the organisation of European Enforcers Co-ordination Sessions, which are intended to involve all EU national enforcers of financial disclosures in the development of meaningful co-ordination of enforcement. This mechanism does not appear to go as far as some industry participants consider desirable: the European Federation of Accountants, a leading voice on institutional oversight arrangements for financial disclosures in EU Member States, has called for the establishment of a new specialised body to work with CESR in the co-ordination of enforcement of financial disclosures through involvement in information-gathering, peer review and other functions.[67]

In broad terms, the emerging institutional oversight arrangements for financial disclosures are similar to those for core securities law disclosures: some control over the nature and powers of the national bodies that have oversight responsibilities, plus an EU-wide forum in which those bodies can come together to share views and experiences and, it is hoped, develop common approaches and practices. The details differ in many important respects (for example, delegation by financial oversight agencies is widely permitted; and European Enforcers Co-ordination Sessions are likely to be a much more modest type of network than CESR). Furthermore the arrangements are on a different legal footing to those in core securities law because they are derived from non-binding CESR Standards rather than enforceable EU legislative measures; but it is unclear whether this difference will have much practical significance.[68]

---

[66] Committee of European Securities Regulators, *Standard No. 2*, p. 5.

[67] European Federation of Accountants, *European Enforcement Coordination* (Discussion Paper, November 2003), available via http://www.fee.be/publications/main.htm (accessed May 2004). See also European Federation of Accountants, *The Role of Accounting and Auditing in Europe* (Position Paper, May 2002), available via http://www.fee.be/publications/main.htm (accessed May 2004).

[68] Inter-Institutional Monitoring Group for Securities Markets, *Second Interim Report Monitoring the New Process for Regulating Securities Markets in Europe* (*The Lamfalussy Process*) (Brussels, December 2003), pp. 34–5 discusses whether there is a need for CESR Standards which are not formally legally binding to be given greater authority by being adopted as Commission Recommendations. The IIMG suggests that any such move would encounter significant hurdles. It favours peer pressure within CESR as a mechanism to support CESR Standards.

A pertinent question at this juncture is why it is that the oversight of financial disclosures is dealt with within its own distinct structure rather than simply being subsumed within the institutional arrangements for securities disclosures and thus treated as being the direct responsibility of securities regulators. This does not seem to be because of some fundamental distinction in the substantive nature of financial disclosures and other types of disclosures since such no such distinction can easily be established. In principle securities regulators could be responsible for overseeing the accuracy of financial disclosures and enforcing compliance, as much as they are for other types of issuer disclosure. In practice the likelihood is that they often will be involved in any event, because inaccurate financial statements could, depending on the circumstances, infringe the disclosure requirements in the Prospectus or Transparency Directives or amount to market abuse contrary to the Market Abuse Directive, thereby giving rise to the need for understandings between agencies on the exercise of their overlapping powers.[69] Vesting primary responsibility for financial disclosures in securities regulators would not necessarily preclude the involvement in oversight and enforcement of bodies with specialist expertise that is not available to securities regulators from their internal resources so long as delegation is permitted; but would allow them to control the extent of reliance on such bodies. Having the same type of institution with primary responsibility for financial disclosures in all of the Member States could be conducive to the development of more effective pan-European supervision than where this responsibility is vested in national agencies with potentially widely-differing status and responsibilities.

The European Commission seems to have been attracted to the arguments for vesting primary responsibility for the oversight of financial disclosures in securities regulators: 'Securities supervisors also have a critical role in ensuring that listed companies comply with financial reporting requirements... In the EU securities markets regulators must be actively involved in enforcement issues.'[70] Yet the IAS Regulation reflects this viewpoint only to the extent of identifying CESR as the main body with which the Commission intended to liaise in the development of a

---

[69] Transparency Directive, rec. 18 explicitly recognises the possibility of overlapping powers. It provides that Member States may designate an authority other than the securities regulator as the competent authority for examining that information is drawn up in accordance with the relevant reporting framework and taking appropriate measures in case of discovered infringements; such an authority need not be of an administrative nature.

[70] European Commission, *EU Financial Reporting Strategy*, p. 9.

common approach to enforcement.[71] That CESR is responsible for leading the pan-European co-ordination effort, notwithstanding that the securities regulators represented on CESR may not be the agencies with primary responsibility for enforcement of financial disclosures in their home State, is a rather odd institutional settlement. It could be a ploy to encourage a gradual shift of responsibility onto securities regulators at national level. If so, this suggests that the explanation for why the EU has not moved more explicitly to concentrate national level power in securities regulators in this respect lies more in the political realities of what can feasibly be pushed for at EU level than in some fundamental principle.

In the general field of securities regulation and supervision, institutional diversity between Member States is diminishing as more and more of them converge on the single regulator model.[72] De facto convergence around a particular institutional model by Member States creates an environment in which objections to a proposal for EU-wide institutional standardisation which is consistent with that model are likely to be muted.[73] There have not yet been equivalent processes of convergence by Member States around any particular infrastructure model for the oversight of financial disclosures. It is therefore likely that any attempt to impose from the centre a rigid institutional model would attract a welter of objections from

---

[71] IAS Regulation, rec. 16.

[72] EU Member States that have opted for the single regulator model include the United Kingdom, Sweden, Denmark, Germany, Austria, Belgium and Ireland: E. Wymeersch, 'Co-operation between Authorities in the Community: The Case of Banking, Insurance and Securities Supervision', Paper for Yale Law School Center for the Study of Corporate Law Symposium, *Assessing Corporate Law Reform in a Transatlantic Context* (21 October 2003). Finland has concentrated power in one agency in respect of banking and securities market activity, but insurance is separately regulated: ibid.

France's regulatory infrastructure is still based on the traditional sectoral distinctions between banking, insurance and securities markets but the institutional arrangements for the regulation of securities markets have recently been rationalised: ibid. Italy, Spain, Portugal and Luxembourg also have segregated systems: ibid.; but the Italian position is under review as part of the response to the Parmalat scandal: ibid. Hungary and the Czech Republic are amongst the new EU Member States (accession May 2004) to have adopted the single regulator model: ibid.

See also R. M. Lastra, 'The Governance Structure for Financial Regulation and Supervision in Europe' (2003) 10 *Columbia Journal of Economic Law* 49, 50–2.

[73] It is significant that, despite the trend towards the single regulator model, one area where significant institutional differences remain between Member States is with regard to the role of exchanges in the supervision of issuers. This has generated controversy with regard to certain aspects of the institutional oversight model in core securities law, as is discussed further in ch. 7.

various interests groups in Member States and thus would probably fail to carry the necessary political support to be formally adopted as EU law.

Recent UK experience illustrates the sort of manoeuvring that can still take place at national level over institutional responsibility for financial disclosures. Historically, the Financial Services Authority (FSA) held supervisory powers over the entirety of issuers' financial disclosures but, in practice, it acted only in relation to prospectuses and interim accounts leaving another body, the Financial Reporting Review Panel (FRRP), to exert control over inaccuracies in annual accounts.[74] As part of its national response to Enron, the British Government established a review of auditing and accounting issues from which emerged a proposal to expand the role of the FSA in the enforcement of financial disclosures, working alongside the FRRP.[75] A particular aspect of the enhanced role envisaged for the FSA was that of identifying the high-risk cases that most merited investigation.[76] This proposal was not implemented in the end. Instead the new institutional framework expands the role of the FRRP to include proactive, investigatory responsibilities bypassing the FSA.[77] According to reports, this change of direction came about because the FSA had sought but failed to win political backing for a larger role than the one envisaged for it by the review group, and would not countenance assuming a more limited role.[78] That this kind of turf war, demanding a response that is attuned to local conditions and path-dependencies, can still occur is an indication why the time does not yet appear ripe for a mandatory direction from the EU on the location at national level of oversight responsibilities for financial disclosures.

The degree of separation of ownership and control and the degree of employee involvement in governance vary widely across the corporate sector in EU Member States.[79] Board structures differ, and the operation

---

[74] Co-ordinating Group on Audit and Accounting Issues, *Final Report* (London, DTI, URN 03/567), p. 60. This report is available via http://www.dti.gov.uk/cld/cgaai-final.pdf (accessed May 2004).

[75] Co-ordinating Group, *Final Report*, pp. 57–62.

[76] Statement by the Secretary of State for Trade and Industry, 30 January 2003, available via http://www.dti.gov.uk/cld/sos-statement290103.pdf (accessed May 2004).

[77] The legal underpinning for this arrangement is to be provided by the Companies (Audit, Investigations and Community Enterprise) Bill 2003.

[78] R. Bruce, 'A Proactive Policeman', *Financial Times*, 24 April 2003, Appointments & Accountancy, p. 2.

[79] M. J. Roe, *Political Determinants of Corporate Governance* (Oxford, Oxford University Press, 2003), p. 4.

of mechanisms of market-based control vary depending on the level of dispersal of ownership and the extent of reliance on securities market or bank-based financing.[80] Factors such as these combine to make corporate governance an intensely sensitive area for EU policy-makers.[81] Whilst the fallout from Enron has sparked an increased level of debate that may eventually culminate in some new regulatory requirements, early intervention to dictate an institutional model for the supervision of corporate governance seems unlikely. Even though the arguments in principle for concentrating in securities regulators disclosure supervisory responsibilities can be applied to corporate governance disclosures as much as to financial disclosures,[82] EU sensitivity about intervention in corporate governance,[83] traditional deference to Member States on supervision, and the diversity of institutional models whereby corporate governance disclosures are currently monitored and enforced in EU Member States,[84] all seem to combine to rule this out as a realistic short-term political option. In announcing the Company Law Action Plan, the Commission in fact avoided detailed discussion of national institutional responsibilities for the monitoring and enforcement of the proposed corporate governance disclosure requirements. Its only, rather loose, proposal was for the creation of an European Corporate Governance Forum to help encourage coordination and convergence of national codes and of the way they are enforced and monitored.[85] The review group, whose work was highly influential in

---

[80] L. Enriques, 'Bad Apples, Bad Oranges: A Comment from Old Europe on Post-Enron Corporate Governance Reforms' (2003) 38 *Wake Forest Law Review* 911, 934.

[81] This is reflected in European Commission, *FSAP Action Plan*, p. 15 where 'long-standing legal and socio-economic traditions' are cited to explain only modest proposed intervention in EU corporate governance.

[82] E. Ferran, 'The Role of the Shareholder in Internal Corporate Governance' (2003) 4 *European Business Organization Law Review* 491.

[83] J. C. Coffee, 'The Future as History: The Prospects for Global Convergence in Corporate Governance and Its Implications' (1999) 93 *Northwestern University Law Review* 641, 667–71 argues that securities law harmonisation within the EU has largely succeeded while corporate law harmonisation has been largely frustrated for a variety of reasons including that changes to securities law do not appear to challenge long-established social policies, and that such changes can be largely accomplished at the administrative level and do not require national legislatures to act, thereby inviting political rivalries to enter the picture.

[84] Weil, Gotshal & Manges, *Comparative Study Of Corporate Governance Codes Relevant to the European Union And Its Member States* (Brussels, European Commission, 2002), available via http://europa.eu.int/comm/internal_market/en/company/company/news/corp-gov-codes-rpt_en.htm (accessed May 2004) indicates the wide variations that exist across Member States with regard to institutional responsibility for corporate governance disclosure.

[85] European Commission, *Modernising Company Law*, pp. 16–17.

shaping the Commission's thinking in the Company Law Action Plan, did address the issues in more depth but (unsurprising given the discussion thus far in this section) thought that Member States should be free to implement corporate governance disclosure requirements as they thought fit, through company law, securities law, listing rules or otherwise.[86] Thus, what is currently envisaged in high-level EU policy circles with regard to institutional responsibilities for corporate governance disclosures is even less interventionist than in relation to financial disclosures: tolerance for diversity in institutional responsibilities at national level and, here, not even a general steer in the form of specification of minimum requirements that responsible bodies would be expected to meet.

D   US regulatory requirements as a catalyst for institutional remodelling in Member States: recent experience on auditor oversight

If it is right to say that wide institutional diversity at national level effectively precludes EU intervention to impose a single institutional model on a pan-European basis, this turns the spotlight onto factors that may encourage Member States to remodel their own supervisory structures, and to do so in a way that results in de facto convergence around a particular model. De facto 'bottom up' convergence can dissipate resistance to EU intervention and help convert such intervention into more of a tidying-up exercise than an attempt to lead from the top.

Clearly there are many circumstances that could trigger an overhaul of national supervisory structures. The need to respond to local scandals that expose failings in the existing supervisory structure is an obvious one: the Italian Government's announcement of reform of its financial regulatory system in response to the Parmalat scandal serves as a good recent example of this factor at work.[87]

The controversial outreach of the auditor oversight provisions in the US Sarbanes-Oxley Act of 2002 to foreign auditors of SEC-registered foreign issuers has recently operated as a powerful agent for institutional change in EU Member States.[88] The UK and France have revised their

---

[86] High Level Group of Company Law Experts, *A Modern Regulatory Framework*, pp. 61–2.

[87] S. Delaney, 'Parmalat Spurs Call For Reform In Business: Italian Government Plans To Strengthen Oversight', *Washington Post*, 20 January 2004, p. EO1.

[88] Sarbanes-Oxley Act of 2002, § 106. The controversy provoked by this development is surveyed in European Federation of Accountants, *European Coordination*, sec. 4.

auditor oversight arrangements in ways that look designed to mirror the US model.[89] Similar reform is under discussion in Germany,[90] although there are also some in Germany who are advocating more radical change in the form of a European oversight body similar to the US Public Company Accounting Oversight Board (PCAOB).[91] The underlying motivation for these changes is obvious: they are designed to enable audit firms based in these European countries to obtain favourable supervisory treatment from the PCAOB.[92]

Such developments in Member States have the potential to rebound on what it is feasible to propose at EU level: if national trends are already moving towards PCAOB-style auditor oversight bodies, it would be reasonable to expect this trend to enhance the political feasibility of an initiative to apply this model on a pan-European basis. Recent developments in EU policy with regard to auditor oversight support this expectation.

Auditing took up little space in the original FSAP with just a brief suggestion that International Standards on Auditing might be the appropriate minimum standard to be satisfied in order to give credibility to published financial statements.[93] This brevity could be a little misleading

---

[89] The UK has established a Professional Oversight Board for Accountancy and has introduced a Bill to strengthen the system of audit regulation and also the infrastructure for the enforcement of financial disclosures: Companies (Audit, Investigations and Community Enterprise) Bill 2003. The French Financial Security Act 2003 has established an Auditor Oversight Board: Enriques, 'Bad Apples', 918–19. Ireland has also established an independent audit supervisory body, the Irish Auditing and Accounting Supervisory Authority (IAASA). In this case, the reforms were instigated before Enron *et al.* in response to local financial scandals. The IAASA is also responsible for monitoring financial disclosures. Its legal underpinning is derived from the Companies (Auditing and Accounting) Act 2003.

[90] T. Baums and K. E. Scott, 'Taking Shareholder Protection Seriously? Corporate Governance in the United States and Germany' *Stanford Law School John M. Olin Program in Law and Economics* Working Paper No. 272 (November 2003), ssrn abstract = 473185.

[91] A. Michaels, 'Germany Plans Pan-European Audit Regulator', *Financial Times*, 12 March 2003, p. 26.

[92] Under the Final Rules Relating to the Oversight of Non-US Public Accounting Firms (PCAOB Release No. 2004–005, June 2004), there is a 'sliding scale' regulatory procedure for non-US auditors, which is intended to be less stringent in those countries where audit control is closest to the US. See further Public Company Accounting Oversight Board, *Oversight of Non-US Public Accounting Firms* (Washington, PCAOB, Briefing Paper, October 2003).

[93] European Commission, *FSAP Action Plan*, p. 7. ISAs are produced by the International Auditing and Assurance Standards Board, which functions as an independent standard setting body under the auspices of the International Federation of Accountants. Further details are available via: International Auditing and Assurance Standards Board, About IAASB, http://www.ifac.org/IAASB/ (accessed May 2004).

if the FSAP's character as a summary of various projects already on the EU's policy agenda is overlooked. In fact the European Commission had been giving some attention to the role of statutory auditors during the 1990s on the basis that enhancing the reliability of financial disclosures through high-quality audit went hand-in-hand with the IAS/IFRS adoption project and was thus an important contribution to the establishment and the functioning of the single market.[94] The lack of a properly harmonised view at EU level concerning the statutory audit was also recognised to be something that could become a serious handicap for European companies seeking access to international capital markets.[95]

Yet, although a discussion of auditing matters was certainly taking place at EU level before the market downturn in the early 2000s,[96] the specific proposals emanating from such discussion were rather modest and restrained. In November 2000 the Commission addressed the issue of public oversight of auditors through a Recommendation on minimum quality assurance standards for statutory audits.[97] A consultation on auditor independence was launched soon afterwards, and this too culminated in a Recommendation issued by the Commission in May 2002.[98] A Recommendation is meant to act as a form of best practice benchmark for Member States but it is not binding under EU law; the record of their use in relation to securities markets is that they are often ignored.[99]

Latterly, the EU has begun to revisit its light-touch approach to the regulation of auditors.[100] The new initiatives are explicitly acknowledged

---

[94] European Commission, *Statutory Audit in the European Union: The Way Forward* (COM (1998) 143) provides background. This Communication announced the establishment of a Committee on Auditing. A brief summary of the Committee on Auditing's role is available via, European Commission, Committee on Auditing, http://www.europa.eu.int/comm/internal_market/en/company/audit/committt/index.htm (accessed May 2004).

[95] European Commission, *Statutory Audit*, para. 1.3. EU-wide regulation of auditors had been attempted during the 1980s (Eighth Council Directive 84/253/EEC of 10 April 1984 on the approval of persons responsible for carrying out the statutory audits of accounting documents, OJ 1984 No. L126/20) but this Directive only laid down minimum requirements and contained major interpretative uncertainties (in particular there was a requirement for 'independence' but this crucial concept was undefined).

[96] The establishment of the Committee on Auditing was designed to institutionalise this discussion: European Commission, *Statutory Audit*, para. 1.4.

[97] Commission Recommendation 2001/256/EC of 15 November 2000 on quality assurance for the statutory audit in the European Union: minimum requirements, OJ 2001 No. L91/91.

[98] Commission Recommendation 2002/590/EC of 16 May 2002 on statutory auditors' independence in the EU: a set of fundamental principles, OJ 2002 No. 191/22.

[99] Moloney, *EC Securities Regulation*, p. 19.

[100] European Commission, *Reinforcing the Statutory Audit in the EU* (COM (2003) 286).

by EU bodies to be in direct response to the collapse of Enron and subsequent financial reporting scandals.[101] Whatever else Enron and other similar market abuses revealed, it rapidly became received wisdom that significant conflicts of interest in the relationships between auditors and their clients lay at the heart of the problems.[102] With policy-makers wordwide grappling with the challenges of finding solutions to these problems, and the US leading the regulatory response with tough new statutory requirements for auditor independence,[103] rotation of audit partners[104] and the establishment of a new infrastructure for the public oversight of auditors,[105] doing nothing was not a realistic option within the EU.[106] In particular EU institutions felt obliged to acknowledge the inadequacies of non-binding instruments as a policy tool in the post-Enron environment.[107]

The broad features of the emerging post-Enron EU regime for auditor regulation are as follows:[108]

– modernisation of the existing Directive on the approval of persons recognised to conduct statutory audit work;
– a shift to the style of law-making now in favour for core EU securities law: that is, a framework Directive augmented by implementing measures;
– establishment of a two committee structure broadly equivalent to the institutional arrangements for securities law-making: an Audit Regulatory Committee to assist the Commission under comitology procedures in the passing of implementing measures; and an Audit Advisory Committee to act as a preparatory discussion forum between regulators and the audit profession;[109]

---

[101] Ibid., pp. 3–4.
[102] See, e.g., 'The Lessons from Enron', *Economist*, 9 February 2002, p. 9. For a sceptical view of the magnitude of the problems directly resulting from the provision by auditors of multiple services to audit-client companies: G. J. Benston, 'Accountants and Public Accounting Before and After Enron' (2003) 52 *Emory Law Journal* 1325, 1340–7.
[103] Under the Sarbanes-Oxley Act of 2002, § 201 auditors are prohibited from providing non-audit services (other than tax) to companies whose accounts they audit.
[104] Sarbanes-Oxley Act of 2002, § 203.
[105] The Public Company Accounting Oversight Board (PCAOB) established under the Sarbanes-Oxley Act of 2002, § 101.
[106] Hopt, 'Modern Company', p. 223.
[107] European Commission, *Reinforcing*, p. 5.
[108] Ibid., p. 5; European Commission, *Proposal for a Directive of the European Parliament and of the Council on statutory audit of annual accounts and consolidated accounts and amending Council directives 78/660/EEC and 83/349/EEC* (COM (2004) 177).
[109] The Audit Regulatory Committee would be new but the Audit Advisory Committee would be a new name for the existing Committee on Auditing.

- adoption of the International Standards on Auditing as common standards for all EU statutory audits from 2005, subject to certain improvements in their quality and in the standard-setting processes;
- minimum requirements for public oversight of auditors imposed on Member States by Directive; and
- establishment of a co-ordination mechanism at EU level to link up national systems of public oversight into an efficient EU network.

It is the last two proposals – for specification of minimum requirements for public oversight bodies and the establishment of a co-ordination mechanism – that relate most specifically to the general theme of this chapter. These proposals broadly follow the pattern that we have seen elsewhere but they are towards the less interventionist end of the spectrum: the European Commission disowns any intention to give a blueprint for the establishment of an effective public oversight mechanism;[110] the principles of public oversight proposed in the draft Directive are fairly high-level and thus seem likely to leave room for variations in the characteristics of the national agencies that are responsible for auditor oversight at national level;[111] and precisely how these organisations are to be linked together into some European co-ordination mechanism is not yet clear.

The inclusion of provision for public oversight of auditors on the EU's legislative agenda has become part of a settlement with the US PCAOB of the dispute over the outreach of the Sarbanes-Oxley Act.[112] The gist of the settlement is that if the EU brings its laws on auditors, including public oversight arrangements, more closely into line with those of the US, EU audit firms that operate in the US may qualify for a more favourable supervisory treatment from the PCAOB. EU audit firms will still be required to register with the PCAOB (this was previously a sticking point) but there is a quid pro quo in the form of a proposed new EU law whereby foreign (including US) firms will be required to register in the EU (subject to derogation for firms that are subject to third country systems of oversight that are deemed, by the Commission, to be 'equivalent' to those

---

[110] European Commission, *Proposal for a Directive on statutory audit*, explanatory memorandum, p. 7.

[111] Ibid., draft Directive, art. 31. A sticking point could be the proposal that the majority of the persons involved in the public oversight mechanism be non-practitioners. This may attract criticism from the accountancy profession who may press for greater freedom to permit more self-regulatory, practitioner involvement.

[112] 'EU, US Reach Agreement on Auditor Oversight', *EU Business*, 25 March 2004, http://www.eubusiness.com/afp/040325190124.kiarp1sl (accessed May 2004).

within the EU).[113] Despite this gesture towards reciprocity, to all intents and purposes the PCAOB looks like the winner in this settlement, and the Commission now faces the potentially hard task of selling the deal to the Member States and to the European Parliament. However, it seems unlikely that the Commission would have agreed to this settlement if it had not been fairly comfortable about the likely level of support for it amongst Member States. Hence the fact that these proposals broadly follow a pre-existing trend in some major EU States to move in the direction of US-style public auditor oversight bodies is particularly significant.

Events that are sufficiently serious as to spark a regulatory reaction such as the Sarbanes-Oxley Act do not come along too often. This means that regulatory overspill from the US may only intermittently drive the development of regulation and supervision within Member States. Thus the speed of supervisory convergence that may come about via this mechanism is unpredictable. Nonetheless the example does serve to make the point that harmonisation is not the only mechanism that can produce a common approach: innovation by one country that is then followed by 'copycat' actions in other countries can also achieve this result.

E   Does lack of uniformity in EU-wide supervision of securities market activity matter?

The Lamfalussy Committee identified the large number and the different characteristics of the bodies involved in supervision as impediments to efficient and effective pan-European supervision.[114] The review of the institutional oversight of issuer disclosure contained in this chapter indicates that some rationalisation has taken place since then, particularly in the core securities field, but that political realities have precluded the emergence of a system that in principle might seem more conducive to efficiency and effectiveness, wherein securities regulators play the lead supervisory role for all types of issuer disclosure. This chapter suggests that further refinement of EU-wide supervisory structures is likely to depend significantly on Member States leading the way through change at the domestic level and that regulatory spillover from the US is likely to be a powerful, if intermittent, agent for such change.

However, examining whether the EU has the supervisory structure that is best suited to address the needs of an integrated market might be said to miss the real point. Just as strong markets are built by the people who operate within them rather than being the creatures of some form of

---

[113] European Commission, *Proposal for a Directive on statutory audit*, draft Directive, art. 46.
[114] *Lamfalussy Report*, pp. 15–16.

central planning, effective supervision depends more on people and how they work in practice than on structures as they appear on paper. The imbalance in knowledge, experience and expertise between securities regulators from countries that have large, long-established, internationally significant securities markets and securities regulators from countries where securities markets are small and/or relatively recently established, and where financing of the corporate sector is still largely bank-based, cannot be ironed out by institutional remodelling.[115] The best that remodelling can do is to provide an infrastructure to facilitate the sharing of expertise and experience, the forging of closer links between agencies and the individuals within them, and the promotion of common practices and standards. This is CESR's role, but even its strongest supporters would be unlikely to claim that it has achieved much more than a good beginning in this respect.

Does it matter that a truly pan-European regime for the supervision of securities market activity is still some way off and that its emergence is dependent on numerous variables, many of which are deeply rooted in different socio-economic, political and cultural traditions across Europe and which therefore cannot be changed simply by changing institutional models? Is the gap between common rules for securities market activity and a common system to supervise their implementation and enforcement not merely indicative of a broader and well-known phenomenon within the EU market integration project: that the reality often falls short of the rhetoric? At a broad policy level, there is reason to care about supervisory deficiencies on the grounds that they represent impediments to the realisation of the range of economic benefits that studies suggest would flow from the establishment of a truly integrated EU securities market.[116] At another level, uneven standards of supervision across the EU would matter greatly if they were to result in downgrading by association, that is if Member States with high-quality oversight and enforcement systems were to find themselves on a lesser footing in their external relations with the rest of the world because of their association with poorer-quality national supervisory regimes elsewhere in the EU.

The European Commission plays a prominent role in 'speaking for Europe' in international dialogue on the regulation of financial markets,

---

[115] Ch. 2 considers the varying degrees of securities market development across the EU.
[116] These studies are considered in ch. 2.

particularly with regard to US regulatory authorities.[117] CESR has also begun to assert itself internationally, and has established links with the SEC.[118] Audit firm oversight, on which the deal was brokered with the PCAOB by the European Commission, is an example of this dialogue at work, and it is one which Commission officials hope will set a precedent for the future.[119] The full impact of this deal for Member States will take some time to work out and it is dependent on certain changes to EU law, as discussed earlier. It appears that the PCOAB does not intend, at least in the short term, to treat the EU as a block for the purposes of determining the appropriate degree of intensity of US scrutiny of its audit firms and that it will instead look at firms on a country-by-country basis.[120] Assuming this interpretation is correct, it indicates that the Commission's role in conducting negotiations collectively on behalf of Member States did not lead on this occasion to standardised treatment prejudicial to EU firms that operate within high-quality national oversight regimes. As such, this example serves to allay fear about downgrading by association. However, the strengthening of the European (Commission/CESR) voice in international dialogue and the accumulation of formal and informal constraints on Member States' striking their own reciprocal deals with regulatory authorities in the rest of the world, create a new dynamic that needs to be carefully monitored to ensure that the benefits and burdens of a collective approach remain balanced in favour of Member States.

---

[117] Mark Sobel, the US Deputy Assistant Secretary for International Monetary and Financial Policy, has spoken of a strong mutual interest in close co-operation on financial market regulation and has outlined the mechanics of such co-operation, which include regular meetings between Commission officials and representatives from the US Treasury, the SEC, and the Federal Reserve: The United States Mission to the European Union, *European Financial Services Action Program Good for World Economy*, 29 January 2004, available via http://www.useu.be/Categories/Tax%20 and%20Finances/Jan2904SobelFSAP.html (accessed May 2004). A. Schaub, 'Testimony of Director-General, DG Internal Market of the European Commission before the Committee on Financial Services, US House of Representatives', 13 May 2004, http://europa.eu.int/comm/internal_market/ en/finances/general/2004–05–13-testimony_en.pdf (accessed May 2004) takes up the same theme.

[118] Committee of European Securities Regulators, 'Director of the SEC Office of International Affairs and the Secretary-General of the Committee of European Securities Regulators Announce Enhanced Cooperation and Collaboration', CESR Press Release, CESR/04–278, 26 May 2004.

[119] Schaub, 'Testimony'.

[120] 'Holier Than Thou'; D. Dombey, 'Sarbanes-Oxley and Europe – US Legislation Finds a Friend Across the Water', *Financial Times*, 23 April 2004, Understanding Corporate Governance Supplement, p. 9.

7

Regulatory competencies: the end of exchange-based regulation and supervision of issuers in the EU?

A Scope of chapter

This chapter considers the role of stock exchanges in performing regulatory and supervisory functions relating to issuers.[1] One reason why this issue has come into the foreground of policy discussions is because of the evolution of exchanges from organisations with tightly controlled member ownership into companies with shares that can be freely traded. Historically, even though some exchanges had the formal organisational structure of private sector bodies, they were seen as quasi-public bodies and the notion that stock exchanges would discharge public interest responsibilities was part of the everyday fabric of securities regulation. As organisations with the ownership structure of ordinary commercial companies, new-style exchanges must now embrace the objective of shareholder-value maximisation. This new shareholder-value orientation of exchanges and the increasingly competitive environment in which they now operate intensifies debate about the willingness of exchanges to carry out regulatory responsibilities in the public interest and also about whether, or to what extent, it is appropriate for them to do so.[2]

The EU market integration agenda gives a distinctive character to European debate about exchange-based regulation and supervision of

---

[1] J. Black, 'Mapping the Contours of Contemporary Financial Services Regulation' [2002] *Journal of Corporate Law Studies* 253 uses 'enrolment' analysis to examine the role of various actors, including exchanges, in the regulatory process.

[2] A leading article on exchanges as regulators is P. G. Mahoney, 'The Exchange as Regulator' (1997) 83 *Virginia Law Review* 1453. Mahoney is not concerned specifically with questions about the impact of changes to organisational and ownership structures on the ability of exchanges to act as regulators. However, general concerns about whether exchanges make good regulators acquire an enhanced intensity when they are considered in connection with exchange demutualisation: see International Organization of Securities Commissions Technical Committee, *Issues Paper on Exchange Demutualization* (IOSCO, 2001), available via http://www.iosco.org/pubdocs/pdf/IOSCOPD119.pdf (accessed May 2004) and R. S. Karmel, 'Turning Seats into Shares: Causes and Implications of Demutualization of Stock and Futures Exchanges' (2002) 53 *Hastings Law Journal* 367, 421–7.

issuers. According to the influential *Lamfalussy Report*, the number and diversity of organisations involved in EU securities regulation is a barrier to the achievement of a fully-integrated market.[3] Europe still has a lot of stock exchanges and there are even some proposals to establish new ones.[4] The market integration perspective thus provides an additional reason to question the merits of exchanges as regulators and supervisors of issuers.

There are two key issues arising in relation to the role of stock exchanges as regulators and supervisors of issuers. The first concerns the demarcation of the boundaries between State and market with regard to rule-making functions: which matters should be addressed by way of detailed State rules applying directly to issuers and which matters should be left for private ordering between exchanges and issuers, with the State confined to an indirect role via its supervisory regime for exchanges?[5] Increasingly it is legislation passed by EU central bodies that determines where these lines are drawn in European securities regulation. However, in areas not covered by EU-wide legislation or where room has been left for Member States to adopt local rules that are more prescriptive than the general EU standards, it is for national authorities to exert control over where these lines are set.

The second issue is the role of stock exchanges in supervising issuers' compliance with mandatory regulatory requirements. This situation assumes mandatory rules set by the State (either EU-wide or through additional national intervention) but turns the spotlight instead onto the appropriateness of the State looking to exchanges to discharge functions

---

[3] Lamfalussy Committee, *The Regulation of European Securities Markets: Final Report* (Brussels, 15 February 2001) (*Lamfalussy Report*), pp. 15–16.

[4] The UK Department of Trade and Industry (DTI) has announced an initiative to encouraging the DTI's local agencies to assess the feasibility of launching low-cost, Internet-based, share-trading systems regionally: W. Kay, 'Time Investment Power Went Back to the People' *Independent* 6 September 2003, Features, p. 2.

[5] The regulatory regime applicable to an exchange will typically oblige it to maintain an orderly market, a requirement that will embrace monitoring and disciplining the issuers that it has admitted to trading: see, e.g. the UK requirements for recognition as an investment exchange as set out in Financial Services and Markets Act 2000 (Recognition Requirements for Investment Exchanges and Clearing Houses) Regulations 2001 (SI 2001 No. 995).

Other ways in which State control could be maintained over exchanges that have power to write regulatory rules for issuers include: dictating aspects of the exchange's internal organisational and corporate governance structure, requiring it to follow specified procedures and processes so as to ensure transparency in the exercise of its rule-making powers, making its rules conditional on the approval of the securities regulator, and the imposition of ongoing disclosure and other requirements so as to facilitate regular accountability to the regulator in respect of its supervisory functions: IOSCO, *Issues Paper*, p. 9.

with regard to monitoring compliance with those requirements under some form of oversight by the State.

This chapter reviews the general debate on the regulatory and supervisory role of stock exchanges that has been prompted by the trend towards demutualisation (section B) and then considers the issues through the prism of the EU market integration agenda (section C). This chapter contends that market integration considerations point towards reducing the role of exchanges in issuer regulation and supervision as part of a general rationalisation of regulatory competencies within the EU so as to promote the development of a credible pan-European regulatory and supervision system. However, this does not mean that exchanges must necessarily be completely stripped of regulatory and supervisory functions in relation to issuers, save for their obligation to monitor issuers as part of their general duty to maintain orderly markets. New legislative initiatives under the EU Financial Services Action Plan (FSAP)[6] threatened totally to divest exchanges of regulatory and supervisory functions, a policy choice that was arguably made without giving sufficient weight to the potential benefits that could flow from their continued involvement. The immediate threat has receded but it is evident that influential voices within the European Commission and elsewhere still see the longer-term trend as being away from significant exchange involvement in the regulation and supervision of issuers within the EU.[7] Yet over-vigorous pursuit of this policy without sensitive regard

[6] European Commission, *Financial Services: Implementing the Framework for Financial Markets: Action Plan* (COM (1999) 232) ('*FSAP Action Plan*').

[7] Directive 2003/71/EC of the European Parliament and of the Council of 4 November 2003 on the prospectus to be published when securities are offered to the public or admitted to trading and amending Directive 2001/34/EC, OJ 2003 No. L345/64, art. 21 provides for a review of interim arrangements that permit exchange involvement by December 2008 but at the same time provides a mandatory cut-off point for this interim arrangement by December 2011. The Transparency Directive, art. 20 contains a similar provision (this Directive secured final political agreement in May 2004 but will not be published in the Official Journal until autumn 2004; references to specific provisions of the Directive in this chapter are to an unofficial version available via http://europa.eu.int/comm/internal_market/en/finances/mobil/transparency/directive–unofficial_en.pdf (accessed May 2004)). The specification of a fixed cut-off point raises questions about the purpose of the review and suggests that re-opening the possibility of preserving exchange involvement beyond 2011 could be difficult. See also European Commission, *Proposal for a Directive of the European Parliament and of the Council on the harmonisation of transparency requirements with regard to information about issuers whose securities are admitted to trading on a regulated market and amending Directive 2001/34/EC* (COM (2003) 138), explanatory memorandum, p. 20.

to the potential benefits of exchange involvement in the oversight of issuers could be a mistake.

B   Exchanges as regulators of issuers and the impact of demutualisation: issues and responses

Demutualisation: changes to organisational structures as a response to growing competitive pressures

Historical studies demonstrate that in the nineteenth century stock exchanges competed for the business of issuers that sought to raise finance from foreign investors and, in doing so, exploited new methods of communication such as telegraph and, later, the telephone and telex.[8] So, in a sense, technology-driven competition between providers of facilities for the issuance and trading of securities is nothing new. Yet technological advances that have facilitated new methods of securities trading and rapid worldwide information transmission, coupled with deregulatory measures that have removed exchange controls and given foreign investment firms access to national markets,[9] have presented market infrastructure providers with the prospect of competitive challenges on an unprecedented scale.[10] Exchanges and providers of alternative securities trading services are beginning increasingly to compete with each other for business that, in

---

[8] Generally, R. Michie, *The London Stock Exchange: A History* (Oxford, Oxford University Press, 1999), 70–142.

[9] In Europe, Council Directive 93/22/EEC of 10 May 1993 on investment services in the securities field, OJ 1993 No. L141/27.

[10] Thus far, competition between exchanges and alternative trading systems has not become as significant a phenomenon in Europe as it has in the US. A 2000 study by the Forum of European Securities Commissions (FESCO, the forerunner to the Committee of European Securities Regulators, CESR) found that there were then twenty-seven alternative trading systems operating in Europe, with the majority of these being UK authorised firms. In equity markets, these alternative trading systems were starting to attract business by offering services not provided by traditional exchanges, such as after-hours trading, direct access for institutional investors, and trading platforms for unlisted securities. See, generally, Forum of European Securities Commissions, *The Regulation of Alternative Trading Systems in Europe: A Paper for the EU Commission* (FESCO/00–064c, 2000), pp. 6–7.

   The growing US competition between traditional exchanges and alternative trading systems and its implications for regulatory policy are considered by J. R. Macey and M. O'Hara, 'Regulating Exchanges and Alternative Trading Systems: A Law and Economics Perspective' (1999) 28 *Journal of Legal Studies* 17.

the past, would often have gone virtually automatically to local exchanges because of strong issuer and investor bias towards their home market.[11]

As a result, established stock exchanges have come under pressure to reduce trading costs, to improve clearing and settlement facilities, to raise more capital to fund the development and maintenance of cutting-edge technological infrastructures[12] and to adopt more transparent management structures that meet prevailing notions of good corporate governance practice. Demutualisation is currently the favoured organisational response to these pressures.[13] Demutualisation is not a precisely defined term in

[11] 'In equity markets, the development of new trading systems has often signalled incipient additional competition for exchanges that had previously enjoyed near monopolies': Committee of European Securities Regulators, *Standards for Alternative Trading Systems* (CESR/02–086b, 2002), p. 2.

For a sceptical view of the erosion of exchanges' natural monopolies through international competition see B. M. Ho, 'Demutualization of Organized Securities Exchanges in Hong Kong: The Great Leap Forward' (2002) 33 *Law and Policy in International Business* 283. But for a view that organised stock exchanges operate in exceedingly competitive environments see J. R. Macey and H. Kanda, 'The Stock Exchange as a Firm: the Emergence of Close Substitutes for the New York and Tokyo Stock Exchanges' (1990) 75 *Cornell Law Review* 1007.

[12] Some have questioned whether the need for capital is a real driver of exchange demutualisation. Using the example of the Amsterdam Stock Exchange, which returned capital to its members on demutualisation, Steil argues that capital needs are often something of a smokescreen and that in reality market officials resort to demutualisation to break the stranglehold of existing members which is frustrating their expansion plans: B. Steil, 'Changes in the Ownership and Governance of Securities Exchanges: Causes and Consequences' *Wharton Financial Institutions Center* Working Papers 02–15, available via http:// fic.wharton.upenn.edu/fic/papers/02/0215.pdf (accessed May 2004).

[13] For differing views on the economic case for the greater efficiency of for-profit exchanges in times of increasing competition and decreasing homogeneity of interests between members: O. Hart and J. Moore, 'The Governance of Exchanges: Members' Cooperatives versus Outside Ownership' (1996) *Oxford Review of Economic Policy* 53; C. Pirrong, 'A Theory of Financial Exchange Organization' (2000) 43 *Journal of Law and Economics* 437; Steil, 'Changes'). On the organisational form of enterprise generally: H. Hansmann, *The Ownership of Enterprise* (Cambridge, Mass., Belknap Press, 1996). See also R. Lee, *What is an Exchange?* (Oxford, Oxford University Press, 1998).

It is not new for exchanges to respond to market pressures by changing their internal structures – for example the London Stock Exchange became a not-for-profit mutual organisation in the immediate aftermath of the Second World War having previously been owned by outside shareholders: Michie, *The London Stock Exchange*, pp. 330-52; F. Donnan, 'Self-regulation and the Demutualisation of the Australian Stock Exchange' (1999) 10 *Australian Journal of Corporate Law* 1, 5.

Of fifty-two exchanges represented at the 1999 meeting of the International Federation of Stock Exchanges, fifteen had demutualised, fourteen had member approval to demutualise and another fifteen were actively contemplating demutualisation: IOSCO, *Issues Paper*, p. 3. Steil, 'Changes', provides a table listing twenty securities and futures exchanges that he considered to be demutualised as at the end of 2001.

this context[14] but Steil has helpfully identified the key feature characteris-
ing what is typically regarded as a demutualised exchange as being that
members can freely sell their equity stake in the exchange to non-members.[15]
Through demutualisation in this sense, exchanges acquire outside shareholders and become exposed to the same shareholder-value maximising
pressures as affect ordinary commercial companies whose shares are publicly
traded. A fairly recent practice, in which the Australian Stock Exchange
was an early pioneer[16] and which other exchanges, including the London
Stock Exchange[17] and Deutsche Börse[18] later followed, is for exchanges to
quote their own securities or those of their holding company. Demutualisation and public listing can facilitate co-operative alliances and agreed
mergers between exchanges but, as the London Stock Exchange discovered
in 2000 when it became the target of a bid from Sweden's OM Gruppen,
being public can also expose exchanges to market discipline including the
possibility of hostile takeover.[19]

The New York Stock Exchange and NASDAQ have lagged behind their
counterparts elsewhere in the world in embracing demutualisation. The

[14] In particular, exchange 'demutualisation' is not a term that is reserved for the conversion
of exchanges into corporate form. Several of the exchanges that demutualised in the late
1990s /early 2000s, such as the Deutsche Börse and Paris Bourse (Steil, 'Changes') and the
London Stock Exchange (London Stock Exchange, *About the Exchange*, available via http://
www.londonstockexchange.com/about/about_05.asp (accessed May 2004)) were already
in corporate form before demutualisation. In these cases demutualisation concerned the
process whereby their equity was opened up to public ownership.

[15] Steil, 'Changes'.

[16] R. Humphry, 'ASX Demutualisation – The First Four Months', Speech by Managing Director, Australian Stock Exchange to CEDA, Melbourne, 18 February 1999, text available via
http://www.asx.com.au/shareholder/l3/AA180299_AS3.shtm (accessed May 2004). The
first stock exchange to demutualise was the Stockholm Stock Exchange (1993) but it did
not admit its own securities until some time later. Ho, 'Demutualization', provides a
detailed, critical study of the Hong Kong experience on exchange demutualisation.

[17] The London Stock Exchange became a private limited company in 1986. In 2000 its shareholders voted for it to become a public limited company. Dealing in its shares began
initially through an off-market trading facility operated by Cazenove and Co. It then listed
its own securities in July 2001. London Stock Exchange, *About the Exchange*, provides
a summary of the London Stock Exchange's steps towards becoming a publicly quoted
commercial company.

[18] The Deutsche Börse was taken public in 2001 and is now listed on the Frankfurt Stock
Exchange: J. Adolff, B. Meister, C. Randell and K. D. Stephan, *Public Company Takeovers in
Germany* (Munich, Verlag CH Beck, 2002), pp. 67–8.

[19] C. Bradley, 'Demutualization of Financial Exchanges: Business as Usual?' (2001) 21 *Northwestern Journal of International Law and Business* 657. The OM bid for the London Stock
Exchange was made at a time when its shares were publicly trading but had not yet been
listed.

NYSE, a member-owned organisation incorporated under the not-for-profit laws of the State of New York,[20] considered the demutualisation question in the late 1990s[21] but dropped the issue after discussions with the SEC.[22] NASDAQ has begun the move towards demutualisation[23] but has not completed the transformation to being a listed company.[24] A compelling explanation for the relative slowness of the major US operators is that, as dominant players in the securities markets, they have been insulated from the competitive pressures that have forced lesser exchanges to move in the direction of full demutualisation.[25] Pressure for change may be coming from a different direction, however. The furore surrounding the August 2003 announcement[26] by the NYSE of the startlingly large compensation package awarded to its Chairman, Richard Grasso,[27] focused attention on its internal governance structure and reignited debate about its possible demutualisation. According to the SEC Chairman, the remuneration package raised serious questions regarding the effectiveness of the NYSE's governance structure.[28] Some well-placed critics of the NYSE's handling of events raised demutualisation as the way of resolving the governance problems on the basis that this would inject

---

[20] New York Stock Exchange, *About the NYSE*, available via http://www.nyse.com/about/p1020656067652.html?displayPage = %2Fevents%2F1063105216026.html (accessed May 2004) outlines the NYSE's organisational structure.

[21] R. Karmel, 'Self-Regulation and Governance at the United States Securities and Commodities Exchanges' in D. Frase and H. Parry, *Exchanges and Alternative Trading Systems* (London, Sweet & Maxwell, 2002), pp. 62–72.

[22] One sticking point was the loss of regulatory functions which the SEC would have insisted upon if the NYSE has chosen to demutualise: R. Aggarwal, 'Demutualization and Corporate Governance of Stock Exchanges' (2002) 15 *Journal of Applied Corporate Finance* 105.

[23] Karmel, 'Self-Regulation'; Aggarwal, 'Demutualization'.

[24] NASDAQ, *Report Regarding NASDAQ Corporate Governance* (May 2003), available via http://www.nasdaqnews.com/about/Reports/NDQ_Corporate_Governance0503.pdf (accessed May 2004).

[25] Steil, 'Changes'.

[26] New York Stock Exchange, 'NYSE Announces New Contract For Dick Grasso Through May 2007', NYSE Press Release, 27 August 2003, available via http://www.nyse.com/press/p1020656068695.html?displayPage = %Fpress%2F1020656068695.html (accessed May 2004).

[27] $139.5 million in accrued savings, benefits and incentives, in addition to a continuing base salary of US $1.4 million and a possible annual bonus of at least US $1 million. The details of the compensation package are set out by the Chairman of the NYSE Committee on Compensation in: H. C. McCall, 'Letter to SEC Chairman, William H. Donaldson', 9 September 2003, available via http://www.nyse.com/pdfs/donaldsonletter.pdf (accessed May 2004).

[28] W. H. Donaldson, 'Letter to NYSE Regarding NYSE Executive Compensation', 2 September 2003, available via http://www.sec.gov/news/speech/spch090203whd.htm (accessed May 2004).

greater transparency into the organisation of its affairs.[29] Although the short-term response to this pressure was an internal reorganisation that fell short of demutualisation, it is evident that this has not put to rest concerns about the NYSE's internal governance and practices[30] and that the option of demutualisation and public listing continues to command some powerful support.[31]

Exchanges as regulators and supervisors of issuers: possible functions, and how the assessment of their role is affected by demutualisation

All securities exchanges, irrespective of their organisational form, ownership structure and precise regulatory status, are in a position potentially to perform regulatory and supervisory functions in relation to issuers that seek access to their facilities. To the extent that rule-writing functions have not been pre-empted by the State, they can limit entry to their facilities to applicants satisfying specified qualitative criteria, make entry conditional upon disclosure of specified information, and make continued access to those facilities conditional upon satisfaction of specified disclosure and qualitative requirements. Qualitative admission criteria, initial disclosure requirements and continuing obligations are one means by which securities exchanges can compete with each other to attract business from issuers of securities. As Mahoney puts it: 'self-interested stock exchange members will produce rules that investors want for the same reasons that self-interested bakers produce the kind of bread that consumers want'.[32] This view, which is a variant on the 'race to the bottom' or 'race to the top' debate that took place in US corporate law,[33] implies that a dropping of standards is not an

---

[29] E.g. press coverage of remarks by Francis Maglio, a NYSE member, at an NYSE special governance meeting on 6 September 2003 that changing the exchange's ownership structure would improve its 'transparency and integrity': A. Posteinicu, 'Calls for NYSE to Demutualise', *Financial Times*, 8 September 2003, p. 21.

[30] E.g. 'John Reed's Modest Proposal. Too Modest. The Big Board Must Regulate Itself No Longer', *Economist*, 22 November 2003, p. 14; 'Mr Thain Moves In: A Rescue Squad Begins Work at America's Leading Stock Exchange', *Economist*, 10 January 2004, p. 64.

[31] A. Posteinicu and D. Wighton, 'NYSE Members Keep Listing Question Afloat', *Financial Times*, 8 March 2004, p. 28.

[32] Mahoney, 'The Exchange as Regulator', 1459. For a similar comment see D. R. Fischel, 'Organized Exchanges and the Regulation of Dual Class Common Stock' (1987) 54 *University of Chicago Law Review* 119, 123. See also N. J. Clausen and K. E. Sørensen, 'Competition and Co-operation between Stock Exchanges in Europe – Legal Aspects and Challenges' (2002) 3 *European Business Organization Law Review* 371, 381.

[33] Fischel, 'Organized Exchanges', 127–32.

inevitable consequence of increased competition between exchanges. Tough standards may make good business sense because they should appeal to issuers that want to signal to investors that they are associated with a premium brand.[34] Not all exchanges may see an advantage in upgrading disclosure standards, so it is possible to envisage a new international trading environment, as outlined by Coffee, in which high and low disclosure exchanges could both persist, each attracting a different core constituency of issuers.[35]

Several commentators have used the example of Germany's Neuer Markt to make the point that exchanges may choose to adopt high standards as a competitive business strategy.[36] From its inception the operators of that market stressed high disclosure and transparency standards as being central to its commercial branding. Olaf Stanhammar, Chairman of OM Gruppen, the operator of the commercial Swedish Stock Exchange, has also been quoted as a supporter of high regulatory and supervisory standards as being critical to an exchange's commercial success.[37]

Recent research relating to EU accession countries provides some evidence to support the thesis that strong regulation and supervision can help stock exchanges to thrive.[38] A study by Claessens *et al.* reported that the four countries with the highest regulation scores – Hungary, Poland, Slovenia and Estonia – saw an increase of 52 per cent in the number of firms listed between 1996 and 2002. The four countries with the lowest scores – Latvia, the Czech Republic, Lithuania and Slovakia – experienced a decrease in the number of firms listed, by 31 per cent. The four countries with the highest regulation scores increased their market capitalisation per GDP by 191 per cent, whereas the four countries with the lowest scores increased their market capitalisation per GDP by only 11 per cent. This study did not however explicitly distinguish between regulation imposed by the exchanges themselves and State regulation. Furthermore its authors cautioned against over-interpretation of the data, noting that there were many other

---

[34] K. Cain, 'New Efforts to Strengthen Corporate Governance: Why Use SRO Listing Standards?' (2003) 3 *Columbia Business Law Review* 619.

[35] J. C. Coffee, 'Racing Towards the Top? The Impact of Cross-listings and Stock Market Competition on International Corporate Governance' (2002) 102 *Columbia Law Review* 1757.

[36] Steil, 'Changes'; Coffee, 'Racing', 1804–6.

[37] Aggarwal, 'Demutualization', 109–10.

[38] S. Claessens, R. Lee and J. Zechner, *The Future of Stock Exchanges in European Union Accession Countries* (London, Corporation of London, Centre for European Policy Research, May 2003), available via http://www.cepr.org/pubs/fse/fse.pdf (accessed May 2004).

factors, alongside the quality of regulation and supervision, determining the number of companies listed on a market and their capitalisation.

A major reservation about relying on exchanges to regulate and supervise issuers is doubt about the credibility of their commitment to vigorous monitoring and enforcement.[39] The Neuer Markt is cited in this context too. This market was eventually forced to close in 2002, in part because it was a victim of the bursting of the dotcom bubble, but also crucially in part because of a shattered reputation for the enforcement of high standards. Press coverage at the time of closure noted that: 'mis-stated accounts and poor levels of transparency were a regular feature of Neuer Markt company news'.[40] The Neuer Markt's fate can be interpreted as an isolated incident but it is also possible to view it as signalling a more systemic problem – that is, rather than it being a case where the operators of a specific market failed to reinforce its professed adherence to high standards with effective monitoring and credible enforcement, it bears out general concerns about monitoring and enforcement being inevitable and inescapable weak spots in regulatory systems that rely heavily on exchanges as regulators and supervisors.

Demutualisation adds new dimensions to the race to the top/bottom debate surrounding reliance on exchanges for the regulation and supervision of issuers, mainly in the direction of adding to concerns that this could lead to a socially damaging lowering of standards.[41] Whilst it is true that in a competitive environment all exchanges, whatever their organisational form, may be tempted to lower their admission and disclosure requirements for issuers and to relax their monitoring and enforcement efforts in order to attract business,[42] the fear is that these temptations may intensify to an unacceptable level once an exchange acquires outside shareholders looking for high returns on their investments and with investment horizons that may not extend beyond the short term. There is

---

[39] J. D. Cox, 'Premises for Reforming the Regulation of Securities Offerings: An Essay' (2000) 63 *Law and Contemporary Problems* 11, 32–4, however, presents a counterview ('The proposition that the exchanges would be aggressive, or even vigilant, regulators is becoming a weaker and weaker proposition by the day.') See also M. Kahan, 'Some Problems with Stock Exchange-Based Securities Regulation' (1997) 83 *Virginia Law Review* 1509.

[40] L. Lewis (ed.), 'Market Mover: Neuer Markt', *Independent on Sunday*, 29 September 2002, Business Section, p. 4.

[41] Exchange demutualisation has implications across the complete range of regulatory functions that exchanges might be called upon to perform (i.e. regulation of issuers, market surveillance and discipline, supervision of member firms, and fair treatment of customers: Karmel, 'Turning Seats into Shares', 421). The discussion in this chapter reflects the scope of the book as a whole and it is therefore largely confined to exchanges as regulators and supervisors of issuers.

[42] IOSCO, *Issues Paper*, p. 6.

also the concern that pressure to relax monitoring and enforcement efforts could intensify once an exchange has demutualised.[43] Against the business case for tough monitoring and enforcement policies as a way of attracting business, lies the possibility that demutualised exchanges with outside shareholders might hesitate to check new applicants too closely or take enforcement action against their existing issuers for fear of losing business.[44] Suspending trading in securities could damage market liquidity and result in the loss of transaction fees.[45] Demutualised exchanges might also underinvest in their supervisory and enforcement infrastructure because the benefits of good regulation are hard to quantify.[46]

Entrepreneurial individuals who are good at running commercial businesses do not necessarily make good regulators, and vice versa. Thus, as well as the conflicts of interest that are inherent in combining a commercial business and a significant regulatory function in one organisation, there are also potential problems with managing tensions in the internal culture of the organisation and of achieving a structure that enables quite different functions to be discharged effectively whilst retaining an overall coherence. The corporate governance of such organisations is also potentially problematic. How, for example, is the pay of the executive directors of a demutualised exchange to be determined – by reference to comparison with other industry players or to other regulatory figures?[47] Again the 2003 furore surrounding the NYSE's Chairman's pay package illustrates the point, with some of the extensive criticism in that case being to the effect that the award was excessive for an executive who served as a federally authorised regulator of the securities industry.[48] Charges were also rife

---

[43] Ibid., p. 7.

[44] Ibid., p. 7.

[45] Ibid., p. 7.

[46] Ibid., p. 7.

[47] Among the companies included in a 'comparator group' used by the NYSE for the purposes of setting its Chairman's controversial pay package were Fannie Mae, AIG, American Express, Wells Fargo, Citigroup, GE Capital and FleetBoston: V. Boland and A. Posteinicu, 'Chief's Deal Matched That of his Peers', *Financial Times*, 11 September 2003, p. 31.

[48] B. White and K. Day, 'Grasso Critics Extend to NYSE Board', Washingtonpost.com, 16 September 2003. The *Financial Times* Lex Column captured the mood with the following opening sentences of an intensely critical article: 'Put aside the fact that Dick Grasso is chairman of the New York Stock Exchange, not the head of a bank, and the conflicts of interest that derive from his combination of ludicrous pay and regulatory powers. Leave, for now, the fact that Kenneth Langone, co-founder and lead director of Home Depot, chaired the NYSE's compensation committee while Mr Grasso sat on Home Depot's board.': Lex Column, 'Counting the Blessings', *Financial Times*, 15 September 2003, p. 20.

of flagrant disregard of fundamental tenets of good corporate governance by the NYSE in that those who were influential in deciding the Chairman's pay had conflicts of interest, such as being attached to firms regulated by the NYSE.[49] Although the NYSE was a mutual firm, the same issue could arise in a more intense form in the context of a fully demutualised exchange. A commercial company that is also a regulator is always liable to be vulnerable to the 'Caesar's wife' charge of personally falling below the governance standards that it requires of its regulated issuers.

There are also other more specialised concerns about demutualised exchanges performing regulatory and supervisory functions in relation to listed companies. A new problem created by demutualisation is that an exchange which is the regulator of listed companies will struggle to carry out those functions credibly in relation to itself as a self-listed company.[50] Not new, but arguably arising in a more intense form post-demutualisation, is the conflict of interest that an exchange may face in regulating and supervising its direct competitors, i.e. other exchanges and trading systems whose securities have been admitted to its market.[51] This issue arose in Australia in 1998–9 when the demutualised Australian Stock Exchange (ASX) became involved in a contested takeover bid for the Sydney Futures Exchange. The rival bidder, Computershare, was a public company listed on ASX, thus giving rise to a sharp potential conflict between ASX's role as supervisor of Computershare as a listed entity and its commercial interests as a competitor in the takeover bid.[52]

Post-demutualisation cutting of the regulatory and supervisory pies: different approaches around the world

So what is the solution to the problems relating to the distribution of regulatory and supervisory responsibilities that are created or intensified

---

[49] E.g. Boland and Posteinicu, 'Chief's Deal'.

[50] IOSCO, *Issues Paper*, pp. 8–9.

[51] Ibid., pp. 7–8.

[52] J. Segal, *Market Demutualisation and Cross Border Alliances: The Australian Experience*, Speech by Deputy Chair, Australian Securities & Investments Commission at Fourth Roundtable on Capital Market Reform in Asia (April 2002), text available via http://www.asic.gov.au/asic/pdflib.nsf/LookupByFileName/Tokyo_Paper_0402.pdf/$fileTokyo_Paper_0402.pdf (accessed May 2004). The problem was resolved by an ad hoc, publicly announced arrangement whereby ASX undertook not make any substantive supervisory decisions about Computershare without first consulting with the Australian Securities & Investments Commission (ASIC) and acting in accordance with advice provided by ASIC, until the issue of the rival bids was resolved: ibid.

by exchange demutualisation? The immediate response to this question is that there can be no universally 'right' solution, as IOSCO has noted.[53] The solutions that are adopted in any particular country or region will necessarily be path-dependent, shaped by established local conditions and existing circumstances. Nor is any specific solution likely to be static because it is liable to change in response to market developments and the emergence of new pressures. As a pioneer of exchange demutualisation, Australia fittingly provides a valuable illustration of the latter point. ASX generally retained its regulatory and supervisory responsibilities for issuers on demutualisation but the conflicts of interest flowing from self-listing were addressed by making the Australian State regulator, the Securities & Investments Commission (ASIC), responsible for ASX's compliance as a listed entity, and the oversight regime in respect of ASX's supervisory obligations was strengthened.[54] However, the potential conflict highlighted by the Computershare/ASX rival bids situation triggered another look at the regulatory infrastructure and resulted in the formation of a special purpose subsidiary, ASX Supervisory Review Pty Ltd (ASXSR), which has the role of ensuring the continued integrity, efficiency and transparency of ASX's supervision of its markets.[55] This response has been described as 'a corporate governance solution to conflict issues'. This solution does not separate completely the market and regulatory roles but Australian commentary makes it plain that the ASX regulatory and supervisory model is likely to remain continually under review.[56]

International comparisons in fact reveal various different responses to the post-demutualisation distribution of regulatory and supervisory responsibilities in respect of listed issuers. The Toronto Stock Exchange established a discrete business unit to separate market regulation from for-profit business operations.[57] A separate company (NASDR) was established to assume regulatory functions in relation to NASDAQ.[58] In Singapore, the demutualised Singapore Stock Exchange retained frontline regulatory and supervisory responsibilities for issuers but governmental

---

[53] Segal, *Market Demutualisation.*
[54] Principally, (i) more detail in the legislation on the obligations of exchanges, (ii) more accountability to ASIC in respect of supervisory functions, and (iii) specific power for ASIC to give directions: Segal, *Market Demutualisation.*
[55] ASXSR role is outlined on its website: ASX Supervisory Review, *Our Role*, available via http://www.asxsr.com.au/role.htm (accessed April 2004).
[56] ASXSR, *Our Role.*
[57] Bradley, 'Demutualization', 692–3.
[58] Karmel, 'Turning Seats into Shares', 424–7.

oversight of the exchange was intensified and some issuer disclosure requirements were upgraded from privately enforceable Exchange listing requirements to mandatory State rules.[59] Hong Kong broadly followed the Australian approach by leaving the demutualised Hong Kong Stock Exchange (HKEx) as the listing authority (except in relation to itself) under governmental oversight.[60] Under the German Exchange Act of 21 June 2002,[61] passed after the demutualisation of the Deutsche Börse in 2001, a Board of Admissions within the Frankfurt Stock Exchange (which is itself a legal entity under German law, separate and distinct from its administrator and operator, Deutsche Börse AG) was made responsible for listing matters; the composition of the Board of Admissions is regulated by the Act, which includes a specific provision to the effect that at least one half of its members must be individuals not professionally involved in the exchange trading of securities.[62]

The demutualisation of the London Stock Exchange (LSE) triggered a major restructuring of regulatory and supervisory responsibilities for issuers in the UK. Historically the LSE had been the primary regulator of issuers admitted to its markets[63] but its demutualisation resulted in a significant shift in the balance of power, with the Financial Services Authority (FSA), the UK's single financial regulator, assuming many of the functions in relation to issuers that the LSE had previously performed.

---

[59] L. B. Ngiap, 'Regulation of a Demutualized Exchange (Singapore)' in S. Akhtar (ed.), *Demutualization of Stock Exchanges: Problems, Solutions and Case Studies* (Manila, Asian Development Bank, 2002), pp. 177–83.

[60] P. Ashall, 'Regulation of Stock Exchanges and ATS in Hong Kong' in D. Frase and H. Parry (eds.), *Exchanges and Alternative Trading Systems* (London, Sweet & Maxwell, 2002), pp. 167–77.

A Standard & Poor's review of HKEx in 2004 saw no evidence of any major conflicts around HKEx's dual accountability to both shareholders and the public at large. S&P did not believe that the HKEx had ever misused its regulatory influence to benefit its own financial performance. On the other hand, S&P noted that ongoing public debate over the appropriateness of HKEx's regulatory role vis-à-vis listed companies, while being itself a listed company, might eventually lead to changes to HKEx's regulatory role as well as its overall governance structure: Standard and Poor's *Corporate Governance Score: Hong Kong Exchanges and Clearing Limited, Hong Kong* (Hong, Kong, February 2004), available via http://www.acga-asia.org/loadfile.cfm?SITE_FILE_ID = 216 (accessed April 2004).

[61] An English language version text of this Act is available via http://www.boersenaufsicht.de/exchange_act.htm (accessed April 2004).

[62] § 31.

[63] B. R. Cheffins, 'Does Law Matter: The Separation of Ownership and Control in the United Kingdom' (2001) 30 *Journal of Legal Studies* 459, 473–6, 480–2 considers the LSE's twentieth-century regulatory role in relation to issuers.

It was, however, only in relation to the LSE's main market, the officially listed segment, that there was significant change. Despite demutualisation, the LSE remained the frontline supervisor of issuers admitted to its second-tier market, the Alternative Investment Market (AIM), under the general supervision of the FSA. It is not clear whether the different approach to the two segments of the LSE's market was a deliberate policy choice to provide diversity within the regulatory framework through variable degrees of State control over issuers admitted to different trading platforms or was an inadvertent consequence of the fact that the changes took place at a time of intense regulatory activity in the UK. The entirety of the financial regulatory structure was under review at that time and it is thus at least plausible to suggest that the implications of demutualisation for the location of responsibility for the regulation and supervision of AIM-issuers might have been too low down the priority list to attract serious attention.

The key to understanding another feature of the post-demutualisation distribution of regulatory responsibilities in the UK may also lie in placing it in the broader context of contemporaneous events. Exchanges can be involved in the regulatory process for issuers in a number of different ways: they can be rule-makers and supervisors of compliance with those rules, or they can supervise compliance with rules that have been set by the State, or they can perform some combination of these functions. Pre-demutualisation, the LSE had performed a combination of functions in relation to issuers admitted to trading on its main market: it both gave effect to the mandatory State rules (largely derived from Directives) on admission to official listing, prospectuses and periodic disclosures, and also wrote and gave effect to its own additional rules. The regulatory reorganisation triggered by the LSE's demutualisation could have been an opportunity to examine the appropriate place for setting the boundary between mandatory State rules and requirements set by a private organisation. An option that could have been explored was to effect the reorganisation by slimming down the LSE's existing *Listing Rules* to the mandatory core necessary to give effect to the Directives on official listing, passing responsibility for this core over to the FSA, and converting the remaining requirements into the LSE's own requirements for admission to trading. Instead, the FSA assumed from the LSE its role as competent authority for the implementation of the EU Directives, and also took over, in their entirety, the additional elements of the LSE's *Listing Rules*, which comprised an accumulated body of rules and standards that, over the years, the LSE had chosen to impose on issuers. Oversight or deliberate planning? It seems likely that a number of factors were at work. It is clear that there was a strong desire on the part of all the parties, the LSE, the FSA, and the Government, to make the regulatory transfer with as little disruption as possible.[64] Preserving continuity was seen to be crucial and it was consistent with that aim for the entirety of the LSE's listing regime to pass over to the FSA. For the Government officials and FSA staff immersed in the enormous task of securing the passing of the Financial Services and Markets Act 2000 and writing the secondary legislation and regulatory rules to make the new regime effective, not having to overhaul the *Listing Rules* at the same time was surely a welcome relief. That it was an interim solution adopted in a period of considerable pressure is an interpretation that is supported by the FSA's consultative document that preceded the transfer of regulatory responsibilities from the LSE to the FSA.[65]

It is noticeable that the view that exchanges can distinguish themselves in the competitive market for listing business by the quality of their regulatory requirements appears not to be one that particularly concerned the LSE at the time of its demutualisation. The behind-the-scenes discussions between the Government and the LSE on this issue are unknown but it does seem that the LSE was broadly content to lose its frontline regulatory role for listing.[66]

In the wider market, the shift of regulatory responsibility from the LSE to the FSA did not generate much public controversy at the time it took place.[67] It was widely regarded as the correct response to demutualisation:

---

[64] Financial Services Authority, *The Transfer of the Listing Authority to the UKLA* (London, FSA, Consultation Paper 37, 1999), sec. 1.

[65] Financial Services Authority, *The Transfer of the Listing Authority*, paras. 1.4 and 1.7.

[66] A London Stock Exchange press release 'New Arrangements for UKLA Listing Authority', 4 October 1999 stated that: 'In the light of the new ownership structure the Exchange intends to create, the Treasury has agreed with the Exchange that it would be appropriate for the role of Listing Authority to be transferred and that the Financial Services Authority (FSA) will become UK Competent Authority for Listing.'
A statement from the Chancellor of the Exchequer (Gordon Brown MP) suggested that the transfer was at the initiative of the LSE: 'But, in the light of its proposal to demutualise and turn itself into a commercial company, the Exchange has suggested that it would no longer be appropriate for it to continue to exercise its Listing Authority function. I share this view and accordingly I am planning that this function should be transferred to the Financial Services Authority.': HM Treasury, 'Financial Services Authority to Become UK's Competent Authority for Listing Announces Gordon Brown, HMT Press Release, 4 October 1999.

[67] See, e.g., *Hansard*, HL, vol. 611, col. 898 where the Opposition Spokesman (Earl of Northesk) raised some muted objections but conceded that the change had to be made because of the London Stock Exchange's decision that it was no longer appropriate for it to discharge this role.

'a positive and forward-looking move'.[68] Since then, events have combined to cast a still rosier glow over the move. Although it may have been
an interim solution adopted in a hurry and without full regard to the
significance of the expansion of direct State control over issuers, as time
has gone on, as listed issuers have become accustomed to the FSA as their
main regulator, and especially as new controversies and catastrophes,
such as major corporate collapses, the piercing of the dotcom bubble and
the spectacular misjudgement by the NYSE on its Chairman's pay, have
put regulatory systems under intense scrutiny, the concentration of regulatory and supervisory power in the FSA has acquired a lustre that not
even its strongest supporters could surely have anticipated. The natural
tendency is for failures and scandals to trigger calls for stronger, more
effective regulation and, in that environment, a regulatory model which
locates wide-ranging powers with a State regulator that has a heavy armoury
of enforcement tools at its disposal naturally appears in a good light.

Careful management of the post-transfer period by the FSA also helped
the system to bed down securely. At the outset it was possible to present
the transfer largely as 'business as usual' in a new home because, at the
operational level, the transfer in effect meant that employees of the old
LSE listing department largely stayed together and simply continued their
work under a new employer.[69] A separate branding – the UK Listing
Authority – was put in place so as to distinguish the listing function from
the rest of the FSA's activities. Since then, institutionally the FSA's listing
function has started to evolve away from its LSE-origins: senior staff of
the relevant department no longer necessarily come from the ranks of
old-LSE employees;[70] there has been considerable staff turnover;[71] and the
UKLA department has been merged into a broader Markets Division of
the FSA covering both primary and secondary markets.[72] The character of
the *Listing Rules* has also begun to change as these requirements become
more integrated with the rest of the FSA Handbook though, again, the

---

[68] F. Banks, 'Discrepancies in FSA's Role', *Times*, 2 December 1999, Business Section.

[69] Financial Services Authority, *Transfer of the Listing Authority*.

[70] A. Gibson, 'On the Move', *Times*, 31 May 2001, Features, noting the appointment as head
of the UKLA department of Ken Rushton, who had previously been director of the Institute of Business Ethics, following a long career with ICI.

[71] H. Davies, 'Rethinking the Listing Regime' Speech by FSA Chairman at Annual Listing
Rules Conference, June 2002, available via http://www.fsa.gov.uk/pubs/speeches/sp98.html.

[72] Financial Services Authority, 'FSA Announces Merger of UK Listing Authority and Markets
and Exchanges Division' FSA Press Release, 8 October 2003; United Kingdom Listing
Authority, *List!*, Issue No. 4, November 2003.

process of revising these rules has been carefully managed with extensive consultation with market participants.[73]

Feedback from market participants suggests that there is broad contentment with the way in which the FSA has performed the role of frontline regulator and supervisor of officially listed issuers.[74] According to a PricewaterhouseCoopers study commissioned by the FSA, based on their post-transfer experiences, market participants 'generally viewed such separation [of exchange and regulator] very positively.'[75]

The UK's successful move from exchange to State-based regulation and supervision of listed issuers provides a powerful example of markets being willing to trade the benefits of being regulated by an exchange that, as a market participant itself, should be sensitive and responsive to market needs and driven by competition to attain high standards of professional competence, for the superior ability of the State to avoid conflicts of interest and to deliver credible enforcement. However, it also demonstrates that context and local circumstances matter, and that the answers to questions about the appropriate distribution of regulatory and supervisory powers may depend more on these than on some preordained universal regulatory model. An important contextual consideration is that significant aspects of the regulatory regime operated by the LSE were already dictated by the State; that regulation of officially listed issuers was already not simply a matter of private contract probably made the switch to the FSA feel less dramatic than it might otherwise have done. The local attention to careful

---

[73] Financial Services Authority, *Review of the Listing Regime* (London, FSA, Discussion Paper 14, 2002); Financial Services Authority, *Review of the Listing Regime* (London, FSA, Consultation Paper 203, 2003).

[74] Financial Services Authority, *Feedback Statement on Review of the Listing Regime* (London, FSA, Feedback Statement 14, 2003), para. 1.4 reports responses supportive of the UK's listing regime.

[75] PricewaterhouseCoopers, *Primary Market Comparative Regulation Study: Key Themes* (2002) (which appears as Annex A to FSA, *Review of the Listing Regime* (Discussion Paper)), p. 4.

It has been argued that: 'listed companies in the United Kingdom sacrificed a valuable regulator of corporate governance and did not receive a comparable benefit from the FSA after it usurped the LSE's role as the UK's listing authority': K. S. Burke, 'Regulating Corporate Governance Through the Market: Comparing the Approaches of the United States, Canada and the United Kingdom' (2002) 27 *Journal of Corporation Law* 341, 379. The author is right to suggest that the LSE's demutualisation did not make the loss of its regulatory role inevitable but that it was a move in the wrong direction is a view that is not supported by prevailing market sentiment.

management of the post-transfer period also helped because this facilitated a good fit between the new regulatory and supervisory model and the UK's market environment.

In noting the importance of contextual conditions and the absence of a universally applicable response to the challenges created or intensified by exchange demutualisation, it is useful to return here to the fact that the FSA only directly regulates issuers admitted to markets for officially listed securities such as the LSE's main market. Regulation and supervision of issuers admitted to other markets, such as AIM, remain to a large extent exchange-based though there is some public control over prospectus content. Thus recent UK experience demonstrates that, even within one country, there may be room for more than one post-exchange demutualisation regulatory model. However, whether this particular form of diversity will survive in the longer term is now in doubt because of recent EU regulatory developments.

C   Competitive exchanges and EU market integration

Existing diversity in the regulatory and supervisory roles
played by exchanges in Member States

Pre-FSAP EU laws established a common core of rules on eligibility criteria for official listing, for prospectus disclosure on admission to official listing or in respect of public offers of securities, and for ongoing disclosures by issuers whose shares had been admitted to official listing. The common core did not generally preclude individual Member States from imposing their own additional requirements and the institutional arrangements for oversight and enforcement were left to Member States' discretion. This allowed for considerable diversity between Member States on the role that stock exchanges have historically played in issuer regulation and supervision. Overall, the UK's concentration of responsibility (at least for the officially listed segment) in the State regulator stands out as being relatively unusual, though there are some similarities with France where the State securities regulator, the Authorité des Marches Financiers (AMF), also plays a significant regulatory and supervisory role in relation to issuers.[76]

---

[76] Euronext, *Paris Listing Process. IPO Guidelines*, available via www.euronext.com (accessed May 2004).

Germany is among a large group of EU countries where stock exchanges are still in the forefront of issuer regulation and supervision.[77]

Exchange-based regulation and supervision as a mechanism for promoting EU market integration

General arguments for exchange-based regulation and supervision fit within the broader discussion of the merits of self-regulation as compared to regulation by the State. As industry participants, exchanges have direct access to the sort of knowledge and expertise that should enable them to produce good rules.[78] There are incentives for exchanges to devote resources to regulation and supervision in order to secure competitive advantages.[79] Some European exchanges have pointed to their heavy historical investment in the development of infrastructures and skill-bases to carry out supervisory functions effectively in support of their claim not to be cut out of these functions in the future.[80]

The EU market integration objective presents a further argument in favour of locating regulatory and supervisory responsibilities with exchanges:

---

[77] Committee of European Securities Regulators, *Summary of the Answers to a Questionnaire on the Way in Which Prospectuses are Controlled, Scrutinised and Approved in All Member States and on the Deadlines Allowed for the Publication of the Prospectus Once it has Been Approved by the Competent Authority* (CESR/02–100b, 2002), indicates that stock exchanges were then involved in prospectus approval in nine countries (Austria, Denmark, Germany, Greece, Iceland, Luxembourg, Netherlands, Norway and Sweden). The Irish Listing Rules are available via www.ise.ie (accessed May 2004).
See also Finland's position as discussed in M. J. Sillanpää, 'Finland' in J. lau Hansen, (ed.), *Nordic Financial Market Law* (Copenhagen, DJØF Publishing, 2003) pp. 138–45 and PricewaterhouseCoopers, *Primary Market Comparative Regulation Study*, pp. 14–16 which notes that in Continental Europe the functions that the FSA performs with regard to assessing whether applicants meet eligibility criteria for official listing tend to be discharged by stock exchanges.

[78] IOSCO, *Issues Paper*, p. 6.

[79] Ibid., p. 7.

[80] Federation of European Stock Exchanges, *Regulatory Responsibilities of European Exchanges: First Analysis on Issues of Regulatory and Market Structure Raised by the European Commission in their Directive Proposals on Prospectuses and on Market Abuse* (2001), available via http://www.fese.be/initiatives/european_representation/2001/regulatory_responsibilities. pdf (accessed May 2004). FESE functions as the common voice for the established regulated markets vis-à-vis the European Union institutions and as a forum for discussion for their members.

through mergers and alliances and simply through attracting foreign listings, EU stock exchanges are increasingly becoming transnational in the
operation of their own businesses;[81] it could therefore be a logical policy
choice to devolve regulatory and supervisory responsibilities for issuers to
them with a view to promoting a concomitant growth in their transnationalisation.

The best-known EU stock exchange alliance is Euronext, which represents a merger of the Amsterdam, Brussels and Paris stock exchanges (the
original members) and the Lisbon exchange BVLP (Bolsa de Valores de
Lisboa e Porto) which joined in 2002.[82] Nordic and Baltic exchanges are
also coming together. OM Gruppen, the operator of the Stockholm
Exchange and HEX, the Finnish exchange operator, merged in 2003 and,
by 2004, the merged group had grown also to control the Latvian, Estonian
and Lithuanian exchanges.[83] The OMHEX exchanges are then linked to
other Nordic exchanges (Copenhagen, Iceland and Oslo) in the NOREX
alliance.[84] The Deutsche Börse has a joint venture with the Swiss Exchange
SWX to provide EUREX, a marketplace for futures trading and clearing.[85]
The Deutsche Börse is also reportedly developing links with the Milan Stock
Exchange.[86] The LSE failed in an attempt to merge with the Deutsche
Börse in 2000 and since then has not yet entered into formal alliances with
other EU exchanges for equities trading. It has, however, established a
derivatives market, EDX, in conjunction with OM of Sweden and, through
this, has established links to the exchanges in Copenhagen, Oslo and
Stockholm.[87] The LSE's recent strategy for developing greater competition

---

[81] A. N. Licht, 'Stock Exchange Mobility, Unilateral Recognition, and the Privatization of
Securities Regulation' (2001) 41 *Virginia Journal of International Law* 583, 592–4 provides
a list of some of the more significant mergers and alliances.

[82] LIFFE (London International Financial Futures and Options Exchange) was acquired.
Data on Euronext generally available via www.euronext.com (accessed May 2004).

[83] A. Skorecki, 'Lithuania Exchange Joins Baltic Collection', *Financial Times*, 31 March
2004, p. 45.

[84] www.norex.com, and P. E. Skaanning-Jorgensen, 'NOREX' in J. lau Hansen (ed.), *Nordic
Financial Market Law*, pp. 321–40.

[85] Deutsche Börse, *Annual Report 2003*, available via http://deutsche-boerse.com.

[86] 'Swallow Me, Swallow: All to Play for Among Europe's Exchanges', *Economist*, 11 May
2002, p. 99.

[87] London Stock Exchange, *About EDX London*, available via www.londonstockexchange.
com (accessed May 2004).

across European markets has involved establishing new trading services for foreign-EU (specifically Dutch) equities.[88]

Counter considerations

In some respects the transnationalisation of EU exchanges remains at an early stage despite the various alliances and mergers just mentioned. A key area of underdevelopment in the context of this discussion is that exchange alliances have not yet borne fruit in the form of common rulebooks governing listing.[89] On Euronext, issuers must choose a point of entry to the market from one of the four constituent exchanges and conform to the requirements of that national system.[90] NOREX is also broadly an amalgam of exchanges that have their own distinct listing rules, though the position is evolving.[91] Thus the reality currently falls short of a truly transnational regulatory system of regulation for issuers. This is so notwithstanding the fact that the process of rules-convergence is already quite advanced because the exchanges enjoy the benefit of a common 'core' of regulatory requirements provided by the existing Directives on listing. An inference that can be drawn from the current position is that the potential competitive advantages that could flow from having common rule books for the entirety of their market is not yet a major priority for the European exchange alliances.

A statement by a spokesperson for the London Stock Exchange suggests that at least some market operators might regard the prospect of assuming new responsibilities for issuer regulation as more of a burden than a benefit at a time when so many other aspects of their business are changing in response to new competitive pressures: '[Loss of responsibility for issuer regulation] has given us greater strategic flexibility. The shedding of

---

[88] London Stock Exchange, *EUROSETS Dutch Trading Service*, available via http://www.londonstockexchange.com/trading/dutchtradingservice.asp (accessed May 2004). This move was widely seen to be an attempt by the LSE to exploit perceived Dutch dissatisfaction with the Francophile orientation of Euronext by establishing favourable arrangements for secondary trading in Dutch equities: see e.g, 'Dutch Auction: Can the LSE Snatch Dutch Equities Trading from Euronext?', *Economist*, 6 March 2004, p. 85, suggesting strains in the Euronext alliance. Euronext has responded by announcing plans to offer trading in the biggest UK stocks on its own platform: N. Cohen, 'Euronext Plan for UK Trades', *Financial Times*, 22 March 2004, p. 23.

[89] Harmonisation of listing rules has lagged behind harmonisation of trading rules: Clausen and Sørensen, 'Competition and Co-operation', 383–7.

[90] www.euronext.com (accessed May 2004).

[91] Skorecki, 'Lithuania Exchange'.

regulatory responsibilities has meant we can take a sharper customer focus.'[92] Thus it is by no means clear that EU exchanges would have appropriate incentives to devote resources to the task of filling the regulatory gap if the policy of mandatory provision of detailed regulatory rules for issuers were to be sharply reversed in favour of devolving responsibility for this to exchanges.

Furthermore, there is no certainty on the direction that regulation might take if it were to be left generally[93] in the hands of exchanges and they were willing to engage in vigorous use of their powers. Would, for example, the Euronext alliance, the LSE and Deutsche Börse all converge around broadly the same standards with perhaps only some differences at the margins? Or would they maintain quite different rules as part of their competitive strategy to distinguish themselves from each other? It is hard to say what would happen in a world of wide exchange discretion over regulatory requirements for issuers, but it is clear that choices would reflect the exchanges' self-interested assessments of appropriate regulatory requirements rather than the broad social welfare considerations that underpin the market integration project. Thus placing too much reliance on exchanges as regulators could impede rather than advance the integration project in that it could lead to socially detrimental levels of fragmentation and to the persistence of barriers to truly pan-European issuance and investment activity.

On the supervisory side, there is a longstanding recognition that a large and diverse number of supervisory organisations is an impediment to effective and efficient pan-European supervision.[94] Furthermore, exchanges that are business competitors could not be expected easily to co-operate with each other in the development of pan-European strategies for effective supervision. Thus their involvement in supervision could undermine the trust that is needed for a network of EU-supervisors to operate successfully. A question about trust also arises in relation to the operation

---

[92] Quoted in V. Boland and A. Skorecki, 'Grasso Has Gone, but Questions Remain for the Big Board: Message to New York: The Future is Listed', *Financial Times*, 19 September 2003, p. 19.

[93] In this model there would still be supervisory control over the exchanges themselves.

[94] *Lamfalussy Report*, pp. 15–16. See also the FESCO (later CESR) discussions on the need to reconsider the regulatory role of exchanges in the light of demutualisation and the emergence of new competition: Forum of European Securities Commissions, *A 'European Passport' for Issuers – A Report for the EU Commission* (FESCO/00–138b, December 2000); Forum of European Securities Commissions, *The Regulation of Alternative Trading Systems in Europe*; Committee of European Securities Regulators, *Standards for Alternative Trading Systems*.

of the passport principle. The effectiveness of the principle of open issuer access to the entirety of the EU marketplace so long as an issuer has obtained relevant regulatory approvals and is supervised by the authorities in one State (usually the State of its registered office), depends on national regulators trusting each other, and there are concerns that exchange participation in the regulation and supervision of issuers in individual Member States would not foster the necessary levels of trust.[95]

Competition between traditional exchanges and alternative trade execution mechanisms places a further question-mark against the wisdom of looking to exchange to discharge significant regulatory and/or supervisory obligations in relation to issuers. Most bond trading activity in the EU already takes place outside traditional exchanges.[96] Whilst the position is markedly different as regard equities, where alternative mechanisms account for only 1 per cent of equity trading volumes, the financial trading landscape is changing.[97] If competitive forces move the EU to a position where much issuance and trading activity takes places outside traditional exchanges, a regulatory and supervisory regime that is based around exchanges, narrowly defined, could become too limited in its coverage.

A way forward

There are thus arguments for and against involving exchanges in the regulation and supervision of issuers within the EU. Two factors that powerfully militate against the extreme deregulatory option of simply handing everything over to exchanges are that: first there is evidence that at least one major exchange (the LSE) does not want to assume a heavy responsibility for the detailed oversight of issuers; and second, even if EU exchanges were all willing to act as vigorous regulators and supervisors, this approach would be unlikely to fulfil EU market integration objectives. However, ruling out such a radical deregulatory policy shift as an unsuitable solution based on the EU's particular needs does not necessarily mean

---

[95] See further below for consideration of the seriousness of the 'trust' problem in the context of institutional responsibility for prospectus approval.

[96] European Commission, *Proposal for a Directive of the European Parliament and of the Council on investment services and regulated markets, and amending Council Directives 85/611/EEC, Council Directive 93/6/EEC and European Parliament and Council Directive 2000/12/EC* (COM (2002) 625), explanatory memorandum, p. 8.

[97] Ibid.

that exchanges should play no role whatsoever in issuer regulation and supervision. A more nuanced approach may be desirable.

In considering what role, if any, exchanges could usefully play in the EU regulation of issuers, an appropriate starting point is at the boundaries of the EU regulatory regime. The presence of exchanges and their potential role as regulators of issuers could usefully be regarded as relevant considerations in determining the appropriate location of such boundaries – that is, rather than exchanges being simply passive recipients of regulatory crumbs that fall off the harmonisation table, leaving room for exchanges to write the rules in certain areas could be regarded as a positive policy choice. This approach would imply potential continuing diversity in institutional rule-making competencies across Member States, but in areas where a common approach may be undesirable in any case.

Quarterly reporting by issuers is an example of such an area.[98] The case for and against a mandatory EU-wide requirement for quarterly reporting was considered at length during the passage of the Transparency Directive, and the European Commission's original proposal for such a rule did not make it into the final version of the Directive. Debate revealed strong support for leaving the desirability of quarterly reporting to be determined by market participants. The imposition of quarterly reporting requirements is a technique that some European exchanges have used in the past to enhance their reputation for tough standards.[99] It is thus reasonable to suppose that exchanges will continue to exploit whatever freedom they are allowed in future to make use of this technique where they deem it to be in their business interests to do so.

Another area where there is room for exchanges to play a useful regulatory role is in relation to qualitative standards for admission, particularly with regard to equity securities. Within the EU at present, there are specific qualitative admission criteria for issuers seeking official listing, including a prescribed minimum market capitalisation, period of existence and proportion of shares distributed to the public, albeit with power for competent authorities to derogate from these minima in certain prescribed circumstances.[100] Generally, the concept of a special 'official' segment of the

---

[98] The rejection of the Commission's proposal to introduce mandatory quarterly reporting in the Transparency Directive is considered further in ch. 5.

[99] Coffee, 'Racing', pp. 1804–6.

[100] Council Directive 79/279/EEC of 5 March 1979 coordinating the conditions for the admission of securities to official stock exchange listing, OJ 1979 No. L66/21, later consolidated into Directive 2001/34/EC of the European Parliament and of the Council of 28 May 2001 on the admission of securities to official stock exchange listing and on information to be published on those securities, OJ 2001 No. L184/1.

securities markets is in terminal decline because the FSAP Directives establish a uniform regulatory regime across all regulated markets, a category that embraces some second-tier markets as well as main markets. However, somewhat inconsistently with the general trend, the specific qualitative criteria for admission to official listing are to be retained.[101] These criteria are in addition to the characteristics of different classes of instruments that regulated markets will be required under the Financial Instruments Markets Directive (ISD2) to take into account when assessing eligibility for admission to trading to different market segments.[102] The degree of intervention that will take place under the latter Directive is not yet clear because the details are to be supplied by future implementing measures.[103]

The policy choice to retain specific qualitative admission criteria for the listed segment in addition to the broader supervisory oversight of exchanges' admission requirements that will be effected via the Financial Instruments Markets Directive (ISD2), seems to reflect the European Commission's view that admission conditions are 'the front-line of defence in ensuring the quality of the instruments which are traded on markets'.[104] However, it is an odd policy choice. There is a compelling counter-view against the need for intervention to establish quality or merit-based controls in the form of detailed mandatory minimum admission criteria.[105] Admission criteria provide a mechanism whereby exchanges can spell out the particular segments of the issuer market that they are keen to attract and screen out those that they do not. Exchanges have strong incentives to pay attention to admission criteria since the quality of

---

[101] Transparency Directive, art. 28 indicates that the parts of the old Admission Directive (consolidated into CARD, arts. 42–63) on qualitative conditions remain valid.

[102] Directive 2004/39/EC of the European Parliament and of the Council of 21 April 2004 on markets in financial instruments amending Council Directives 85/611/EEC and 93/6/EEC and Directive 2000/12/EC of the European Parliament and of the Council and repealing Council Directive 93/22/EEC, OJ 2004 No. L145/1, art. 40.

[103] Federation of European Stock Exchanges, *Response to CESR's Call for Evidence on the First Provisional Mandate on implementing measures for the FIMD (ISD2)* (January 2004) argues that it is crucial that regulated markets be allowed to adapt admission rules to the policy they themselves see appropriate for all instruments that they admit. This comment is available via http://www.fese.be/initiatives/european_representation/2004/fimd2_feb2004. htm (accessed May 2004).

[104] European Commission, *Upgrading the Investment Services Directive* (COM (2000) 729), para. 4.1.

[105] See further on merit regulation R. Kraakman, P. Davies, H. Hansmann, G. Hertig, H. Kanda, K. J. Hopt, and E. B. Rock, *The Anatomy of Corporate Law* (Oxford, Oxford University Press, 2004), pp. 207–12.

the issuers that they admit to trading goes to the heart of their brand.[106] This is an area where, rather than allowing the last remnants of an old, defunct regulatory concept (i.e. special rules for a special market segment) to limp on, the EU might have done better to leave exchanges to their own devices under broad supervisory oversight from their regulator.[107]

On the supervisory side, exchanges have regulatory obligations to maintain orderly markets[108] and these will oblige them to have systems in place to monitor and discipline listed issuers. To this extent their supervisory role is uncontroversial. However, there is scope for more debate with regard to specific supervisory roles that they might be asked to discharge in relation to issuers. Within the EU, this debate has focused particularly on the question of supervisory responsibilities for the vetting of prospectuses.

Historically, exchanges have been widely involved in prospectus scrutiny in the EU. Even in the UK, outside the listed sector prospectus vetting currently remains a private function.[109] Advocates of privately organised vetting of prospectuses argue that it is cheaper than vetting by the State[110] and point to the concentration of expertise in respect of this function in exchanges rather than State regulators.[111]

---

[106] Macey and Kanda, 'The Stock Exchange as a Firm', 1023–4, 1040–2, 1048, (discussing ways in which stock exchanges can act as reputational intermediaries and considering, with reference to the New York and Tokyo Stock Exchanges, whether other entities, such as rating exchanges, compete with exchanges to perform quality signalling functions with regard to issuers).

[107] Leaving room at EU level would not preclude intervention at Member State level to mandate an allocation of regulatory responsibilities that is appropriate for local circumstances. This approach would require Member States to examine the issue individually. For an example of a Member State doing so see Financial Services Authority, *Review of the Listing Regime* (Consultation Paper), pp. 27–8 where the FSA asks whether qualitative admission criteria that exceed minimum EU specifications should continue to be set by the FSA or should be left to exchanges.

[108] Financial Instruments Market Directive, arts. 36–46.

[109] E.g., on AIM: London Stock Exchange, *AIM Rules*, available via http://www.londonstock-exchange.com/cmsattach/1814.pdf (accessed May 2004).

[110] For example on costs, in 2003 the average costs associated with AIM listings in the UK were around £500,000 (with around £75,000 of this comprising legal fees, and around £50–75,000 going to the nominated advisor, which judges whether the applicant is suitable for admission and guides it through the admission process, including in relation to prospectus disclosures): Growth Company Investor, *The AIM Guide 2003* (London, Growth Company Investor, 2003) xxix–xxx. £500,000 is regarded as around the minimum for costs associated with a full listing and the figure can rise significantly for a full listing: London Stock Exchange, *A Practical Guide to Listing* 24, available via http://www.londonstockexchange.com/livecmsattach/1222.pdf (accessed May 2004).

[111] Federation of European Stock Exchanges, *Regulatory Responsibilities*.

A specific argument against exchange-based vetting of prospectuses has, however, gathered weight in recent EU debate. This is that for exchanges to perform this function could undermine the operation of the prospectus passport. As is discussed in chapter 5, the new Prospectus Directive provides a prospectus 'passport' regime whereby an issuer, armed with a prospectus approved by its home State (generally the State of its registered office), is to be free to offer its securities into host Member States without having to comply with any additional prospectus disclosure requirements imposed by the hosts. FESCO (the predecessor body to CESR) argued that the effective operation of the passport regime depended on trust between the vetting body and the hosts, a quality that it considered likely to be lacking where the vetter was a commercial organisation such as an exchange.[112]

FESCO's view was reflected in the early drafts of the Prospectus Directive. The draft Directive provided that the competent authority for the purpose of granting prospectus approval had to be an administrative authority, thereby precluding exchanges from performing this role.[113] A recital in the draft explained why:[114]

> A variety of competent authorities in Member States, having different responsibilities, creates unnecessary costs and overlapping of responsibilities without providing any additional benefit . . .
>
> The private for-profit nature of certain entities may raise conflicts of interest and is unsuitable for ensuring protection of the market and investors. In each Member State a competent authority should be designated to approve prospectuses. It should be established as an administrative authority and in such a form that its independence from economic actors is guaranteed and conflicts of interest are avoided.

The final version of the Prospectus Directive adopted in July 2003 is, however, noticeably different. Gone are the references in the recitals to for-profit entities being unsuited to the performance of regulatory functions. On the specifics of prospectus approval, although final responsibility for approval is located with State regulators, they are permitted to delegate their tasks to other entities including exchanges.[115]

---

[112] Forum of European Securities Commissions, A 'European Passport' for Issuers.

[113] European Commission, Proposal for a Directive of the European Parliament and of the Council on the prospectus to be published when securities are offered to the public or admitted to trading (COM (2001) 280), draft Directive, art. 19.

[114] Rec. 24.

[115] Art. 21.

This revision was a political compromise secured after extensive lobbying by exchanges.[116] The European Parliament, in particular, was satisfied that exchanges had developed streamlined and top-quality procedures for prospectus scrutiny and approval, and had established structures to detect, address, and avoid conflicts of interest.[117] The compromise has a limited shelf-life until 2011, with a review scheduled to take place by 31 December 2008, but, at least for now, it leaves some room for exchange-based supervision.

The scheme for the allocation of supervisory responsibilities under the Transparency Directive (which, as discussed in chapter 5, regulates issuers' periodic financial disclosures and certain other matters) follows that of the Prospectus Directive: State regulators are primarily responsible but for a limited period of eight years from the entry into force of the Directive (with a review after five years) they can delegate tasks.[118]

EU law-making processes are often criticised for producing legislation whose quality has been undermined by messy compromises that were politically necessary to secure its passage.[119] Yet in resisting the 'publicisation'[120] of supervisory functions as regards issuers that would have resulted from a concentration of non-delegable powers in State agencies, on this occasion the political processes seem to have produced a sensible, interim result. Judging when uniformity is necessary for the development of the single market and when Member State diversity can be allowed to continue is one of the trickiest questions facing EU policy and law-makers.[121] In principle rationalisation of the number and characteristics of EU securities

---

[116] In particular by the Federation of European Stock Exchanges, *Regulatory Responsibilities*.

[117] European Parliament Committee on Economic and Monetary Affairs, *Report on the proposal for a European Parliament and Council directive on the prospectus to be published when securities are offered to the public or admitted to trading* (A5–0072/2002) (Rapporteur: Christopher Huhne), amendment 56, justification.

[118] Transparency Directive, art. 20.

[119] For example, D. Cruickshank, Speech by the Chairman of the London Stock Exchange, 'The Impact of the EU Financial Services Action Plan on the Regulation of the EU Securities Market', Guildhall, London, 6 March 2003 where the EU law-making processes were described in scathing terms, including phrases such as: 'almost unadulterated national self-interest', 'single-issue deals and messy compromises' and 'the path of least resistance'. The text of the speech is available via http://www.londonstockexchange.com/newsroom/speeches/speech19.asp (accessed May 2004).

[120] This term is borrowed from G. Ferrarini, 'Pan-European Securities Markets: Policy Issues and Regulatory Responses' (2002) 3 *European Business Organization Law Review* 249.

[121] HM Treasury, Financial Services Authority and Bank of England, *The EU Financial Services Action Plan: A Guide* (July 2003) p. 19. This guide is available via http://www.fsa.gov.uk/pubs/other/fsap_guide.pdf (accessed May 2004).

regulatory and supervisory bodies does seem both desirable and, with the expansion of the EU, an inevitable necessity. This is a powerful consideration against allowing exchanges to play the role that they once did: some form of reorganisation is needed. But the assumption that for-profit exchanges are entirely unsuited to perform regulatory or supervisory functions, as was embodied in the first draft of the Prospectus Directive, was arguably an overly simplistic response to a complex question that needs to be addressed sensitively. The blanket assertion of unsuitability was plainly inconsistent with international evidence indicating widespread acceptance around the world of the principle that exchanges can continue to act in regulatory and supervisory capacities despite their demutualisation. Other countries seem to have managed to find acceptable structural solutions to address conflict of interest concerns and to devise mechanisms for public enforcement of exchange requirements so as to meet deficiencies in that regard.[122] Furthermore, in the closely related field of corporate governance disclosure, even EU policy-makers seem content to allow exchanges to continue to play a leading supervisory role, an odd stance if in fact exchanges are so unfitted to the task of supervision as the original version of the Prospectus Directive suggested.[123]

The interim solution of locating primary responsibility for issuer supervision with State regulators addresses concerns about not over-populating the pan-European network of entities involved in the development of cross-border supervision or undermining its likely effectiveness by including within it commercial organisations that are aggressively competing with each other. This seems sensible: the development of a credible pan-European system of supervision is a top priority and central intervention to determine the number and character of the national bodies that are entitled to participate at the pan-European level is justifiable.

From this perspective, it therefore looks right to confine exchanges to a delegated role at national level. Whether their participation at that level will undermine the trust on which the system of open issuer access to the entirety of the EU market, so long as there is compliance with home State requirements depends, is a rather uncertain proposition. Whereas it is easy to see why competing exchanges might not want to share with each other commercially sensitive data on how they manage their relationships with issuers admitted to their markets and monitor their activities, it is less

---

[122] Cain, 'New Efforts', 652 noting Swedish and Australian arrangements for State agencies to enforce rules of demutualised stock exchanges.
[123] See further ch. 6.

obvious why they (and other bodies) would not trust each other's professional competence and integrity in performing specific tasks, such as prospectus vetting, and would not be prepared to rely on the supervisory oversight to which exchanges are subject and the assumption of primary responsibility by national securities regulators as adequate safeguards against abuse.

The breathing space provided by the Directives thus usefully provides an opportunity to see whether EU exchanges can still perform supervisory functions in relation to issuers effectively, and whether the concerns that are thought to result from demutualisation and greater competition actually do materialise in a serious form. There are some indications that the die is already cast in favour of eventually stripping exchanges of supervisory functions, but this is an issue that deserves to be looked at in an unbiased way and on which decisions should be based more on empirical evidence of exchanges' performance than on preconceived notions of the capabilities or incapabilities that flow from the adoption of new organisational forms.

BIBLIOGRAPHY

Adolff, J., Meister, B., Randell, C. and Stephan, K. D., *Public Company Takeovers in Germany* (Munich, Verlag CH Beck, 2002)

Aggarwal, R., 'Demutualization and Corporate Governance of Stock Exchanges' (2002) 15 *Journal of Applied Corporate Finance* 105–13

Alcock, A., 'Public Offers in the UK: The New Regime' (1996) 17 *Company Lawyer* 262–8

Alexander, K., 'Establishing a European Securities Regulator: Is the European Union an Optimal Economic Area for a Single Securities Regulator?' *Cambridge Endowment for Research in Finance* Working Paper No. 7 (December 2002)

Andenas, M., 'The Financial Market and the Commission as Legislator' (1998) 19 *Company Lawyer* 98–103

Arlman, P., Speech by FESE Secretary General, at Globalisation 5, a FEAS/FESE Conference, Prague, 25 February 2004

Arnull, A. M., Dashwood, A. A., Ross, M. G. and Wyatt, D. A., *Wyatt & Dashwood's European Union Law* (4th edn, London, Sweet & Maxwell, 2000)

Ashall, P., 'Regulation of Stock Exchanges and ATS in Hong Kong' in Frase, D. and Parry, H. (eds.), *Exchanges and Alternative Trading Systems* (London, Sweet & Maxwell, 2002), pp. 167–77

Association of British Insurers, *Review of the Listing Regime – ABI Response to FSA Consultation Paper 203* (2004), http://www.abi.org.uk/Display/File/39/FSACP203.doc

August, O., 'Don't Mention the Euro as Germany Prepares for E-Day to Dawn in City', *Times*, 15 July 1997, Business Section

Avgerinos, Y. V., 'Essential and Non-essential Measures: Delegation of Powers in EU Securities Regulation' (2002) 8 *European Law Journal* 269–89

'EU Financial Market Supervision Revisited: The European Securities Regulator' *Jean Monnet* Working Paper 7/03

Regulating and Supervising Investment Services in the European Union (Basingstoke, Palgrave Macmillan, 2003)

Bainbridge, S. M., 'Mandatory Disclosure: A Behavioral Analysis' (2000) 68 *University of Cincinnati Law Review* 1023–60

Baldwin, R. and Cave, M., *Understanding Regulation* (Oxford, Oxford University Press, 1999)

Balk, T., 'Brussels Has to Bear Down on Unfair Taxes' *Financial Times*, 17 February 2003, FT Fund Management, p. 6

Banks, F., 'Discrepancies in FSA's Role', *Times*, 2 December 1999, Business Section

267

Banner, S., 'What Causes New Securities Regulation? 300 Years of Evidence' (1997) 75 *Washington University Law Quarterly* 849–55

Barber, T., 'The Neuer Markt: Celebrations Turn to Reflections', *Financial Times*, 2 December 1999, European Private Equity Survey, p. 3

Barclays Bank, *Response to Inter-Institutional Group* (July 2003)

Baums, T. and Scott, K. E., 'Taking Shareholder Protection Seriously? Corporate Governance in the United States and Germany' *Stanford Law School John M. Olin Program in Law and Economics* Working Paper No. 272 (November 2003)

Becht, M., 'Reciprocity in Takeovers' *European Corporate Governance Institute* Law Working Paper No. 14/2003

Benston, G. J., 'Accountants and Public Accounting Before and After Enron' (2003) 52 *Emory Law Journal* 1325–51

Bhattacharya, U. and Daouk, H., 'The World Price of Insider Trading' (2002) 57 *Journal of Finance* 75–108

Black, B. S., 'The Legal and Institutional Preconditions for Strong Securities Markets' (2001) 48 *UCLA Law Review* 781–849

Black, B. S., Kraakman, R. and Tarassova, A., 'Russian Privatisation and Corporate Governance: What Went Wrong?' (2000) 52 *Stanford Law Review* 1731–1803

Black, J., 'Audacious but Not Successful? A Comparative Analysis of the Implementation of Insider Dealing Regulation in EU Member States' [1998] *Company Financial and Insolvency Law Review* 1–40

   'Decentring Regulation: Understanding the Role of Regulation and Self Regulation in a "Post-Regulatory" World' (2001) 54 *Current Legal Problems* 103–46

   'Mapping the Contours of Contemporary Financial Services Regulation' [2002] *Journal of Corporate Law Studies* 253–87

Blackwell, D., 'OFEX Left on Blocks as AIM Sprints Away', *Financial Times*, 15 March 2004, p. 28

Blommstein, H. J., 'The New Financial Landscape and Its Impact on Corporate Governance' in Balling, M., Hennessy, E. and O'Brien, R. (eds.), *Corporate Governance, Financial Markets and Global Convergence* (Dordrecht, Kluwer Academic, 1998), pp. 41–70

Boland, V. and Posteinicu, A., 'Chief's Deal Matched That of his Peers', *Financial Times*, 11 September 2003, p. 31

Boland, V. and Skorecki, A., 'Grasso Has Gone, but Questions Remain for the Big Board: Message to New York: The Future is Listed', *Financial Times*, 19 September 2003, p. 19

Bolkestein, F., 'Learning the Lessons of the Financial Services Action Plan' Speech/04/50, http://europa.eu.int/rapid/start/cgi/guesten.ksh?p_action.gettxt = gt&doc = SPEECH/04/50|0|RAPID&lg = EN

Bradley, C., 'Demutualization of Financial Exchanges: Business as Usual?' (2001) 21 *Northwestern Journal of International Law and Business* 657–702

Braithwaite, J. and Drahos, P., *Global Business Regulation* (Cambridge, Cambridge University Press, 2000)

Brennan, M. J. and Cao, H. H., 'International Portfolio Investment Flows' (1997) 52 *Journal of Finance* 1851–80

Brennerman, D., 'The Role of Regional Integration in the Development of Securities Markets: A Case Study of the EU Accession Process in Hungary and the Czech Republic' (April 2004, unpublished LL M thesis, Harvard Law School)

British Bankers Association, *BBA Comments on the Lamfalussy Process* (2003)

    BBA Response to CP203: Review of the Listing Regime, http://www.bba.org.uk/bba/jsp/polopoly.jsp?d = 155&a = 1784

Bruce, R., 'Global Harmony Hangs in the Balance', *Financial Times*, 23 February 2004, FT Special Report, *International Accountancy*, p. 1

    'A Proactive Policeman', *Financial Times*, 24 April 2003, Appointments & Accountancy, p. 2

Brussels Bureau, 'Brussels Agenda: Bonds Foreign and Financial', *FT.com*, 1 July 2003

Burke, K. S., 'Regulating Corporate Governance Through the Market: Comparing the Approaches of the United States, Canada and the United Kingdom' (2002) 27 *Journal of Corporation Law* 341–80

Burn, L., 'The EU Prospectus and Transparency Directives' *Practising Law Institute, Corporate Law and Practice Course Handbook Series 1400 PLI/Corp* (December 2003) 15–42

Cain, K., 'New Efforts to Strengthen Corporate Governance: Why Use SRO Listing Standards?' (2003) 3 *Columbia Business Law Review* 619–60

Carlin, W. and Mayer, C., 'Finance, Investment and Growth' (2003) 69 *Journal of Financial Economics* 191–226

Carr, R., 'EU Investment Services Directive Could Kill Off Execution-only Share Trading', *Investors Chronicle*, 25 April 2003, p. 13

Cers, G. and Sakarne, I., 'Country Report on Latvia' (2004) 14 *European Financial Services Regulation* 17–18

Cheffins, B. R., 'Does Law Matter? The Separation of Ownership and Control in the United Kingdom' (2001) 30 *Journal of Legal Studies* 459–83

Choi, S., 'Regulating Investors not Issuers: a Market-based Proposal' (2000) 88 *California Law Review* 279–334

Choi, S. C. and Pritchard, A. C., 'Behavioral Economics and the SEC' (2003) 56 *Stanford Law Review* 1–73

Choi, S. J., 'Assessing Regulatory Responses to Securities Market Globalization' (2001) 2 *Theoretical Inquiries in Law* 613–47

    'Promoting Issuer Choice in Securities Regulation' (2001) 41 *Virginia Journal of International Law* 815–58

Choi, S. J. and Guzman, A. T., 'Portable Reciprocity: Rethinking the International Reach of Securities Regulation' (1998) 71 *South California Law Review* 903–51

Claessens, S., Lee, R. and Zechner, J., *The Future of Stock Exchanges in European Union Accession Countries* (London, Corporation of London, Centre for European Policy Research, May 2003)

Clarotti, P., 'The Completion of the Internal Financial Market: Current Position and Outlook' in Andenas, M. and Kenyon-Slade, S., (eds.), *EC Financial Market Regulation and Company Law* (London, Sweet & Maxwell, 1993), pp. 1–17

Clausen, N. J. and Sørensen, K. E., 'Competition and Co-operation between Stock Exchanges in Europe – Legal Aspects and Challenges' (2002) 3 *European Business Organization Law Review* 371–402

Cleary Gottlieb, *The EU Prospectus Directive – Impact on European Capital Markets* (Alert Memorandum, January 2004)

Coase, R. H., 'The Institutional Structure of Production' in *Essays on Economics and Economists* (Chicago, University of Chicago Press, 1994), pp. 3–14

Coffee, J. C., 'Law and Regulatory Competition: Can They Co-exist? (2002) 80 *Texas Law Review* 1729–36

'Market Failure and the Economic Case for a Mandatory Disclosure System' (1984) 70 *Virginia Law Review* 717–53

'Privatization and Corporate Governance: The Lessons from Securities Market Failures' (1999) 25 *Journal of Corporation Law* 1–38

'Racing Toward the Top? The Impact of Cross-listings and Stock Market Competition on International Corporate Governance' (2002) 102 *Columbia Law Review* 1757–1831

'The Future as History: The Prospects for Global Convergence in Corporate Governance and Its Implications' (1999) 93 *Northwestern University Law Review* 641–707

'The Rise of Dispersed Ownership: The Roles of Law and the State in the Separation of Ownership and Control' (2001) 111 *Yale Law Journal* 1–82

'Understanding Enron: "It's About the Gatekeepers, Stupid"' (2002) 57 *Business Lawyer* 1403–20

'What Caused Enron? A Capsule Social and Economic History of the 1990s' (2004) 89 *Cornell Law Review* 269–309

Coffey, J., 'The Market Abuse Directive – The First Use of the Lamfalussy Process' (2003) 18(9) *Journal of International Banking Law and Regulation* 370–6

Coggan, P., 'Considering Equity Supply', *Financial Times*, 28 July 2003, p. 28

Cohen, N., 'Euronext Plan for UK Trades', *Financial Times*, 22 March 2004, p. 23

Cohn, S. R., 'The Impact of Securities Laws on Developing Companies: Would the Wright Brothers Have Gotten Off the Ground?' (1999) *Journal of Small & Emerging Business Law* 315–66

Committee of European Securities Regulators, *Advice on Level 2 Implementing Measures for the Prospectus Directive* (CESR/03–208, 2003)

Annual Report 2003

CESR In Short, www.cesr-eu.org

'Director of the SEC Office of International Affairs and the Secretary-General of the Committee of European Securities Regulators Announce Enhanced Cooperation and Collaboration', CESR Press Release, CESR/04–278, 26 May 2004

Interim Report on the Activities of the Committee of European Securities Regulators to the European Commission and sent to: the European Parliament (CESR/03–174b, 2003)

Prospectus Consultation Draft Feedback Statement (CESR/03–129, 2003)

Prospectus Consultation Feedback Statement (CESR/03–301, 2003)

Standard No. 1 on Financial Information. Enforcement of Standards on Financial Information in Europe (CESR/03–073, 2003)

Standard No. 2 on Financial Information. Coordination of Enforcement Activities (CESR / 03–317c, 2004)

Standards for Alternative Trading Systems (CESR/02–086b, 2002)

Summary of the Answers to the Questionnaire on Factual Information on the Legislation and Practices of Member States Regarding the Treatment of Third Country Issuers with Respect to the Drawing up and Approval of Prospectuses (Article 20 of the Prospectus Directive) (CESR/03–496, 2003)

Summary of the Answers to a Questionnaire on the Way in Which Prospectuses are Controlled, Scrutinised and Approved in All Member States and on the Deadlines Allowed for the Publication of the Prospectus Once it has Been Approved by the Competent Authority (CESR/02–100b, 2002)

The Role of CESR At 'Level 3' Under the Lamfalussy Process (CESR/04–104b, 2004)

Co-ordinating Group on Audit and Accounting Issues, *Final Report* (London, DTI, URN 03/567/January 2003)

Cox, J. D., 'Premises for Reforming the Regulation of Securities Offerings: An Essay' (2000) 63 *Law and Contemporary Problems* 11–44

'Regulatory Duopoly in US Securities Markets' (1999) 99 *Columbia Law Review* 1200–52

Cox, J. D., Hillman, R. W., and Langevoort, D. C., *Securities Regulation Cases and Materials* (3rd edn, New York, Aspen, 2001)

Craig, P., 'The Nature of the Community: Integration, Democracy, and Legitimacy' in Craig and de Búrca (eds.), *The Evolution of EU Law*, pp. 1–54

Craig, P. and de Búrca, G., *EU Law Text, Cases, and Materials* (3rd edn, Oxford, Oxford University Press, 2003)

Craig, P. and de Búrca, G. (eds.), *The Evolution of EU Law* (Oxford, Oxford University Press, 1999)

Cruickshank, D., Speech by the Chairman of the London Stock Exchange, 'The Impact of the EU Financial Services Action Plan on the Regulation of the EU Securities Market', Guildhall, London, 6 March 2003

Cunningham, L. A., 'Behavioral Finance and Investor Governance' (2002) 59 *Washington & Lee Law Review* 767–838

Dammers, C., 'Life under the Prospectus Directive', http://www.europarl.eu.int/hearings/20021002/econ/dammers.pdf

Danthine, J. P., 'European Financial Markets After EMU: A First Assessment' *National Bureau of Economic Research* Working Paper No 8044 (2000)

Dashwood, A., 'The Constitution of the EU After Nice: Law-making Procedures' (2001) 26 *European Law Review* 215–38

Davies, H. 'Rethinking the Listing Regime' Speech by FSA Chairman at Annual Listing Rules Conference, June 2002

Davies, P. L., 'The European Community's Directive on Insider Dealing: From Company Law to Securities Market Regulation' (1991) 11 *Oxford Journal of Legal Studies* 92–105

Davis, E. P. and Steil, B., *Institutional Investors* (Cambridge, Mass., MIT Press, 2001)

de Búrca, G, 'The Institutional Development of the EU: A Constitutional Analysis' in Craig and de Búrca (eds.), *The Evolution of EU Law*, pp. 55–81

Dehousse, R., 'Regulation by Networks in the European Community: The Role of European Agencies' (1997) 4 *Journal of European Public Policy* 246–61

'Towards a Regulation of Transitional Governance? Citizens' Rights and the Reform of Comitology Procedures' in Joerges and Vos, *EU Committees* (eds.), pp. 109–27

Delaney, S., 'Parmalat Spurs Call For Reform In Business: Italian Government Plans To Strengthen Oversight', *Washington Post*, 20 January 2004, p. EO1

Demirgüç-Kunt, A. and Maksimovic, V., 'Law, Finance, and Firm Growth' (1998) 53 *Journal of Finance* 2107–37

Dermine, J., 'European Capital Markets: Does the Euro Matter?' in Dermine, J. and Hillion, P. (eds.), *European Capital Markets with a Single Currency* (Oxford, Oxford University Press, 1999), pp. 1–30

Deutsche Bank Research, 'Reform of EU Regulatory and Supervisory Structures: Progress Report' (2003) 4 *EU Monitor* (July 2003) (Financial Markets Special)

Deutsche Börse, *Annual Report 2003*, http://deutsche-boerse.com

Docters van Leeuwen, A., 'Interview with CESR Chairman' (2002) 7(3) *The Financial Regulator* 20

Speech by Chairman of CESR, 'A Network of Regulators to Meet the Challenges of Regulating European Capital Markets' (Ref. CESR/03–055), Guildhall, London, 6 March 2003

Dombey, D., 'EU Drops Plan for Mandatory Profit, Loss Data', *Financial Times*, 26 November 2003, p. 28

'EU Rejects Chance to Set Cross-border Takeover Rules', *Financial Times*, 5 July 2001, p. 1

'Parmalat: A Scandal "Made in the EU"', *FT.com*, 20 January 2004

'Sarbanes-Oxley and Europe – US Legislation Finds a Friend Across the Water', *Financial Times*, 23 April 2004, Understanding Corporate Governance Supplement, p. 9

Dombey, D. and Sevastopulo, D., 'No Accord Yet Over European Auditors', *Financial Times*, 16 October 2003, p. 8

Dombey, D. and Skorecki, A., 'MEPs Clear Way For Deal on Borrowing', *Financial Times*, 27 June 2003, p. 8

Donaldson, W. H., 'Letter to NYSE Regarding NYSE Executive Compensation', 2 September 2003, http://www.sec.gov/news/speech/spch090203whd.htm

Donnan, F., 'Self-regulation and the Demutualisation of the Australian Stock Exchange' (1999) 10 *Australian Journal of Corporate Law* 1–33

Doughty, A. and Papp, E., 'Harmonising Legislation in Central Europe' (2004) 14 *European Financial Services Regulation* 11–13

Durnev, A. A. and Nain, A. S., 'The Unanticipated Effects of Insider Trading Regulation', working paper (2004), ssrn abstract = 517766

Eatwell, J., 'New Issues in International Financial Regulation' in Ferran, E. and Goodhart, C. E. (eds.), *Regulating Financial Services and Markets in the 21st Century* (Oxford, Hart Publishing, 2001), pp. 235–54

Eatwell, J. and Taylor, L., *Global Finance at Risk: The Case for International Regulation* (Cambridge, Polity Press, 2000)

Ebke, W. F., 'Company Law and the European Union: Centralized Versus Decentralized Lawmaking' (1997) 31 *International Lawyer* 961–86

Economic and Financial Committee, *Report on EU Financial Integration* (ECFIN/194/02-EN)

Report on Financial Regulation, Supervision and Stability (Brussels, October 2002)

Economic and Monetary Affairs Committee, *Recommendation for second reading on the common position adopted by the Council with a view to adopting a European Parliament and Council directive on the prospectus to be published when securities are offered to the public or admitted to trading* (A5-0218/2003, 13 June 2003)

Edwards, V., *EC Company Law* (Oxford, Clarendon Press, 1999)

Eisenhammer, J., 'Red Faces at Failure to Enact EC law', *Independent*, 30 May 1993, Business on Sunday, p. 6

Enriques, L., 'Bad Apples, Bad Oranges: A Comment from Old Europe on Post-Enron Corporate Governance Reforms' (2003) 38 *Wake Forest Law Review* 911–34

Eurofi, *An Integrated European Financial Market* (Paris, Survey, November 2002)

Euronext, *Paris Listing Process. IPO Guidelines*, www.euronext.com

European Central Bank, *Opinion of the European Central Bank on a proposal for a Directive on the harmonisation of transparency requirements with regard to information about issuers whose securities are admitted to trading on a regulated market* (CON/2003/21) OJ 2003 No. C242/6

Opinion of the European Central Bank on a proposal for a Directive on the prospectus to be published when securities are offered to the public or admitted to trading (CON/2001/36) OJ 2001 No. C344/5

European Commission, *Accounting Harmonisation: a New Strategy vis-à-vis International Harmonisation* (COM (1995) 508)

Action Plan 'Simplifying and Improving the Regulatory Environment' (COM (2002) 278)

Amended proposal for a Directive of the European Parliament and of the Council on the prospectus to be published when securities are offered to the public or admitted to trading and amending Directive 2001/34/EC (COM (2002) 460)

Analysis of Repercussions of the Enron Collapse: A First EU Response to Enron Related Policy Issues (April 2002)

'Commission Consults on the Cross Border Transfer of Companies' Registered Offices', Commission Press Release, 26 February 2004

Committee on Auditing, http://www.europa.eu.int/comm/internal_market/en/company/audit/committ/index.htm

'EU Concerned About US Audit Registration Step', Commission Press Release, 24 April 2003

EU Financial Reporting Strategy: The Way Forward (COM (2000) 359)

European Governance White Paper (COM (2001) 428)

Financial Integration Monitor (SEC (2004) 559)

'Financial Reporting: Commission Welcomes Creation of European Technical Expert Group', Commission Press Release, 26 June 2001

Financial Services: Building a Framework for Action (1998)

'Financial Services: Commission Sets Up Specialist Groups to Take Stock of Action Plan and Look to The Future', Commission Press Release, 27 October 2003

'Financial Services: Commission to set up Expert Forum to Look at Policies from Users' Point of View (FIN–USE)', Commission Press Release, 25 July 2003

Financial Services: The FSAP Enters the Home Strait (FSAP, 9th Progress Report, November 2003)

Financial Services: Implementing the Framework for Financial Markets: Action Plan (COM (1999) 232)

Fostering an Appropriate Regime for the Remuneration of Directors (MARKT/ 23.02.2004)

'Investment Services Directive: Council Agreement is Major Step Towards Integrated EU Equities Market', Commission Press Release, 7 October 2003

Main differences between the Commission draft regulation on draft implementing rules for the Prospectus Directive and the CESR advice (ESC / 42/2003-rev2)

Memorandum of Understanding on a Cross border Out of-Court Complaints Network for Financial Services in the European Economic Area

Modernising Company Law and Enhancing Corporate Governance in the European Union – A Plan to Move Forward (COM (2003) 284)

Online Consultation on Board Responsibilities and Improving Financial and Corporate Governance Information (April 2004), http://www.europa.eu.int/comm/internal_market/accounting/board/index_en.htm

Proposal for a Directive of the European Parliament and of the Council amending Council Directives 73/239/EEC, 85/611/EEC, 91/675/EEC, 93/6/EEC and 94/19/EC and Directives 2000/12/EC, 2002/83/EC and 2002/87/EC of the European

Parliament and of the Council, in order to establish a new financial services committee organisational structure (COM (2003) 659)

Proposal for a Directive of the European Parliament and of the Council on the harmonisation of transparency requirements with regard to information about issuers whose securities are admitted to trading on a regulated market and amending Directive 2001/34/EC (COM (2003) 138)

Proposal for a Directive of the European Parliament and of the Council on insider dealing and market manipulation (market abuse) (COM (2001) 281)

Proposal for a Directive of the European Parliament and of the Council on investment services and regulated markets, and amending Council Directives 85/611/ EEC, Council Directive 93/6/EEC and European Parliament and Council Directive 2000/12/EC (COM (2002) 625)

Proposal for a Directive of the European Parliament and of the Council on the prospectus to be published when securities are offered to the public or admitted to trading (COM (2001) 280)

Proposal for a Regulation of the European Parliament and of the Council on the application of international accounting standards (COM (2001) 80)

Proposal for a Regulation of the European Parliament and the Council on the Law Applicable to Non-contractual Obligations ('Rome II') (COM (2003) 427)

'Provisional Mandate to CESR for Technical Advice on Possible Implementing Measures Concerning the Future Directive on Financial Instruments Markets'

Public Consultation on the Transfer of the Registered Office of Limited Companies (2004), http://www.europa.eu.int/comm/internal_market/company/seat-transfer/ index_en.htm#consult

Reinforcing the Statutory Audit in the EU (COM (2003) 286)

Statutory Audit in the European Union: The Way Forward (COM (1998) 143)

Towards a Reinforced Culture of Consultation and Dialogue – General Principles and Minimum Standards for Consultation of Interested Parties by the Commission (COM (2002) 704)

Upgrading the Investment Services Directive (COM (2000) 729)

European Economic and Social Committee, *Opinion on the Proposal for a Directive of the European Parliament and of the Council on the harmonisation of transparency requirements with regard to information about issuers whose securities are admitted to trading on a regulated market and amending Directive 2001/34/ EC,* OJ 2004 No. C80/128

Opinion on the Proposal for a Directive of the European Parliament and of the Council on the prospectus to be published when securities are offered to the public or admitted to trading, OJ 2002 No. C80/52

European Federation of Accountants, *Enforcement Mechanisms in Europe: A Preliminary Investigation of Oversight Systems* (April 2001), http://www.fee.be/ publications/main.htm

European Co-ordination of Public Oversight (Discussion Paper, September 2003), http://www.fee.be/publications/main.htm

European Enforcement Coordination (Discussion Paper, November 2003), http://www.fee.be/publications/main.htm

The Role of Accounting and Auditing in Europe (Position Paper, May 2002), http://www.fee.be/publications/main.htm

European Parliamentary Financial Services Forum, *Transparency Obligations Directive* (September 2003), http://www.epfsf.org

European Savings Banks Group, *Response to Inter-Institutional Group* (2003)

Evans-Pritchard, A., 'EC Fury at Franco-German Backroom Deal', *Daily Telegraph*, 13 June 2003, p. 34

Fama, E., 'Efficient Capital Markets: A Review of the Theory and Empirical Work' (1970) 25 *Journal of Finance* 383–417

Federation of European Securities Exchanges, Futures & Options Association, International Swaps and Derivatives Association, International Primary Markets Association, International Securities Market Association, London Investment Banking Association, Swedish Securities Dealers Association and European Banking Federation, *Joint Response to the Inter-Institutional Monitoring Group First Interim Report* (June 2003)

Federation of European Stock Exchanges, *Comments on the Commission Proposals for a Transparency Directive* (2003), http://www.fese.be/initiatives/european_representation/2003/transparency_directive_position.htm

Regulatory Responsibilities of European Exchanges: First Analysis on Issues of Regulatory and Market Structure Raised by the European Commission in their Directive Proposals on Prospectuses and on Market Abuse (2001), http://www.fese.be/initiatives/european_representation/2001/regulatory_responsibilities.pdf

Federation of German Industries (BDI), *Lamfalussy Process – Statement on the First Interim Report of May 2003* (2003)

Fellner, G. and Maciejovsky, B., 'The Equity Home Bias: Contrasting an Institutional with a Behavioral Explanation' *Max Planck Institute for Research into Economic Systems* Papers on Strategic Interaction No. 3–2003

Ferran, E., 'Dispute Resolution Mechanisms in the UK Financial Sector' [2002] *Civil Justice Quarterly* 135–55

'Examining the United Kingdom's Experience in Adopting the Single Financial Regulator Model' (2003) 28 *Brooklyn Journal of International Law* 257–307

'The Role of the Shareholder in Internal Corporate Governance' (2003) 4 *European Business Organization Law Review* 491–516.

Ferrarini, G., 'Pan-European Securities Markets: Policy Issues and Regulatory Responses' (2002) 3 *European Business Organization Law Review* 249–92

'Securities Regulation and the Rise of Pan-European Securities Markets: An Overview' in Ferrarini, Hopt and Wymeersch (eds.), *Capital Markets in the Age of the Euro*, pp. 241–88

Ferrarini, G., Hopt, K. J. and Wymeersch, E. (eds.), *Capital Markets in the Age of the Euro* (London, Kluwer Law International, 2002)

Financial Markets Law Committee, *Issue 76 – Transparency Obligations Directive* (January 2004), www.fmlc.org

Financial Services Authority, *Alternative Trading Systems: Policy Statement and Made Text* (London, FSA, 2003)

    Conflicts of Interest: Investment Research and Issues of Securities (London, FSA, Consultation Paper 205, 2003)

    Feedback Statement on Review of the Listing Regime (London, FSA, Feedback Statement 14, 2003)

    'FSA Announces Merger of UK Listing Authority and Markets and Exchanges Division', FSA Press Release, 8 October 2003

    Proposed Changes to the UK Mechanism for Disseminating Regulatory Information by Listed Companies (London, FSA, Policy Statement, November 2001)

    Review of the Listing Regime (London, FSA, Discussion Paper 14, 2002)

    Review of the Listing Regime (London, FSA, Consultation Paper 203, 2003)

    Review of the UK Mechanism for Disseminating Regulatory Information by Listed Companies (London, FSA, Consultation Paper 92, 2001)

    The Transfer of the Listing Authority to the UKLA (London, FSA, Consultation Paper 37, 1999)

Financial Times Survey, *Europe Reinvented* (February 2001)

Fischel, D. R., 'Organized Exchanges and the Regulation of Dual Class Common Stock' (1987) 54 *University of Chicago Law Review* 119–52

Fischer, S., 'Reforming the International Financial System' (1999) 109 *Economic Journal* F557–F576

Forum of European Securities Commissions, A *'European Passport' for Issuers: Consultation Paper* (FESCO/99-098e, 2000)

    A *'European Passport' for Issuers – A Report for the EU Commission* (FESCO/00-138b, December 2000)

    The Regulation of Alternative Trading Systems in Europe: A Paper for the EU Commission (FESCO/00-064c, 2000)

Forum Group, *Financial Analysts: Best Practices in an Integrated European Financial Market* (Brussels, European Commission, September 2003)

Fox, M. B., 'The Issuer Choice Debate' (2001) 2 *Theoretical Inquiries in Law* 563–611

    'The Political Economy of Statutory Reach: US Disclosure Rules in a Globalizing Market for Securities' (1998) 97 *Michigan Law Review* 696–822

    'Required Disclosure and Corporate Governance' (1999) 62 *Law and Contemporary Problems* 113–27

    'Retaining Mandatory Securities Disclosure: Why Issuer Choice is Not Investor Empowerment' (1999) 85 *Virginia Law Review* 1335–1420

    'Securities Disclosure in a Globalizing Market: Who Should Regulate Whom' (1997) 95 *Michigan Law Review* 2498–632

'Self Registration, Integrated Disclosure and Underwriter Due Diligence: An Economic Analysis' (1984) 70 *Virginia Law Review* 1005–34

Fox, M. B., Durnev, A., Morck, R. and Yeung, B., 'Law, Share Price Accuracy and Economic Performance: The New Evidence', working paper (2003), ssrn abstract = 437662

Franks, J., Mayer, C. and Rossi, S., 'Ownership: Evolution and Regulation' *European Corporate Governance Institute* Finance Working Paper No 9 (2003)

Freeman, P., Director of Markets and Compliance, OFEX speaking at an OFEX Financial Services Action Plan Conference, 24 July 2003

Freshfields Bruckhaus Deringer, *The Prospectus Directive* (Client Publication, 2003)

Galati, G. and Tsatsaronis, K., 'The Impact of the Euro on Europe's Financial Markets' *Bank for International Settlements* Working Paper No 100 (July 2001)

Gárdos, I., 'Country Report on Hungary' (2004) 14 *European Financial Services Regulation* 15–16

Gerke, W., Bank, M. and Steiger, M., 'The Changing Role of Institutional Investors – A German Perspective' in Hopt and Wymeersch (eds.), *Capital Markets and Company Law*, pp. 357–86

Gibson, A., 'On the Move', *Times*, 31 May 2001, Features

Gillingham, J., *European Integration 1965–2003: Superstate or New Market Economy* (Cambridge, Cambridge University Press, 2003)

Gilson, R. J. and Kraakman, R., 'The Mechanisms of Market Efficiency' (1984) 70 *Virginia Law Review* 549–643

'The Mechanisms of Market Efficiency Twenty Years Later: The Hindsight Bias' (2003) *Journal of Corporation Law* 715–42

Gimbel, F., 'US Managers Dominate Europe', *Financial Times*, 21 July 2003, FT Fund Management, p. 1

Giovanoli, M., 'Legal Aspects of Standard-Setting' in Giovanoli, M. (ed.), *International Monetary Law* (Oxford, Oxford University Press, 2000), pp. 3–59

Godson, R., 'But Europe is Worse' *Sunday Times*, 10 March 2002, Business Section

Goergen, M. and Renneboog, L., 'Why Are the Levels of Control (So) Different in German and UK Companies? Evidence From Initial Public Offerings' (2003) 19 *Journal of Law, Economics and Organization* 141–75

Gordon, J. N., 'What Enron Means for the Management and Control of the Modern Business Corporation: Some Initial Reflections' (2002) 69 *University of Chicago Law Review* 1233–50

Goshen, Z. and Parchomovsky, G., 'On Insider Trading, Markets, and "Negative" Property Rights in Information' (2001) 88 *Virginia Law Review* 1229–77

Green, D., 'Enhanced Co-operation among Regulators and the Role of National Regulators in a Global Market' (2000) 2 *Journal of International Financial Markets* 7–12

'Philosophical Debate or Practical Wisdom: Competing Visions of the EU's Financial Services Sector', Conference Speech (March 2003)

Gros, D. and Lannoo, K., 'EMU Monetary Policy and Capital Markets' in Dermine, and Hillion (eds.), *European Capital Markets*, 33–75

Growth Company Investor, *The AIM Guide 2003* (London, Growth Company Investor, 2003)

Guenther, D. B., 'The Limited Public Offer in German and US Securities Law: A Comparative Analysis of Prospectus Act Section 2(2) and Rule 505 of Regulation D' (1999) 20 *Michigan Journal of International Law* 871–928

Guerrera, F. and Norman, P., 'European Leaders Invested Heavily in Building a Single Capital Market to Rival the US', *Financial Times*, 4 December 2002, p. 17

Haabu, H., 'Country Report on Estonia' (2004) 14 *European Financial Services Regulation* 14

Haas, P. M., 'Introduction: Epistemic Communities and International Policy Co-ordination' (1992) 46 *International Organization* 1–36

Hansmann, H., *The Ownership of Enterprise* (Cambridge, Mass., Belknap Press, 1996)

Harlow, C., *Accountability in the European Union* (Oxford, Oxford University Press, 2002)

Hart, O. and Moore, J., 'The Governance of Exchanges: Members' Cooperatives versus Outside Ownership' (1996) *Oxford Review of Economic Policy* 53–69

Hartley Brewer, J., 'PM Allows His Frustration to Show at the European Summit As the Day's Business is Strictly for Anoraks', *Sunday Express*, 17 March 2002, p. 11

Heine, K. and Kerber, W., 'European Corporate Laws, Regulatory Competition and Path Dependence' (2000) 13 *European Journal of Law and Economics* 47–71

Heinemann, F. and Jopp, M., *The Benefits of a Working European Retail Market for Financial Services* (Bonn, Europa Union Verlag GmbH, 2002)

Herbert Smith, *Market Abuse: Key Implementation Issues* (Corporate Briefing, April 2004)

Heritier, A., 'The Accommodation of Diversity in European Policy-making and Its Outcomes: Regulatory Policy as Patchwork' (1996) 3 *Journal of European Public Policy* 149–76

Hertig, G., 'Imperfect Mutual Recognition for EC Financial Services' (1994) 14 *International Review of Law and Economics* 177–86

'Regulatory Competition for EU Financial Services' in Esty, D. C. and Geradin, D. (eds.), *Regulatory Competition and Economic Integration* (Oxford, Oxford University Press, 2001), pp. 218–40

Hertig, G. and Lee, R., 'Four Predictions About the Future of EU Securities Regulation' [2003] *Journal of Corporate Law Studies* 359–77

High Level Group of Company Law Experts, *A Modern Regulatory Framework for Company Law in Europe* (Brussels, European Commission, November 2002)

Hix, S., *The Political System of the European Union* (Basingstoke, Palgrave Macmillan, 1999)

HM Treasury, Financial Services Authority and Bank of England, *The EU Financial Services Action Plan: A Guide* (July 2003)

'Financial Services Authority to Become UK's Competent Authority for Listing Announces Gordon Brown', HMT Press Release, 4 October 1999

Flexibility in the UK Economy (March 2004)

Ho, B. M., 'Demutualization of Organized Securities Exchanges in Hong Kong: The Great Leap Forward' (2002) 33 *Law and Policy in International Business* 283–367

Hogfeldt, P., 'The History and Politics of Corporate Ownership in Sweden' *European Corporate Governance Institute* Finance Working Paper No. 30/2003

Hopt, K. J., 'Company Law in the European Union: Harmonisation and/or Subsidiarity' (1999) 1 *International and Comparative Corporate Law Journal* 41–61

'Modern Company and Capital Market Problems: Improving European Corporate Governance after Enron' [2003] *Journal of Corporate Law Studies* 221–68

'The Necessity of Co-ordinating or Approximating Economic Legislation, or of Supplementing or Replacing it by Community Law – A Report' (1976) 13 *Common Market Law Review* 245–77

Hopt, K. J. and Wymeersch, E. (eds.), *Capital Markets and Company Law* (Oxford, Oxford University Press, 2003)

European Insider Dealing (London, Butterworths, 1999)

Hu, H. T. C., 'Faith and Magic: Investor Beliefs and Government Neutrality' (2000) 78 *Texas Law Review* 777–884

Hugin, *About Us*, www.hugincorporate.com

Huhne, C., MEP (Rapporteur to Economic and Monetary Affairs Committee, European Parliament) speaking at an OFEX Financial Services Action Plan Conference, 24 July 2003

Humphry, R., 'ASX Demutualisation – The First Four Months' Speech by Managing Director, Australian Stock Exchange to CEDA, Melbourne, 18 February 1999

Inel, B., 'Assessing the First Two Years of the New Regulatory Framework for Financial Markets in Europe' (2003) 18(9) *Journal of International Banking Law and Regulation* 363–9

'Impact of Enlargement on the Wholesale Banking Markets' (2004) 14 *European Financial Services Regulation* 3

'Implementing the Market Abuse Directive' (2003) (8) *European Financial Services Regulation* 10–12

Inter-Institutional Monitoring Group for Securities Markets, *First Interim Report Monitoring the New Process for Regulating Securities Markets in Europe* (*The Lamfalussy Process*) (Brussels, May 2003)

Second Interim Report Monitoring the New Process for Regulating Securities Markets in Europe (*The Lamfalussy Process*) (Brussels, December 2003)

International Auditing and Assurance Standards Board, *About IAASB*, http://www.ifac.org/IAASB/

International Organization of Securities Commissions, *International Disclosure Standards for Cross-Border Offerings and Initial Listings by Foreign Issuers* (Madrid, IOSCO, 1998)

Statement of Principles for Addressing Sell-side Securities Analyst Conflicts of Interest (Madrid, IOSCO, 2003)

International Organization of Securities Commissions Technical Committee, *Issues Paper on Exchange Demutualization* (Madrid, IOSCO, 2001)

International Primary Market Association, *The International Capital Markets 2000* (London, IPMA, 2000)

International Primary Market Association & European Banking Federation, 'Banking Sector Satisfied with Progress on Prospectus Directive', Joint Press Release, 5 November 2002

Investment Management Association, *Review of the Listing Regime – Responses to Specific Questions Raised*, http://www.investmentfunds.org.uk/investmentuk/publications/Responses/cp203–02.pdf

Jackson, H. E., 'Centralization, Competition, and Privatization in Financial Regulation' (2001) 2 *Theoretical Inquiries in Law* 649–72

'To What Extent Should Individual Investors Rely on the Mechanisms of Market Efficiency: A Preliminary Investigation of Dispersion in Investor Returns' (2003) 28 *Journal of Corporation Law* 671–89

Jackson, H. E. and Pan, E. J., 'Regulatory Competition in International Securities Markets: Evidence from Europe in 1999 – Part I' (2001) 56 *Business Lawyer* 653–91

Jayaratne, J. and Strahan, P., 'The Finance–Growth Nexus: Evidence from Bank Branch Deregulation' (1996) 111 (4) *Quarterly Journal of Economics* 639–70

Jeske, K., 'Equity Home Bias: Can Information Cost Explain the Puzzle?' (2001) 3 *Federal Reserve Bank of Atlanta Economic Review* 31–42

Joerges, C., '"Good Governance" Through Comitology' in Joerges and Vos (eds.), *EU Committees*, pp. 311–38

Joerges C. and Vos, E. (eds.), *EU Committees: Social Regulation, Law and Politics* (Oxford, Hart Publishing, 1999)

Kahan, M., 'Some Problems with Stock Exchange-Based Securities Regulation' (1997) 83 *Virginia Law Review* 1509–20

Kang, J.-K. and Stulz, R. M., 'Why is There a Home Bias? An Analysis of Foreign Portfolio Equity Ownership in Japan' (1997) 46 *Journal of Financial Economics* 3–28

Karmel, R., 'Self-Regulation and Governance at the United States Securities and Commodities Exchanges' in Frase, D. and Parry, H., *Exchanges and Alternative Trading Systems* (London, Sweet & Maxwell, 2002), pp. 55–80

Karmel, R. S., 'Reconciling Federal and State Interests in Securities Regulation in the United States and Europe' (2003) 28 *Brooklyn Journal of International Law* 495–549

'Turning Seats into Shares: Causes and Implications of Demutualization of Stock and Futures Exchanges' (2002) 53 *Hastings Law Journal* 367–430

Kay, W., 'Time Investment Power Went Back to the People', *Independent*, 6 September 2003, Features, p. 2

Khan, M. S. and Senhadji, A. S., 'Financial Development and Economic Growth: An Overview' *IMF* Working Paper WP/00/209 (2000)

Kitch, E., 'The Theory and Practice of Securities Disclosure' (1995) 61 *Brooklyn Law Review* 763–887

Kraakman, R., Davies, P., Hansmann, H., Hertig, G., Kanda, H., Hopt, K. J. and Rock, E. B., *The Anatomy of Corporate Law* (Oxford, Oxford University Press, 2004)

Krijgsman, P., *Brief History: IPMA's Role in Harmonising International Capital Markets 1984–1994* (London, International Primary Market Association, 2000)

La Porta, R., Lopez-de-Silanes, F., Shleifer, A., 'Corporate Ownership Around the World' (1999) 54 *Journal of Finance* 471–517

'Investor Protection and Corporate Valuation' (2002) 57 *Journal of Finance* 1147–70

'What Works in Securities Laws?' *National Bureau of Economic Research* Working Paper 9882 (July 2003)

La Porta, R., Lopez-de-Silanes, F., Shleifer, A. and Vishny, R. W., 'Agency Problems and Dividend Policies Around the World' (2000) 55 *Journal of Finance* 1–33

'Investor Protection and Corporate Governance' (2000) 58 *Journal of Financial Economics* 3–27

'Law and Finance' (1998) 106 *Journal of Political Economy* 1113–55

'Legal Determinants of External Finance' (1997) 52 *Journal of Finance* 1131–50

Lamfalussy Committee, *The Regulation of European Securities Markets: Final Report* (Brussels, February 2001)

The Regulation of European Securities Markets: Initial Report (Brussels, November 2000)

Langevoort, D. C., 'Managing the "Expectations Gap" in Investor Protection: the SEC and the Post-Enron Reform Agenda' (2003) 48 *Villanova Law Review* 1139–65

'Taming the Animal Spirits of the Stock Markets: a Behavioral Approach to Securities Regulation' (2002) 97 *Northwestern University Law Review* 135–88

Lannoo, K., 'The Emerging Framework for Disclosure in the EU' [2003] *Journal of Corporate Law Studies* 329–58

Lannoo, K. and Khachaturyan, A., *Disclosure Regulation in the EU: The Emerging Framework* (Brussels, Centre for European Policy Studies Task Force Report No. 48, October 2003)

Lastra, R. M., 'The Governance Structure for Financial Regulation and Supervision in Europe' (2003) 10 *Columbia Journal of Economic Law* 49–68

lau Hansen, J., 'MAD in a Hurry: The Swift and Promising Adoption of the EU Market Abuse Directive' [2004] *European Business Law Review* 183–221

'The New Proposal for a European Union Directive on Market Abuse' (2002) 23 *University of Pennsylvania Journal of International Economic Law* 241–68

Law Society Company Law Committee, *Review of the Listing Regime* (Committee Paper No. 472, 2004)

Leader Column, 'Concerns About the Lamfalussy Approach', *Financial Times*, 1 December 2003, p. 18

'Uncommon Market: Senseless Decision on Bonds must be Reversed', *Financial Times*, 6 May 2003, p. 20

Lee, R., *What is an Exchange?* (Oxford, Oxford University Press, 1998)

Levin, M., *EU Financial Regulation and Supervision Beyond 2005: An Agenda for the New Commission* (Brussels, Centre for European Policy Studies, 2004)

Levine, R., 'Financial Development and Economic Growth: Views and Agenda' (1997) 35 *Journal of Economic Literature* 688–726

Levine, R. and Zervos, S., 'Stock Markets, Banks, and Economic Growth' (1998) 88 *American Economic Review* 537–58

Lewis, J., 'National Interests: Coreper' in Peterson and Shackleton (eds.), *The Institutions of the European Union*, pp. 277–98

Lewis, K. K., 'Trying to Explain Home Bias in Equities and Consumption' (1999) 37 *Journal of Economic Literature* 571–608

Lewis, L. (ed.), 'Market Mover: Neuer Markt', *Independent on Sunday*, 29 September 2002, Business Section, p. 4

Lex Column, 'Counting the Blessings', *Financial Times*, 15 September 2003, p. 20

'Deutsche Bahn', *Financial Times*, 24 May 2003, p. 16

'The Prodi Plot', *Financial Times*, 19 November 2002, p. 20

Licht, A. N., 'Stock Exchange Mobility, Unilateral Recognition, and the Privatization of Securities Regulation' (2001) 41 *Virginia Journal of International Law* 583–628

Lipska, A. and Miller, J., 'Country Report on Poland' (2004) 14 *European Financial Services Regulation* 21–2

Littleford, D., 'International Financial Reporting Standards: Harmonising Accounting Principles' (2004) 15 (4) *Practical Law for Companies* 23–30

Lomnicka, E., 'The Internal Financial Market and Investment Services' in Andenas, M. and Kenyon-Slade, S. (eds.), *EC Financial Market Regulation and Company Law*, pp. 81–90

London Economics, *Quantification of the Macro-Economic Impact of Integration of EU Financial Markets* (Final Report to The European Commission – Directorate-General for the Internal Market, November 2002)

London Stock Exchange, *A Practical Guide to Listing*, http://www.londonstockexchange.com/livecmsattach/1222.pdf

About EDX London, www.londonstockexchange.com

About the Exchange, http://www.londonstockexchange.com/about/about_05.asp

AIM Rules, http://www.londonstockexchange.com/cmsattach/1814.pdf

EUROSETS Dutch Trading Service, http://www.londonstockexchange.com/trading/dutchtradingservice.asp

'London Stock Exchange Confirms Change to AIM's Regulatory Status', LSE Press Release, 18 May 2004

'New Arrangements for UKLA Listing Authority', LSE Press Release, 4 October 1999 *Statistics*, http://www.londonstockexchange.com/cmsattach/2834.pdf

London Stock Exchange, PR Newswire, Investor Relations Society, Association of British Insurers, Confederation of British Industry, Waymaker, Quoted Companies Alliance, National Association of Pension Funds, Association of Private Client Investment Managers and Stockbrokers, London Investment Banking Association, Institute of Chartered Secretaries and Administrators, British Bankers Association and the Association of Corporate Treasurers, *News Dissemination and the EU Transparency Directive* (Position Paper, October 2003) http://www.treasurers.org/technical/papers/resources/positionpaper 2003.pdf

Louët, S, 'Biotechs Await Single European Financial Market' (2003) 21 (12) *Nature Biotechnology* 1417

Macey, J., 'Regulatory Globalization as a Response to Regulatory Competition' (2003) *Emory Law Journal* 1353–79

Macey, J. R., 'Administrative Agency Obsolescence and Interest Group Formation: A Case Study of the SEC at Sixty' (1994) 15 *Cardozo Law Review* 909–49

'A Pox on Both Your Houses: Enron, Sarbanes-Oxley and the Debate Concerning the Relative Efficacy of Mandatory Versus Enabling Rules' (2003) 81 *Washington University Law Quarterly* 329–55

Macey, J. R. and Kanda, H., 'The Stock Exchange as a Firm: the Emergence of Close Substitutes for the New York and Tokyo Stock Exchanges' (1990) 75 *Cornell Law Review* 1007–52

Macey, J. R. and O'Hara, M., 'Regulating Exchanges and Alternative Trading Systems: A Law and Economics Perspective' (1999) 28 *Journal of Legal Studies* 17–54

Mackintosh, J., 'Brussels Threat to Shareholder Protection', *Financial Times*, 22 June 2002, p. 2

Mahoney, P., 'Mandatory Disclosure as a Solution to Agency Problems' (1995) 62 *University of Chicago Law Review* 1047–1112

Mahoney, P. G., 'The Exchange as Regulator' (1997) 83 *Virginia Law Review* 1453–500

Majone, G., 'Delegation of Regulatory Powers in a Mixed Polity' (2002) 8 *European Law Journal* 319–39

'Functional Interests: European Agencies' in Peterson and Shackleton (eds.), *The Institutions of the European Union*, pp. 299–325

Majone, G. (ed.), *Regulating Europe* (London, Routledge, 1996)

Major, T., 'Deutsche Bank Faces Up to Its Identity Crisis', *Financial Times*, 28 September 2001, p. 23

Mann, B. A., 'Reexamining the Merits of Mandatory Quarterly Reporting' (1992) 6 (4) *Insights* 3–5

Martin, P., 'Ghost of Business Future', *Financial Times*, 11 December 1997, p. 20

Mazey, S. and Richardson, J., 'Interest Groups and EU Policy-making' in Richardson (ed.), *European Union*, pp. 217–37

McCall, B. M., 'Why Europe Needs a Data Source Like Edgar' (June 2004) *International Financial Law Review* 17

McCall, H. C., 'Letter to SEC Chairman, William H Donaldson', 9 September 2003, http://www.nyse.com/pdfs/donaldsonletter.pdf

McGee, A. and Weatherill, S., 'The Evolution of the Single Market – Harmonisation or Liberalisation' (1990) 53 *Modern Law Review* 578–96

McKee, M., 'The Unpredictable Future of European Securities Regulation' (2003) 18 *Journal of International Banking Law and Regulation* 277–83

Michaels, A., 'Germany Plans Pan-European Audit Regulator', *Financial Times*, 12 March 2003, p. 26

Michaels, A. and Parker, A., 'US Warns Europe on Accounting Rules', *Financial Times*, 2 February 2004, p. 1

Michie, R. *The London Stock Exchange: A History* (Oxford, Oxford University Press, 1999)

Milner, M., 'Soros Fined £1.4m for Insider Trading over Privatisation of French Bank', *Guardian*, 21 December 2002, p. 2

Moloney, N., 'Confidence and Competence: the Conundrum of EC Capital Markets Law' [2004] *Journal of Corporate Law Studies* 1–49

　EC Securities Regulation (Oxford, Oxford University Press, 2002)

　'Investor Protection and the Treaty: an Uneasy Relationship' in Ferrarini, Hopt and Wymeersch (eds.), *Capital Markets in the Age of the Euro*, pp. 17–61

Munchau, W., 'Germany to Tighten Financial Regulation', *Times*, 18 January 1992, Business Section

NASDAQ, *Report Regarding NASDAQ Corporate Governance* (May 2003), http://www.nasdaqnews.com/about/Reports/NDQ_Corporate_Governance0503.pdf

New York Stock Exchange, *About the NYSE*, http://www.nyse.com/about/p1020656067652.html?displayPage=%2Fevents%2F1063105216026.html

　'NYSE Announces New Contract For Dick Grasso Through May 2007', NYSE Press Release, 27 August 2003

Ngiap, L. B., 'Regulation of a Demutualized Exchange (Singapore)' in Akhtar, S. (ed.), *Demutualization of Stock Exchanges: Problems, Solutions and Case Studies* (Manila, Asian Development Bank, 2002), 177–83

Nicolaides, P., 'Preparing for Accession to the European Union: How to Establish Capacity for Effective and Credible Application of EU Rules' in Cremona, M., *The Enlargement of the European Union* (Oxford, Oxford University Press, 2003), pp. 43–78

Norman, P., 'Brussels Wise Man "Satisfied" With Reform', *Financial Times*, 2 June 2003, FT Fund Management, p. 4

　'Credit Due to Brussels' Achievement', *Financial Times*, 19 April 2004, Fund Management Supplement, p. 8

　'A Crucial Year For The Single Market', *FT.com*, 11 January 2004

　'EU Tries to Balance Quality and Haste', *FT.com*, 6 April 2003

'EU Urged to Mull Single Financial Watchdog', *Financial Times*, 27 November 2002, p. 3

'Parmalat Changes Mood in Brussels' *FT.com*, 8 February 2004

'A Tiny Committee with Considerable Reach', *Financial Times*, 7 November 2002, p. 16

North, D. C., *Institutions, Institutional Change and Economic Performance* (Cambridge, Cambridge University Press, 1990)

Nowak, E., 'Investor Protection and Capital Market Regulation in Germany' in Krahnen, I. P. and Schmidt, R. H. (eds.), *The German Financial System* (Oxford, Oxford University Press, 2004), pp. 425–49

Nugent, N.,'The Commission's Services' in Peterson and Shackleton (eds.), *The Institutions of the European Union*, pp. 141–63

The Government and Politics of the European Union (4th edn, Basingstoke, Palgrave Macmillan, 1999)

O'Keefe, D. and Carey, N., 'The Internal Market and Investor Protection' in Ferrarini, Hopt and Wymeersch (eds.), *Capital Markets in the Age of the Euro*, pp. 1–16

OECD *Economic Survey – Euro Area 2003*

OFEX, *About Ofex plc*, www.ofex.com

Pagano, M., Röell, A. A. and Zechner, J., 'The Geography of Equity Listing: Why Do Companies List Abroad?' (2002) 57 *Journal of Finance* 2651–94

Pan, E., 'Harmonization of US–EU Securities Regulation: The Case for a Single Regulator' (2003) 34 *Law and Policy in International Business* 499–536

Parker, A. and Pretzlik, C., 'French Call IASB to Account', *Financial Times*, 2 February 2004, p. 28

Parliamentary Select Committee on the European Union, *Towards a Single Market for Finance: the Financial Services Action Plan* (45th Report, London, TSO, 2003)

Partnoy, F., 'Why Markets Crash and What Law Can Do About It' (2000) 61 *University of Pittsburgh Law Review* 741–817

Peterson, J., 'The College of Commissioners' in Peterson and Shackleton (eds.), *The Institutions of the European Union*, pp. 71–94

Peterson, J. and Shackleton, M. (eds.), *The Institutions of the European Union* (Oxford, Oxford University Press, 2002)

Picciotto, S., 'Networks in International Economic Integration: Fragmented States and the Dilemmas of Neo-liberalism' (1997) 17 *Northwestern Journal of International Law and Business* 1014–56

Pirrong, C., 'A Theory of Financial Exchange Organization' (2000) 43 *Journal of Law and Economics* 437–71

Pistor, K., 'Patterns of Legal Change: Shareholder and Creditor Rights in Transition Economies' (2000) 1 *European Business Organization Law Review* 59–107

Pistor, K., Raiser, M. and Gelfer., S, 'Law and Finance in Transition Economies' (2000) 8 *Economics of Transition* 325–68

Posteinicu, A., 'Calls for NYSE to Demutualise', *Financial Times*, 8 September 2003, p. 21

Posteinicu, A. and Wighton, D., 'NYSE Members Keep Listing Question Afloat', *Financial Times*, 8 March 2004, p. 28

Prentice, R., 'Enron: A Brief Behavioral Autopsy' (2003) *American Business Law Journal* 417–44

'Whither Securities Regulation? Some Behavioral Observations Regarding Proposals for its Future' (2001) 51 *Duke Law Journal* 1397–1512

Pretzlik, C., 'European Directives "Could Undermine Plans for More Efficient Capital Markets"', *Financial Times*, 27 January 2004, p. 7

PricewaterhouseCoopers, *Primary Market Comparative Regulation Study: Key Themes* (2002)

Public Company Accounting Oversight Board, *Oversight of Non-US Public Accounting Firms* (Washington, PCAOB, Briefing Paper, October 2003)

Rajan, R. G. and Zingales, L., 'Banks and Markets: The Changing Character of European Finance', *National Bureau of Economic Research* Working Paper No 9595 (2003)

Reciunas, G. and Stasevicius., G, 'Country Report on Lithuania' (2004) 14 *European Financial Services Regulation* 19–20

Reinhardt, N., *The Lamfalussy Process: A Guide and Evaluation* (Brussels, Houston Consulting Europe, April 2004)

Report by a Group of Experts, *The Development of a European Capital Market* (Brussels, European Commission, 1966)

Revell, S., 'The Prospectus Directive' (2003) 14 *Practical Law for Companies* 14–15

Ribstein, L. E., 'Market v Regulatory Responses to Corporate Fraud: A Critique of the Sarbanes-Oxley Act of 2002' (2003) 28 *Journal of Corporation Law* 1–67

Richardson, J., 'Policy-making in the EU: Interests, Ideas and Garbage Cans of Primeval Soup' in Richardson (ed.), *European Union*, pp. 3–26

Richardson, J. (ed.), *European Union: Power and Policy-Making* (2nd edn, London, Routledge, 2001)

Rider, B. A. K., 'The Control of Insider Trading – Smoke and Mirrors!' (2000) 19 *Dickinson Journal of International Law* 1–45

Rider, B. A. K. and Ashe, M., 'The Insider Dealing Directive' in Andenas, M. and Kenyon-Slade, S. (eds.), *EC Financial Market Regulation* (London, Sweet & Maxwell, 1993), pp. 209–40

Roe, M. J., 'Delaware's Competition' (2003) 117 *Harvard Law Review* 588–646

Political Determinants of Corporate Governance (Oxford, Oxford University Press, 2003)

Rogers, W. V. H., *Winfield & Jolowicz on Tort* (16th edn, London, Sweet & Maxwell, 2002)

Romano, R., 'Empowering Investors: a Market Approach to Securities Regulation' (1998) 107 *Yale Law Journal* 2359–430

'The Need for Competition in International Securities Regulation' (2001) 2 *Theoretical Inquiries in Law* 387–562

Rudnick, D., 'Big Guns Voice Concern at Takeover Directive Amendments', *Daily Telegraph*, 6 November 2003, p. 15

Samuel, A., 'Consumer Financial Services in Britain: New Approaches to Dispute Resolution and Avoidance' (2002) 3 *European Business Organization Law Review* 649–94

Schaub, A., 'Testimony of Director-General, DG Internal Market of the European Commission before the Committee on Financial Services, US House of Representatives', 13 May 2004, http://europa.eu.int/comm/internal_market/en/finances/general/2004–05–13-testimony_en.pdf

Schwarze, H. J., 'The European Insider Dealing Directive and its Impact on the Member States, Particularly Germany' in Hopt and Wymeersch (eds.), *European Insider Dealing*, pp. 151–7

Scott, C., 'Analysing Regulatory Space: Fragmented Resources and Institutional Design' [2001] *Public Law* 329–53
    'The Governance of the European Union: The Potential for Multi-Level Control' (2002) 8 *European Law Journal* 59–79

Scott, H. S., 'Internationalization of Primary Public Securities Markets' (2000) 63 *Law and Contemporary Problems* 71–104

Scott, J. and Trubek, D. M., 'Mind the Gap: Law and the New Approaches to Governance in the European Union' (2002) 8 *European Law Journal* 1–18

Securities Expert Group, *Financial Services Action Plan: Progress and Prospects* (Final Report, Brussels, May 2004)

Segal, J., *Market Demutualisation and Cross Border Alliances: The Australian Experience*, Speech by Deputy Chair, Australian Securities & Investments Commission at Fourth Roundtable on Capital Market Reform in Asia (April 2002)

Shackleton, M., 'The European Parliament' in Peterson and Shackleton (eds.), *The Institutions of the European Union*, pp. 95–117

Shaw, J., *Law of the European Union* (3rd edn, Basingstoke, Palgrave Macmillan, 2000)

Shearman & Sterling, *The EU Prospectus Directive – Home Member State for Non-EU-Issuers* (Client Publication, November 2003)

Shiller, R. J., *Irrational Exuberance* (Princeton, N.J.; Princeton University Press, 2000)

Shleifer, A., *Inefficient Markets: An Introduction to Behavioral Finance* (Oxford, Oxford University Press, 2000)

Shojai, S., 'But I Thought I Was Part of a Pan-European Index', *Sunday Business*, 16 September 2001, p. 29

Sillanpää, M. J., 'Finland' in lau Hansen, J. (ed.), *Nordic Financial Market Law* (Copenhagen, DJØF Publishing, 2003), pp. 131–62

Skaanning-Jorgensen, P. E., 'NOREX' in lau Hansen, J. (ed.), *Nordic Financial Market Law*, pp. 321–40

Skeete, H., *Key Trends in the Market Data Sphere*, http://www.afma.com.au/afmawr/pdf/fmc_herbie_skeete.pdf

Skorecki, A., 'AIM Chiefs Query EU Prospectus Proposals', *Financial Times*, 29 May 2003, p. 24

'Equity Ship is Becalmed', *Financial Times*, 11 January 2003, Money Section, p. 3

'European Issuers Get Passport', *Financial Times*, 1 July 2003, p. 47

'Lithuania Exchange Joins Baltic Collection', *Financial Times*, 31 March 2004, p. 45

Skorecki, A. and Buck, T., 'Banks in EU Set for Share Trading Shake-up', *FT.com*, 24 February 2004

Slaughter, A. M., 'Global Government Networks, Global Information Agencies, and Disaggregated Democracy' (2003) 24 *Michigan Journal of International Law* 1041–75

Snyder, F., 'EMU Revisited: Are We Making a Constitution? What Constitution Are We Making?' in Craig and de Búrca (eds.), *The Evolution of EU Law*, pp. 417–77

St Clair Bradley, K., 'The European Parliament and Comitology: On the Road to Nowhere' (1997) 3 *European Law Journal* 230–54

St John, A. B., 'The Regulation of Cross Border Public Offerings of Securities in the European Union: Present and Future' (2001) 29 *Denver Journal of International Law and Policy* 239–60

Standard and Poor's *Corporate Governance Score*: *Hong Kong Exchanges and Clearing Limited, Hong Kong* (Hong, Kong, February 2004), http://www.acga-asia.org/loadfile.cfm?SITE_FILE_ID=216

Steil, B., 'Changes in the Ownership and Governance of Securities Exchanges: Causes and Consequences' *Wharton Financial Institutions Center* Working Papers 02–15

Stigler, G., 'The Theory of Economic Regulation' (1971) 6(2) *Bell Journal of Economics and Management Sciences* 3–21

Stiglitz, J., *Globalization and its Discontents* (London, Penguin, 2002)

Stout, L. A., 'Are Stock Markets Costly Casinos? Disagreement, Market Failure, and Securities Regulation' (1995) 81 *Virginia Law Review* 611–712

'The Mechanics of Market Inefficiency: An Introduction to the New Finance' (2003) 28 *Journal of Corporation Law* 635–69

'The Unimportance of Being Efficient: An Economic Analysis of Market Pricing and Securities Regulation' (1988) 87 *Michigan Law Review* 613–709

Strongin, D. G., 'EU Transparency Obligations Directive' 13 January 2004, http://www.sia.com/international/pdf/SIALuxembourgTOD.pdf

Suckow, S., 'The European Prospectus' (1975) 23 *American Journal of Comparative Law* 50–68

Sun, J. M. and Pelkmans, J., 'Regulatory Competition in the Single Market' (1995) 33 *Journal of Common Market Studies* 67–89

Tassell., T., Rigby, E. and Dombey, D., 'City Trade Bodies Issue Warning on Directives', *Financial Times*, 14 October 2003, p. 8

Thatcher, M., 'European Regulation' in Richardson (ed.), *European Union*, pp. 303–20

Tiebout, C., 'A Pure Theory of Local Expenditures' (1956) 64 *Journal of Political Economy* 416–24

Trachtman, J. P., 'Regulatory Competition and Regulatory Jurisdiction in International Securities Regulation' in Esty and Geradin (eds.), *Regulatory Competition and Economic Integration*, pp. 289–310

Trefgarne, G., 'MEP Wins AIM Concessions', *Daily Telegraph*, 27 February 2002, p. 39

Tridimas, T., *The General Principles of EC Law* (Oxford, Oxford University Press, 1999)

Tsoukalis, L.,'Economic and Monetary Union' in Wallace and Wallace (eds.), *Policy-Making*, pp. 149–78

Tucker, S., 'Quarter Reports Gain Support', *Financial Times*, 11 February 2004, p. 24

United Kingdom Listing Authority, *List!*, Issue No. 4, November 2003

United States Mission to the European Union, *European Financial Services Action Program Good for World Economy*, 29 January 2004, http://www.useu.be/Categories/Tax%20and%20Finances/Jan2904SobelFSAP.html

van der Elst, C., 'The Equity Markets, Ownership Structures and Control: Towards an International Harmonization' in Hopt and Wymeersch, (eds.), *Capital Markets and Company Law*, pp. 3–46

Villiers, T., 'Where Next for the ISD?' *The Parliament Magazine* 3 November 2003, 23–4

Wallace, H., 'The Institutional Setting' in Wallace and Wallace (eds.), *Policy-Making in the European Union*, pp. 3–37

'The Policy Process' in Wallace and Wallace (eds.), *Policy-Making*, pp. 39–64

Wallace, H. and Wallace, W. (eds.), *Policy-Making in the European Union* (4th edn, Oxford, Oxford University Press, 2000)

Warren, M. G., 'The Harmonization of European Securities Law' (2003) 37 *International Lawyer* 211–20

'The Regulation of Insider Trading in the European Community' (1991) 48 *Washington & Lee Law Review* 1037–78

Weatherill, S. and Beaumont, P., *EU Law* (3rd edn, London, Penguin, 1999)

Weil, Gotshal & Manges, *Comparative Study of Corporate Governance Codes Relevant to the European Union And Its Member States* (Brussels, European Commission, 2002)

White, B. and Day, K., 'Grasso Critics Extend to NYSE Board', Washingtonpost.com, 16 September 2003

White, W. R., 'The Coming Transformation of Continental European Banking?' *Bank for International Settlements* Working Paper No 54 (June 1998)

Wincott, D., 'Looking Forward or Harking Back? The Commission and the Reform of Governance in the EU' (2001) 39 *Journal of Common Market Studies* 897–911

Winter, J. W., 'Cross-border Voting in Europe' in Hopt and Wymeersch (eds.), *Capital Markets and Company Law*, pp. 387–426

Wolf, J. and Atkinson, D., 'Spain Rocks Takeover Pact', *Guardian*, 22 June 1999, p. 20

Woolcock, S., 'Competition Among Rules in the Single European Market' in Bratton, W., McCahery, J., Picciotto, S. and Scott, C. (eds.), *International Regulatory Competition and Coordination* (Oxford, Clarendon Press, 1996), pp. 289–321

Wymeersch, E., 'Company Law in Turmoil and the Way to Global Company Practice' [2003] *Journal of Corporate Law Studies* 283–98

'Co-operation between Authorities in the Community: the Case of Banking, Insurance and Securities Supervision', Paper for Yale Law School Center for the Study of Corporate Law Symposium, *Assessing Corporate Law Reform in a Transatlantic Context* (21 October 2003)

'Regulating European Markets: the Harmonisation of Securities Regulation in Europe in the New Trading Environment' in Ferran and Goodhart (eds.), *Regulating Financial Services*, pp. 189–210

Young, A. R. and Wallace, H., 'The Single Market' in Wallace and Wallace (eds.), *Policy-Making*, pp. 85–114

Zerafa, A., 'Country Report on Malta' (2004) 14 *European Financial Services Regulation* 23–4

'A Bit of Give and Take: Another Transatlantic Row over Financial Regulation', *Economist*, 19 October 2002, p. 99

'A Ragbag of Reform', *Economist*, 3 March 2001, p. 93

'A Survey of Europe's Internal Market', *The Economist*, 8 July 1989, special survey

'Actions Speak Louder than Words', *Economist Global Agenda*, 7 May 2003, via www.economist.com

'Big, Bigger, Biggest', *Economist*, 6 April 2002, p. 77

'Bolkestein Sees EU–US Audit Firm Deal by Year End', Forbes.com (9 October 2003)

'Dutch Auction: Can the LSE Snatch Dutch Equities Trading from Euronext?', *Economist*, 6 March 2004, p. 85

'EU, US Reach Agreement on Auditor Oversight', *EU Business*, 25 March 2004

'Europe's Enron', *Economist*, 1 March 2003, p. 63

'Holier Than Thou: European Sanctimony over American Accounting Scandals is Misplaced', *Economist*, 8 February 2003, p. 85

'How to Protect Investors', *Economist*, 27 April 2002, p. 81

'Is Deutschland AG Kaputt?', *Economist*, 7 December 2002, A Survey of Germany, p. 8

'John Reed's Modest Proposal. Too Modest. The Big Board Must Regulate Itself No Longer', *Economist*, 22 November 2003, p. 14

'Labouring with Lamfalussy', *Economist*, 16 June 2001, p. 97

'Mr Thain Moves In: A Rescue Squad Begins Work at America's Leading Stock Exchange', *Economist*, 10 January 2004, p. 64

'Outing the Insiders', *Financial Times*, 1 August 1994, p. 15

'Scrapping over the Pieces – Laborious Efforts Towards a Single Market', *Economist*, 9 March 2002, p. 85

'Signed But Not Sealed', *Economist*, 27 May 2000, p. 113

'Spoilt Choice: Horse-trading on EU-wide Prospectus Rules Could Have a Perverse Outcome', *Economist*, 9 November 2002, p. 101

'Swallow Me, Swallow: All to Play for Among Europe's Exchanges', *Economist*, 11 May 2002, p. 99

'Thatcherites in Brussels (Really)', *Economist*, 15 March 1997, p. 25

'The Lessons from Enron', *Economist*, 9 February 2002, p. 9

'The Pause After Parmalat: Europe's Enron Calls for a Measured but More Determined Response', *Economist*, 17 January 2004, p. 13

'The Perils of Not Sticking to Your Knitting', *Economist Global Agenda*, 12 November 2002

'The Perils of Political Europe', *Economist*, 28 June 2003, p. 52

'The Tower of Babble', *Economist*, 2 August 2003, p. 45

'Trojan Horses', *Economist*, 15 February 2003, p. 77

accession countries   122, 244
accountability
    CESR   103
    Lamfalussy process   95
    pan-European regulatory
        agency   120
Accounting Regulatory
    Committee   214
accounting requirements
    FSAP approach   35, 44
    IAS/IFRS   35, 137, 162–3, 172, 209
        and audits   230
        EU choice   162–4, 212–15, 217
        IAS Regulation   209
        and non-EU issuers   205
    institutional supervision   221
    maximum harmonisation
        approach   55
    responsibility statements   190
    semi-annual accounting
        requirements   138
    SMEs   181
    US GAAP   162–3, 212, 214, 217
Accounting Technical
    Committee   214–15
acquisitions. *See* takeovers
Action Plan for Company Law
    218–19, 227, 228
admission criteria   260–2
Advisory Panel of Financial Services
    Experts (APFSE)   84, 110
advisory services   21
Aerosol clause   108
agency workers   117
Alternative Investment Market
    (AIM)   186, 187, 188, 206, 250
alternative trading systems   206,
    239n10, 259
asset managers   105
Association of British Insurers   158

ASXSR   248
asymmetric information   90–1,
    202–3
audits
    Audit Advisory Committee   231
    Audit Regulatory Committee   231
    conflicts of interest   231
    draft Directive   232, 233
    international standards   232
    Prospectus Directive   138
    Sarbanes-Oxley Act   113, 228, 231,
        232, 233
    statutory auditors   230
    supervision   228–33, 235
Australia, stock exchanges   241, 247,
    248
Austria   225n72, 255n77

Babel Tower   160–7
banking
    bank finance   14, 15, 219
    British Bankers Association
        93, 158
    changes   16–17
    Committee of European Banking
        Supervisors (CEBS)   48
    European Banking Federation   93
    Lamfalussy process   124
    pan-European supervision   47–8
Belgium   35–6, 186, 225n72
Bhattacharya, U.   33, 34
Bolkestein, Frits   48, 49n191, 50n198
bond markcts
    advisory services   21
    alternative trading systems   206, 259
    denominations   172
    financing mergers and
        acquisitions   15–16
    flexibility   109
    and FSAP approach   45

bond markets (cont.)
  growth 19
  location 173
  pan-European market 20
  research 20–1
  standard equivalence issues 162
  supervision, thresholds 173–5
Bretton Woods system 22
British Bankers Association 93, 158

Canada, Toronto Stock
  Exchange 248
Claessens, S. 244
Coffee, J. C. 244
comitology 66, 68, 74, 91n132
Committee of European Securities
  Regulators (CESR)
  accountability 103
  consultation 84, 95–6, 181–2
  CSER-Fin 80
  CSER-Pol 80
  decisions 81
  effectiveness 48, 56, 221, 234, 235
  guidelines 79, 100
  legitimacy 102–7
  Markets Participants Group 106
  meetings 80
  mutual dependence 152
  peer review 79–80, 112
  positive role 101–2
  power 88, 103–4
  and protectionism 103
  relations with EU
    Commission 88–91, 102–5
  resources 80, 89, 124
  and retail investors 106–7
  role 6–7, 47, 78–80, 215,
    224–5, 234
  and special interest groups 104–7
  standards 222–3
  website 7
Common Agricultural Policy 117
company law. See also corporate
  governance
  Action Plan for Company
    Law 218–19, 227, 228
  diversity of national regimes
    226–8

and FSAP 218
  state of incorporation 56
competition, regulatory
  competition 46–50
Computershare 241, 248
consultation
  CESR 84, 95–6, 181–2
  fatigue 98
  Lamfalussy process 84, 92–8
convertible securities,
  prospectuses 168
cooperation, national regulators
  209, 220
Copenhagen criteria 39n154
COREPER 75, 76
corporate governance
  Anglo-American model 118
  codes of best practice 218
  Company Law Action Plan
    218–19, 227, 228
  demutualised stock
    exchanges 246–7, 248, 265
  disclosures 128, 129, 130, 209,
    218–19
  diversity of regimes 226–8
  EU sensitivity 227
  European Corporate Governance
    Forum 227
Czech Republic 40, 225n72, 244

Daouk, H. 33, 34
debt securities. See specialist debt
  securities
Demirgürç-Kunt, A. 13
demographic changes 22
Denmark 31n112, 255n77, 256
derivatives 16, 168, 173, 214
Deustche Bank 17, 32n117
directives. See also Lamfalussy process
  application 213
  issuer disclosure 134–5,
    159–60, 208
  legislative process 67–70
directors
  disqualification 193, 219
  remuneration 130, 218, 246–7, 252
disclosure. See issuer disclosure
dotcom bubble 245

Economic and Financial Committee
(EFC) 75
EDX 256
enforcement. *See also* supervision
alternative to further
regulation 46–50
convergence 47
issuer disclosure 188–93
civil liability 189, 190–1, 196
criminal liability 189–90
multi-jurisdictional
litigation 191
national systems 46, 111
pan-European regulatory
agency 60, 119–22
and regulatory competition 52
sanctions 220
Enron 192, 203, 215–16, 226, 227, 231
Estonia 244, 256
EU Commission
Guardian of the Treaty 102
and lobbysts 104
policy entrepreneur 86
relations with CESR
88–91, 102–5
resources 86
role in Lamfalussy process 86–91
EU Council, ascendancy 117–18
EU securities markets
2000 downturn 18
alternative trading
systems 239n10
changes 15–21
and economic growth 11–14
forces for growth 21–4, 41
fragmentation 9, 19–21, 122
growth 9, 15–24
infrastructure 21
integration. *See* single securities
markets
regulation. *See* regulation of EU
securities markets
size 17–18
EUREX 256
euro 8–9, 12, 21, 23
Euronext 256, 257
European Banking Federation 93
European Central Bank 8, 76–7

European Commission
Recommendations 230
and regulatory agencies 120–1
relations with Council 117–18
European Corporate Governance
Forum 227
European Court of Justice,
jurisprudence 73, 116
European Economic and Social
Committee 76
European Federation of
Accountants 223
European Monetary Union
(EMU) 8–9, 23
European Parliament
Economic and Monetary Affairs
Committee 76, 83–4, 109–10
and Lamfalussy process 66–7, 85,
87, 109–11
legislative power 74
and Prospectus Directive 93
European regulatory agency
accountability 120
alternative to Lamfalussy
process 60, 119–22, 123
and EU Commission 120–1
option 2
remoteness 120
supporters and opponents 120
Treaty changes 121
European Securities Committee
77–8, 95, 107–9
European Union
accession countries 39, 40
Constitution 7, 12
governance 123–4
Lamfalussy process. *See* Lamfalussy
process
legal personality 7
legislation, primary legislation 61
legislative competence 29–30
original aims 8
policy making 59, 60
state-like attributes 11–12
terminology 7
euro-securities 170
exchange controls 239
execution only dealings 106

financial development, benefits   11–14
financial reporting
    accounting standards   212–17
    accuracy   221
    audits   230
    post-Enron   215–17
    single regulator model   225–6
    supervision   219–26
Financial Reporting Review Panel
    (FRRP)   226
financial scandals   215–16, 228, 231
Financial Services Action Plan (FSAP)
    approach, assessment   11, 111–18
    and audits   229–30
    balance   2
    and corporate governance   218
    criticisms   1
    development   2–5, 215
    impact   2
    Lamfalussy process. *See* Lamfalussy
        process
    objective   1
    policy choices   43–5, 238
    post-FSAP phase   204
    regulation option   43–5
    regulatory convergence   46
    and retail investors   105–7
    Securities Expert Group   87
    shift of legislative centre   105, 111
    significance   204
    timetable   95, 124
    uniform regulatory regime   11, 261
Financial Services Authority
    157–9, 193–4, 226, 249–54
Financial Services Committee
    (FSC)   75
Finland   255n77, 256
FIN-NET   49–50
FIN-USE   107
Forum of European Securities
    Commissions (FESCO)
    47, 79, 263
France
    audit supervision   228–9
    Autorité des Marchés
        Financiers   254
    and CAP   117
    growth of securities market   15

insider dealing   31n112, 33
issuer disclosure regime   35–6
and pan-European regulatory
    agency   120
protectionism   94
regulators   225n72, 254
second-tier markets   186
and single financial market   113
stock exchange   21, 256
free movement of capital   3, 29
free movement of persons   3, 29
freedom to supply services   3, 29,
    115–16
fund management   20, 105

Germany
    auditor oversight   229
    banking sector   17, 18
    and CAP   117
    Deutsche Börse   21, 241, 249, 256
    Frankfurt Stock Exchange   249
    growth of securities market   15
    implementation record   111n212
    insider dealing   31, 32, 33
    investor protection regulation   38–9
    issuer disclosure regime   36
    Neuer Markt   18, 36, 244
    and single financial market   112–13
    single regulator model   225n72
    stock exchange regulation   255,
        255n77
    and Takeover Directive   110, 116,
        117
    and temporary workers   117
Gibraltar   117
globalisation   115
Grasso, Richard   242, 246–7, 252
Greece   255n77
guidelines. *See* standards

home bias
    asymmetric information   202–3
    and issuer disclosure regime
        202–4
    retail investors   9, 179
home states
    choice   156–7, 173–4
    existing listing preferences   154

identification
  non-equity securities 173–4
  non-EU issuers 205
  Prospectus Directive 147–9
  rigidity 150–3, 202
  Transparency Directive 149–50
  supervision of disclosures in host
    states 152
Hong Kong 249
Hungary 225n72, 244

Iceland 78, 255n77, 256
information
  asymmetric information 90–1,
    202–3
  dissemination 193–7
    assessment 204
    commercial companies 194–5
    national regulators 195
    publication mechanisms
      195–6
    standards 196
    UK 193–4
    websites 195–6
  inside information 197–200
  issuers. See issuer disclosure;
    periodic disclosures;
    prospectuses
  and market prices 128
  overload 178
inside information 197–200
insider dealing
  effect of EU legislation 30–4
  enforcement 32–3
  FSAP approach 44
insurance
  Lamfalussy process 124
  representation of interests 105
  supervision 48
Inter-Institutional Monitoring Group
  (IIMG) 87, 105
International Organisation of
  Securities Commissions
  (IOSCO) 140, 248
International Primary Market
  Association 93
Investment Management
  Association 158

investment services
  directive 3
  freedom to supply 115–16
  FSAP approach 44
investor protection
  effect of integrated regulation 10, 45
  effect on market growth 42
  EU competence 29
  EU legislation 30
  FSAP approach 43–5
  national systems 46
  origins of legislation 28
  Prospectus Directive 137
  regulatory competition 52
  strategic choices 41–57
  supervision and enforcement
    alternative 46–50
Ireland 225n72, 229n89, 255n77
issuer disclosure
  agency problems 129–30
  assessment of new regime 200–7
  centrality 127–33
  corporate governance
    disclosures 130, 209,
    218–19, 226–8
  credibility 132
  directives 134–5, 208
    assessment 159–60
  directors' disqualifications 193, 219
  dissemination of
    information 193–7, 204
  effect of past EU legislation 34–8
  effectiveness of Lamfalussy
    process 131–2
  enforcement 188–93, 219
  EU legislative history 135–8
  EU policy choices 129–30
  EU supervision 132
  financial disclosures 212–17
    supervision 219–26
  FSAP regime 2, 44, 45
  functions 127–9
  identification of home states
    147–56
    choice 160
    effect on EU issuers 153–5
    effect on non-EU issuers
      155–6, 205

issuer disclosure (cont.)
    rigidity 150–3, 202
    state of trading v state of
        incorporation 151–2, 160
  information overload 178
  inside information 197–9
  language 201–2
    financial information 160–4
    non-financial information 151,
      164–6
    translations 166–7
  listed and unlisted securities 186
  and market abuse directive
    197–200
  non-EU issuers. *See* non-EU issuers
  passport mechanism 144,
    201–2, 263
  periodic. *See* periodic disclosures
  prospectuses. *See* prospectuses
  retail securities 175–9
  role of stock exchanges 133
  second-tier stock markets
    185–8, 206–7
  and single securities market
    objective 200–7
  SMEs and start-ups 179–85
  specialist debt securities 167–75
  supervision. *See* supervision
  wholesale securities 200–1
issuers
  admission criteria 260–2
  categories 139, 140
  choice of home states 156–7, 173–4
  disclosure. *See* issuer disclosure
  mobility 52, 56, 150, 154, 156
  representation of interests 105
Italy 15, 33, 94, 186, 225n72,
  228, 256

La Porta, R. 27, 37
Lamfalussy, Alexandre 6, 61, 65n18
Lamfalussy process
  allocation of institutional
    responsibilities 67–74
  application 6
  assessment 84–111, 119, 123–6
  Commission's role 86–91
  consultation 84, 92–9

description 61–84
directives 67–70
ESC role 107–9
and European Parliament 66–7,
  85, 87, 109–11
guiding principles 73
impact 7
institutional cooperation 67
and issuer disclosure 131–2
legitimacy 92, 96–8
level 1 61, 62, 68–71, 99
level 2 61, 63, 68, 74, 81–2, 100–2
level 3 61, 64, 79, 100–2
level 4 61, 64
level boundaries 99–102, 124
level structure 61
limitations 111–18
new committees 75–81
pan-European regulatory agency
  alternative 119–22, 123
private sector involvement 83–4
Regulations 70–1
and retail investors 105–7
special interest groups 104–7
and Takeover Directive 118
transparency 82–3, 92–9
Lamfalussy Report 4n10, 6, 47, 61,
  69, 79, 87, 99, 237
language
  accessible language 179
  financial information 160–4
  issuer disclosure 201–2
  non-financial information 151,
    164–6
Latvia 244, 256
law. *See* regulation of EU securities
Law Society, Company Law
  Committee 158
Lee, R 244
legislation. *See* Lamfalussy process;
  regulation of EU securities
  markets
legitimacy
  CESR 102–7
  EU governance 123–4
  Lamfalussy process 92, 96–8
Levine, R. 13
Lisbon summit 65, 213

Lithuania   244, 256
lobbying   59, 104–7, 110, 120
Lopez-de-Silanes, F.   27, 37
Luxembourg   35–6, 162, 167, 173,
       206, 225n72, 255n77

Maastricht Treaty   8
Mahoney, P. G.   243
Maksimovic, V.   13
market abuse
   directive   71–2, 135, 197–200
   foreign issuers   205
   FSAP approach   44
   inside information   197
   and issuer disclosure   197–200
   Lamfalussy process   92
   level 1 process   68–9
   level 2 process   81–2
   territoriality   199
market prices
   and corporate governance   128
   and information   128
   and inside information   197
   irrationality of retail
          investors   175–6
   and issuer disclosure regimes   130
Markets Participants Group   106
maximum harmonisation
   accounting requirements   55
   disadvantages   145
   prospectuses   138–45, 159–60, 179
member states. See also home states
   compromises   116–17, 124,
          210, 264
   corporate governance   226–8
   enforcement of issuer
          disclosure   189–93
   opposition to EU securities
          regulation   116
   protectionism   20, 94, 103, 110,
          115, 117, 155
   regulators. See national regulators
   supervision and enforcement
          systems   111, 132
   Treaty obligations   116
mergers and acquisitions. See takeovers
minimum harmonisation
       55, 111, 141

Moloney, Niamh   29, 106
monopolies, national regulators   151

NASDAQ   248
national regulators
   accounting standards   221
   consistency   209
   convergence   228
   cooperation   209, 220
   coordination   223
   delegation of responsibilities   220
   designation   220
   institutional diversity   237, 258,
          260
   issuer disclosure   46, 111
   lack of uniformity   219, 221–2,
          233–5
   mutual trust   259
   powers under securities
          directives   208–9
   sanctions   220
   single regulator models   225
   turf wars   226
Netherlands   15, 21, 240n12, 256
non-EU issuers
   choice of supervision
          authority   149, 150, 151,
          155–6, 205
   issuer disclosures   132, 137, 149,
          150, 156–7, 205
   listing in UK   157–9
   periodical disclosures   150,
          156–7
   prospectuses   137, 149
   standardising language of financial
          information   160–4
   statistics   161
NOREX   256, 257
Norway   31n112, 78, 255n77, 256

OFEX   187, 188
OM Gruppen   241, 244, 256
OMHEX   256

Parmalat   217n32, 225n72, 228
passport system
   concept   3–4
   cost savings   26

passport system (cont.)
  effectiveness   259
  issuer disclosures   144, 150,
      201–2, 263
  language issues   164
  securities offerings   4–5
peer review, CESR role   79–80, 112
pensions   20, 48
periodic disclosures   35
  civil liability   189, 190–1
  criminal liability   189–90
  enforcement by member
      states   189–93
    multi-jurisdictional
        litigation   191
  EU legislative history   135–8
  identification of home state
      149–50
    rigidity   150–3, 202
  language
    financial information   160–4
    non-financial information   151,
      164–6
  national differences   146
  quarterly reporting   183–5,
      203, 260
  responsibility statements   190
  retail securities   175–9
  SMEs and start-ups   182–5
  standards, and issuer mobility   154
  supervision   264
  Transparency Directive   145–7
    assessment   159–60
    discretion to exceed
        requirements   156–9
  wholesale securities   173
Poland   244
Portugal   21, 225n72, 256
prices. *See* market prices
PricewaterhouseCoopers   253
privatisations   23–4
proportionality   52, 70–1,
    142, 145
Prospectus Directive
  additional national
      requirements   5, 141–2
  adoption   134
  assessment   159–60

derogations   140, 141
  dividing lines   139
  identification of home state
      for   147–9
    rigidity   150–3
  implementing Regulation   139
  maximum harmonisation   138–45
  objective   137
prospectuses
  disclosure standards   140
  enforcement by member
      states   189, 191–3
  EU legislative history   135–8
  EU legislative process   92–3
  EU regulation   35, 44, 55
  exemptions   169–70
  FSAP cost savings   26
  identification of home states
      147–9
    non-equity securities   173–4
    rigidity   150–3
  language
    accessible language   179
    financial information   160–4
    non-financial information   151,
      164–6
    translation of summaries
      166–7
  maximum harmonisation
      138–45, 179
  new types of securities   140–1
  passport regime   263
  publication mechanisms   195
    central access   195
  retail securities   179
  SMEs and start-ups   180–2
  specialist types of securities   139
  start-up companies   140
  summaries
    retail-investor friendly   179
    translation   166–7
  translation   5
  types of issuers   139, 140
  vetting   262–4, 266
  wholesale securities   170–3
protectionism   20, 94,
    103, 108, 110, 115–16,
    117, 155

quarterly reporting   183–5, 203, 260

registered offices, and identification of
  home states   151–3
regulation of EU securities markets
  boundaries between states and
    markets   237
  catalyst for changes   38–41
  counter-productive regulation
    45, 58
  creative effect   10, 25–8
  and financial development   9–10
  FSAP option   43–5
  historical record   3–5, 10, 24–41
  issues   59
  Lamfalussy model. See Lamfalussy
    process
  limitations   111–18
  listing particulars   34
  maximum harmonisation
    approach   55, 138–45,
    159–60, 179
  minimum harmonisation
    approach   55, 111, 141
  and national opposition   115
  over-reliance on   2
  pan-European regulatory
    agency   8, 60, 119–22, 123
  policy objectives   8, 177
  public offers   3, 4–5
  regulatory competition   50–7
  response to globalisation   115
  stock exchange role. See stock
    exchanges
  strategic policy choices   41–57
  supervision and enforcement
    alternative   11, 46–50
  uncertainty as to effect   41–3, 178
  uniformity   11, 261
Regulations
  accounting standards   213
  direct application   139, 213
  legislative process   70–1
regulatory competition   50–7
retail investors
  cognitive weaknesses   175–6
  dispute resolution   49
  execution only dealings   106

home bias   9, 179
information overload   178
irrationality   175, 178
and issuer disclosure   175–9
official encouragement   175
over-confidence   178
representation of interests   105–7
retail securities
  issuer disclosure   175–9
  and maximum
    harmonisation   179
  translation of prospectus
    summaries   166–7

sanctions, breach of securities
  directives   220
Santer, Jacques   118n246
Sarbanes-Oxley Act   113, 228, 231,
  232, 233
second-tier markets
  European markets   186
  issuer disclosure   185–8, 206–7
  unregulated markets   187–8, 206–7
securities directives
  breach, sanctions   220
  main directives   134–5, 208
  supervision system   219–28
securities markets
  alternative trading
    systems   239n10
  and bank financing   14
  and economic growth   11–14
  EU. See EU securities markets
  function of financial markets   12
  international access   239
Shleifer, A.   27, 37
Singapore   248–9
single market
  development process   59
  EU objective   8, 29
  financial services   4
  impact on securities law   3–4
  securities. See single securities
    markets
single securities markets
  advantages of collective
    action   112–14
  benefits   9, 12–14

single securities markets (cont.)
　　and disclosure regime　200–7
　　and dissemination of
　　　　information　193
　　and diversity of regulators　237
　　FSAP approach　11, 43–5
　　and home bias　202–4
　　mixed approach　11, 56
　　objective　1
　　passport concept　3–4
　　policy objectives　8, 177
　　regulation history　3–5, 10, 25–41
　　regulatory competition
　　　　alternative　50–7
　　role of diversity　53–6
　　strategic choices　41–57
　　supervision and enforcement
　　　　approach　46–50, 60, 119–22
　　through stock exchange
　　　　regulation　255–66
　　variables　9
Slovakia　244
Slovenia　244
SMEs
　　finance sources　26
　　FIN-USE representation　107
　　issuer disclosures　45, 179–85
　　periodic disclosures　182–5
　　prospectuses　109, 179–82, 180–2
Snyder, Francis　92
Soros, George　33
Spain　15, 117, 186, 225n72
special interest groups　104–7
specialist debt securities
　　issuer disclosure　167–75
　　modified prospectus
　　　　requirements　170–3
　　non-regulated markets　206
　　periodic disclosures　173
　　prospectus exemptions　169–70
　　supervision, threshold　173–5
standards
　　accounting. *See* accounting
　　　　requirements
　　audits　232
　　CESR competence　101–2
　　CESR function　79
　　CESR standards　222–3

FSAP approach　114
information dissemination　196
IOSCO disclosure standards　140
positive role　101
standardising language of financial
　　information　160–4
stock exchanges　243–6
Stanhammar, Olaf　244
start-ups
　　issuer disclosure　179–85
　　periodic disclosures　182–5
　　prospectuses　180–2
Steil, B.　241
stock exchanges
　　accession countries　244
　　admission criteria　260–2
　　alternative trading
　　　　systems　239n10
　　Australia　241, 247, 248
　　Baltic stock exchanges　256
　　Belgium　21, 256
　　competition　239, 242
　　Czech Republic　40
　　demutualisation　238, 239–43
　　Denmark　255n77, 256
　　directors, remuneration　246–7
　　EDX　256
　　EU numbers　21
　　EUREX　256
　　Euronext　256, 257
　　evolution　236
　　Finland　256
　　France　21, 256
　　Germany　21, 241, 249, 256
　　Hong Kong　249
　　Italy　256
　　London Stock Exchange　21,
　　　　240n13, 241, 249–54,
　　　　256–7, 259
　　NASDAQ　241–2
　　Netherlands　21, 240n12, 256
　　New York Stock Exchange
　　　　241–3, 252
　　NOREX　256, 257
　　numbers　237
　　OMHEX　256
　　Portugal　21, 256
　　pressures　240, 242

prospectus vetting   266
quasi-public bodies   236
regulatory functions   236–9, 243–7
    conflicts of interest   246, 247, 265
    and corporate governance
        246–7, 248, 265
    delegated role   265
    and demutualisation   246–7
    diversity among member
        states   254–5
    issuer disclosure   133, 262–4
    mechanism for EU market
        integration   255–66
    post-demutualisation
        approaches   247–54
    prospectus vetting   262–4
    reduction   238, 266
    self-listing   247
Scandinavia   256
Singapore   248–9
standards, and competition
    243–6
Sweden   241, 244,
    255n77, 256
Switzerland   256
Toronto Stock Exchange   248
transnationalisation   256, 257
Stockholm summit   65
subsidiarity   52, 70–1, 144–5, 210
supervision
    alternative to further
        regulation   46–50
    audits   228–33
    banking   47–8
    boundaries   260
    convergence   46–8, 132, 209,
        210–11, 221, 228
    and financial scandals   215–16
    identification of home states
        147–56
    rigidity   150–3, 202
    insurance   48
    issuer disclosure
        diversity   219
        EU strategy   219–20
        generally   132, 208–11, 219–28
        inside information   199
        new regime   160

periodic disclosures   264
prospectuses   262–4
lack of uniformity   211
national regulators
    coordination   223
    institutional diversity   237, 258,
        260
    lack of uniformity   219, 222–3,
        233–5
    monopoly   151
    securities directives   208–9,
        219–20
national systems   46, 111
occupational pensions   48
pan-European regulatory
    agency   60, 119–22
pan-European system   265
post-Enron   215–17
and regulatory competition   52
standards, and issuer mobility   154
stock exchange role. See stock
    exchanges
US model   228–33
wholesale securities   173–5
Sweden   31n112, 116, 225n72, 241,
    244, 255n77, 256
Switzerland   17, 33, 256

takeovers
    banking sector   17
    financing   15–16
    and market prices   128
    Takeover Directive   110, 116–18
    UK code   54
temporary workers   117
terminology   5–7
Tower of Babel   160–7
transaction costs, reduction   26
transition economies   25
translations   166–7, 202
transparency   67, 76, 82–3,
    92–9, 120
Transparency Directive. See also
    periodic disclosures
    adoption   134, 137
    approach   145–7, 163
    assessment   159–60
    contents   137–8

Transparency Directive (cont.)
 discretion to exceed
  requirements 156–9
 identification of home state
  149–50

United Kingdom
 Alternative Investment Market
  (AIM) 186, 187, 188, 206,
  250
 audit supervision 228–9
 bond market 167, 173, 206
 City Code on Takeovers and
  Mergers 54
 dissemination of
  information 193–4
 EDX 256
 Financial Services Authority 157–9,
  193–4, 226, 249–54
 hostility to regulation 42
 influence on EU regulation 53–4
 insider dealing 33
 issuer disclosure regime 35, 157–9
 Listing Rules 146, 193, 250
 London Stock Exchange 240n13,
  241, 249–54, 256–7, 259
 and pan-European regulatory
  agency 120
 regulators' turf war 226
 second-tier markets 186, 187, 206
 securities market financing 219
 and single financial market 112–13
 single regulator model
  225n72, 254
 and Takeover Directive 116, 117
 and temporary workers 117
 UK Listing Authority 252
United States
 alternative trading
  systems 239n10
 corporate law 243
 and EU 113, 232, 233, 235

financial reporting 217
foreign issuer disclosures 140
fund managers 20
impact of regulation on EU
 36–7, 189
insider dealing 33
international bonds 162
investment banks 21
issuer disclosure 127
 pace-setting 189
 quarterly reporting 203
 SMEs 180, 183
NASDAQ 241–2, 248
New York Stock Exchange
 241–3, 252
Public Company Accounting
 Oversight Board
 (PCAOB) 229, 232, 233, 235
regulatory model 210–11,
 228–33
Sarbanes-Oxley Act 113, 228, 231,
 232, 233
size of securities market 18
v EU 113–14

Vishny, R. W. 27

websites
 disclosure of inside
  information 199
 issuer information 195–6
wholesale securities
 issuer disclosure 167–8, 200–1
 periodic disclosures 173
 prospectuses
  exemptions 169–70
  language 167
  modified requirements 170–3
 supervision, threshold 173–5

Zechner, J. 244
Zervos, S. 13